Mixed Methods in Criminol

Mixed Methods in Criminology is the first book to bring together the discipline of criminology with the mixed methods research strategy, which has become increasingly prominent within criminological teaching and research.

The book is structured so that it charts the course of a criminological mixed methods study. Starting with an introduction to mixed methods and its implications for criminology and criminological research, the book then works systematically through the planning stages of a research project. Developing research questions, aims, and objectives is discussed alongside literature searching skills and the project planning process, before the principles and practice of ethical research are summarised. Next come chapters on philosophy, mixed methods design, combining the data, research design and sampling, data collection methods, and data analysis, delivering a comprehensive overview of how to undertake a mixed methods research project in practice. This is followed by a chapter on troubleshooting, which provides useful advice from experienced mixed methods researchers, before a detailed account of how to write-up mixed methods research is presented. The book concludes with a range of real-life mixed methods case studies to demonstrate how the techniques outlined in this book have been employed in reality and to inspire new criminological mixed methods projects.

Providing straightforward, easy-to-follow guidance, *Mixed Methods in Criminology* is the essential student companion for any criminological mixed methods research project. Drawing on the authors' years of experience teaching research methods, the book is written in a supportive and encouraging tone that will serve as a reference and guide for those embarking on their adventures 'in the field'.

Vicky Heap is Senior Lecturer in Criminology and Fellow of the Sheffield Institute for Policy Studies at Sheffield Hallam University. She conducts research and lectures in the areas of anti-social behaviour, crime prevention, and research methods. Her current research examines victims' experiences of anti-social behaviour and the implementation of the Community Trigger and Community Remedy policies from the Anti-Social Behaviour, Crime and Policing Act (2014).

Jaime Waters is Senior Lecturer in Criminology and Fellow of the Sheffield Institute for Policy Studies at Sheffield Hallam University. She has been teaching criminological research methods since 2004 and publishes on methodological issues. Her main research interests include illegal drug use, gambling, and emotional labour, and she published her first research monograph, *Illegal Drug Use Through the Lifecourse* (with David Moxon, Routledge), in 2017.

Mixed Methods in Criminology

Vicky Heap and Jaime Waters

LONDON AND NEW YORK

First published 2019
by Routledge
2 Park Square, Milton Park, Abingdon, Oxon OX14 4RN

and by Routledge
711 Third Avenue, New York, NY 10017

Routledge is an imprint of the Taylor & Francis Group, an informa business

British Library Cataloguing in Publication Data
A catalogue record for this book is available from the British Library

Library of Congress Cataloging in Publication Data
Names: Heap, Vicky, 1983– author. | Waters, Jaime, author.
Title: Mixed methods in criminology / Vicky Heap and Jaime
    Waters.
Description: Abingdon, Oxon ; New York, NY : Routledge, 2018. |
    Includes bibliographical references.
Identifiers: LCCN 2018036528 | ISBN 9781138309456 (hardback)
    | ISBN 9781138309463 (pbk.) | ISBN 9781315143354
    (ebook)
Subjects: LCSH: Criminology—Methodology. | Mixed methods
    research.
Classification: LCC HV6018 .H43 2018 | DDC 364—dc23
LC record available at https://lccn.loc.gov/2018036528

ISBN: 978-1-138-30945-6 (hbk)
ISBN: 978-1-138-30946-3 (pbk)
ISBN: 978-1-315-14335-4 (ebk)

Typeset in Bembo
by Swales & Willis Ltd, Exeter, Devon, UK

Contents

13 Case studies   260

CATRIN ANDERSSON

Figures

Tables

Foreword

The debate between qualitative and quantitative approaches to research methodology is one of the all-time great debates in the social sciences, right up there with 'nature versus nurture' or 'structure versus free will'. What makes these arguments 'great' is that they are essentially unwinnable, so they can just go on and on. Indeed, many a career has been spent (fruitfully or not) debating one side or the other of the quant versus qual fight. The only way such battles end, in fact, is sheer exhaustion. Neither side will ever concede, but eventually both will simply move on to more fruitful pursuits.

Elsewhere, I have argued that we are finally reaching this stage with the methods debate in criminology. That is, when historians of social science look back on the so-called paradigm wars in a few decades' time, I predict they will scratch their heads and wonder: but why didn't they just go both ways? (Maruna, 2010). Mixed methods qual-quant designs, as outlined in this incredibly useful text, are the future of social science research.

Mixed methods might be uniquely well suited to a historically pragmatic and interdisciplinary field of study like criminology. Unlike, say, economics or anthropology, criminology has no allegiance to any particular methodology; indeed, our field has developed something of a reputation for being a 'rendezvous' discipline (Rock and Holdaway, 1998) open to all comers. The one unifying thing that makes a criminologist a criminologist is not the methods she uses, or even the theories she ascribes to, but rather the subject she is studying. And our subject includes some of the most urgent and pressing questions any society faces: why are some neighbourhoods more dangerous than others? What leads a society to genocide? How can communities reduce the problems of domestic violence or sexual assault? Our job is clear, then: we need to use every possible tool at our disposal to answer these important questions.

In this regard, those criminologists insisting on using uni-methods (either qual-only or quant-only designs) are the ones who have some explaining to do. After all, human behaviour is famously complex, and never more so than efforts to solve the mysteries of our darker impulses. We are simultaneously interpretivist and positivist creatures, animated both by mechanical laws and our unique perceptions. Ignoring one of these aspects of human lives is essentially like trying to win a boxing match with one arm behind your back.

Not for readers of this book, though. Heap and Waters outline everything a budding criminologist needs to know to deliver the 'one-two punch' in research design. It should be essential reading for students of crime everywhere.

Shadd Maruna, Professor of Criminology,
Queen's University Belfast

Acknowledgements

We would like to express our gratitude to a range of people who have supported us throughout the production of this book. First, we would like to thank Professor Shadd Maruna, a mixed methods champion, for writing the Foreword and for his encouragement. Thank you to Dr Catrin Andersson for supporting the process, preparing the 'case studies' chapter, and providing feedback on draft chapters. Also, thank you to the case study authors who kindly provided information about their mixed methods research: Dr James Banks, Beth Collinson, Dr Michelle Cubellis, Dr Joanna Large, and Dr Deborah Platts-Fowler, as well as everyone that contributed their thoughts to the 'troubleshooting' chapter, especially Jacky Burrows and Anne Robinson. We would like to recognise and thank Professor Rachel Armitage, Jennifer Herrera, and Professor Ann Macaskill for giving us permission to use their research documents as examples.

We are indebted to our Sheffield Hallam colleagues who have contributed towards our thinking about mixed methods and research methods in general, in particular: Dr Liz Austen, Richard Lynch, and Sue Parkinson. Much of this book reflects conversations we have had with our students to nurture and facilitate their development as researchers, which has been invaluable in helping us to articulate research methods in a relatable way. A big thank you to our students Gemma Agnew and Zoe Rodgers, who read and commented upon draft chapters. We were also fortunate to have Dr Jake Phillips and Christa Waters read the book for us and they provided a range of thoughtful comments and suggestions. Many thanks to Hannah Shakespeare and Matthew Bickerton at Routledge for their support and assistance from the outset.

Special thanks to Samantha Jefferson-Heap for reading many drafts, embracing research methods (you love it really), and being generally amazing. Finally, thank you to everyone who has lived through this writing experience with us. We know you are pleased/relieved/ecstatic it is all over . . . until next time ☺

1   Introduction to mixed methods

CHAPTER OVERVIEW

- Introduction
- Quantitative and qualitative research strategies
- Introducing mixed methods
- Why use mixed methods in your research?
- Mixed methods vs multiple methods
- Mixed methods in criminology
- Chapter outlines
- Summary
- Learning questions

Introduction

Welcome to *Mixed Methods in Criminology*!

This book shows you how the mixed methods research strategy can be productively utilised in the discipline of criminology and criminal justice. Mixed methods is a relatively new methodological strategy, which has become increasingly prominent over the last three decades or so (Mayoh and Onwuegbuzie, 2015), and in particular since the turn of the 21st century (Plano Clark and Creswell, 2008). It is an approach where both quantitative and qualitative methods and data are employed in the same research project, and it is now frequently used across many disciplines in the social, behavioural, and health sciences in situations where it can greatly assist in the exploration of complex and multi-faceted phenomena.

The recent growth of mixed methods is the result of a variety of different factors. Chief among these has been pressure from governmental funding bodies, private funding bodies, and other stakeholders, who are increasingly demanding that mixed methods are used in order to explore social policy issues (Hesse-Biber, 2010). One result of this growth has been an explosion in the number of mixed methods publications, of which this book is a part. The discipline of criminology and criminal justice has been especially keen to embrace mixed methods, in some way because of the particular issues and complexities that studying crime, deviance, and victimisation entails.

This book delivers a step-by-step guide on how to carry out your own mixed methods research project. The two main objectives of this book are:

- To show how the mixed methods research strategy can be used within the discipline of criminology.
- To provide you with a practical guide on how to approach and design your own criminological mixed methods research project.

This first chapter delivers a comprehensive introduction to the topic of mixed methods. It will begin with a brief discussion of quantitative and qualitative research strategies, the component parts of mixed methods research. It will then go on to present an overview of mixed methods itself, discussing its emergence as an explicitly recognised methodological strategy over recent years. Some of the advantages and disadvantages of the mixed methods strategy will be explored, before we go on to consider why using mixed methods is a good option for many research studies. Then, we will distinguish mixed methods from so-called 'multiple methods' or 'multi method' approaches and examine the use of mixed methods in the discipline of criminology. All this will provide the foundations for the chapters that follow. The chapter ends by outlining the rest of the book.

Throughout the book, you will be introduced to the terminology that is associated with mixed methods research. As mixed methods is an emerging field, terminology and definitions are often contested and used in contradictory or inconsistent ways by different authors (Teddlie and Tashakkori, 2010). It is therefore vital to have a sound understanding of the concepts that are being referred to and the terminology used to describe them. Where there is debate and dissensus over terminology, we will make this clear. The 'Glossary of key terms' at the end of the book will also assist you in this regard.

Quantitative and qualitative research strategies

A **research strategy** is an overall general approach to a research project. **Quantitative** and **qualitative** research strategies are the building blocks of **mixed methods** research. It is therefore crucial to understand them before going on to discuss the mixed methods research strategy itself. Whilst some researchers favour quantitative over qualitative, and others the opposite, one of the key features of the mixed methods strategy, as we will see over the course of the book, is that neither quantitative nor qualitative is seen as being inherently superior; the needs of the project dictate which strategy, if any, should take priority. This point will become clear over the forthcoming chapters. For now, let us concentrate on the basics of the quantitative and qualitative strategies (for further detail, see www.simplypsychology.org/qualitative-quantitative.html).

Quantitative research

The quantitative strategy prioritises numbers. Its focus is on producing and analysing numerical data. When researchers first became interested in learning about the social world, this tended to be the way that they sought to measure it, borrowing from the established disciplines of the natural sciences (physics, chemistry, and biology) in the early 1800s. Quantitative research has four main concerns:

- Measurement (e.g. how much crime?)
- Causality (e.g. what causes crime?)

- Generalisation (e.g. can findings apply elsewhere?)
- Replication (e.g. can the research be repeated to yield similar findings?)

Caulfield and Hill (2014: 229) sum up the quantitative strategy as a 'systematic approach to research that relies upon statistical analysis'. Examples of quantitative criminological research include large-scale victimisation and crime surveys (e.g. Crime Survey for England and Wales, Uniform Crime Report, US Victimisation Survey Data, United Nations crime data), structured observations, quantitative content analysis, secondary data analysis of existing datasets from crime statistics (police-recorded crime, court, prison, and probation statistics), and smaller/local crime and victimisation questionnaires.

Quantitative research is often criticised for its attempts to measure the social world in the same manner as the physical sciences attempt to measure the natural world, without taking into account the considerable differences between the two, most notably the idea that individuals in the social world can react to being measured and alter their behaviour. Concerns have also been repeatedly raised that the quantitative measurement of the social world can sometimes seem rather artificial and spurious, that the quantitative research process disconnects data from everyday life, that the measures typically used tend to lack complexity and can dehumanise people, and that quantitative work can suffer from reverse operationism (the overly deductive operationalisation of concepts) (see, for example, Bryman, 2016: 167). It is also worth noting that the cost and practicalities of quantitative research are often prohibitive, especially for student researchers or those working alone. Large-scale probability questionnaires, for instance, require a great deal of time to set up, ready access to participants, some efficient means of distribution, and enough time for what could be a significant amount of data entry. In recent years some of the time and costs involved have been reduced because of the growth in online data collection tools, but the advance of technology has not alleviated all the problems associated with quantitative research. Table 1.1 provides a summary of some of the advantages and disadvantages of quantitative data and data collection. Our ordering of 'quantitative' before 'qualitative' throughout this book reflects this historical quirk and our desire for consistency, and does not represent a favouring or perceived superiority of the quantitative strategy.

Qualitative research

The qualitative strategy prioritises the production of data that usually takes the form of words, but can also take the form of pictures, or indeed anything other than numbers. It 'has a long and distinguished history in the social sciences, arising in part from dissatisfaction with quantitative approaches' (Noaks and Wincup, 2004: 3). In the social sciences, the seminal work of the Chicago School in the 1920s and 1930s was vital in establishing qualitative research as a viable alternative to quantitative research.

Qualitative research involves the collection of data through the process of, for example, interviews, focus groups, or observations, and it tends to be much more open-ended than quantitative research. It is an 'approach to research that focuses upon the gathering of in-depth data through which meaning can be derived' (Caulfield and Hill, 2014: 229), paying close attention to context and the so-called 'lived experience' of the participants. If quantitative research can be viewed as dehumanising the participants of research, then qualitative seeks to address this and often attempts to view the world through the eyes of the researched. Analysis of the data often precedes attempts to discern key themes or repeated tropes. Examples of qualitative criminological research might include studies that seek to investigate the attitudes of people committing crime, that focus on the experiences of victims of crime, or that explore how criminal justice practitioners carry out and view their work. Such studies seek to understand how people experience their own lives and place that understanding in some kind of wider social context.

Table 1.1 Advantages and disadvantages of quantitative and qualitative research (adapted from University of Southampton, 2017)

	Advantages	*Disadvantages*
Quantitative	• Allows the research problem to be stated in very specific and clear terms • Allows the clear and precise specification of both the independent and the dependent variables under investigation • Potential for more objective conclusions, testing of hypotheses, and determination of causality • Potential for data to have high levels of reliability because of the controlled nature of observations, laboratory experiments, mass questionnaires, etc. • Eliminates or at least minimises subjective judgements • More readily allows for longitudinal measurements to be made	• Risk of failure to provide the researcher with information on the context of the situation where the studied phenomenon occurs • Potential for a lack of control over the environment in which participants respond, for instance in a large-scale questionnaire administered online • Possibly limits the scope of study to that which is outlined in the original research proposal because of the closed nature of questions and the exceedingly structured format • Does not encourage the continuous evolution of a research project on the basis of ongoing findings because of its tightly defined focus and highly structured nature
Qualitative	• Potential to obtain a more realistic feel of the world that cannot be gained from the numerical data and statistical analysis used in quantitative research • Offers flexibility during data collection, subsequent analysis, and interpretation of collected information as different means to carry out these phases of the research are available • Provides a holistic view of the phenomena under investigation • Offers the potential to interact with the research subjects in their own language and on their own terms • Potential for rich and in-depth descriptions based upon primary and unstructured data	• Possibility of departing from the original objectives of the research in response to the changing nature of the context • Potential to arrive at different conclusions based on the same information depending on the personal characteristics of the researcher • Inability to investigate causality in a conclusive manner • Difficulties in explaining the difference in the quality and quantity of information obtained from different respondents and arriving at different, non-consistent conclusions • Ideally requires a capable and preferably experienced researcher to obtain the relevant information from the respondent • Lacks consistency and reliability because the researcher is able to employ a variety of different probing techniques and the respondent has control over what is revealed

A range of criticisms have been levelled at the qualitative strategy. Some consider qualitative research to be too subjective because it is heavily reliant upon the researcher themselves to interpret and understand the data. It has also been suggested that qualitative projects suffer from a lack of replicability; this is in large part because the researcher is so integral to the nature of the data collected and the analysis that is carried out. The lack of transparency inherent in much qualitative research can also be problematic; once again, this derives from the fact that case selection and data analysis are far more dependent upon the researcher. Qualitative data have also been criticised because it is often difficult to generalise from its findings given that it regularly utilises non-probability sampling techniques with relatively few participants. Table 1.1 outlines some of the advantages and disadvantages of qualitative research.

Moving beyond quantitative and qualitative research

In recent years, there has been increasing unease with research strategies that see quantitative and qualitative as diametrically opposed and irreconcilable opposites. Researchers have steadily come to reject the sense that they must necessarily be in one of two opposed 'camps', either quantitative or qualitative. Moving beyond this traditional division in research strategy is crucial to the whole notion of mixed methods research.

As Bryman (2016) has argued, whilst there self-evidently are differences between quantitative and qualitative research, it is important not to exaggerate them. For example, qualitative research sometimes exhibits features normally associated with a natural science model, such as quantification, and quantitative research aims on occasions to engage with what would normally be seen as a rather interpretivistic stance. In the end, Bryman goes on to suggest that research strategies are more self-determining in relation to epistemological commitments than is often appreciated (see Chapter 4 – Philosophy). What is therefore important to recognise here is that whilst quantitative and qualitative strategies are often taught and treated as separate and distinct entities, there is in fact a great deal of overlap between the two, particularly when the practicalities of real-world research are considered. The two strategies can potentially be complementary rather than opposed. Once this has been acknowledged, the adoption of a mixed methods approach begins to look increasingly sensible in certain contexts.

Introducing mixed methods

Mixed methods is the systematic bringing together of quantitative and qualitative research strategies into one coherent research approach. Over recent years it has steadily become more influential across a range of different disciplines. As Hesse-Biber (2010: 2) points out, it has a long pre-history, with the classic European studies of poverty conducted by Frédéric Le Play (in 1855), Charles Booth (from 1892–1897), and Bohm Rowntree (in 1901) utilising both quantitative and qualitative methods, 'including the use of demographics analysis, participant surveys and observations, and social mapping techniques'. Nevertheless, it has only been during the last quarter-century or so that mixed methods has become rigorous and systematised enough to be properly considered as a genuine third strategy alongside its constituent quantitative and qualitative parts.

Mixed methods, despite its increasing systematisation over recent years, is still far from a unified approach. A number of different definitions of mixed methods have been proposed, with varying emphases, as Table 1.2 shows. Some researchers focus

Table 1.2 Selected definitions of mixed methods research

Author	Definition
Creswell	'An approach to research in the social, behavioural, and health sciences in which the investigator gathers both quantitative (closed-ended) and qualitative (open-ended) data, integrates the two, and then draws interpretations based on the combined strengths of both sets of data to understand research problems. A core assumption of this approach is that when an investigator combines statistical trends (quantitative data) with stories and personal experiences (qualitative data), this collective strength provides a better understanding of the research problem than either form of data alone' (2015: 2).
Denscombe	'1 A preference for viewing research problems from a variety of perspectives. 2 The combination of different types of research within a single project . . . In most cases this means mixing "qualitative" and "quantitative" components. 3 The choice of methods based on "what works best" for tackling a specific problem' (2014: 146–147).
Johnson and Onwuegbuzie	'Mixed methods research is the class of research where the researcher mixes or combines quantitative and qualitative research techniques, methods, approaches, concepts or language into a single study or set of related studies' (Johnson et al., 2007: 120).
Morse and Niehaus	'the use of two (or more) research methods in a single study, when one (or more) of the methods is not complete in itself' (2009: 9).
Tashakkori and Teddlie	'working primarily within the pragmatist paradigm and interested in both narrative and numerical data and their analyses' (Teddlie and Tashakkori, 2009: 4). 'a type of research design in which QUAL and QUAN approaches are used in types of questions, research methods, data collection and analysis procedures, and/or inferences' (2003: 711).
Heap and Waters	The systematic and rigorous bringing together of quantitative and qualitative research methods and data into a coherent whole, where this whole is greater than the sum of its individual component parts, in order to answer a central research question.

on the epistemological and ontological aspects of mixed methods when attempting to delineate its essence. Others focus upon more practical matters of, for example, data collection, analysis, and interpretation (Creswell, 2015). It has also been positioned 'within a transformative perspective, such as feminism or disability theory' by some researchers (Creswell, 2015: 1).

Our own approach is to focus attention on the methodological practicalities. Our starting point is for the central research question to be foregrounded, because this should govern the decision to use mixed methods, which we view as a pragmatic tool that allows better answers to research questions to be produced. This also chimes with our view of the philosophical underpinnings of mixed methods research (see Chapter 4 – Philosophy). That said, our definition also emphasises the data collection, data analysis, and overall interpretation and synthesis, and it draws on the definitions offered in Table 1.2.

We would therefore define mixed methods as the systematic and rigorous bringing together of quantitative and qualitative research methods and data into a coherent whole, where this whole is greater than the sum of its individual component parts, in order to answer a central research question. To be clear, this definition emphasises what we feel are the four key features of mixed methods research:

- It puts the central research question at the heart of the project, stressing that the use of mixed methods is a practical response to the challenge of answering such a question.
- It highlights a preference for viewing a research problem from a variety of perspectives.
- It requires the combination of quantitative and qualitative strategies within a single project (contrast this with Morse and Niehaus' (2009) definition in Table 1.2).
- It underlines that the choice of methods should be based on what works best for tackling the specific problem at hand (following Creswell's (2015) and Denscombe's (2007) definitions in Table 1.2).

As well as considering what mixed methods is, it can also be helpful to think about what mixed methods is not. Perhaps most importantly, mixed methods is not simply the gathering of quantitative and qualitative data in an unstructured manner, with no thought paid to the design of the study or the combining of the data. Morse and Niehaus (2009: 10) are unequivocal regarding this: they argue that mixed methods is

> NOT a *blending* [emphasis in original] of research methods. We do not collect data in a willy-nilly fashion and then try to think of a way to combine it in the analysis so we can 'see what we have got'. Mixed method designs are not, as we have heard them described, like a stir fry, a collection of nuts, or a more expensive drink.

Instead, a mixed methods project is far more systematic than this. Close attention must be paid, for example, to the nature of the combining of the quantitative and qualitative components of the project. Table 1.3 highlights in more detail what does and does not constitute mixed methods research.

Table 1.3 What mixed methods is, and what it is not (adapted from Creswell, 2015: ch. 1)

Mixed methods is:	Mixed methods is NOT:
<ul><li>The collection and analysis of quantitative and qualitative data in response to a central research question</li><li>The rigorous use of both quantitative and qualitative methods</li><li>The combination or integration of quantitative and qualitative data using a specific type of mixed methods design</li><li>The underpinning of the adopted mixed methods design with a research philosophy or theory</li></ul>	<ul><li>Simply the gathering of both quantitative and qualitative data</li><li>Merely the application of the 'mixed methods' label onto a study that does not systematically combine quantitative and qualitative components</li><li>The adoption of a 'mixed model' approach to quantitative research, in which investigators conduct statistical analysis of fixed and random effects in a database</li><li>An evaluation technique, for example formative plus summative evaluation, even where both quantitative and qualitative data are utilised in performing such evaluation</li><li>Merely the addition of some qualitative data to a quantitative project without the underlying mixed methods design and methodological decisions</li><li>The collection of multiple forms of qualitative data, or the collection of multiple forms of quantitative data. This is known as 'multi method' research</li></ul>

Advantages and disadvantages of mixed methods

There are both advantages and disadvantages to mixed methods research. These should be taken into account when considering whether to adopt a mixed methods strategy and when planning a mixed methods project. The main advantages and disadvantages, as suggested by Denscombe (2014), are summarised in Table 1.4 and discussed below.

Advantages of mixed methods

1   *Allows for a better understanding of the phenomenon under study*: By combining quantitative and qualitative **components** it is possible to create a more comprehensive, detailed, and nuanced understanding of whatever phenomenon is being researched. Whilst a quantitative questionnaire might reveal a statistically significant relationship between two concepts, a series of qualitative interviews might shed greater light on the precise nature of that relationship. Using either of the methods in isolation would of course lead to some understanding, but when quantitative and qualitative methods are used in combination a far fuller picture is likely to be revealed.

2   *A practical, pragmatic approach that is problem-driven*: A key strength of the mixed methods strategy is that the methodological components for a study can be selected based on the practical needs of the project, as there is no need to stick religiously to either qualitative or quantitative methods. The project, and in particular the central research question, guides the selection of the methodological components to be used, and not the other way around. Indeed, many researchers have long been of this pragmatic persuasion, and the growth of mixed methods as an increasingly legitimate and systematised approach has validated their use of what can often seem like 'common sense', practical decision-making in the research process, so long as these decisions can be explicitly justified. See Chapter 4 – Philosophy for a more detailed discussion of pragmatism and its association with mixed methods.

3   *The strengths of the qualitative components of the work compensate for the weaknesses of the quantitative components, and vice versa*: Mixed methods research benefits greatly from the fact that components can effectively compensate for each other. For instance, the lack of depth and nuance provided by a quantitative questionnaire can be addressed by combining it with qualitative semi-structured interviews. Likewise, the quantitative questionnaire provides a potentially much bigger sample, the possibility of statistical analysis and a broader picture of the phenomenon under study, things that the qualitative semi-structured interview cannot readily provide. In this way, mixed methods research allows for the best of both worlds, harnessing the different strengths of both quantitative and qualitative strategies in a single research endeavour.

4   *Encourages clearer links to be drawn between different methods and different kinds of data*: Because the success of a mixed methods project hinges, at least in part, on the way that quantitative and qualitative methods and data are combined, mixed methods researchers are encouraged 'to provide an explicit account of how and why the different methods and data complement each other. Good mixed methods avoids an arbitrary "mix and match" approach' (Denscombe, 2014: 160). This can make for robust, defensible projects with explicit justifications of the methodological decisions that have been made.

Table 1.4 Advantages and disadvantages of mixed methods research (adapted from Denscombe, 2014: 160–161)

Advantages	Disadvantages
1 Allows for a better understanding of the phenomenon under study	1 Increase in time and cost
2 A practical, pragmatic approach that is problem-driven	2 Researcher needs skills in multiple methods
3 The strengths of the qualitative components of the work compensate for the weaknesses of the quantitative components, and vice versa	3 Findings from different components may not corroborate one another
4 Encourages clearer links to be drawn between different methods and different kinds of data	4 Underlying philosophy (pragmatism) open to misinterpretation

Disadvantages of mixed methods

1 *Increase in time and cost*: Put simply, as mixed methods research requires a minimum of two components to be carried out, it is very likely to be more time consuming and more financially costly than a project involving only one component. Also, bear in mind the increased time likely to be necessary for the analysis of the collected data. The increase in time and cost is a particular issue for undergraduate student researchers, who are likely to be working to a strict deadline, over a maximum of a single academic year, and who are unlikely to have much in the way of resources to fund the project, if indeed they have anything at all for this purpose. Because of this, you need to think extremely carefully at the outset about what is and what is not feasible within the constraints that you are working under.

2 *Researcher needs skills in multiple methods*: Researchers conducting a mixed methods project must have the requisite skills to carry out both the quantitative and qualitative components of the work. As Hesse-Biber (2010: 21–22) bluntly, but helpfully, puts it, 'researchers must ask themselves whether they have the training . . . necessary to carry out a mixed methods study [and] jumping on the mixed methods bandwagon without really thinking through the implications of doing so may yield research of dubious quality or research that does not add theoretical value and understanding to a research project'. This is, of course, not an issue in projects that adopt only a single method, where a researcher can focus their efforts on the mastery of one particular technique. Mixed methods projects allow no such luxury and therefore require a capable, committed, and motivated researcher prepared to develop a wider range of skills.

3 *Findings from different components may not corroborate one another*: It is perfectly possible in mixed methods projects that the inferences from the different components might not corroborate one another. The results of the qualitative component might point in a very different direction to the quantitative results, and vice versa. This can have serious implications when you come to think about the overall answer to your central research question. In such a situation, you will need to think very carefully about why any disparity exists and what this tells you about the phenomenon under study.

4 *Underlying philosophy (pragmatism) open to misinterpretation*: Denscombe (2014: 161) suggests that 'there is a common-sense use of the word pragmatic which implies expediency and a certain lack of principles underlying a course of action. There is the danger, then, that the mixed methods strategy is associated with this understanding

of the word and thus becomes regarded as an approach in which "anything goes"'. As Denscombe goes on to point out, and as Chapter 4 – Philosophy in this book will show, this is not actually the case with mixed methods, where pragmatism has a very specific meaning that does not allow for a lax, *laissez faire* attitude towards the construction of a mixed methods project. A mixed methods strategy should not be used as an excuse to throw lots of individual components into a pot in the hope that an answer to the central research question will emerge as if by magic out of the stew (see Karp, in Hesse-Biber, 2010: 23, who uses the metaphor of 'sprinkling', for further discussion of this point).

Ultimately, it is clear that there are a number of difficulties associated with the mixed methods strategy. However, rather than being seen as reasons not to engage in mixed methods research, these should be seen as challenges or obstacles that you need to consider, and your study should be planned in such a way as to minimise their impact. By doing so, you can ensure that your work harnesses the very significant strengths of the mixed methods approach in order to provide robust answers to your central research question.

Why use mixed methods in your research?

Mixed methods often represents the best option for a research project, because it allows for the uniting of quantitative and qualitative methods in order to provide a broader, more wide-ranging, and comprehensive answer to the central research question. This is because mixed methods projects allow for the application of both quantitative and qualitative techniques to a single issue. Imagine a criminological project with a central research question focused upon the effects of recent reforms to the probation service in the UK. This might be partly addressed through the application of quantitative components looking at, among other things, the effectiveness of probation interventions measured by reoffending rates, or levels of subsequent employment among individuals who have passed through the probation system. However, such an approach in isolation would only give a partial account, despite many different quantitative components being utilised. Qualitative components seeking the views, opinions and experiences of, for example, probation staff on the ground, service users, managers, and so on could buttress the quantitative findings and provide context, nuance and greater depth to the study. Similarly, these qualitative components alone can only provide a partial answer to the question at hand; they in turn are supported by the quantitative analysis.

As this example shows, by combining quantitative and qualitative components, a great deal more can be accomplished within the scope of a single project. The strengths of both quantitative and qualitative methods can be aggregated, and the two compensate for each other's weaknesses and blind spots. For instance, a quantitative questionnaire might be able to answer questions like 'how much?', 'how many?', 'how often?', 'what percentage?', and a qualitative interview might be able to answer questions like 'why did that happen?', 'why is that the case?', and 'how did you come to that understanding?'. In combination, more comprehensive answers can be provided, and a fuller understanding of a given topic can be arrived at. Indeed, the mixed methods strategy is often the only realistic and practical means by which a detailed and robust answer to the central research question can be constructed. Thus, ultimately, you would use mixed methods in your research when it offers you the best way to provide a sophisticated answer to your central research question.

Mixed methods vs multiple methods

As noted in Table 1.2, we draw a distinction between mixed methods research and so-called '**multiple methods**' or '**multi methods**' research, although care should be taken as some authors use the terms interchangeably. We define mixed methods research as the use of *both* quantitative and qualitative methods and data within a single study. That is, to qualify as a mixed methods study by our definition, a piece of work must include at least one qualitative component *and* one quantitative component.

Multiple methods research, on the other hand, is a study that involves the use of more than one component, but there is no requirement to use both quantitative and qualitative methods and data. Thus, a study that used two quantitative components to answer a central research question would qualify as a multiple methods study, but not as a mixed methods study on our definition. The term 'multi methods' is used in a similar manner; Hesse-Biber (2010: 3) uses it to refer to the combination of two or more qualitative methods (such as in-depth interviewing and participant observation) in a single research study, or the combination of two or more quantitative methods (such as a questionnaire and structured observation) in a single research study. Once again, this would not qualify as a mixed methods study by our definition as such work must include at least one qualitative *and* one quantitative component.

There are, of course, merits to the multiple methods and multi methods approaches, and in certain instances they will be wholly appropriate to the task at hand. However, our focus in this book is on the mixed methods strategy alone. Once again, it is important to exercise care when researching these topics, as some authors will use the terms interchangeably, and use the label 'mixed methods' to describe what we would class as a multiple methods or multi methods study, or the label 'multiple methods' or 'multi methods' to describe what we would class as a mixed methods study.

Mixed methods in criminology

The focus of this book is on the use of mixed methods within the discipline of criminology. Mixed methods is becoming increasingly prominent in criminology (Maruna, 2010). Indeed, the funders of criminological research projects now often specify that mixed methods are required for projects that they are prepared to support. It is therefore vital that criminology students understand mixed methods in order to be able to effectively evaluate studies carried out by other researchers and academics as well as carry out their own studies.

Criminology is frequently referred to as an 'applied' discipline because the knowledge it produces very often has practical applications. This is rather distinctive for an academic discipline in the social sciences. Criminological research routinely has a direct influence on governmental policy or the activities of criminal justice agencies, for example. The mixed methods approach to research, with its pragmatic persuasion (see Chapter 4 – Philosophy) and its focus on doing what is required in the circumstances in order to address the central research question, therefore has a natural affinity with criminology where direct and defensible answers to 'real-world' questions are often necessary.

There are a great many instances of the mixed methods strategy being adopted in criminological research. For example, Waters' (2009) PhD research on illegal drug use among older adults utilised a quantitative component, an analysis of the British Crime Survey to ascertain the levels of drug taking among the target population, and a qualitative component, a series of semi-structured interviews exploring the drug careers of the sample throughout their lifecourse. This approach is fairly typical, combining the use of a large-scale quantitative dataset to uncover patterns at the macro level with a qualitative supplement to add depth and understanding. Cabrera (2011: 77) 'critically examines white male college students' racial ideologies and the experiences that influence racial ideology formation [highlighting] how racial privilege is recreated in higher education'. The study began with qualitative interviews which informed the researchers' emerging understandings of the field and generated themes and concepts that were fed into the subsequent quantitative phases of the study, which consisted of two successive waves of a questionnaire. This is a good example of another common approach, where an exploratory initial phase of the work guides the later phases, with the qualitative and the quantitative complementing each other. Banks et al.'s (2018) research into families living with problem gamblers used a large-scale online quantitative questionnaire in order to recruit participants for qualitative semi-structured interviews, as well as to inform that subsequent phase of the research. Clearly this is not exhaustive, but it gives a flavour of the many ways that the mixed methods strategy has been put to work in criminology. Chapter 5 – Mixed methods design will cover these and other examples in greater detail.

Chapter outlines

The book is structured so that it charts the course of a research project. It works in a logical order; beginning with the planning stages of your project, guiding you through what is required at each stage of the process of a mixed methods study, and ending with advice on writing-up and presenting your inferences and meta-inferences.

Following this introduction, Chapter 2, *Creating a mixed methods question and project planning*, guides you through the first steps towards creating a mixed methods research project. It provides a comprehensive introduction to the research planning process, starting with the driving force behind mixed methods research, the central research question. Literature searching is then discussed, alongside the processes of creating subsidiary research questions, research aims and research objectives. The chapter concludes with an overview of the next steps required to start planning your project, detailing a range of decisions that you will be required to make along the way.

Chapter 3 considers *Ethics*, and the importance of undertaking ethical practice in mixed methods criminological research. First, an outline of the role of research ethics is defined, considering the four ethical principles of: avoiding harm; consent and deception; privacy, anonymity, and confidentiality; and complying with the laws of the land. This is contextualised by exploring the bodies and institutions responsible for governing research ethics. Second, we apply the ethical principles to a range of practical considerations that mixed methods researchers will have to navigate throughout their research project, including examples and templates.

Chapter 4, on *Philosophy*, discusses the epistemological and ontological underpinnings of mixed methods research. As mixed methods is neither solely quantitative nor qualitative, the traditional (if contested) divisions between positivism and interpretivism and objectivism and constructivism are not so sharp. As such, pragmatism (Denscombe, 2002; Tashakkori and Teddlie, 1998) will be introduced as the most appropriate epistemological approach for those working on mixed methods projects, alongside multiple realities (Onwuegbuzie et al., 2009), as the most apt ontological position. The chapter ends by bringing together pragmatism and multiple realities into a coherent overall philosophical approach towards mixed methods research.

Chapter 5 covers *Mixed methods design*. Two key questions, the priority question and the sequence question (Bryman, 2016; Denscombe, 2014), are discussed. The priority question considers the weighting of the quantitative and qualitative components of the research.

The sequence question is related to the order in which the quantitative and qualitative components of the research are carried out. The chapter will then look at how the answers to the sequence and priority questions serve to create the overall design of the research.

Chapter 6 focuses on *Combining the data*. Initially, the chapter provides an overview of the terminology used by mixed methods researchers when combining the data, to familiarise the new mixed methods researcher with the variety of terms in use. The core aspects of Greene et al.'s (1989) framework for combining quantitative and qualitative data are then explained, namely: triangulation, complementarity, development, initiation, and expansion. For each of the five methods proposed, an outline of the process is provided, alongside an example of where this has been employed in criminological research. Step-by-step guidance is provided to help students make justifiable methodological decisions about how to combine their data in practice.

Chapter 7 details *Research design and sampling*. Starting with research design, five different designs are considered (cross-sectional, case study, longitudinal, experimental, and comparative), with reference to how they can be utilised in a mixed methods project. A range of different sampling techniques are then discussed, including probability (random, systematic, and stratified), non-probability (convenience, purposive, snowball, theoretical, and quota), and sampling that can be either probability or non-probability depending on how it is used (cluster and multi-stage).

Chapter 8 concentrates on *Data collection methods* and how they can be used in your research project. It supports you in making informed decisions about which data collection methods you are going to adopt, and how you will connect them in practice. Five common primary data collection methods are discussed (questionnaires, interviews, focus groups, observations, and media analyses), as well as secondary data analysis. The chapter ends with a discussion of the way that the data collection methods introduced in this chapter can be deployed within research projects that adopt the basic mixed methods designs (introduced in Chapter 5 – Mixed methods design) and ways to combine the data (introduced in Chapter 6 – Combining the data).

Chapter 9 looks at *Data analysis*. This chapter is divided into two parts: quantitative data analysis and qualitative data analysis. While we cannot be exhaustive with this chapter (there are entire textbooks dedicated to data analysis), we do give you a good starting point for analysing your data and carrying out a mixed methods project. Quantitative data analysis covers levels of measurement, independent and dependent variables, hypotheses, univariate analysis including measures of central tendency and frequencies, and bivariate analysis including crosstabs and correlation (Cramer's V, Spearman's rho, and Pearson's r). Qualitative analysis covers how to undertake a simple thematic analysis, based on the process of data authentication, the creation of sensitising concepts, coding, moving from codes to themes, and generating themes.

Chapter 10, on *Critique*, details how to fully appraise a mixed methods research project. It provides a thorough overview of the evaluative terms associated with the quantitative strategy (reliability and validity) and qualitative strategy (trustworthiness and authenticity), which should be applied to the inferences generated by each component. It then moves on to introduce and apply mixed methods-specific evaluative terms to assess the meta-inferences (inference quality and inference transferability).

Chapter 11 covers *Troubleshooting*; that is, how to deal with those situations where research does not go according to plan. Because of the nature of mixed methods research, in particular the fact that two or more pieces of data collection are taking place, there is greater opportunity for things to go wrong. Thus, the chapter looks at the potential solutions to common problems that may be encountered in mixed methods research.

Also included is a worked example to show how troubleshooting might operate in a real-life situation, and top tips for success from experienced mixed methods researchers.

Chapter 12 turns your attention to *Writing-up*. This chapter guides you through the process of writing-up a mixed methods research project. Providing step-by-step instructions, it outlines the elements that should be included in a written account. It also addresses technical issues such as structuring arguments and presenting data. The final part of this chapter details a checklist for students to follow when writing-up their work.

Finally, Chapter 13 consists of a number of *Case studies* of actual criminological mixed methods research projects, kindly contributed by researchers in the field. They are included in order to provide concrete illustrations of the process of mixed methods studies and the themes and ideas introduced in the earlier chapters as they apply in 'real-world' research endeavours.

At the back of the book you will find the 'Glossary of key terms'. This defines all the key terms that have been used over the course of the book. Terms that are included in the glossary will appear in **bold** type on their first use. It is important to ensure that you understand the key terms as you are working through the book.

Summary

This chapter provides an introduction to the topic of mixed methods in criminology. Starting with a discussion of quantitative and qualitative research strategies and their associated strengths and weaknesses, we then look at how they are brought together in mixed methods projects. Key terms and definitions are introduced; we define mixed methods as *the systematic and rigorous bringing together of quantitative and qualitative research methods and data into a coherent whole, where this whole is greater than the sum of its individual component parts, in order to answer a central research question.* Some of the advantages and disadvantages of mixed methods are explored, before considering why mixed methods is a useful strategy, and concluding that it is of utility when it offers the best way of addressing a central research question. Next, we distinguish the mixed methods strategy from the so-called 'multiple methods' or 'multi methods' approaches. Finally, we suggest that the mixed methods strategy has something of a natural affinity with criminology, as its pragmatic nature fits well with what is often seen as an applied discipline with real impacts in the world of policy. We end by providing an outline of the rest of the book.

We hope that this book will offer you a useful 'how to' guide as you consider your own mixed methods project. Remember that mixed methods is challenging and requires hard work on your part, but it can undoubtedly be 'exciting to do, rewarding, and [can] often produce results that are broader and of more significant impact than research that uses one method alone' (Morse and Niehaus, 2009: 9). By the time you have finished reading this book you will have developed your research skills and be able to produce comprehensive and impactful conclusions. We wish you the best of luck as you embark on your own criminological mixed methods journey!

Learning questions

- What is the mixed methods strategy?
- What is the difference between mixed methods and multiple methods?
- How is mixed methods research having an impact upon the discipline of criminology?

2 Creating a mixed methods question and project planning

CHAPTER OVERVIEW

- Introduction
- Developing a mixed methods research project
- Research questions
- Literature searching
- Research aims
- Research objectives
- Clarifying your ideas and planning your project
- Initial mixed methods project planning checklist
- Summary
- Learning questions

Introduction

Planning a mixed methods research project can be a daunting task. The process will require you to make many decisions that are inter-related, particularly in the early stages, and will impact the final structure and outcomes of your project. This chapter will help you to begin your research journey by guiding you through each step of the project planning process. The first part outlines two key features of conducting mixed methods research, undertaking a systematic process and using mixed methods terminology. We then explain how to create an appropriate mixed methods central research question, including all the practical factors that need to be taken into consideration. Once you have an idea about the central research question you wish to answer, you can begin the process of literature searching and we provide a range of tips to locate the most relevant literature and how this may re-shape your question. This is followed by guidance on how to create appropriate mixed methods research aims and objectives. We then introduce some of the interconnecting decisions you will need to make throughout your initial project planning. Once you are familiar with the types of decisions a mixed methods project will entail, an outline of the next steps to begin creating your project will be provided. We give an insight into the series of decisions you will have to make when you begin to formulate your mixed methods project, ready for you to utilise the information that follows in Chapters 4–9. The chapter concludes with a step-by-step checklist to help you through the first part of the mixed methods project planning process.

Developing a mixed methods research project

We define mixed methods research as: the systematic and rigorous bringing together of qualitative and quantitative research methods and data into a coherent whole, where this whole is greater than the sum of its individual component parts, in order to answer a **central research question**. A mixed methods research project relies upon the researcher undertaking a **systematic process**, but what does 'systematic' mean in practice? The dictionary definition of systematic is something that is 'done or acting according to a fixed plan or system; methodical' (Oxford Dictionary, 2018). This translates into a mixed methods context by ensuring your research follows an orderly and well-justified process. See Box 2.1 for a range of characteristics associated with a systematic research project.

Box 2.1   Characteristics of a systematic research process

- Meticulous planning

  ○ Creating a written plan and continually updating it
  ○ Keeping resources (e.g. notes) together and filing them in order
  ○ Following the research process (see Figure 2.1)
  ○ Making links between philosophy, combining the data, mixed methods design, research design, sampling, data collection and data analysis
  ○ Deciding on your plan before commencing data collection

- Scheduling and undertaking tasks in a logical order

  ○ Setting aside enough time to complete tasks
  ○ Finishing one task before starting the next (where possible and relevant)
  ○ Completing the stages of the research process in the correct order

- Carrying out the research according to plan

  ○ Following the correct processes and techniques
  ○ Creating milestone deadlines

- Producing a write-up that accurately reflects your project

  ○ Writing-up an account that demonstrates and reflects the project plan
  ○ Editing and re-writing to produce a polished piece of work

---

The notion of working systematically may seem quite overwhelming when beginning to think about undertaking a mixed methods research project because of all the decisions that need to be made. Feelings of uncertainty about what your new project will look like in reality are completely normal. Essentially, all mixed methods research projects follow a

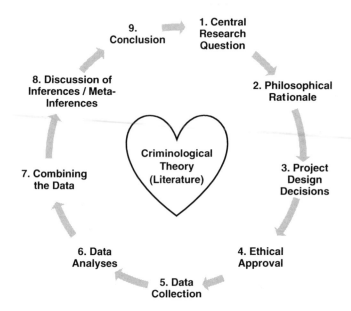

Figure 2.1 The mixed methods research process.

very similar structure. The process illustrated in Figure 2.1 details all the stages you need to undertake to complete your project. You will note that criminological theory is at the heart of the process. This is because theory and research from the discipline will help you to shape your own research project. You will also be adding to the field and extending our knowledge about a criminological topic (even if your contribution is small). Generating new knowledge is one of the key reasons for undertaking research, hence why criminological theory is at the heart of the research process. Criminological theory helps researchers to make sense of their inferences/meta-inferences (findings) and inform their conclusions. For more about the role of theory in research see Chapter 4 – Philosophy. Answering one central research question can lead to the generation of another, hence the circular process.

During the initial stages of your project, the most important thing to remember is that mixed methods research requires careful planning because of the multiple quantitative and qualitative components. You may not be familiar with some of the terminology used in Figure 2.1, such as **inferences** and **meta-inferences**, which are mixed methods specific. We use a range of mixed methods terminology throughout the book that we detail in Table 2.1, alongside information about the chapter that explains this term in detail. It is important that you grasp basic mixed methods language at the outset as this will enable you to be more precise in your initial planning. Comprehensive information about mixed methods project development can be found in Chapters 4–9. To help with your planning, make detailed notes of all your ideas as you go along (no matter how big or small) so you can keep track of your thinking. This will help you to manage the multiple decisions that need to be made and will provide evidence to help you to justify your methodological decisions.

Table 2.1 Introducing key mixed methods terminology

Mixed methods term	Definition	For details see chapter . . .
Component	Constituent parts of your mixed methods design that, when combined, make up your mixed methods research. They are either quantitative or qualitative. Mixed methods requires a minimum of one quantitative component and one qualitative component.	We refer to this term throughout the book.
Inferences	The conclusions and interpretations from each single component (quantitative or qualitative) of a mixed methods research project.	These two terms are used and contextualised throughout the book.
Meta-inferences	The conclusions and interpretations drawn from across all of the quantitative and qualitative components.	
Pragmatism	An epistemological position often adopted in mixed methods research. Pragmatism seeks to bypass the debates around positivism and interpretivism by taking a practical stance that focuses on the research questions at hand, utilising the most appropriate research tools available to provide the 'best' possible outcome.	4 – Philosophy
Multiple realities	An ontological position often associated with mixed methods research. It suggests that there is no single 'correct' ontological understanding of the social world, and instead there are multiple understandings of reality that each have some validity.	4 – Philosophy
Abductive	Refers to the relationship between theory and research, where there is a back-and-forth relationship between theory generation and theory testing, with theories being successively tested and developed as the research progresses (see 'deductive' and 'inductive' for related approaches).	4 – Philosophy
Mixed methods design	The element of a mixed methods study where decisions on the priority question and the sequence question are made. The answers to these questions, and the way the answers are combined, result in an overall mixed methods design.	5 – Mixed methods design
Sequence question	A question that researchers must answer when designing a mixed methods project: In what order do the qualitative and quantitative components occur, simultaneously or sequentially?	5 – Mixed methods design
Priority question	A question that researchers must answer when designing a mixed methods project: Are the qualitative and the quantitative components of equivalent priority or is one component of greater priority than the other?	5 – Mixed methods design

Combining the data	How we refer to the 'mixing' of inferences to generate meta-inferences.	6 – Combining the data
Triangulation	Used in mixed methods research where two or more methods are used to investigate the same phenomenon. The aim is to seek a convergence and corroboration of the inferences generated from each research component.	6 – Combining the data
Complementarity	Used in mixed methods research where two or more methods are used to investigate distinct, albeit often overlapping, aspects of a phenomenon in order to produce rich, deep understanding.	6 – Combining the data
Development	A technique of mixed methods research involving the employment of a sequential design, with the inferences drawn from the first component used to help inform the development of the second component. This approach is employed to increase the robustness of the findings and any concepts generated as a result.	6 – Combining the data
Initiation	Refers to mixed methods research where new perspectives or paradoxes emerge. This may not have been the purpose of the mixed methods design, but the inferences generated from each component of the research allow for further analysis to be undertaken to create new knowledge and ideas.	6 – Combining the data
Expansion	Refers to mixed methods research that provides breadth and depth to the exploration of a particular phenomenon. This approach reflects the philosophically pragmatic notion of selecting the most appropriate tool for the job at hand.	6 – Combining the data

Research questions

A central research question is 'the overarching question that defines the scope, scale and conduct of a research project' (Gilbert, 2008: 512). In mixed methods research, the central research question drives the creation of the research project because all subsequent decisions you make will be focused on answering that question. To a large extent, it is the question itself that influences the decision to undertake mixed methods research in the first place (Onwuegbuzie and Leech, 2006). Therefore, it is important to spend some time thinking about how to create a clear and researchable question; and it should be a question, ending with a question mark.

When creating a mixed methods research project, the type of question you pose will influence the decisions you make about philosophy, mixed methods design, each of the data collection components, data analysis and how you combine them. These decisions will ultimately shape what the overall mixed methods project will look like. To create a mixed methods central research question, you need to ensure it is broad enough to cover both quantitative and qualitative research strategies. The language used in the central research question should be neither too deductive nor too inductive in approach, allowing for the inclusion of both research strategies (see Chapter 4 – Philosophy). For example, a mixed methods central research question should avoid the use of explicitly quantitative terms such as 'measurement' or 'relationship'. A generic mixed methods central research question could be as simple as: 'What are public perceptions of anti-social behaviour?'

Central research questions and subsidiary questions

We advocate the creation of one central research question per project, with **subsidiary questions** employed where appropriate, based upon the needs of the research. A subsidiary, or sub-question, is a question that helps you to answer your central research question, but is component specific. Particular quantitative and qualitative concerns can be acknowledged by using subsidiary questions that relate to the strategy employed by each component (either quantitative or qualitative). See Figure 2.2 for a visualisation, with examples of quantitative and qualitative subsidiary questions.

There is a connection between the research question you intend to answer and the way you will combine the data from your quantitative and qualitative research components. If you employ subsidiary questions for each research component, your inferences can be combined in four different ways: complementarity, development, initiation, and expansion. This is because the different components of the research will seek to answer slightly different, but related questions. The inferences generated by answering the subsidiary questions will combine to create the meta-inferences that will answer the overarching central research question. In contrast, you may decide that you only need to have one central research question and no subsidiary questions, in which case you will employ triangulation to combine your data (where two or more methods are used to investigate the same phenomenon). We discuss this further in Chapter 6 – Combining the data.

The philosophical pragmatism that underpins mixed methods research, and the idea of using the best tools for the job at hand, will drive the decisions you make about whether to employ subsidiary questions in your study (see Chapter 4 – Philosophy). These interconnections highlight the complex and dynamic nature of mixed methods research questions (Plano Clark and Badiee, 2010). However, if you focus on what you would like your research to find out and how you plan to combine the inferences from each component, creating a mixed methods central research question and any subsidiary questions should not prove too daunting a task.

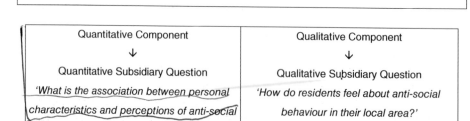

Mixed Methods Central Research Question
'What are public perceptions of anti-social behaviour?'

Quantitative Component	Qualitative Component
↓	↓
Quantitative Subsidiary Question	Qualitative Subsidiary Question
'What is the association between personal characteristics and perceptions of anti-social behaviour?'	*'How do residents feel about anti-social behaviour in their local area?'*

Figure 2.2 Visualisation of a mixed methods central research question and subsidiary questions.

Choosing a topic

When set the challenge of creating a research project it can be difficult to know where to start, especially if you can choose any topic. When thinking about the area you would like to research it may be useful to consider your interests, preferences for certain types of research, previous learning, adjacent learning, and career plans (Box 2.2). These factors are not necessarily mutually exclusive, but thinking about each one in turn should help you to identify your research topic.

Box 2.2   Things to consider when choosing a research topic

- Area(s) of criminology you find interesting
- Preferences for types of research (from Davies, 2011)
- Previous learning
- Adjacent learning
- Career plans

A helpful starting point is to consider what aspect(s) of criminology you find particularly interesting. It may also help you to think about why you chose to study criminology in the first place. What are the topics that you love learning about? Has being a victim of crime or real-life experience of the criminal justice system fuelled your interest in criminology? What criminological debates engage and/or enrage you? What part of criminology would you like to change, contribute to, and expand? For example: is it youth justice? Drugs? Prisons? Mentally disordered offenders? Anti-social behaviour? The list of criminological areas is extensive. Assessing your personal interests is a very important consideration because a research project is usually a substantial piece of work that can last for a semester or a whole year. Therefore, selecting a topic that excites you will help you to maintain your engagement and momentum throughout the process. Making a list of topics, or drawing a mind-map of some of the issues associated with a topic, may provide a helpful visualisation of your thought processes. You might also find it advantageous to list the topics or debates you do not wish to study, as this can help to clarify the things you really like. Talking these ideas through with a peer on your course can be useful too, along with discussing it with someone you know well, but who has no knowledge of criminology – known as the Grandma test (see Box 2.3).

Box 2.3   The Grandma test

Selecting a research topic can be challenging, so it can be very useful to talk through your ideas with someone that has no criminological knowledge, like your Grandma (other relatives, childhood friends, or neighbours are just as good). This is because they know you well enough to challenge your thinking, and their lack of criminological training means that they are likely to pose questions that you may think are too obvious. Considering these foundational-type questions can help to crystallise your thought process. Moreover, if you cannot persuade your Grandma about your research idea, it is unlikely you are going to convince the academic marking your work. Bear in mind that your entire research project, in terms of both the process and meta-inferences, should be accessible and make sense to a non-criminologist. Therefore, starting out with a clear central research question is the basis to achieve this.

Relatedly, Davies (2011) suggests there are four different types of research: policy-related research, intervention research, theoretical research, and critical research (see Box 2.4). When thinking about your research options you may find it useful to consider which type of research your chosen topic best relates to, as well as the type of research you would feel most confident conducting. For example, some people are really interested in policy-related research but less enthused by theoretical research. One of the strengths of mixed methods is that it provides the opportunity to combine a range of research types by selecting different types for different components. For instance, a research project could have one quantitative component that reflects intervention research and one qualitative component that embodies theoretical research. You can just as easily employ quantitative or qualitative methods for each of the different types of research.

Box 2.4   Types of research (Davies, 2011)

Policy-related research

Linked to criminal justice policy, this type of research focuses on collecting data to inform the creation of policies relating to actors within the criminal justice system, such as victims, offenders, and the general public. For example, a mixed methods project might investigate police discrimination relating to stop-and-search policies, with a central research question of: How do black, Asian, and ethnic minority people perceive police and stop-and-search policies?

Intervention research

This focuses on the evaluation of programmes that intend to have a specific outcome, such as drug rehabilitation or family intervention programmes. The research usually tests whether the intervention has been successful or not. For example, a mixed methods project could assess the success of the Troubled Families programme; an initiative designed to provide support to families to stop and prevent anti-social behaviour. An appropriate central research question would be: To what extent has the Troubled Families programme been effective in reducing anti-social behaviour?

Theoretical research

Understanding and explaining human behaviour are the primary concerns of theoretical research in criminology. This could relate to a variety of criminological topics, particularly when considering human action in relation to social and criminal justice institutions. The focus is on developing a deeper understanding of a phenomenon rather than a policy or intervention programme. For example, a mixed methods project may explore the reasons why people consume recreational drugs, with a central research question such as: Why do people use recreational drugs?

Critical research

Combining elements of policy-related research and theoretical research, critical research considers human actions and policies, with reference to social structure and theory. For example, a critical research mixed methods project could examine gendered perspectives of victim-focused policy, with a central research question of: What differences do different genders encounter when reporting rape?

As well as being interested in your research topic and knowing which type of research you wish to conduct, you can also focus your ideas strategically. By the time you are asked to undertake a criminological research project you will have already completed a range of core learning about the subject. You can draw upon the materials from previous modules/units and learning experiences to start thinking about what questions remain unanswered and the types of new research that you could undertake to answer them. You will need to carry out some preliminary reading about your topic area before being able to formulate a question, so basing your research on a topic that you have already studied means that you can utilise the existing reading list. Re-visiting previous materials and notes may also help to remind you about the topics that interest you. Furthermore, examining topics you have already studied can help you to appreciate the variety of criminological areas that can be studied.

It is important that your research is relevant to the discipline so your meta-inferences contribute towards the creation of new knowledge. An example of a relevant research project would be a study that investigates public perceptions of prisoners. It has criminal justice policy relevance and there is a substantial body of existing literature and research, which can be used to refine ideas and help to identify how the new project has the potential to add to knowledge of the field. In contrast, a research question that attempts to examine something inconceivable would be deemed irrelevant, such as considering whether all offenders should be imprisoned on an island. This example sounds a little extreme, but serves to highlight how research questions should keep real-world, relevant, and realistic concerns in mind.

In addition to considering your previous criminological experiences, think about the topics you will be studying while you are conducting your research project (adjacent learning). It can be advantageous to link your taught module learning to your research project. This is because similar topics will have common foundational reading. Furthermore, you will have the opportunity to ask the person delivering the content any questions arising from your research. This can often be in addition to the individual supervising your research, who may not be an expert in that area, thus maximising the potential support available.

Finally, think about whether your mixed methods research can link to your career ambitions. Are you currently volunteering with a criminal justice agency or third sector organisation? If so, what research would assist their core business? Alternately, if you are considering a career in the police, prison service or with probation, what are the current issues facing these criminal justice institutions? Conducting research, such as a dissertation, in a relevant and/or topical area may enhance a future job application and give you something to discuss during a recruitment event or interview.

Types of research questions

When starting to think about the topic you would like to investigate, it is important to know and understand the different types of questions that you can pose. De Vaus (2001) suggests there are two types of research questions: **descriptive research questions** and **explanatory research questions**; see Box 2.5.

Box 2.5   Descriptive vs explanatory research questions (De Vaus, 2001)

Descriptive research

Descriptive research finds out what is going on, such as: how much crime is there in an area? Descriptive questions allow researchers to create a benchmark, which in turn creates the opportunity for explanatory research. Examples of descriptive research questions for student projects include:

- What is the extent of anti-social behaviour on campus?
- What is the level of student trust in the police?
- What do students think about security staff in nightclubs?

Explanatory research

Explanatory research finds out why something is going on. For instance: why does an area experience a certain crime rate? Examples of explanatory research questions for student projects include:

- Why is there anti-social behaviour on campus?
- Why do students trust or mistrust the police?
- Why are students negative about nightclub security staff?

According to De Vaus (2001), the type of question you select will fundamentally affect the purpose of your research project. Therefore, a good starting point is to ask yourself which type of research question you would like to investigate: a descriptive research (what) question or an explanatory (why) research question? Or, consider whether your mixed methods project could incorporate both.

Practical considerations

When formulating a mixed methods central research question it is essential to be realistic about what you will be able to achieve. It is likely that your research will be subject to a range of practical constraints. These restrictions will require you to balance time, resources, and ethical considerations. To illustrate, you might have limited time to complete your project because of competing deadlines. It is likely your research will span either one semester (possibly 12 weeks) or an academic year, and during that time you will have other assessments to complete, alongside your non-academic life. Therefore, your research questions should be answerable within the given timescale.

It is also important to consider the resources at your disposal. You may not have the financial means to collect the data you desire. Carefully reflect on the potential cost of your research and see where any savings can be made. For example, universities often loan equipment such as audio recorders to students free of charge which saves you having to buy your own, or you could use telephony technology such as Skype or FaceTime to avoid paying travel costs (encryption and data security are discussed in Chapter 3 – Ethics). Resources might not just be financial in nature: you may not have access to your desired participants because there is insufficient time to build relationships, so build these potential restrictions into your question formulation process.

Furthermore, you will also have to consider the ethical implications of your proposed question at the outset. Novice researchers are unlikely to be granted ethical approval by their university to undertake research with vulnerable groups, such as children, victims of crime or prisoners, because of the potential harms that participants and the researcher may suffer. For instance, an undergraduate student is unlikely to be given permission to interview victims of child sexual exploitation, or serial killers in prison (topics that students are often interested in). Therefore, if you would like to research a sensitive topic, think about the different possible ways you could do this. To illustrate, if you are desperate to research serial killers, you could navigate the ethics process by conducting a public perception survey about your target group or use secondary data collected by an experienced researcher, rather than trying to research them directly. Always try to think about what you can potentially do, rather than focusing on what you cannot. See Chapter 3 – Ethics for information about how a mixed methods project can facilitate and enhance research into sensitive subjects.

Concepts in your central research question

Once you have decided on the topic you would like to research and considered all the constraints within which you have to work, the challenge of writing the question begins. The first part of writing a question is thinking about the **concepts** that will make up your question. According to De Vaus (2014: 41), 'concepts are simply tools which fulfil a useful shorthand function: they are abstract summaries of a whole set of behaviours, attitudes and characteristics which we see as having something in common'. Consequently, concepts are the building blocks of research questions. The term originates from the quantitative strategy, but it is still applicable for mixed methods research question development because it helpfully allows us to group ideas together in a manageable way and provides a starting point for your literature search. For example, if your research project is going to examine public perceptions of anti-social behaviour, the two concepts you are interested in are: public perceptions and anti-social behaviour. If you are investigating gender and drug use, the two concepts will be personal characteristics (because this is a more general way of thinking about gender) and drugs.

To get to the stage of identifying your concepts, you will need to start narrowing down the field of study you would like to research. It is helpful to think of this as a funnelling process, as shown in Figure 2.3.

As a starting point, your central research question should contain two concepts. This will help to avoid over-complication and make it a manageable project. Below is a list of concepts that you may find useful. Ideally your question should contain an actor-based concept, which will be the factor that influences and/or impacts upon the criminological concept (similar to an independent variable and dependent variable in quantitative research).

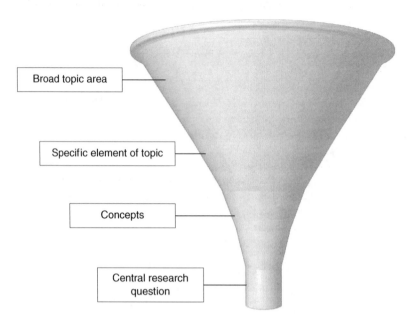

Figure 2.3 Funnelling big ideas into concepts for a central research question.

Actor-based concepts

- Perceptions or attitudes (reflects people's opinions about a topic)
- Personal characteristics (includes age, gender, ethnicity, etc.)

Criminological concepts

- Anti-social behaviour
- Crime prevention
- Desistance
- Drugs
- Fear of crime
- Police
- Prison
- Probation
- Victimisation
- Young people

Creating a question

Once you have selected your chosen topic area, considered the practical constraints, and identified the concepts you wish to research, you can begin the process of piecing together your central research question and any subsidiary questions. Being able to answer your central research question is the fundamental reason you are undertaking your research project. Plus, in mixed methods research the question drives all the subsequent planning decisions you will make. Therefore, this is a crucial part of the project planning process that will require time and careful consideration.

It is good practice to draft more than one potential central research question. Box 2.6 contains some examples of good and not so good research questions. Once you have a fair idea about the question you would like your research to answer, you should spend some time thinking about and refining the wording. Generally, central research questions should not be too lengthy. Therefore, try to refine your question into 12 words or fewer. This can be challenging and may require numerous drafts and re-drafts. This is a completely normal (and sometimes frustrating) part of the process. The other thing to ensure during this refinement stage is that your question finishes with a question mark, so it reads like a question. This may sound obvious, but can sometimes be overlooked.

Writing your very first mixed methods central research question can be difficult. Bryman (2016: 83) has produced evaluative criteria for research questions, which can be used as a checklist to ensure your central research question has the desired characteristics:

✓   Is it clear?
✓   Is it researchable?
✓   Is there some connection(s) to established theory and research?
✓   If you have a central research question and subsidiary questions, are they linked?
✓   Is there the prospect of making an original contribution to the field?
✓   Is the research question neither too broad nor too narrow?

Box 2.6   Examples of good and not so good mixed methods central research questions

Good mixed methods central research questions

- How do victims navigate the criminal justice system?
- What are public perceptions of anti-social behaviour?
- Why has hate crime increased post–Brexit?
- How does gender influence fear of crime?
- What are students' opinions of recreational drug use?

Not so good mixed methods central research questions

- Men commit more crimes than women. (Not a question and not an original contribution.)
- How does gender affect drug use, domestic violence, and homelessness? (Not researchable – too broad and too many concepts to research in one project.)
- What is the relationship between gender and fear of crime? (Not mixed methods – biased towards the quantitative strategy.)
- How do people feel about hate crime? (Not mixed methods – biased towards the qualitative strategy.)
- Are you afraid to walk alone in your local area after dark? (Too narrow – this reads more like a questionnaire question than a central research question.)

Refining and altering questions

Students are often concerned that once they have formulated a central research question and/or subsidiary questions, they are final and cannot be changed. This is not the case, because questions can be refined throughout the research process. Ideally, once you have started your data collection the wording of your central research question will not change dramatically, but up until that point there is a good degree of flexibility. Many research questions will inevitably change as more knowledge is gained about the topic being researched, which is a common part of the research process. Box 2.7 provides an example of how a central research question might progress through the refinement stages.

Box 2.7   Example of the refining process for a central research question

Drafting a strong central research question takes time and perseverance. Below are some examples of how a central research question might evolve from a first draft to a final draft. In reality it may take more (or fewer) stages to get to the point where you are happy with the question you have produced. Having gone through the process of idea generation and refinement, we are interested in:

Concepts: personal characteristics and anti-social behaviour

First draft, after preliminary reading and considering interests: Why do young people commit anti-social behaviour in their local community?

Second draft, taking into account practical constraints: Why do young people commit anti-social behaviour? *Local community omitted because the researcher cannot focus on the one community they have access to, because of their inability to travel there for financial reasons.*

Third draft, thinking about ethical approval: What do people think about adults committing anti-social behaviour? *'Young people' omitted as the target sample because of concerns about not obtaining ethical approval because children under 18 are seen as a vulnerable group (see Chapter 3 – Ethics). Asking the opinions of adults seems a more practical approach.*

Final draft, following the main literature review: What are public perceptions of anti-social behaviour? *Wording refined to reflect how the literature articulates people's thoughts about anti-social behaviour, namely 'public perceptions'. It is fewer than 12 words and poses a question. Subsidiary questions can now be developed to reflect quantitative and qualitative concerns.*

Literature searching

To formulate a central research question and subsidiary question(s), you must have some appreciation of the related criminological literature to inform your thinking. However, once a central research question has been formulated, a thorough review of the literature relating to your topic is required. According to Punch (2016: 70), this is necessary because you need to 'identify the literature that is relevant to the study and be familiar with it [and] locate the present study in relation to the literature'. You should develop an understanding of the literature to learn about previous research that has been conducted in the area, so the findings of previous studies can be utilised to inform your research project. Locating your study in relation to existing research findings will help you to identify what new knowledge your project will create. For example, you might replicate a study with a different sample of the population. Furthermore, reading about the work of previous researchers and the types of methodology they employed should help you to make a range of informed project planning decisions to ensure your research project is as successful as possible (see Figure 2.1, Boxes 2.16 and 2.17, and Chapter 5 – Mixed methods design).

Starting your **literature review** will be the first substantial task of your research project after question formulation, and it is neither a quick nor straightforward process. You will need to search for, locate, and consider numerous different literature sources and start to organise the topics/sub-topics that emerge into a coherent order, which sets the scene for your research. Students often ask how many sources they should read before their literature search is 'done'. Unfortunately, there is no set number of items that need to be read because different criminological topics have different amounts of literature. At this point it is easier to consider what the finished product needs to look like. When your final written-up literature review is complete, it should cover all the main topics related to your central research question. Therefore, you need to read enough literature relating to your research area to cover all the core areas and to know you have read enough. For example, a literature review related to a question that investigates public perceptions of anti-social behaviour would include sections on: defining and measuring anti-social behaviour, theoretical approaches to anti-social behaviour, anti-social behaviour legislation and public perceptions of anti-social behaviour. After completing some initial reading, the main areas related to your research question will start to become apparent because you will see those topics recur regularly throughout your reading – make a note of them. It is important at this initial stage of your research project to be really organised so you do not waste time or lose any information; to this end you may find the tips in Box 2.8 helpful. Plus, neatly organising your research project from the outset helps to feed into the principles of conducting a systematic research process, explained earlier in Box 2.1.

Box 2.8   Top tips for organising your literature review sources

- Maintain a list of all the literature you have accessed.
- Document which pieces of literature you intend to use and which you have rejected, noting why they have been rejected.
- At the top of any notes you make, always write out the full reference for the source, using the referencing format adopted by your institution (e.g. APA 6th). You may also wish to save this information electronically in specific referencing software such as Endnote.

(continued)

(continued)

- Keep a record of page numbers for direct quotations.
- Where possible, start filing your notes according to the sub-topic they relate to.
- As you develop your body of notes, start to plan an outline of your literature review that lists the relevant areas and think about what order these might be presented in. Using sub-headings with bullet-point notes can help.

Types of literature sources

There are a variety of different types of literature that you should consult, with each source providing you with different types of information; see Box 2.9.

Box 2.9 Different types of literature sources

- Monographs (research-based books)
- Journal articles
- PhD theses
- Textbooks
- Government reports
- Official statistics
- Blogs (academic/non-academic)
- Websites (official criminal justice system/other miscellaneous sites)

A sensible starting point for any project is to consult a criminology textbook such as Newburn (2017) *Criminology* (3rd edition). This is the type of source you would read initially to get an idea about a topic for your research project. However, a criminology textbook is problematic for a literature review because it is not a **primary source**. A primary source is the original version of a document. Textbooks are a **secondary source** because they provide the author's interpretation of the research that has been undertaken, rather than the researcher's own account. Although textbooks are written by authoritative figures within the discipline, they can only reflect a fraction of the information contained in the original piece of work. Therefore, textbooks should be used to identify key studies that have taken place within a topic, which can be followed up and read as a primary source. Some students are daunted by this prospect, mistakenly under the impression that they will not be able to 'say it better' than the textbook author who has already summarised the original work. There is no need to worry here because you are not in competition with the textbook author. Reading the primary source will give you a much greater insight into the research that took place, providing more depth to the findings presented and the methodological process undertaken.

The best sources to utilise for a literature review are monographs (books based on research projects) and journal articles. This is because these resources are focused on empirical research and produced directly by the researchers themselves. These sources will contain information about the findings and the methodology. Monographs and journal articles are written by experts in the field you are researching and before publication go through an intense peer-review process by other academic specialists. This means their ideas are scrutinised to ensure that the research is rigorous and the conclusions drawn accurately reflect the data. Using these sources in your literature review will help you to build a strong and coherent overview of up-to-date knowledge in the area, and will demonstrate to the person marking your work that you know where to access the most reliable information about your topic. PhD theses are similar, as the purpose of a PhD is to provide a new contribution to knowledge. All UK PhD theses are required to be sent to the British Library upon completion. Hence, their catalogue contains over 480,000 doctoral theses (British Library, 2018), which can be searched by keyword (see http://ethos.bl.uk/Home.do;jsessionid=CCF311DD23328CEB1E14F46 2D1D8BAF4).

Government reports and official statistics are useful sources to include in your literature review because they provide up-to-date details on a range of criminological topics. This information is a helpful addition to a literature review because it reflects the 'official' perspective relating to your topic area (Finch and Fafinski, 2016) and can help you to contextualise your arguments. However, their utility is limited by the often political nature of government reports; for example, some of the statements may be based on political ideology as opposed to research evidence. Similarly, official statistics should be viewed with caution because of changing counting rules and the crimes/victims that are unaccounted for, known as the 'dark figure of crime'. Being aware of and acknowledging these weaknesses in your writing should allow you to provide a balanced account of these data in your literature review. See Box 2.10 for a list of websites to search for these sources.

Box 2.10   Sources of government publications and official statistics

England and Wales

- Home Office publications: www.gov.uk/government/publications?departmen ts%5B%5D=home-office
- Ministry of Justice publications: www.gov.uk/government/publications?depar tments%5B%5D=ministry-of-justice
- Police-recorded crime and the Crime Survey for England and Wales accessible via the Office for National Statistics: www.ons.gov.uk/people populationandcommunity/crimeandjustice
- Local police-recorded crime: www.police.uk

Scotland

- Scottish Government crime and justice publications: www.gov.scot/Topics/ Statistics/Browse/Crime-Justice/Publications
- Scottish Crime and Justice Survey: www.gov.scot/Topics/Statistics/Browse/ Crime-Justice/crime-and-justice-survey

(continued)

(continued)

Northern Ireland

- Department of Justice publications: www.justice-ni.gov.uk/publications
- Northern Ireland Crime Survey: www.justice-ni.gov.uk/articles/northern-ireland-crime-survey
- Local police-recorded crime: www.police.uk

USA

- FBI Uniform Crime Reporting Program: https://ucr.fbi.gov/ucr-publications
- Bureau of Justice Statistics publications: www.bjs.gov/index.cfm?ty=pbo
- National Crime Victimization Survey: www.bjs.gov/index.cfm?ty=dcdetail&iid=245

Canada

- Statistics Canada 'Crime and Justice' Publications: www150.statcan.gc.ca/n1/en/subjects/crime_and_justice
- Statistics Canada 'Results and documentation of surveys and statistical programs – Crime and Justice': www150.statcan.gc.ca/n1/en/type/surveys?MM=1
- Uniform Crime Reporting Survey: www23.statcan.gc.ca/imdb/p2SV.pl?Function=getSurvey&SDDS=3302

Australia

- Australian Bureau of Statistics Publications: www.abs.gov.au/Crime-and-Justice
- Recorded Crime Offenders: www.abs.gov.au/ausstats/abs@.nsf/0/DA308C67766C3735CA257751001BD477?Opendocument
- Recorded Crime Victims: www.abs.gov.au/ausstats/abs@.nsf/0/DA3DED213BAE8114CA257178001B6949?Opendocument

New Zealand

- Ministry of Justice publications: www.justice.govt.nz/about/publication-finder
- Crime and Safety Survey: www.justice.govt.nz/justice-sector-policy/research-data/nzcass

The least useful sources for a literature review are blogs and websites. Often favoured by students because they can be found with a 'quick Google', blogs and websites do not contain the same academic integrity as monographs and journal articles. This is because anyone can post a webpage or article on the internet and there is no guarantee that the information reported is correct. Remember, algorithms employed by search engines such as Google are configured to prioritise relevance and popularity, not academic authority. Having said that, some useful criminology-related blogs and articles do exist, such as through independent news outlet 'The Conversation', the London School of Economic Politics and Policy blog, and the Sheffield Institute for Policy Studies blog. These sources are written by academics and are usually based on a research publication, so if you find something like this, always search for the primary source, which will likely be a journal article. Websites vary hugely in their content. Some run by criminal justice charities, such as the Howard League for Penal Reform or the Prison Reform Trust, can provide valuable insights into current debates and policies. In contrast, websites such as Wikipedia, the free online encyclopaedia which can be edited by anyone, should be avoided at all costs! There is no academic scrutiny of their content and using these sources as part of your literature review will jeopardise the quality of your understanding, putting the value of your entire project at risk. Essentially, proceed with caution as far as blogs and websites are concerned.

Overall, your literature search should seek to gather information about your topic from a variety of sources; see Table 2.2. However, certain types of sources, such as monographs, journal articles, and PhD theses, are more valuable to researchers because they will contain findings from empirical research and details about others' research methodology. Consequently, try to ensure your final set of literature from your main literature search (see Box 2.14) has a larger proportion of monographs and journal articles than other sources.

Selecting relevant sources for a mixed methods project

As well as the type of literature source, you should consider the nature of the information being gathered from each source. From the literature, you are seeking to understand where your research is situated in the field, by identifying the research methods used by previous studies and their findings. For a mixed methods research project, you should try to ensure your literature review details a range of previous research that reflects the quantitative and qualitative components being used in your study. For example, if you intend to use a quantitative component to examine public perceptions of anti-social behaviour, you should attempt to locate similar previous quantitative research from the field. Equally, if your qualitative component seeks to explore residents' perspectives of local anti-social behaviour, then you should try to find research that has also used a qualitative strategy. Additionally, attempt to find mixed methods research relating to your question, remembering that mixed methods is an emerging trend in criminology so you may have difficulty. Adopting this approach will help you to situate your study within the current field of knowledge and provide you with specific information about the research methods employed. Locating and accessing previous studies which align to the components in your proposed research might not be possible and will depend on your central research question/subsidiary question(s). If at the end of your main literature search you cannot find any studies that relate to the research you intend to conduct via your different components, simply state that your research will provide an original contribution in that field of study. It is not necessarily a bad thing if previous studies cannot be found, but it is a good idea to include some details about the closest, most relevant previous work.

The other aspect you should take into account is the context within which the research took place, specifically the country of origin. This is important because different countries have markedly different criminal justice systems, which can mean that research from one country may not provide a very good insight into the same topic in another. For example, a mixed methods project examining public perceptions of anti-social behaviour in the UK will differ greatly to a study conducted in the USA because the term anti-social behaviour is not really applicable. Instead, the term 'disorder' is used in the USA to describe similar behaviours and incidents are tackled by very different sanctions. Equally, any studies on perceptions of policing or the death penalty will not transfer well between the UK and the

Table 2.2 Pros and cons of literature sources

Source	Pros	Cons	Usefulness Rating/5*
Monographs	• Written by the researcher(s) • Contains findings and research methods • Current knowledge • Peer-reviewed	• Not all monographs will be available in all libraries, especially older ones	*****
Journal articles	• Written by the researcher(s) • Contains findings and research methods • Current knowledge • Peer-reviewed	• Can sometimes be difficult to read (technical language) • Not all journals will be available in all libraries	*****
PhD theses	• Cutting-edge research • Available online • Peer-reviewed	• Could be too niche	****
Textbooks	• Introduces main theories and research studies • Provides a clear overview • Signposts to original research	• Secondary information • Does not provide the full account • May not be the most up-to-date account	***
Government reports	• 'Official' • Easily accessible	• May not present both sides of an argument • Can lack criminological theory	***
Official statistics	• 'Official' • Easily accessible • Produced regularly	• Missing data e.g. dark figure of crime • May not collect data relating to your topic • May be biased	***
Academic blogs (university affiliated e.g. LSE Politics and Policy http://blogs.lse.ac.uk/politicsandpolicy or the Sheffield Institute for Policy Studies https://sheffieldinstituteforpolicystudies.com/blog)	• Easily accessible • Contains key points from research project • Signposts to primary source	• Should not be used instead of the primary source	***
Criminal justice websites	• Easily accessible • Current • Written by practitioners • May link to research projects	• May not contain empirical research • Little/no scrutiny process • Not peer-reviewed	***
Other websites	• Easily accessible • Readable	• No scrutiny process, no way of knowing if the information is correct • Unlikely to contain empirical research • Author may be unknown • Likely to be a secondary account	*
Non-academic blogs (not university affiliated)	• Easily accessible • Readable	• Little/no scrutiny process • Unlikely to contain empirical research	*

USA because of the divergent approach to criminal justice policy taken by these countries. In contrast, research that investigates the experiences of certain crime types, such as burglary or domestic violence, may transfer better. Overall, this does not mean you cannot use studies outside of your home country in your research where they are relevant; you just have to make sure you create your research based on the criminal justice context you are studying and acknowledge any contextual differences from the literature in your written work.

Library catalogue and searching techniques

There are numerous online systems that you can use to search for literature for your mixed methods research project. However, the most powerful tool at your disposal is your institution's library catalogue facility. This is because it will be configured to find the sources that your institution has access to and it can be set up to locate sources that your institution does not have access to, but can be requested through either the inter-library loan (books) or document supply services (journal articles). Google Scholar is a useful secondary tool to use for your literature review as it will allow you to cross-check your hits from the library catalogue and it may generate some different sources. However, be prepared not to be able to access these straight away. If there is a source from Google Scholar, such as a journal article, that you are unable to obtain but would really like to, it is a good idea to seek advice from your librarian. Your library staff are the experts at finding literature so seek their help where possible. Alternatively, you could email the author to request a copy, or look for open-access versions available through online platforms such as ResearchGate (www.researchgate.net) or Academia (www.academia.edu). Before starting your literature search check to see if your library runs any courses on literature searching, as these will be specific to your library catalogue software.

A more advanced method for finding literature is through searching electronic databases, which will be accessible to you through your library webpages. Other methods of finding literature include searching criminology and criminal justice journal websites and publishers' websites. Finch and Fafinski (2016) provide a thorough overview of how to access literature using these methods in their text *Criminology skills* (2nd edition).

The difference between producing a satisfactory and an excellent literature search is down to the key terms you use to search for the literature; in effect, you get out what you put in. Many textbooks and online resources provide a detailed step-by-step account of how to conduct an online search for literature sources, which is far beyond the detail we can cover in this chapter; see Box 2.11 for a list of resources and Chapter 9 – Data analysis for an overview of Boolean searching techniques.

Box 2.11   Detailed literature searching resources

- Finch, E. and Fafinski, S. (2016). *Criminology skills* (2nd ed.). Oxford: Oxford University Press. See Chapter 2 – Books, Journals and Articles, section 2.4 'Finding Articles'
- Online video tutorial 'Search Smarter, Search Faster' produced by the University of Sydney on YouTube: https://youtu.be/Oa66AxTbjxA
- Online interactive tutorial 'Searching Effectively Using AND, OR NOT' produced by Colorado State University: https://lib2.colostate.edu/tutorials/boolean.html

To begin your search, be that in your library catalogue, a database or journal website, you will need to create a list of keywords to search with. Knowing the best keywords to use for your topic takes some perseverance because some authors refer to topics slightly differently. Keep trying to develop your keywords, and your keyword selection skills, based upon your reading and understanding of the topic. Persistence with your search is essential. If you do not find many sources straight away, do not give up! Revise your keywords and search again (and again) until you begin to build a collection of relevant literature. For a mixed methods project you may need to refine your keywords even further because you will ideally like to find a variety of quantitative, qualitative, and mixed methods literature. This will involve you including specific keywords in your search that relate to all of the strategies, as shown in Box 2.12.

Box 2.12   Research strategy-specific keywords for literature searching

Quantitative

- Association
- Measurement
- Relationship

Qualitative

- Understanding
- Experiences
- Detailed

Mixed methods

- Mixed methods (many mixed methods studies have this as a keyword in journal articles)
- Triangulation (often used as a default for mixed methods analysis – see Chapter 6)
- Pragmatism (for more details on research philosophy, see Chapter 4)

Hidden gems: utilising reference lists

Conducting an online search to locate literature for your project can sometimes prove frustrating, as it is difficult to determine if you have discovered all the relevant literature. Once you have identified the main previous studies related to your topic, the sources themselves can provide a helping hand. This is because the researchers' work you are reading will cite previous research studies. Therefore you can use their reference lists to identify other key studies that are similar to your research. If you look at the reference lists for between three and five similar studies, which have all been published within a timeframe of about five years, you should be able to identify studies that are repeatedly cited and these are likely to be the most important pieces of research. If your own searching process has not located these studies, make finding them a top priority. It would then be useful to examine the reference lists of these articles too, to ensure you have a good coverage of the topic.

Reviewing the literature through a critical lens

Finding a range of relevant sources to be part of your literature review is only part of the process. Once you have identified the relevant sources, you need to read everything carefully to identify the key points that are useful to your literature review. However, the purpose of a literature review is not to be purely descriptive of others' work. You should aim to analyse and evaluate previous work to provide an overarching critical appraisal of your research topic. Denscombe (2017: 374) suggests that a literature review should 'compare and contrast the works and arrive at conclusions about their relative merits and failings'. In order to achieve this, Burns and Sinfield (2012: 201) suggest trying to develop a critical attitude, 'a habit of approaching the world in a questioning and critical way; a desire to rid ourselves of purely instinctive, emotional or belief-based responses and develop the habit of analysis, interpretation and evaluation'. You may even find yourself in a position where you are reviewing literature written by your research supervisor. In this situation it is still okay to be critical about their work; they will be expecting the same treatment as the other authors you refer to. Developing a critical attitude takes time and practice. There are many useful textbooks which explain how to be critical; see Box 2.13 for some suggestions. Furthermore, your institution may offer critical writing workshops that can be undertaken as an addition to your criminological studies.

Box 2.13   Useful resources to develop critical thinking and critical writing

- Burns, T. and Sinfield, S. (2012). *Essential study skills: The complete guide to success at university* (3rd ed.). London: SAGE. See Chapter 13 – How to think effectively: Analytical and critical thinking.
- Cottrell, S. (2011). *Critical thinking skills: Developing effective analysis and argument* (2nd ed.). London: SAGE. The whole text is valuable, but specifically Chapter 8 – Where's the proof? Finding and evaluating sources of evidence.
- Metcalfe, M. (2006). *Reading critically at university*. London: SAGE. More technical than the other texts, this book provides 13 different ways of undertaking a critique. Chapter 14 – Writing-up your critique is also helpful.
- Shon, P. (2015). *How to read journal articles in the social sciences* (2nd ed.). London: SAGE.
- University of Manchester (n.d.). The Academic Phrasebank. [online] Available at: www.phrasebank.manchester.ac.uk.

Ending the literature search and re-refining your question

Even though criminology is a relatively new discipline, there is a wealth of literature available. This can often make it difficult for students to decide when the literature searching process is complete. Fundamentally, the literature reviewing process does not stop until almost the end of your project because you will likely need to re-visit the searching process, possibly revising your search terms once your inferences have been generated. These additional searches allow you to look for literature that corresponds to the inferences and meta-inferences you have generated that were not expected, enabling you to

determine whether your findings confirm or contradict existing research. It is good practice to formulate a literature searching plan to avoid becoming bogged down with doing
too much searching at the expense of undertaking your data collection and analysis; see
the stages of the literature searching process in Box 2.14.

Box 2.14   Stages of literature searching

1   Scoping to determine initial central research question/subsidiary question(s)
2   Main extensive search
3   Supplementary search post-analyses for each component
4   Final supplementary search upon the production of meta-inferences

---

One of the hardest decisions to make about literature searching is when to end the
main extensive search. This is because there is no clear point at which to do this and you
will not want to miss anything out. You will be nearing the end of the main search when
you notice you are no longer finding new sources, or you appear to find repeats of the
same source. This indicates that you have found the most important pieces of literature.
The next challenge is to write up your literature review, with comprehensive guidance
on how to create a synthesised literature review provided in Chapter 12 – Writing-up.

Once you have completed the main search, it is worth re-visiting your central research
question and any subsidiary question(s) to ensure that they reflect what you found in the
literature and it is still the research you wish to carry out. For example, the literature
you have read may indicate that you need to tweak one of the concepts in your central
research question. For instance, a question that initially focused on age differences may be
re-positioned to examine gender differences to reflect the debates uncovered in the literature review. At this early planning stage, it is okay to make slight changes to your research
question as it is just part of the refinement process. The overall process of research question refinement is visualised in Box 2.15.

Box 2.15   Stages of a mixed methods central research question

Initial question (first thoughts)

Working question (post-literature review)

↓

Emerging question (post-data collection and analysis)

↓

Final question (decided before meta-inferences finalised)

Research aims

During the initial project planning stage, you should create an overarching aim for your mixed methods research. This should be what your project broadly hopes to achieve, and includes phrases such as:

- To test the relationship between . . . (quantitative)
- To assess the hypothesis that . . . (quantitative)
- To explore attitudes towards . . . (qualitative)
- To describe feelings about . . . (qualitative)

There is no set number of aims to include, but there should be at least one. For a mixed methods project you may find it useful to include an overall aim for the whole project, plus an aim for each research component. Re-visiting these statements will assist your quest to retain the original vision for your research throughout the lengthy project process. It will also help you to neatly express your intentions to those reading your written work, with the **research aims** and objectives situated at the end of your literature review; see Chapter 12 – Writing-up for more information.

Research objectives

Creating a set of **research objectives** will help to **operationalise** your central research question, any subsidiary question(s) and your research aim by specifically detailing what it is you intend to do in your research project. To operationalise means to put into practice, therefore defining your objectives should help to give some context and purpose to your research aim. We recommend you create three research objectives for your mixed methods project:

Objective 1: intended purpose

Denscombe (2002, 2010) talks about how contemplating the purpose of your research can provide direction to a project. Denscombe (2002: 28) suggests working through the following to ascertain the purpose of your project. Specifically, you might consider whether your research is attempting to:

- forecast some outcome
- explain the causes or consequences of something
- criticise or evaluate some theory or belief
- describe something
- develop good practice
- empower a social group.

Objective 2: intended method

Linked to purpose, it is also valuable at this stage to start framing your research ideas by stating the methods that you intend to use. This does not have to be detailed, but should indicate the components you propose to make up your mixed methods project, how you will combine the data, as well as the mixed methods design, research design, sampling, data collection methods, and data analysis technique. The information in this objective can be edited and refined as part of the project planning process to reflect the decisions you ultimately make.

Objective 3: intended outcomes

This final objective also relates to objective 1 about purpose, but requires you to think more specifically about the end-product of your research project. For students, this may be the production of an assessment paper or dissertation. Alternatively, it might be that you have conducted some policy-related research in partnership with a local organisation or charity, so you may produce a briefing note or set of recommendations that can be circulated to those with an interest in your inferences and meta-inferences. It is useful to consider and articulate the impact that your research might have.

Ideally, your central research question, subsidiary question(s), the research aims, and your research objectives should fit together to create a coherent starting point for your project. Boxes 2.16 and 2.17 provide two examples: a model set of questions, aims, and objectives to demonstrate good practice, and an example of poorly constructed questions, aims, and objectives that highlight what you should avoid. It is vitally important that your questions, aims, and objectives are clear and accurately reflect the research you intend to carry out.

Box 2.16   Aligned questions, aims, and objectives

Example of well-constructed questions, aims, and objectives

Central research question: What are public perceptions of anti-social behaviour?

Subsidiary question 1: What is the association between personal characteristics and perceptions of anti-social behaviour? (Quantitative component)

Subsidiary question 2: How do residents feel about anti-social behaviour in their local area? (Qualitative component)

Aim: The aim of this project is to analyse the connection between different people's perceptions of anti-social behaviour based on their personal experiences.

Objective 1: The intended purpose is to describe how people's experience of anti-social behaviour impacts on their perceptions of anti-social behaviour.

Objective 2: The intended method is mixed methods, adopting a simultaneous convergent parallel design with equal priority. A quantitative questionnaire will assess the association between personal characteristics and perceptions of anti-social behaviour, with qualitative interviews used to explore people's experiences of anti-social behaviour. Both components will employ a cross-sectional research design and use non-probability sampling. The inferences will be combined using complementarity.

Objective 3: The intended outcome is to better understand the factors that drive public perceptions of anti-social behaviour, with a view to sharing the findings with criminal justice stakeholders who are able to implement policies to ameliorate perceptions and reduce anti-social behaviour.

Well-constructed questions, aims, and objectives explained: The central research question is fairly broad and avoids using language that privileges either the quantitative or qualitative strategy. In contrast, the subsidiary questions use the language related to the component they reflect, for example the quantitative term 'association' is used in the quantitative subsidiary question. The aim is a broad, general statement with the objectives highlighting how this will all be operationalised.

Box 2.17   Aligned questions, aims, and objectives

Example of poorly constructed questions, aims, and objectives

Central research question: How effective is the youth justice system?

Subsidiary question 1: –

Subsidiary question 2: –

Aim: The aim is to work out if the public interpret the view that the youth justice system delivers protection to the public and young offenders.

Objective 1: The purpose of this project is to see if the youth justice system is effective.

Objective 2: The method being used is mixed methods.

Objective 3: The outcome will be that it will be seen that the youth justice system is not effective.

Poorly constructed questions, aims, and objectives explained: The central research question is too broad and possibly unachievable within the context of a student project; the youth justice system is a multi-faceted collection of organisations and actors. It also indicates a quantitative concern around effectiveness, rather than a neutral mixed methods approach. There are no subsidiary questions to clarify the central research question; this is not necessarily a problem if the central research question is clear. However, in this instance a lack of subsidiary questions means the already problematic central research question has not been further clarified. The aim gives a little additional insight into the remit of the research, but is simultaneously confusing because it introduces the notion of public perceptions of youth justice, as well as the effectiveness of the system for the young people involved. The objectives are poor too because they fail to accurately operationalise the aim by not providing enough detail. Objective 1 essentially repeats the question and does not heed any of Denscombe's (2002) suggestions. Objective 2 only states the overarching research strategy being employed, without indication of the data collection methods or what information they will collect. Finally, objective 3 assumes a conclusion without the research having been undertaken.

Clarifying your ideas and planning your project

Deciding on your central research question, subsidiary question(s), research aims, and objectives is a significant milestone. Once these choices have been made, numerous further planning decisions are required to shape the development of your mixed methods research project. With a central research question in mind, and a commitment to pragmatism (selecting the best tools for the job, see Chapter 4 – Philosophy), it is useful to divide the project up into its component parts.

Initially, you will need to think about exactly how you are going to go about answering your question. There are a range of factors that will influence your decision-making process, for example practical and ethical concerns will shape your decisions as much as philosophical or mixed methods design concerns. For mixed methods, the range of decisions you will need to make will be more complex than a single method. You will need to ensure the different quantitative and qualitative components work together to create a coherent overall project. In order to comprehend the types of decisions you will need to make as part of the holistic planning process, you must understand the topics covered in Chapters 4–9, namely: philosophy, mixed methods design, combining the data, research design, sampling, data collection and data analysis.

According to Heap and Waters (2018), when undertaking a mixed methods research project for the first time, it might be difficult to think about all of these different elements at once. You may therefore find it useful to work through the following four areas of decision-making, shown in Box 2.18.

Box 2.18   Areas of decision-making for planning mixed methods projects (adapted from Heap and Waters, 2018)

Area 1:

- Central research question/subsidiary questions
- Literature review
- Aims and objectives
- Philosophical rationale

Area 2:

- Mixed methods design (priority and sequence decisions)
- Proposed way of combining the data
- Research design

Area 3:

- Data collection methods
- Sampling
- Methods of data analysis

Area 4:

- Ethical approval and access

Once the philosophical rationale and central research question have been settled upon, the consideration of the remaining issues is not necessarily a linear process and it does not have to occur in any particular order. In other words, the decisions made on each of the above points are not independent of each other, and decisions in one area will influence those in another, and vice versa. As you work through each area of decision-making, you will see your project begin to 'build'. This process, and the requisite decisions, will make more sense once you have read Chapters 4–9 of this book.

Planning your mixed methods project is not something that will happen quickly because of the variety and complexity of the decisions that need to be made, and that is normal. It is also worth remembering that initial planning decisions are not final and should be discussed with your research supervisor to clarify your decision-making rationale. Ultimately, the overall aim of the planning process is to create a robust and defensible overall methodology, where each decision makes sense in terms of the others, and in terms of the project as a whole. Having a clear plan also makes the rest of the project easier to undertake and creates a better outcome.

Initial mixed methods project planning checklist

To assist with your initial planning, we have created a checklist to help you develop a systematic approach which can be followed when creating your mixed methods research project. We have tried to put these items in the most logical successive order, but you may find that you skip parts of the checklist and re-visit them later.

- Central research/subsidiary question development:
  - Initial thinking about potential research topics using previous learning materials/ interests
  - Think about question type and research type
  - Consider practical and ethical constraints
  - Decide on a topic
  - Create concepts for the central research/subsidiary question(s)
  - Generate, revise, and select initial central research question/subsidiary question(s)

- Literature searching:
  - Create a list of keywords
  - Attend institutional training on literature searching (if available)
  - Search the library catalogue
  - Search the reference lists of key articles
  - Search Google Scholar
  - Search databases, journal searches, and publishers' websites
  - Review the literature critically and make orderly notes
  - Create a literature review framework to gradually build throughout the project
  - Re-visit central research/subsidiary question(s) and revise, if necessary, to create your working question

- Research aims:
  - Broad overview of research intentions (possibly one per research component)

- Research objectives:

  o   Objective 1: intended purpose
  o   Objective 2: intended methods
  o   Objective 3: intended outcome

- Read Chapters 4–9 in order to understand the background/terminology behind the decisions that need to be made during the next part of the planning process:

  o   Philosophy
  o   Mixed methods design
  o   Combining the data
  o   Research design and sampling
  o   Data collection
  o   Data analysis

- Work through Heap and Waters' (2018) decision-making process:

  o   Area 1: philosophy
  o   Area 2: way(s) of combining the data, mixed methods design, research design
  o   Area 3: data collection, sampling, methods of analysis
  o   Area 4: ethical approval

Summary

This chapter introduces how to plan a mixed methods research project. The emphasis has been on highlighting the characteristics of a systematic research process by detailing the initial stages involved in research planning. Undertaking a single method research project is a complicated task, but a mixed methods research project is even more complex because of the multiple decisions that need to be made about the individual research components and the project as a whole. Following the process outlined in this chapter should make creating your mixed methods project a more straightforward and enjoyable endeavour. The key to success is to progress through the different stages as logically as possible: considering the topic you would like to research, practical, and ethical constraints, thinking about your research in terms of concepts, as well as drafting and generating an initial central research question and subsidiary question(s). Once a question has been decided upon, the task of reviewing the literature can begin, safe in the knowledge that any research questions can still be refined until the latter stages of the project. Building an understanding of the literature will scaffold into decisions about research aims and research objectives, which in turn should fuel methodological decisions.

The decisions made in the early stages of a project act as the foundations for the methodological decisions that follow. Therefore meticulously approaching the start of your research with rigour will provide the platform for you to make a range of justifiable decisions later on. Ultimately, all of these decisions are linked together so the better prepared you are to make these decisions, the easier it will be to make them.

Learning questions

1   What are the key elements of a mixed methods central research question?
2   How should research aims and objectives for mixed methods research be formulated?
3   What do we mean when we talk about a systematic research process?

3 Ethics

CHAPTER OVERVIEW

- Introduction
- The importance of ethical research
- Key principles
- Governing research ethics
- Situating ethics in a criminological mixed methods context
- Mixed methods ethics in practice
- Ethics checklist
- Summary
- Learning questions

Introduction

This chapter introduces, and underlines the importance of, ethical practice in the context of mixed methods criminological research. It is in two parts. First, we set the scene by defining and outlining the role of research ethics and how this has developed within the discipline of criminology, using infamous case studies to highlight past unethical practice and ongoing debates. Following this, we explain four principles that are widely regarded as the key to upholding ethical research practice, namely: avoid harm; consent and deception; privacy, anonymity, and confidentiality; and comply with the laws of the land. Ethical research practice does not exist in a vacuum, so we investigate how ethics is governed. We explore this internationally, nationally, and by higher education institutions to contemplate what this means for student researchers. Second, our attention turns to a range of practical factors for mixed methods researchers to consider, such as the benefits of using mixed methods to explore sensitive research topics by combining primary and secondary data. We then talk through a range of ways to ensure you uphold ethical principles by giving tips about how to obtain ethical approval for your research, as well as guidance about the research materials you will need to produce for inspection, such as information sheets and consent forms. The chapter concludes with an ethics checklist to make sure you have thought about and prepared for all the necessary ethical responsibilities relating to your mixed methods research project.

The importance of ethical research

Ethics play a pivotal role in all research, regardless of disciplinary boundaries. Many texts have been written about research ethics and we do not have space within a single chapter to cover all the contested debates here. Nevertheless, there is a shared belief within social research that the creation of new knowledge should not be at the expense of human safety. Oliver (2010: 12) summarises this well by saying, 'there is a fundamental moral requirement to treat . . . people in accord with the standards and values which affirm the essential humanity'. However, research ethics only developed as a concern in the middle of the 20th century. Subsequently, there are examples from early social research where these values were not upheld. For example, the Stanford Prison Experiment (1973) is a famous case where research participants suffered harm as a result of taking part in the study – see Box 3.1 for further information. This, coupled with other ethically unsound studies, such as Milgram's (1963) obedience study, Latané and Darley's (1968) bystander effect experiment, and Humphreys' (1970) investigation into homosexual behaviour in public toilets, contributed towards a greater regulation of social research activities to ensure the welfare of everyone involved.

Box 3.1   The Stanford Prison Experiment (Zimbardo, 1973)

American psychologist Zimbardo (1973) created an experiment via a mock prison setting to investigate the 'psychology of imprisonment' as demonstrated by two groups of participants who role-played as either prison guards or prisoners. Twenty-four undergraduate male students from American universities volunteered and were randomly assigned to the roles. Neither group was given any training, but both groups quickly took on their given roles. Planned to last two weeks, the experiment was halted after six days because of the physical and psychological harm inflicted by the guards on the prisoner group. The guards were physically and verbally aggressive, exhibited unpredictable behaviour, and demonstrated dehumanisation of the prisoners. Precautions such as participant personality testing and informed consent were taken, and the research was conducted by experienced researchers. However, the end result demonstrated harm to the participants regardless of the good intentions, which meant the ethical principle of avoiding harm was not upheld.

As a result of the increasing number of studies where harm was being caused to participants, social research became subject to greater scrutiny, which you can read about later in this chapter in the section titled 'Governing research ethics'. However, greater regulation of ethical concerns has not necessarily made the research planning process any easier for researchers. To illustrate, Winlow and Hall (2012) suggest that ethics committees (which govern research in universities) attempt to control the production of knowledge, which marginalises risky research and stifles criminological inquiry. This notion may be felt most by those who plan to investigate criminological issues that push the boundaries of ethical practice and/or investigate sensitive topics such as gangs and organised violence. Even if a research project is given approval to take place, situations still arise in the heat of the research moment that can lead to questions being raised about the ethical credentials of a study. Recent ethnographic research undertaken by Goffman (2014), who studied a black neighbourhood in Philadelphia, USA, has been hotly debated because of the suggestion she was involved in the commission of a crime while undertaking her research. This incident meant that the ethical principle to comply with the laws of the land was not upheld. For more details, see Box 3.2.

Box 3.2   On the run (Goffman, 2014)

Goffman (2014) conducted an ethnographic study for six years in Philadelphia, USA, where she immersed herself in a predominantly black neighbourhood to gain a deeper understanding of the lives of its residents. Referred to as '6th Street' (not its real name), Goffman followed the day-to-day events of friends, Chuck, Tim, Reggie, Mike, Ronnie, Alex, and Anthony, as well as their girlfriends and mothers. She contends that policing and surveillance practices have transformed poor black neighbourhoods into communities that consist of suspects and fugitives. Goffman (2014: 8) suggests 'a climate of fear and suspicion pervades everyday life, and many residents live with the daily concern that the authorities will seize them and take them away'.

In an article in *The New Rambler* titled 'Ethics on the Run', Lubet (2015) questions the reliability and integrity of Goffman's account, suggesting that certain stories relating to law enforcement activity were implausible. Most problematic from an ethics perspective is Lubet's discussion of Goffman's role in the commission of a crime. In brief, Chuck, one of the core participants, was murdered and the remaining 6th Street Boys went to seek revenge. Goffman drove the car containing the 6th Street Boys, who were carrying guns, to find the people who killed Chuck. No one was identified by the group and nobody was shot that night. However, Lubet suggests that under Pennsylvanian law, Goffman's behaviour amounted to conspiracy to commit murder, thus she committed a crime in her research pursuits, something he confirmed with four current or former prosecutors. Lubet (2015: 9) concludes by saying,

> perhaps it takes a legal ethics professor to point out that participant-observers have no privilege to facilitate crimes of violence. Eminent sociologists appear to have considered Goffman's offense – if they considered it at all – at worst an excusable misjudgement or perhaps a mere legal technicality.

Goffman (2014: 263) detailed the incident at length in her book, stating, 'looking back, I'm glad I learned what it feels like to want a man to die – not simply to understand the desire for vengeance in others, but to feel it in my bones'. Do you think this valuable research insight justifies committing a crime? Should the knowledge that criminality was involved discredit the findings?

Goffman's (2014) work demonstrates that ethically questionable studies have not been confined to the past, as the quest to better understand our social world continues. It shows how ethical dilemmas in criminological research stimulate a continually evolving debate and highlights the importance of researchers understanding the core ethical principles, knowing how to apply them in practice, and making informed and justifiable decisions about their conduct when collecting data.

Key principles

A useful starting point to begin thinking about your own research practice is to consider the principles of ethical research. There is a degree of overlap between the different principles (Bryman, 2016) and there is no agreed wording between academics about the principles themselves, which you might notice when reading other textbooks. Each ethical principle will be discussed in turn, with the following four considered (adapted from Bryman, 2016; Caulfield and Hill, 2014; Denscombe, 2017; and Finch and Fafinski, 2016):

- Avoid harm
- Consent and deception
- Privacy, anonymity, and confidentiality
- Comply with the laws of the land

Avoid harm

Put simply, conducting research should not cause harm to any party involved, be that participants or researchers. As a result, researchers have the responsibility to ensure that the risk of harm is minimised by protecting their own and participants' interests. Harm is a broad term, encompassing physical, psychological and stress-related factors, all requiring the careful consideration of the researcher before data collection takes place. As such, researchers must plan ahead for the sake of their participants and themselves.

From a participant's perspective, they should not be harmed during the research, nor should they suffer any long-term negative effects because of taking part. The consensus is that participants should not encounter any greater risks than those posed by everyday life. This is quite subjective, as one individual's daily risk factors will differ from another's. However, it is a useful foundation for researchers to consider their ethical duties and should act as a salient reminder not to take any unnecessary risks that could result in harm. Denscombe (2017) highlights five harm-related factors that researchers should take into account:

1 *Prevent physical harm*: Physical safety should be taken into consideration. This will depend on the type of research you are conducting, but it spans a variety of scenarios, ranging from the safety of your participants travelling to and from the research site, to the prospect of them potentially facing physical retribution from those they may be discussing during the research.

2 *Avoid psychological harm*: This should be a prominent concern in criminological research because of the nature of the discipline and the potentially vulnerable nature of research participants. Denscombe (2017: 342) says that 'researchers therefore need to anticipate the likelihood that their investigation might be perceived as intrusive, touch on sensitive issues, or threaten the beliefs of the participants'. When the research is likely to explore delicate topics, participants should be provided with information about where they can seek help or support and be fully debriefed once the data collection is finished.

3   *No personal harm from disclosing information*: During the data collection process, participants may disclose details that outside of the research context could lead to detrimental consequences for them personally. For instance, an interviewee may disclose offending behaviour that, should it come to the attention of the police, could lead to criminal charges. This is a complex aspect of research ethics, which will be discussed further from a practical perspective in the 'Mixed methods ethics in practice' section of this chapter.

4   *The benefits of the research*: Researchers should be mindful to ensure that participants benefit from research. This might not be directly, but it should be explained to the participants that people in similar situations to themselves stand to benefit from their participation in the research. It is important to highlight that the research is taking place for a purpose, rather than just for the sake of it.

5   *Treating people fairly and equally*: The research should not discriminate against participants whose experiences should be heard. Denscombe (2017: 343) states, 'the research design should be sure to represent the interests of all relevant people, including the underprivileged, the weak, the vulnerable and minority groups'. The British Society of Criminology Statement of Ethics (2015) also warns against the devaluation of personal worth, which includes being humiliated and treated disrespectfully. Ensuring equal and just treatment will also enhance the representativeness of your sample, so there are research motives as well as ethical reasons for treating people fairly.

Central to safeguarding your participants from harm is their right to choose not to answer certain questions, and to withdraw from the research if they no longer wish to take part. They should be able to do this without having to give a reason, facing further questions, or encountering any repercussions from the researcher or anyone else. This means that at any point during the research process, including once the data have been collected, the participant can cease to take part and have all data they have contributed confidentially destroyed. The option to withdraw from the research should be made clear to the participants in advance of their decision to participate, which is explained later in the chapter in the section on 'Mixed methods ethics in practice'.

In order to protect researchers, points 1 and 2 from Denscombe's (2017) factors also apply: avoid physical and psychological harm. From a health and safety perspective, you should be mindful of your own personal safety when travelling back and forth to research sites. It is good practice to tell someone (family, friends, or your research supervisor) that you are conducting fieldwork, where it is taking place (if this does not compromise participant **confidentiality**), and what time you will be finished, and to check in with that person when you have finished. Similarly, you should take your own mental well-being into consideration as some of the topics participants disclose may be upsetting, with an example being the unexpected disclosure of criminal victimisation. As a student, you should be able to seek support from your research supervisor and broader institutional support services, as well as mainstream helplines such as the Samaritans, which offers a safe place to talk about anything troubling you. It is good practice to create your own procedure about how you plan to deal with such an event and who you would speak to if required. Similarly, it can be useful to write a research journal throughout your project, noting any concerns as you progress through your research.

Your safety, in addition to your participants' safety, will also be protected by making sensible decisions about the research you intend to conduct. Novice researchers are unlikely to have the skills to deal with a distressing situation, for example if a vulnerable interviewee discloses details that make them extremely upset. Therefore, when deciding on your research question you should not undertake any research that is beyond your competency, which could put you and your participants at risk. Your research supervisor should be able to help you decide your boundaries if you are not sure. As a researcher, you also have the responsibility to accurately represent the findings that you produce. Failing to do so could result in harm because it could lead to resources being misallocated, which could be to the detriment of the public. Similarly, you should take care to fairly represent others' data if using secondary data in one of your research components (see Chapter 8 – Data collection methods). You have the responsibility to use others' data with integrity and not make claims beyond the scope of the data itself. Misrepresenting data harms the reputation of the research community and could jeopardise prospective research projects. For instance, discovering that findings have been misrepresented could diminish public trust in social research. The importance of avoiding harm cannot be overstated. The safety of those involved in the research is paramount and should be kept in mind during all aspects of the research process.

Consent and deception

Potential research participants must be provided with information about the nature of the research project and their anticipated role, in order to provide **informed consent** to take part. This information should be provided in a format accessible to the participants and far enough in advance for the individual to be able to ask any further questions, and to make a knowledgeable judgement about whether to take part or not. This seems a straightforward principle, but it is one of the most contested aspects of research ethics because of debates about how informed potential participants need to be. Participants must be told about the nature of the research. However, researchers can withhold information that is likely to elicit a change in behaviour. For instance, research into gendered perspectives about the treatment of prisoners may refrain from detailing the gendered aspect of the research, in order to avoid participants responding in a stereotypically gendered fashion which could alter and bias the results.

Research participants should give their consent voluntarily and without **coercion** (being forced). According to the British Society of Criminology Statement of Ethics (2015), to secure participation in criminological research, there should be no **implicit coercion** (where individuals are under the impression that they have no choice but to take part) or **explicit coercion** (where an obvious threat of harm is made to secure consent). Furthermore, undue influence must not be used either. This is where researchers offer an excessive or inappropriate reward to obtain consent and could include, for instance, if a lecturer is researching student perceptions of prisoners and part of passing the course requires students to take part in the research, which is inappropriate and coercive. Ultimately, potential research participants should feel that they can decline to take part in the research without being disadvantaged. The notion of voluntary participation is linked to the ability of participants to withdraw at any time (discussed in the 'avoid harm' section), which is something that should be explained from the outset.

The most common way a researcher can demonstrate that informed consent has been achieved is by the participant signing a **consent form**. Usually containing a set of statements relating to the terms of the research, the consent form represents a written agreement that the participant has given their informed consent. This provides an audit trail for the researcher and gives them some protection should a participant later question their initial consent. However, sometimes written consent forms can act as a barrier to securing participants because they fuel rather than prevent concerns (Bryman, 2016). If participants decline to participate, do not take this personally as it is simply part of the research process. In some circumstances, practical constraints mean the completion of a written consent form is not possible. To illustrate, a participant may not want to sign their name in case of being identified as undertaking illegal activity. Methods of obtaining proof of informed consent in these situations are discussed in the section that considers 'Mixed methods ethics in practice'.

Due to the nature of criminological study, there is often the desire, and requirement, to research the experiences of vulnerable people. The British Society of Criminology Statement of Ethics (2015: 7) suggests these include: 'children and young people, those with a learning disability or cognitive impairment, or individuals in a dependent or unequal relationship'. An example of those within a dependent or unequal relationship within the criminal justice would be prisoners. Extra care is needed with these groups as they may not be able to provide voluntary and/or informed consent. To illustrate, prisoners may feel they are unable to refuse research participation because of a fear of facing negative consequences such as a reduction in privileges. Consequently, they may feel implicitly coerced into participating in research. The British Society of Criminology Statement of Ethics (2015) attempts to provide an extra layer of protection for such participants by stating that institutions should avoid giving consent on their clients' behalf, known as group assent, where possible. Similarly, passive assent, where consent is assumed unless expressively objected to, should also be avoided. Fully informed, voluntary consent should be sought in all circumstances. When a study would like to recruit children and young people as participants, consent must be sought from an adult responsible for them at the time of the research. The British Society of Criminology Statement of Ethics (2015) says that researchers should be mindful of child protection issues and be prepared for any instances of abuse disclosure. More information about children participating in research can be found on the Research Ethics Guidebook website (www.ethicsguidebook.ac.uk/Research-with-children-105). Researchers must seek permission to access vulnerable participants, which is determined through an **ethical approval** process that is outlined in the 'Governing research ethics' section of this chapter.

Informed consent applies to **overt research**, which is where participants have the study clearly explained to them in advance and voluntarily take part. In contrast, **covert research**, where the participants do not know they are taking part in a study, and/or the researcher does not reveal their real identity, does not secure informed consent in advance. Participants are unable to provide informed consent as they do not know they are research participants at the point in time they are participating. Consequently, they are not given the opportunity to refuse to take part. This type of research could entail the observation of public behaviour, crowds rioting or football hooliganism. A criminological example is Winlow et al.'s (2001) covert research into the occupational culture of bouncers, which focused on the realities of violence within their role in the night time economy. Covert research demonstrates that upholding ethical practice is not straightforward. The British Society of Criminology Statement of Ethics (2015: 6) suggests covert research 'may be allowed where the ends might be thought to justify the means'. This sentiment reflects the importance of many discoveries about the social world that have been exposed by covert research, for instance the undercover research into police cultures by Holdaway (1984) and Young (1991). You may read about covert research in your literature review, because studies adopting this approach have made a strong contribution to the field of criminology. However, the skills and resources required to undertake this type of research mean that covert research is unlikely to be possible at undergraduate level.

Similar to the idea of covert research is the notion of **deception**. This is where researchers deliberately misrepresent the details of their study to withhold information from participants (who have provided their informed consent). The rationale for this approach is to elicit information or observe behaviour from the participants that might not be revealed if the full details of the study are known. The classic example is Milgram's (1963) obedience study, where he advertised for participants to take part in research about memory and learning, when in fact he was testing the extent to which people would comply with orders to inflict extreme harm on others. A detailed account of Milgram's infamous study can be found in his original article published in the *Journal of Abnormal and Social Psychology* (issue 67: 371).

Bryman (2016) suggests that deception is objectionable for two reasons: firstly, it is undesirable because it is unpleasant for participants. Secondly, research involving deception has the potential to damage the reputation of social research, which could lead to difficulties recruiting participants in the future. However, the researcher must balance the use and extent of deception against the potential significance of the findings and risk of harm posed to the participants and researcher(s). As mentioned earlier in this section, it is common for researchers to omit minor details about the research topic to avoid biasing participants' responses. However, deception on the scale of Milgram's (1963) study was extreme, with harmful psychological consequences for the participants. Deception in research covers a broad spectrum, with many examples pushing the boundaries of deception and risk, such as the work of Young (1991), who served as a police officer while collecting inside information about police culture. Once covert research or research involving deception is complete, the researcher must debrief the participant, explaining the true nature of the research and why covert methods or deception were employed. The participant is then given the chance to consent or request that their data are withdrawn from the research. For these types of research, informed consent is still required; it is just secured at the end of the data collection process. Research that involves deception is not out of reach for the student researcher, but the type and extent of the deception must be very carefully considered.

Privacy, anonymity, and confidentiality

Privacy, **anonymity**, and confidentiality are closely linked. As highlighted when discussing the avoidance of personal harm, a participant's right to privacy should be respected at all times. Researchers should not invade participants' privacy by respecting their right not to answer certain questions that they might consider to be too personal, even though the research has been consented to. To illustrate, a participant may not wish to reveal why they served time in prison.

One of the core principles of ethical research is upholding the anonymity of participants. This means that they should not be identifiable as having taken part in a study. Anonymity is preserved by withholding a participant's name and any other details that might identify or associate them with the research. This includes details that when disclosed together might identify someone, such as disclosing their gender, age, ethnicity, occupation, and marital status all at the same time. The provision of anonymity allows participants to talk freely about their experiences without the fear of being identified. It is particularly relevant to criminological research, where participants may disclose unlawful or deviant behaviour, as well as sensitive and/or embarrassing information. Consequently the research is more likely to uncover more detailed information about the topic of study. Anonymity is maintained by either assigning a **pseudonym** (fake name) or a number/letter identification (e.g. participant 1 or participant a). Keeping participants' details anonymous also relates to how any data are managed and stored, which will be discussed in the next section, 'Comply with the laws of the land'. In some instances anonymity can be absolute, in the sense that the researcher does not know the participants' details at all.

Closely aligned to anonymity is the issue of confidentiality, which should be promised to participants. However, because of the types of issues discussed in criminological research, for example offending behaviour, drug consumption, and victimisation experiences, researchers should consider the level of confidentiality they are willing to offer participants. This is because in some circumstances participants may disclose something that the researcher may not be able to keep confidential, such as the participant admitting to ongoing sexual offences involving children. To an extent, the central research question will mitigate this, for instance a study into the perceptions of drug users is unlikely to facilitate any risky confessions. However, when sensitive subjects are to be discussed, researchers have two options: **absolute confidentiality** and **limited confidentiality**.

1   *Absolute confidentiality* is where all information is kept confidential no matter how serious a disclosure may be. Finch and Fafinski (2016) suggest four reasons for adopting this approach:

   i)   Any future threats to offend may not materialise and any existing offences may be uncovered by the authorities without the disclosure of the researcher. Furthermore, historical offences cannot be undone.
   ii) The core differences between the role of the researcher and the role of the police; it is not the researcher's role to encroach on police duties. Plus, any disclosures may be fabricated.
   iii) Breaches of confidentiality may affect the recruitment of future participants or lead to participants not disclosing information, decreasing the value of the research.
   iv) The researcher initiated the disclosure, so the participant should not be detrimentally affected by something that they would not have said, had it not been for participating in the research.

2   *Limited confidentiality* is where a researcher makes it clear to participants in advance that certain disclosures cannot be treated confidentially, such as criminal offences that have taken place. Limited confidentiality may be used when investigating a risky topic such as domestic violence or child sexual exploitation. It may also be employed when there is a perceived risk of the participant harming themselves.

The decision to utilise absolute or limited confidentiality is also, to an extent, influenced by the law. Box 3.3 outlines the British Society of Criminology's warning about the legal issues associated with confidentiality in criminological research.

Box 3.3   The British Society of Criminology's Statement of Ethics (2015: 11–12): confidentiality

'Researchers in the UK have no special legal protection that requires them to uphold confidentiality (as medical staff and lawyers do). Researchers and their data can be subject to subpoena where they may have evidence relating to a case. This legal situation should be taken into account by researchers when they offer confidentiality. Rather than absolute confidentiality, researchers may consider making the limits of confidentiality clear to respondents.

In general in the UK people who witness crimes or hear about them before or afterwards are not legally obliged to report them to the police. Researchers are under no additional legal obligations. There exists a legal obligation to report information about three types of crime to the relevant authorities:

   i) Where a person has information in relation to an act of terrorism, or suspected financial offences related to terrorism (Terrorism Act 2000).
  ii) Where a person has information about suspected instances of money laundering (Proceeds of Crime Act 2002). Although this legislation is aimed at those working in the regulatory sector, this legislation could potentially cover researchers. This is a complex area and researchers are advised to seek legal advice.
 iii) Where the researcher has information about the neglect or abuse of a child, there is a long-standing convention that researchers have responsibility to act. There is no legal obligation to do so, however Section 115 of the Crime and Disorder Act 1998 gives power for individuals to disclose information to specific relevant authorities (engaged in crime prevention) for the purposes of the Act.'

Issues of confidentiality and disclosure are some of the most contested and complex ethical issues in criminological research. Your research supervisor will be able to provide guidance about the type of confidentiality you should offer to the participants in your research. It is normal practice for research supervisors to be expected to take reasonable steps to ensure the integrity of their students' research, and they are held accountable for this by their institution. We will examine 'Governing research ethics' later in the chapter.

Comply with the laws of the land

When undertaking social research it is vital that you uphold the law. The formulation of the central research question is pivotal here, as some types of research are likely to precipitate law-breaking; for example, research into the sharing of child sexual abuse images online. Consequently, care should be taken to select a research topic that is not going to put you at any risk of breaking the law, especially as a student researcher.

A substantial legal consideration relates to how you handle the data you collect. This includes the personal and/or contact details of your participants and the raw data itself. The **General Data Protection Regulation (GDPR)** came into force in May 2018, replacing the Data Protection Act (1998). The new legislation operates at a European level and is intended to strengthen data protection rules in European Union member states, and will continue to be upheld after the UK withdraws from the European Union; full information can be found online at www.eugdpr.org. The GDPR maintains many of the principles of the Data Protection Act (1998), with the key changes mainly relating to how organisations collect and store personal data, and increased fines for institutions that breach data security. Under the GDPR data processing must be lawful, fair, and transparent, with researchers classed as either a data controller (someone who decides the purpose and processing of personal data) or a data processor (someone who processes personal data on behalf of a data controller). Since the change in legislation, researchers must specify what their lawful basis is for data processing, which in the case of academic research is part of a university's function. It is likely that your university will have a generic statement about this that all researchers can use. Ask your research supervisor for details of this if required.

Essentially, you should keep participant data anonymised and confidential (notwithstanding the debate about absolute and limited confidentiality), and make provisions to destroy the data at the end of the project, unless there is a requirement for it to be placed in a repository. The GDPR places an emphasis on making it clear to participants how their research data are handled. There are a variety of practical solutions to ensure you do not breach the GDPR, which will be outlined in the 'Mixed methods ethics in practice' section of this chapter.

Other technological laws and rules should be observed that relate to entities such as internet service provider agreements, any user agreements that have been made (such as any usage rules or conditions that have been placed on secondary data that you have downloaded, such as the Crime Survey for England and Wales dataset), copyright laws, and any information technology usage terms and conditions stipulated by your institution.

Aligned with the principles of avoiding harm and maintaining privacy, the Human Rights Act (1998) should be complied with. In relation to research, Article 8 of the European Convention on Human Rights, which respects an individual's right to private and family life, home and correspondence, is the most applicable.

Governing research ethics

Ethics is a complex and contested part of social research. Therefore, to ensure ethical studies are conducted, layers of governance are in place to scrutinise research practice. Figure 3.1 demonstrates how rules and regulations are reflected internationally, nationally, through educational institutions and by individual researchers. This section will provide a brief introduction to the governance of research ethics, with the purpose of helping you to see where your research fits into the 'bigger picture' of ethical research. This is necessary because before you will be able to undertake your mixed methods research project, you will have to apply for and be granted ethical approval. Ethical approval is given once the plans for your research project are deemed to uphold ethical research practice by the relevant **gatekeeper**. A gatekeeper is a person or body that controls access to something. There are a range of gatekeepers involved in social research and we will explain the roles of these different gatekeepers, which control the access to criminological research.

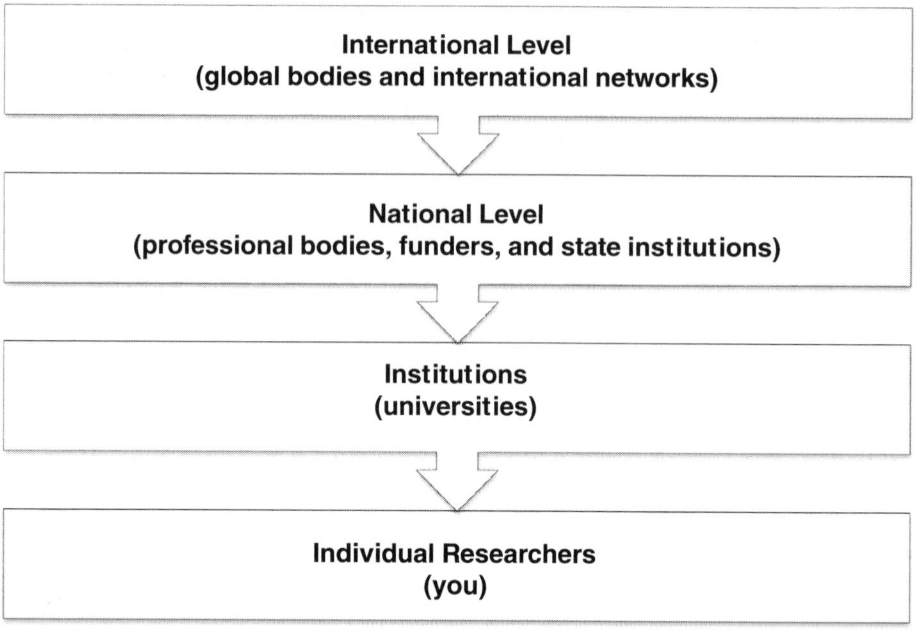

Figure 3.1 The hierarchy of research governance.

International level

Although they may not always act as day-to-day ethical gatekeepers themselves, international bodies set the standards for ethics policies by creating a framework of acceptable practices that filter down the hierarchy of governance. Bodies such as the World Health Organization (www.who.int/ethics/research/en), which operate internationally as well as having their own research committee, have created a set of guidelines detailing their expectations for health-related research (which includes criminological research with, for example, mentally disordered offenders). Others, like the European Network of Research Ethics Committees (www.eurecnet.org/index.html), aim to enhance the cooperation and shared ethical practice between researchers in member states by bringing groups together as part of a joined-up network. These organisations demonstrate the priority afforded to conducting ethical research on a global scale.

National level

Conducting ethical criminological research is influenced at a national level by three main types of organisations: professional bodies, funding organisations including research councils and state departments, and state institutions that act as gatekeepers for the populations they manage (such as Her Majesty's Prison and Probation Service).

A **professional body** is an organisation that aims to further the interests and knowledge related to a profession. In the UK, the professional body for criminology is the British Society of Criminology, which was created in 1951, with links as far back as 1931 when it was called the Association for the Scientific Treatment of Criminals. Professional bodies often publish a **code or statement of ethics**, with the expectation that membership of their society implies an acceptance of the general principles within the code/statement. The British Society of Criminology Statement of Ethics (2015: 2) states that the purpose of the document is 'to provide a framework of principles to assist the choices and decisions which have to be made to reflect the *principles, values* and *interests* of all those involved in a particular situation' [original emphasis], many of which are discussed in the 'Ethical principles' section of this chapter. Similar organisations exist across the globe, with details of a range of professional bodies for criminology, as well as some from aligned disciplines (psychology and sociology), detailed in Table 3.1.

Funding organisations, which include the Economic and Social Research Council (ESRC), invite applications to fund criminological research ranging from postgraduate studentships to multi-million-pound international projects. There is the expectation that those applying for ESRC funding abide by the Framework for Research Ethics they have produced. Although similar to the Statement of Ethics produced by the British Society of Criminology (2015), researchers have to be mindful of any specific requirements associated with the codes of ethics produced by potential funders if they wish to secure a successful application to fund their research.

In addition, state departments, such as the Home Office and Ministry of Justice, also commission criminological research, which often has further ethical constraints. Research within state institutions such as the National Health Service or prisons requires ethical

Table 3.1 Website details for professional bodies related to criminology and aligned disciplines

Professional body	Homepage and related research ethics contents
British Society of Criminology	www.britsoccrim.org www.britsoccrim.org/new/docs/BSCEthics2015.pdf
European Society of Criminology	www.esc-eurocrim.org/index.php
American Society of Criminology	www.asc41.com/index.htm www.asc41.com/code_of_ethics_copies/ASC_Code_of_Ethics.pdf
Academy of Criminal Justice Sciences (USA)	www.acjs.org/default.aspx www.acjs.org/?page=Code_Of_Ethics&hhSearchTerms=%22 ethics%22
Australian and New Zealand Society of Criminology	www.anzsoc.org www.anzsoc.org/cms-the-society/code-of-ethics.phps
British Sociological Association	www.britsoc.co.uk www.britsoc.co.uk/publications/ethics
American Sociological Association	www.asanet.org www.asanet.org/membership/code-ethics
The Australian Sociological Association	https://tasa.org.au https://tasa.org.au/about-tasa/ethical-guidelines
British Psychological Society	www.bps.org.uk https://beta.bps.org.uk/sites/beta.bps.org.uk/files/Policy%20-%20Files/Code%20of%20Ethics%20and%20Conduct%20%282009%29.pdf
American Psychological Association	www.apa.org www.apa.org/ethics/code/committee-2016.aspx
Australian Psychological Society	www.psychology.org.au Members-only access to ethics information

approval from a state gatekeeper; for example, because of the potentially vulnerable nature of the participants, research in prisons, young offenders' institutions, the National Probation Service and Community Rehabilitation Companies (probation) is governed by Her Majesty's Prison and Probation Service (HMPPS) (which between 2004 and 2017 was known as the National Offender Management Service). Accessing these participants requires navigation of the HMPPS National Research Committee, which at the time of writing meets monthly to discuss applications. Students can apply for access through HMPPS, with all the necessary paperwork provided online (www.gov.uk/government/organisations/her-majestys-prison-and-probation-service/about/research). The application form asks if ethical approval has been obtained from a relevant ethics committee, which will be situated in your university, and can add time to the research process as two levels of ethical approval are required. It is strongly advised to seek the support and guidance of your research supervisor before making an application to a state gatekeeper, such as HMPPS.

One of the ethical complications that can arise when undertaking research on behalf of another organisation is the politics of research. If you are working with a local agency or voluntary organisation, possibly accessing their clients as research participants, it is imperative to be transparent about your research questions and proposed design decisions to build a strong dialogue about your project. This should hopefully avoid the situation where any results you produce are dismissed or ignored and that they instead reflect the ethical principles about voluntary and informed consent. These issues can arise when the results are not as anticipated by the funders, with Raynor (2008: 81–82) suggesting there has been the emergence of 'an approach to publication and dissemination which sometimes looks suspiciously like a loss of interest in results which do not fit'. He is referring to research conducted for the Home Office in the early 2000s, which produced results that did not align with the ideology of the governing political party at the time. Furthermore, there have been additional concerns about the research methodologies used in state-funded research, which have been perceived to produce the 'wrong answer' (Raynor, 2004). These issues may seem a little detached from a student project; however, this highlights the importance of methodological decision-making and being able to justify why specific decisions have been made. Project planning decisions should be made with good ethical practice in mind, to ensure the integrity of the research and the welfare of everyone involved.

Overall, criminological researchers' ethical practice is shaped by a range of stakeholders at a national level. Unless applying for access through a state gatekeeper, such as HMPPS, these matters are unlikely to directly affect you or your research, but the impact of national-level policies and the scrutiny that researchers face shape how universities operate their ethics governance processes at an institutional level.

Institutions

Universities are responsible for ensuring that any research conducted in their name, be that by students or staff, upholds sounds ethical practice. All institutions will have a governance process for research ethics. In the UK, they are referred to as Research Ethics Committees, whereas in the USA they are termed Institutional Review Boards. Every institution will have their own rules and regulations about research ethics, but the underlying imperative is that no research can be undertaken until it has been approved by the university.

When undertaking your mixed methods research project, you will be informed about the administrative requirements to obtain ethical approval. In your application, you will need to demonstrate how you intend to uphold the ethical principles we have already discussed to ensure you safeguard your participants, maintain the integrity of social research, and avoid putting yourself at risk.

Individual researchers

As a student researcher, it is your responsibility to be aware of the ethical principles and how your actions uphold them. Acknowledgement of the ethical principles should be built in to your research planning process as well as your real-life research practice, such as data collection.

The remaining sections of this chapter focus on implementing the ethical principles in a mixed methods research context. Firstly, a range of mixed method considerations are outlined, relating to offsetting ethical concerns with secondary data or media analysis, and the initial planning required to secure ethical approval in a mixed methods project. Secondly, a comprehensive range of practical considerations are outlined to ensure you have all the requisite information to gain ethical approval, the knowledge to create a range of research materials, and the ethical insight to support your participants through the research process.

Situating ethics in a criminological mixed methods context

The second part of this chapter draws upon the four ethical principles already discussed and applies them to the research planning process, including where they cut across practical tasks. The purpose of this part of the chapter is to help you to link the ethical principles to your research planning in order to meet a range of project milestones, such as obtaining ethical approval from your Research Ethics Committee or Institutional Review Board, and producing the ethics-related materials that will be distributed to your participants.

Ethics in a mixed methods context does not vary greatly from a single method project; however, there are two main differences:

1   The pragmatic nature of mixed methods can be utilised to mitigate ethical concerns by creating a component that offsets factors such as covert research, deception, and the requirement for participants from vulnerable groups.
2   Mixed methods research is likely to require extra scrutiny and ethical approval because of the multiple quantitative and qualitative components, which may have different sets of participants (samples).

Offsetting ethical concerns

Mixed methods projects are driven and shaped by the central research question. Many students are attracted to the subject of criminology by the prospect of studying serial killers, serious violence and offending behaviour. However, when it comes to creating a research project a student's interest in gruesome crimes and understanding offending behaviour can create ethical barriers. For instance, undergraduate students are unlikely to be able to interview imprisoned serial killers about their modus operandi because of concerns about potential harm to the student due to a lack of research experience, as well as possible harm to participants. Furthermore, there may be issues with accessing prisoners because of the necessity to receive approval from Her Majesty's Prison and Probation Service, plus concerns about prisoners' ability to provide voluntary consent resulting from the unequal relationship involved. In such circumstances, mixed methods research can provide students with the opportunity to study high-profile and/or macabre topics by combining primary and secondary data analysis or media analysis across quantitative and qualitative components. Primary data analysis is where the researcher collects and analyses data they collected for the purpose of answering their central research question. In contrast, secondary data analysis is where researchers who have not been involved in data collection re-analyse an existing dataset to answer a new research question, which can be quantitative or qualitative. See Chapter 8 – Data collection methods for more details about this.

Consequently, a student that would like to pursue an investigation into victims' experiences of domestic violence, which would be unlikely to secure ethical approval because of concerns surrounding the avoidance of harm, could employ mixed methods to overcome this problem. For example, a qualitative secondary dataset detailing the experiences of domestic violence that was collected by an experienced researcher could be obtained from a data repository. It could be re-analysed by the student to answer their own central research question. This could be supplemented by a primary quantitative data collection component that explores public perceptions of the support services available for victims of domestic violence, to complement the findings from the secondary data analysis. Alternatively, if an appropriate secondary dataset could not be found, a media analysis of newspaper or magazine articles could be undertaken to explore reported experiences of domestic violence. These approaches allow students to research an area that they are interested in, and employing mixed methods offsets some of the issues with using secondary data alone, such as the data not neatly reflecting the central research question, which can be catered to by the other component. This idea is further explored in Chapter 11 – Troubleshooting.

We have created Table 3.2 to showcase a range of ideas about how mixed methods projects can combine primary and secondary data/media analysis to allow for traditionally off-limits topics to be studied by students. The intention of the table is to highlight a range of potential options, rather than to be a comprehensive list. Ethical approval will still need to be considered carefully for all of these projects.

Table 3.2 Ethically sound options for investigating risky topics using mixed methods

Topic area	Reasons why ethical approval denied for student researchers	Possible mixed methods alternatives
Serial killers Child/young offenders Prisoners Rape/sexual assault Paedophilia Drug use Domestic violence	• Inexperienced researcher • Potential harm to researcher and participants • Potential for incriminating or distressing disclosures • Potential unequal relationship between participant and researcher • Potential health and safety concerns • Possible access issues	Quantitative: • Questionnaires with perceptions/attitudinal questions • Secondary analysis of large questionnaire datasets Qualitative: • Research interviews or focus groups about perceptions/attitudes • Secondary analysis of research interview data or focus group data • Media analysis

Managing multiple ethical concerns

As described in detail in Chapter 2 – Creating a mixed methods central research question and project planning, undertaking a mixed methods project requires an extra level of organisation and administrative prowess because of the multiple research components involved. Consequently, in relation to research ethics, one of the most important factors is that you schedule enough time to complete the ethical approval process for all of your planned quantitative and qualitative components. The period of time required to do this will vary depending on how many components you would like to implement, the nature of the data collection methods you plan to use, and the sampling technique you intend to employ. To illustrate, if you plan to have three components – quantitative questionnaire, qualitative interview and qualitative media analysis – you will have multiple ethical dilemmas to consider and decisions to make regarding each component, as well as the requisite paperwork to complete and submit to obtain ethical approval. From an ethics perspective you will have to take into account the ethical principles for each of the quantitative and qualitative components. The next section details all of the different decisions you will need to make in practice.

Mixed methods ethics in practice

In practice, you will need to consider how you are going to uphold the ethical principles in your research project, namely aspects relating to: avoid harm; consent and deception; privacy, anonymity, and confidentiality; and comply with the laws of the land. As a researcher, it is your responsibility to identify the issues relating to your project, from each component, and take the appropriate steps to mitigate them.

Mixed methods specifics

Ethical considerations for mixed methods research have the potential to be complex given that distinct data collection methods are combined. The purpose of data collection is to try to capture the reality of individuals' experiences while operating within the bounds of the relevant ethical framework. When conducting mixed methods research, you may need to be extra vigilant when considering ethics because different methods of data collection are likely to be used. For instance, your qualitative method may include interviews with participants, while your chosen quantitative method could focus on gathering secondary data, which has already been collected. There are very different ethical implications for these two methods because the first involves interaction with human beings and the latter may be data which are publicly available online. Consequently, the risk of harm and other ethical concerns is potentially high for interviewing but not so high for secondary data. You will generally have one ethical approval form per project, even if it includes two or more data collection methods. Therefore you must consider the ethical implications early in the project planning process.

Obtaining ethical approval

All research conducted within a university setting must obtain ethical approval from the relevant committee before any contact is made with potential participants. You will be told about the specific requirements for your institution by your research supervisor and/or module leader, although the general requirements are broadly similar. The types of research-related questions posed on an ethical approval form are as follows:

- What is the title of your research?
- What is the background of the study and scientific rationale?
- What is the central research question?
- Is ethical approval required from any other governing bodies (e.g. HMPPS/NHS)?
- What methods are going to be used, including the proposed data analysis?
- What are the arrangements for sampling participants?
- What is the potential for participants to benefit from participating in the research?
- Are there any possible negative consequences of participating in the research, and how will these be limited?
- What are the arrangements for obtaining consent?
- What are the arrangements for ensuring participant confidentiality and/or anonymity?
- How will participants be told about their right to withdraw?
- If your research involves vulnerable participants, what safeguarding procedures will be in place during data collection?
- What are the arrangements for debriefing participants?
- What are the data storage arrangements?
- How will the findings be disseminated?

A lot of information is required by the gatekeeper that decides upon ethical approval. Therefore, before you can complete this process you will need to have completed all your project planning decisions which include: your central research question, philosophical rationale, the mixed methods design (including priority and sequence decisions), the proposed way of combining the data, research design, sampling, data collection, and methods of data analysis. However, if you adopt an exploratory or explanatory design (see Chapter 5 – Mixed methods design) and are designing one data collection tool as a result of another, you can apply for ethical approval in stages. Further to these details, you are usually requested to provide copies of all the materials that will be disseminated to potential/actual participants, such as: participant invitation letter/posters, **information sheet**, consent form, research instruments (e.g. questionnaire/interview schedules), and **debriefing** materials. If you require additional ethical approval from an organisation such as HMPPS, you will need to declare this on your institutional paperwork. You will find that state gatekeepers will often ask whether your research has been granted institutional ethical approval, so before submitting any request for access, check the sequence which applications should be submitted in, including any deadlines and when you are likely to receive a response.

In addition to research-related questions, you are also likely to be asked a range of health and safety questions, such as:

- Where will the data collection take place?
- How will you travel to and from the data collection venue?
- How will you ensure your own personal safety while at the research venue?
- What provisions will be made to ensure someone else knows where you are going (without compromising anonymity), how you are getting there, when you expect to return, and what to do should you not return on time?
- What are the potential risks to your health and safety other than the research venue and the research topic?

The sub-sections that follow provide a range of practical advice that relates to developing ethically sound research practice, the planning for which will help you to complete your ethical approval paperwork. In addition, ethics during data collection and post-project responsibilities are considered, as upholding ethical principles in practice runs throughout the duration of your research.

Ethics and secondary data

Undertaking secondary data analysis involves re-analysing data that were collected by someone else in order to answer new research questions. As these data already exist, some students mistakenly think there are no ethical concerns. However, there are a number of ethical factors to take in account. Firstly, you should ensure that the dataset that you intend to re-analyse was collected in an ethical manner. This is likely to be determined by where you locate the data. For example, official repositories such as the UK Data Service, which is funded by the ESRC, will only publish datasets that uphold ethical principles. However, it is good practice to review the paperwork to check ethical principles were adhered to. Studies funded by the ESRC will stipulate that all researchers obtain consent from their participants for the deposit of their data. Avoid using a secondary dataset from an unofficial website, such as that of an individual researcher, as there is no guarantee that the research was scrutinised for sound ethical practice before data collection took place. A list of reputable sources of secondary data can be found in Chapter 8 – Data collection methods.

Secondly, you must ensure you access the data ethically. To illustrate, at the time of writing, the UK Data Service has three categories of data:

1   Open data: Freely available without having to register.
2   Safeguarded data: Requires registration.

    a   Standard access: Requires user and project registration.
    b   Special conditions: May require the depositor's permission and other special conditions.
    c   Special licence: For more detailed datasets, additional licences are required.

3   Controlled data: Requires registration and data are only accessible via their Secure Lab (data cannot be downloaded); additional training is also necessary.

As a researcher, you must be mindful to obtain the correct permissions and abide by any user agreements that you sign up to. This is likely to include factors such as maintaining the confidentiality of the data and the anonymity of the participants (by not trying to identify individuals), keeping the data secure via a password to ensure they are not disclosed to anyone else, and correctly citing the dataset in your work.

Thirdly, linked to the ethical principles of avoiding harm and deception, it is important that researchers using secondary data do not misrepresent the data by making claims beyond the scope of the information provided. This could be considered as the fabrication or falsification of data, which are both examples of research misconduct (Pitak-Arnnop et al., 2012) and could lead to an academic sanction from your institution.

Sampling potential participants

You should bear in mind ethical considerations when recruiting participants for your research project. Many students will often resort to recruiting friends or family for their research (which biases the sample), because accessing vulnerable groups through official channels (such as HMPPS or the NHS) is difficult and time consuming. In such circumstances, consider accessing participants through informal means such as self-help groups or local community organisations. It might be that you can access participants through a charity that you volunteer with or through community partnerships linked to your institution. If you do rely on friends and family as participants, you should be mindful of the existing power dynamics within that relationship, and be especially conscious and protective of confidentiality.

Data management practices

In order to comply with the GDPR and uphold the ethical principles of privacy, anonymity and confidentiality, you must treat participants' data with care. This includes their personal contact details, as well as any data they provide from taking part in the research.

When undertaking your research project you should be mindful about how you use participants' data on a daily basis. For instance, if you are sending an email to all your research participants, always use the 'Bcc' function to ensure their identities are hidden from each other, in order to maintain anonymity. You should also anonymise all data collected through questionnaires, and for interviews this should take place at the point of transcription. Furthermore, care should be taken when working away from campus. For example, accessing your participants' personal details in public comes with the risk of people 'shoulder surfing', which could lead to your participants being identified if you are working while using public transport or in a café. Similarly, ensure that Wi-Fi connections are secure (only use public Wi-Fi if you are working on an encrypted connection) and always use your institutional email for correspondence. If you ever leave a public workspace, do not leave personal data unattended. Ensure you lock your screen and remove any sensitive hard-copy data from the vicinity. If you are speaking to your participants over the telephone or Skype/FaceTime, it is good practice to do so in a private place.

Electronic data should be stored securely. The best place to do this is via your institution's network drive, with students often assigned their own private, password-protected area upon enrolment. University systems are usually backed up daily, securing the existence of your data as they can be recovered. If you need to access your data remotely, they should be temporarily stored on an AES 256-bit encrypted device, with password-protected flash drives available for a small cost through online electrical retailers. If you are using your own computer, ensure it is password-protected, has up-to-date anti-virus software and that the firewall is turned on. This should help to secure the data in the event of theft.

As a general rule, students should dispose of any research data when the project has finished. It is reasonable to keep the raw data long enough to ensure an assessment/module has been successfully passed before disposal. All electronic data should be deleted, wherever they are stored (encrypted flash drive/university network), and removed from the Recycle Bin/Trash application on the computer you are using. Any hard-copy data should be destroyed confidentially. This can either be through shredding the data yourself or depositing them in the confidential waste collection points at your institution. Data should still be stored securely until they are disposed of. Avoid disposing of your data in 'normal' bins or recycling them.

Ways to secure informed consent in practice

For primary research, the process of gaining informed consent from participants usually begins with an invitation letter, poster or social media post that advertises you are recruiting participants. This initial contact with potential participants needs to provide an accurate representation of your research and how to contact you to become involved. In addition, as you are trying to 'sell' research participation to your potential participants, this is a significant opportunity to state the benefits associated with taking part in your research. Remember, the benefits can be to the participant themselves as well as the wider community. You might have different types of invitations for your different components, as the potential participants may be drawn from different samples. Always leave enough planning time to create the necessary paperwork. See Figure 3.2 for an example invitation letter.

If a potential participant is interested in taking part in your research, the next step is to send them the information sheet. In mixed methods research it is likely that you will need to adapt your information sheet for all the different components in your research. This is because the quantitative and qualitative components are likely to have different research aims, as well as different conditions in which the research will take place. For example, the conditions of an online quantitative questionnaire will differ from a qualitative face-to-face interview.

The information sheet needs to provide the potential participant with enough information about the study for them to give their informed consent; see Figure 3.3 for an example. Consequently, as a general rule, the following information should be included:

- What the research is about
- The legal basis for the research (linked to GDPR requirements)
- Who is conducting the research
- Why they have been asked to take part in the research
- What participation in the research will involve
- Where the research will take place
- Whether they have to take part or not
- What will happen with the information provided
- Information about anonymity and confidentiality
- How their data will be stored, who is responsible for them, who will have access to them and what will happen to them after the study has finished
- How the data collected will be used
- Debriefing details and the right to withdraw
- Any possible risks or disadvantages
- Support resources
- Contact details for the researcher to discuss participation
- How to find out about the results of the study

It is crucial that the wording you use in your information sheet is accessible to non-criminologists and those that may not be familiar with social research. It should be written with a non-specialist audience in mind. If the information sheet is too complicated, it could mean that participants are not adequately informed about the research. Similarly, anything perceived as too technical or difficult may put off potential participants from signing up. It can be helpful if the text is broken down into sub-headings for ease of reading. Furthermore, a level of legitimacy is added by using institutional headed paper (if available). This document is another example of work that could be put to the 'Grandma test'; see Box 2.3 in Chapter 2 for details.

Providing details about available support services is an important part of the information sheet because it demonstrates that you take the participants' well-being seriously. Box 3.4 displays a range of organisations that are suitable for inclusion on criminological research projects.

Sheffield Hallam University

Don't suffer in silence

Sheffield Hallam University
Howard Street
Sheffield
S1 1WB

September, 2018

Greetings,

We would like to invite you to take part in some new research. Independent researchers from Sheffield Hallam University and the charity ASB Help (www.asbhelp.co.uk) have been asked by [X] to find out about how people have experienced using the Community Trigger. We would like to give you the opportunity to talk about your experiences and how it has affected the ASB you were/are suffering from.

Taking part won't take much of your time. We'd need to speak to you once to conduct an interview, but this would be much more like an informal chat about your experiences than anything formal. It will probably last about an hour to an hour and a half and it will be conducted over the telephone at a time that suits you.

As a thank you for taking part, you will receive a £15 High Street Gift Voucher.

You can choose what you tell us, and can stop the interview whenever you want. You will still receive our thank you gift.

We hope to use the information from all the interviews in presentations, reports and academic writing in the future, but no one will be able to tell it is you if we use your responses, and your real name won't be used. For example we will call our participants A, B, C etc. Only the researchers will have access to the data we collect and it will be stored securely. Once the study has finished, all raw data will be anonymised and stored on the Sheffield Hallam University Research Data Archive, for up to 10 years.

You do not have to take part. If, after we speak, you wish to withdraw the information you've told us, you can do so at any point up until 30 November 2018.

If you are interested in taking part and would like to know more about the study, please let [X] know that they can pass on your details to us. We will then be in touch with you to arrange a convenient time.

Thank you, your input in this research would be really appreciated.

Yours sincerely,

Researcher 1   **Researcher 2**
Senior Lecturer in Criminology   **ASB Help**

Figure 3.2 Example of an invitation letter.

Investigating the Community Trigger in Action

Participant Information Sheet

You are invited to take part in a research study by researchers from Sheffield Hallam University and the charity ASB Help (www.asbhelp.co.uk), looking into how victims have experienced using the Community Trigger.

You have been asked to take part because you activated, or attempted to activate, the Community Trigger in [X].

The study involves you being interviewed <u>once</u> by one of our researchers for approximately one to one and a half hours, about you and your experiences of the Community Trigger.

The interview will take place over the telephone at a convenient time for you and we will electronically record the conversation so that we can write it up later.

We hope to use the information in presentations, reports and academic writing in the future, but no one will be able to tell it is you if we use your responses, and your real name won't be used. For example we will call our participants A, B, C etc.

You do not have to take part, participation is completely voluntary.

If you do take part, all your personal information will be kept completely confidential.

Only the researchers will have access to the data we collect and it will be stored securely. Once the study has finished, all raw data will be anonymised and stored in the Sheffield Hallam University Research Data Archive, where it will remain for up to 10 years. All confidential data will be destroyed.

As a thank you for taking part, you will receive a £15 High Street Gift Voucher.

You can stop and ask questions at any point. You can choose what you tell us, and you can stop the interview whenever you want. You will still receive our thank you gift.

You will be able to discuss your participation in the study with the interviewer after the interview has finished, when you will receive a full de-brief.

If, after the study, you wish to withdraw, you can do so up until 30 November 2018.

You can find out about the results of the study by giving your contact details to the interviewer. The research team will then send you a summary of the findings when the study is complete. The findings will also be published on the [X] website.

The University undertakes research as part of its function for the community under its legal status. Data protection allows us to use personal data for research with appropriate safeguards in place under the legal basis of **public tasks that are in the public interest.** A full statement of your rights can be found at https://www.shu.ac.uk/about-this-website/privacy-policy/privacy-notices/privacy-notice-for-research. However, all University research is reviewed to ensure that participants are treated appropriately and their rights respected. This study was approved by University Research Ethics Committee with Reference No. [X]. Further information can be found at https://www.shu.ac.uk/research/ethics-integrity-and-practice

If you wish to discuss the research afterwards, you can contact the lead researcher, Researcher 1, [email] / [phone number].

You can also write to us at: *Sheffield Hallam University, Howard Street, Sheffield, S1 1WB, UK.*

Figure 3.3 Example of an information sheet.

Box 3.4   Contact details for criminological research-related support organisations

UK

Victim Support

www.victimsupport.org.uk

Provides support for those affected by crime or anti-social behaviour; offers free and confidential advice.

Telephone: 08 08 16 89 111 (dial 141 first to hide your number)

The Samaritans

www.samaritans.org.uk

Offers comprehensive support for anyone in crisis, despairing, or suicidal.

Telephone: free helpline: 0845 790 9090 or ROI helpline: 1850 60 9090

Email: jo@samaritans.org

USA

Victim Connect

https://victimconnect.org

National resource centre where victims of crime can find information about their rights and options.

Telephone: 1-855-4-VICTIM (1-855-484-2846)

Online chat facility: https://chat.victimsofcrime.org/victim-connect

National Suicide Prevention Lifeline

https://suicidepreventionlifeline.org

Free and confidential support for people in crisis or distress.

Telephone: 1-800-273-8255

Canada

National Office for Victims

www.publicsafety.gc.ca/cnt/cntrng-crm/crrctns/ntnl-ffc-vctms-en.aspx

Offers information and support to victims of federal offenders.

consequently distributing and collecting hard-copy consent forms would likely stifle participant recruitment. Therefore when using online questionnaires, it is acceptable to seek informed consent online as part of the questionnaire. To illustrate, the landing page of the questionnaire would act as the information sheet; see Figure 3.6 for an illustration. This should contain all of the same information as a regular information sheet, including the support resources. The consent form is often presented to the potential participant at the same time, or on the next screen. It is usually created in a way that allows the individual to tick/select boxes that indicate their agreement with statements similar to those on a hard-copy consent form; see Figure 3.6. The only amendment to a standard consent form that will likely be required for an online questionnaire relates to the right to withdrawal. As data are usually anonymous at the point of submission, it is impossible for the researcher to identify an individual's data to remove them at their request. Consequently, there should be a statement on the consent form screen to inform potential participants that they will be unable to withdraw from the research once they have submitted their responses.

For qualitative research, for example interviews, participants can be sent the information sheet and consent form electronically. Digital signatures are acceptable and completed forms can be returned to the researcher by email.

Online debriefing would take the form of a screen at the end of a questionnaire, which includes all of the information detailed above, the same as a hard-copy sheet. A copy can also be emailed to participants where relevant.

Sheffield Hallam University

Q1. You are invited to take this short survey on behalf of the Graduate Research and Development 2 module, taught in the Department of Law and Criminology at Sheffield Hallam University.

The purpose of this survey is to create a teaching dataset for the module, which students can use to practice their quantitative data analysis skills.

You will be asked two demographic questions, followed by a set of questions about your attitudes towards the police, and a set of questions about your attitudes towards illegal drug use.

Your participation is voluntary and you can stop completing the survey at any time. However, once you submit your final answer you will be unable to withdraw your data as it will be not be identifiable to you.

Your data will be held confidentially and anonymously. Once complete, the dataset will be made available to students on the Graduate Research and Development 2 module and stored on the module's virtual learning environment.

The University undertakes research as part of its function for the community under its legal status. Data protection allows us to use personal data for research with appropriate safeguards in place under the legal basis of public tasks that are in the public interest. A full statement of your rights can be found at https://www.shu.ac.uk/about-this-website/privacy-policy/privacy-notices/privacy-notice-for-research. However, all University research is reviewed to ensure that participants are treated appropriately and their rights respected.

This data collection has received ethical approval from the Faculty Research Ethics Committee, as part of the module's category approval. Further information can be found at https://www.shu.ac.uk/research/ethics-integrity-and-practice

If you have any questions, please contact the Module Leader, Dr Vicky Heap (v.heap@shu.ac.uk)

Q2. I have read and understood the information provided about this survey and consent to participate.

◯ Yes

◯ No

Survey Completion

0% [_____•_____] 100%

Figure 3.6 Example of an information sheet and consent form as part of an online questionnaire.

During data collection

Ethical practice should be upheld throughout the whole research project and is not solely the preserve of the planning stages. Especially when conducting research with participants in person, thought should be given to how you would react in certain scenarios so you are prepared for a range of difficult circumstances, if they arise. For example:

- What would you do if a participant refused a question?
- How would you react if someone started to cry?
- How would you react if someone told you a really upsetting story?
- What would you do if there was a disclosure of offending behaviour?
- What would you do if there was a disclosure of abuse?

The likelihood of any of the above scenarios materialising depends on the sensitivity of your central research question. The more sensitive the topic, the more prepared you will need to be. If this is your first time conducting research face to face with participants, discuss how you might deal with these things with your research supervisor. Also, think about if you were in that situation; what care and support would you expect from a researcher? There is every possibility that no situations will occur such as those described above, but as a researcher you have to be ready to react quickly, professionally and empathetically if they do.

   As a starting point, if someone refuses to answer a question, that is okay. They have the right to do so and you should avoid invading their privacy by pushing for an answer. It can be unsettling and upsetting for a researcher if a participant starts to cry. If you know your topic is sensitive, be prepared and take some tissues with you. Remind the participant they do not have to answer the question, but if they wish to continue then let them carry on at their own pace. They may wish to pause the interview to allow them to compose themselves and/or get a drink and this is all fine; this might be something you want to offer; you are trying to avoid harm to the participant. If a participant does get upset, remember to re-emphasise the support services available during the de-briefing and tailor your suggestions to their needs, for example providing details about Victim Support or The Samaritans (see Box 3.4). Regarding disclosures, you should have a plan in place with your research supervisor in case this situation arises. Speak to your supervisor about it immediately, maintaining confidentiality where appropriate; they should assist you if any further actions are necessary. As mentioned previously, keeping a written research journal can help you to process your initial thoughts and emotions about the situations you encounter. Box 3.5 provides more details about the role of emotions in criminological research.

Box 3.5   Emotions in research

As part of the ethics process, researchers are routinely asked to think about what they will do so as not to cause harm or distress to their participants. But the harm or distress that research can cause to the researcher themselves is seldom considered, although attention is finally being paid to this hitherto hidden aspect of criminological research (Waters et al., forthcoming). Most research projects have the potential to be emotionally difficult for the researcher, with the pressure of a large volume of work and looming deadlines to contend with. But research projects focused on particularly uncomfortable and sensitive topics, which are not unusual in the discipline of criminology, and which utilise particular methodological approaches, carry the risk of serious emotional distress or harm to the researcher.

Criminological researchers have adopted a variety of approaches when carrying out highly emotive and upsetting research (Waters et al., forthcoming); some researchers have taken a preventative approach, following certain routines to try and keep troubling emotions at bay, whilst others have only sought to deal with difficult emotions after particularly uncomfortable interactions or in moments of crisis. Strategies that have been adopted include:

- Peer support
- Supervisor support
- Writing their emotions down in a diary or field journal
- Creating physical space (e.g. physically removing themselves from the data collection environment, not going straight home or back to the office after data collection, going to the gym)
- Creating psychological space (e.g. gaming, watching 'trashy' TV, reading 'light' magazines)
- Cleansing rituals (e.g. changing clothes, showering, going swimming)
- Counselling

The potential of your research project to affect your emotional health is something that needs to be considered as part of the planning process. A good place to start is to ask yourself what emotions you might feel while carrying out your data collection, and how you might deal with them. Having a pre-arranged plan of action should any emotionally difficult situations arise is also a good idea.

Post-project responsibilities

Once you have completed your research project, it is important to fulfil any commitments made to your participants. For instance, many information sheets offer participants the opportunity to receive a copy of the results once the project is over. Be sure to send these to participants where requested. Similarly, if you offered any incentive for taking part, this should be dispatched in a timely manner. Finally, you must remember your responsibilities towards your participants' data and remember to protect and destroy these as you explained it to them.

Ethics checklist

To assist you with your ethics planning process, we have created a checklist to ensure you do not miss out any key decisions or the production of any important documents. We have tried to put these items in the most logical sequential order, but you may find that in practice you complete the checklist in a different order.

Some of the terminology used in the checklist may be unfamiliar to you at this stage because you are still learning about mixed methods, but once you have read Chapters 4–9, you will have all the information required to make decisions about your ethical approach.

- Have you made all your project design decisions?

  - Central research question
  - Subsidiary question(s)
  - Aim(s)
  - Objectives
  - Philosophical stance
  - Mixed methods design decisions (sequence and priority)
  - Way to combine the data
  - Research design, sampling and data collection method for all components
  - Method of data analysis

- Have you considered how you will avoid harm to participants and the researcher?

  - Physical harm (including health and safety of the researcher when travelling to research sites)
  - Psychological harm
  - Personal harm
  - Outlining the benefits of the research
  - Treating people fairly and equally
  - Right to withdraw
  - Identified support resources that are appropriate for the participants in your study

- Have you thought about informed consent?

  - Sampling any vulnerable groups?
  - Information sheet or section as part of an online questionnaire?
  - Consent form, electronic consent form, or verbal consent?
  - Is there any deception involved?

- What provisions have you made for privacy, anonymity, confidentiality?

  - How will privacy be maintained?
  - What measures will be employed to secure anonymity? Pseudonyms?
  - What level of confidentiality will you offer: absolute or limited?

- Are you complying with the laws of the land?

  - How are you going to process the data?
  - How will the data be stored?
  - What will happen to the data after the project has finished?
  - Will you be using secondary data and have you registered to use them?

- Have you completed the correct ethical approval paperwork for your institution?
- Have you created all the research materials for each component that requires scrutiny as part of the ethical approval process?

  - Invitation letter/poster
  - Information sheet (or similar for online questionnaires), with support resources detailed
  - Consent form
  - Debriefing information
  - Research instrument(s) (e.g. questionnaires, interview schedule . . .)

- Do you need to apply to an external gatekeeper for ethical approval (e.g. HMPPS)?

Summary

This chapter has introduced the key ethical principles and detailed how they can be applied to your mixed methods research project. To secure the integrity of both your research and the discipline of criminology, it is important that you consider and reflect upon how you will implement the key ethical principles of: avoid harm; consent and deception; privacy, anonymity, and confidentiality; and comply with the laws of the land.

Prominence has been given to demonstrating how to plan an ethically sound mixed methods project. Multiple decisions need to be made about research ethics in advance of your project starting because you will be required to seek and obtain ethical approval from your institution for your research to take place. Many of these decisions will be put into practice when creating the range of research materials that you will present to your participants, which are likely to include items such as: invitation letters, information sheets and support information, consent forms, data collection instruments and debriefing resources. Navigating the research ethics process for a mixed methods project can be onerous, because you are likely to need different sets of research materials for each research component. However, like all aspects of a mixed methods project, if you are organised, it will run smoothly. Your research supervisor can help you with research ethics, so be sure to consult them for support and guidance throughout the ethical approval process.

Learning questions

1   What are the four key ethical principles?
2   What are the additional ethical dimensions when carrying out mixed methods research?
3   What documents do you need to complete before starting your project?

4 Philosophy

Introduction

This chapter introduces you to the world of research philosophy. This is a topic that is probably not something that you think about every day, so we begin by looking at why it is important to understand research philosophy. The discussion in Chapter 1 on quantitative, qualitative, and mixed methods research strategies is of great relevance here, as we will see. The second part of the chapter involves a discussion of epistemology (the study of the theory of knowledge) and the epistemological positions of positivism, interpretivism, and pragmatism. Third is a section on ontology (the study of what constitutes social reality) and the ontological positions of objectivism, constructionism, and multiple realities. The chapter ends by suggesting that pragmatism and multiple realities can be brought together to form a coherent overall philosophical approach to mixed methods research. Overall, this chapter will help you to understand what research philosophy is, why it is important in criminological research, and how it applies to mixed methods.

The importance of research philosophy

Research is the creation of new knowledge. It involves observation, measurement, and the capture of data, information, and experience in order to build a picture of and understand the social and criminological world that is around us. That social world is made up of all human social interaction, interpersonal practices, social behaviour, and social institutions. Many researchers hope to create objective knowledge of this world through their work; that is, knowledge that is 'discovered' in a value-free way and can be considered as impartial truth, uninfluenced by the researcher's own beliefs and prejudices. However, according to Creswell (2015: 8), we 'all bring our understanding of the nature of the world and our assumptions about what information needs to be collected . . . to our study of a research problem', as well as our 'general beliefs and assumptions about research'. What Creswell is getting at here is the idea that how you understand the world around you has a massive, if often unacknowledged, influence on how you go about studying and researching that world. So as a criminological researcher your inherent understanding of the social world will affect the way you see and therefore collect and interpret data about the social world. As a result of this, some researchers believe the knowledge that they create is **subjective**, and is at least partly a result of the researcher's own 'meaning making', influenced by their personal experiences, beliefs, feelings, and so on. Thus, it is incredibly important to understand research philosophy and in particular the impact your own beliefs and feelings about the social world could have on your research.

If research is the creation of new knowledge, then the next logical question must be 'what is knowledge?' On the face of it this might seem like a very straightforward question. But it leads immediately to a series of related questions that give a clue as to the complexity of this field:

- How do we know what knowledge is?
- What standards determine whether something can be considered as knowledge or is invalid as knowledge?
- How do we create knowledge through the research process?

The above questions fundamentally underpin research philosophy and how you answer them will provide clues to your own personal research philosophy. They also feed into a series of further questions that are specific to the discipline that you are working in. In criminology, for example, we might ask: what should be considered as crime? What constitutes a valid measurement of crime and are official statistics sufficient? How far can crime be understood through the experiences of one lawbreaker or prisoner? It is therefore important to understand the philosophical foundations of research so that we can understand the research itself (the process, findings, conclusion, implications, impact, and so on) and what type of 'knowledge' is being produced.

In sum, the topics we choose to research, the questions we choose to answer, and how we choose to carry out the research to answer these questions are all underpinned by our own research philosophy. Different disciplines, including criminology, also have their own dominant, often unconscious, philosophical traditions that prioritise certain topics and types of research over others. This means that disciplinary imperatives help shape which criminological phenomena – which people, places, and institutions – we as criminologists study and research. This is all linked to what we believe counts as 'real' or 'proper' knowledge.

Competing philosophical frameworks

As noted above, it is important to realise that different fields of academic study are dominated by different philosophical frameworks. Even within the field of criminology, different sub-fields will privilege different frameworks. For example, feminist criminological researchers will likely hold a very different philosophical position as compared to positivist and post-positivist researchers. When engaging with, evaluating and thinking critically about any piece of research, including your own, it is extremely useful to be aware of these differences. It is also helpful to realise that different fields of research will 'differ in terms of the importance of making these philosophical assumptions explicit or implicit in a study' (Creswell, 2015: 8); some may value explicit discussion of their underlying philosophical framework, whilst others may not. However, regardless 'of your field, it is important to acknowledge that our values and beliefs shape our orientation to research, how we gather data, the biases we bring to research, and whether we see our investigations as more emerging or fixed' (Creswell, 2015: 8).

One of the key debates in terms of research philosophy concerns the relationship between research and theory. The schism between the **deductive** and **inductive** approaches hinges around the role of theory in the research endeavour. A more recently developed third orientation, the so-called **abductive** approach, seeks to bridge the gap between the deductive and the inductive and is potentially useful in mixed methods research, as we will see in what follows.

.The deductive approach to research sees the creation of knowledge about the social world and social phenomena as something that starts with theory. Hypotheses are created based upon pre-existing theory and knowledge and data are then collected to either prove or disprove that theory. This 'top-down' approach (see Figure 4.1) is closely linked to the **quantitative research strategy** and it is akin to how most natural science research is conducted. For example, a deductive piece of research might start with a theory about the relationship between gender and fear of crime based on the work of previous researchers in the field, and from this develop a hypothesis stating that women are likely to be more fearful of crime than men. This hypothesis could then be tested through, for instance, a questionnaire that ascertained the respondents' gender and their perceptions of crime and victimisation. A deductive approach to research tends to be taken by those researchers who are more positivistic, objectivist, and quantitative in outlook (this will be discussed in further detail below). Traditionally this has been the more prevalent approach to criminological research.

The inductive approach to research takes precisely the opposite position. It holds that our knowledge and understanding of the social world and specific social phenomena should be derived from the data itself in advance of any theoretical speculation. Thus, according to this approach data should be collected first and theory is built afterwards. The end result is a theory that is constructed directly out of the data that have been collected, and so it might be said that theory 'emerges' from the data. This is a bottom-up approach which generates conclusions by drawing generalities from the findings (see Figure 4.1). The inductive approach is more readily associated with a **qualitative** research strategy. To return to the example of research on gender and the fear of crime, an inductive approach might begin with interviews in which individuals explored their perceptions, thoughts, and feelings about crime and victimisation. The data collected from these interviews could then be analysed and a theory regarding the influence of gender on fear of crime constructed. An inductive approach is generally taken by researchers who are more interpretivistic, constructionist, and qualitative in outlook (this will be discussed in further detail below).

With the deductive approach being closely associated with quantitative research, and the inductive approach with qualitative research, mixed methods researchers have developed an alternative in the guise of the 'abductive' approach, which better marries with the aims and objectives of mixed methods and avoids the need to 'take sides' in the age-old inductive/deductive debate. As Morse and Niehaus (2009: 39) put it, abduction is 'a third mode' of inquiry where the aim 'is to move back and forward between induction and deduction throughout the research by first developing conjectures and then systematically testing these conjectures'; 'conjectures' in this context simply refers to ideas produced by 'imaginative thinking' (Charmaz, 2009: 138) based on prior knowledge or intriguing preliminary findings, which are then examined back in the field. Rather than the theory generation associated with inductive approaches, or the theory testing associated with deductive approaches, by blending the two the abductive approach is geared towards problem solving and thus it fits in well with the pragmatic leanings of mixed methods (see Figure 4.1). How might this movement between the inductive and the deductive work in practice? One example, to return to our focus on gender and fear of crime, might be a study that begins with in-depth interviews exploring people's thoughts, feelings, emotions, or experiences of crime. This would help develop a broad understanding of the area and assist in the development of conjectures or even nascent theory (this is akin to the inductive approach). Following this, these conjectures or theories regarding the fear of crime could be tested through, for example, an online questionnaire administered to a larger number of people (deductive). Then, the research might carry out focus groups with a select number of females and a select number of males in order to concentrate on a particular aspect of the fear of crime and to hone the developing theory further (inductive). It is this 'back and forth' between the inductive and deductive, and the process of continual development and refinement, that is vital in the abductive approach.

In sum, criminological research does not happen in a vacuum. We all come to research with a prior range of beliefs that shape our understanding of what research, knowledge, and data are. You might have a good understanding of your own philosophical underpinnings or you may not; they may be explicitly or implicitly held. You might read pieces of research where the philosophical framework is explicitly stated and you may come across others where it is not. But in all cases, there is always an underlying philosophical framework guiding the research, and influencing the interpretation, analysis, and understanding of the social world in general as well as the particular phenomenon under study.

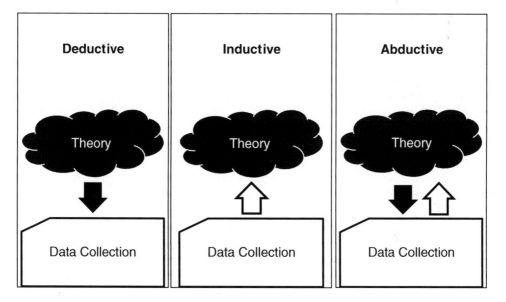

Figure 4.1 Relationships between theory and data collection.

Epistemology

Epistemology is the branch of research philosophy concerned with the theory of knowledge. It considers our methods of acquiring knowledge, how we come to 'know' things and what justifications we have for considering something as 'truth' and accepting it as valid. Different disciplines, and even different sub-disciplines, will have their own particular epistemologies and ways of knowing about the social world. Some people consider knowledge to be something that is fixed and unchanging, while others consider it to be something transient and permanently in flux. Some people see knowledge as something that can be objectively observed, while others consider it as something that is subjectively created. Think about the questions in Figure 4.2. Your answers will depend on your own position in relation to these epistemological debates.

The term 'paradigm' is sometimes used instead of 'epistemology', and sometimes in conjunction with it. 'Paradigm' is a

> term deriving from the history of science, where it was used to describe a cluster of beliefs and dictates that for scientists in a particular discipline influence what should be studied, how research should be done, and how results should be interpreted.
>
> (Bryman, 2016: 694)

As this suggests, the term 'paradigm' has many different meanings in addition to being a synonym for epistemology; Masterman (1970), for example, identified 21 distinct uses of the term. Given this, it is important to take care in your reading and ensure you are clear about what terms are being used and what ideas they are referring to.

Two key epistemologies utilised in the discipline of criminology are **positivism** and **interpretivism**. In simple terms, the debate between the two hinges upon 'the question of whether the social world can and should be studied according to the same principles, procedures, and ethos as the natural sciences' (Bryman, 2016: 24).

Positivism

Historically, social research tended to be positivistic in nature. This was due to its evolution out of the natural sciences as academics increasingly became interested in the social world around them. In the early days of this process social researchers effectively mimicked the manner in which physicists, biologists, and chemists used empirical observation to objectively measure natural phenomena. Thus positivism is 'an approach to social research that seeks to apply the natural science model of research to investigations of social phenomena and explanations of the social world' (Denscombe, 2002: 14). The positivistic epistemological approach is underpinned by six basic assumptions (outlined in Figure 4.3).

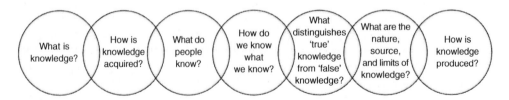

Figure 4.2 Epistemological questions.

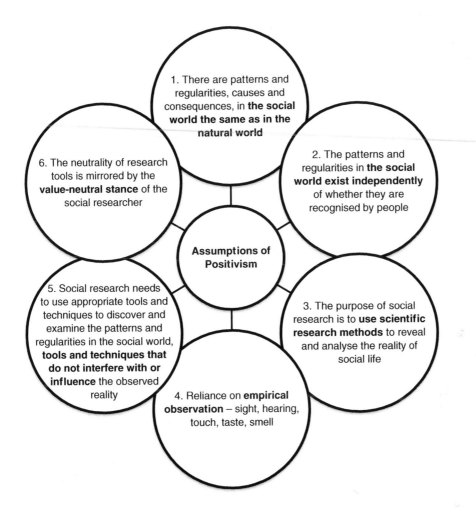

Figure 4.3 Assumptions of positivism (adapted from Denscombe, 2002: 14–16).

These assumptions provide the foundations for a number of key principles of positivism (Bryman, 2016) that inform its deployment in any research endeavour. The most vital of these principles are phenomenalism, objectivism, and scientism. Phenomenalism is the idea that only knowledge confirmed by the senses (sight, hearing, taste, touch, smell) is genuine knowledge. Objectivism holds that knowledge creation, and therefore research, should be value free; it is completely **objective** and free from subjective standards. Scientism suggests that there is a clear distinction between the 'scientific' and the 'normative'. Positivists argue that the 'scientific' is what can be 'known' through the five senses, and if knowledge is not 'learned' through the five sense then it is not 'scientific', and it is therefore 'normative'. This 'last principle is implied by the first [phenomenalism] because the truth or otherwise of normative statements cannot be confirmed by the senses' (Bryman, 2016: 24). It is clear from these principles how closely positivist social research is aligned with research in the natural sciences.

Positivism therefore provides us with a very clear idea about what constitutes 'real' knowledge and how that 'real' knowledge is to be created. Knowledge that is not generated in line with these assumptions and principles is held to be invalid; it cannot qualify as real knowledge. The epistemology of positivism aligns closely with the objectivist **ontology** (see the next section on ontology), the quantitative research strategy (see Chapter 1 – Introduction to mixed methods) and the deductive, theory testing approach (see Table 4.2).

In sum, positivism adopts the natural science model in order to create knowledge about the social world. It relies on the senses (what can be seen, heard, smelt, tasted, and touched) to learn about the social world and holds that we can objectively measure and learn about that world. Positivism was first used in the natural sciences and was adopted by the developing social science movement as it began to emerge from the shadow of these so-called 'hard' sciences.

Interpretivism

A sense of unease with positivistic approaches to social research had emerged by the beginning of the 20th century, and it gained increasing momentum from the 1960s. Social scientists, including criminologists, began to question the usefulness of the positivistic outlook and approach to research, and the natural science model more generally. Social researchers queried not only whether you *could* measure the social world in the same manner as the natural world, but in fact whether the two *should* be measured in the same way. In particular, it was argued that the positivistic, natural science model is often not a practicable research approach, that it can be ethically dubious when used to study people and their societies, and that it cannot always answer the types of questions asked by social scientists (Denscombe, 2002). In the discipline of criminology, the focus was beginning to move beyond the task of simply 'measuring' crime and identifying those supposedly with a criminal propensity, and towards attempts to understand people's lived experiences in relation to crime, deviance, victimisation, and the criminal justice system. In addition to this, there was an increasing acknowledgement that positivism and the natural science model tends to operate as an 'ideal' approach to research, and in reality the manner in which purportedly objective research is conducted is often very different, even within the natural sciences.

The general loss of faith in positivism saw its status as the predominant research philosophy challenged in many disciplines, including criminology. The interpretivist epistemology emerged as an alternative that fundamentally questioned many of the basic assumptions of positivism. Interpretivism recognises that the researcher cannot necessarily separate themselves from their social research environment and is 'founded upon the view that a strategy is required that respects the difference between people and the objects of the natural sciences and therefore requires the social scientist to grasp the subjective meaning of social action' (Bryman, 2016: 26). This recognition of the subjective nature of knowledge about the social world is central to interpretivism and represents its key point of departure from positivism. The five key assumptions of interpretivism are outlined in Figure 4.4.

Clearly, interpretivism proffers a very different theory of knowledge as compared to positivism. The notion of objective knowledge about the social world is rejected in favour of a view that sees research as producing contextually limited and provisional truths, shot through with the values of the researched and the researcher. The epistemology of interpretivism is generally aligned with the constructionist ontology (see the next section on ontology), the qualitative research strategy (see Chapter 1 – Introduction to mixed methods) and the inductive, theory-generating approach (see Table 4.2).

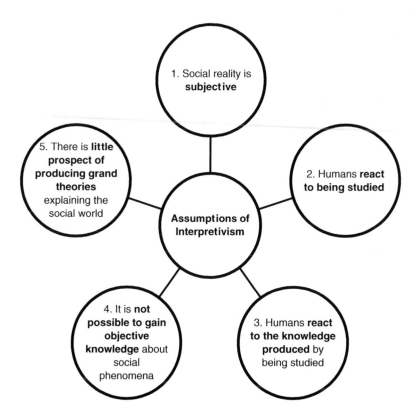

Figure 4.4 Assumptions of interpretivism (adapted from Denscombe, 2002: 18–20).

Not everybody is relaxed about the emergence of interpretivism and the challenge it poses to positivism. There have been a number of criticisms of interpretivism (Denscombe, 2002). Some of the most forceful suggest that interpretivism:

- Lacks authority – if interpretivism challenges the idea that there are single, all-encompassing, and objectively 'correct' explanations of social phenomena, then it follows that any explanation offered by a researcher under the interpretivist banner must suffer from a certain lack of authority (Denscombe, 2002).
- Lacks rigour – the methods and analyses utilised in interpretivist research might be considered by those of a positivist bent to be unscientific and lacking in rigour. In particular, interpretivist research rarely utilises statistical analyses and often employs an emergent research design where the overall methodology develops as the research is conducted rather than being fixed at the outset.
- Results in uncertainty – there is a degree of uncertainty contained within interpretivistic explanations of the social world that might be uncomfortable for some researchers. This is because interpretivist research tends to be much more interested in the understandings, subjectivities and agency of individuals and groups in particular social settings, rather than attempts to provide all-encompassing, generally applicable explanations of social phenomena.

Interpretivists would, of course, contest these points. As the interpretivist approach to research has become increasingly common and accepted in the criminological field, it has developed its own modes of rigour and exactitude, and few would now deny that authoritative pieces of research with far-reaching findings can be produced under interpretivist principles. As for the uncertainty that interpretivist research can result in, interpretivists would claim that this is simply a reflection of the uncertainty inherent in the social world and its amenability to varied interpretations.

As interpretivism increased in importance and influence in the social research field, there was a 'period during which many commentators viewed quantitative and qualitative research as based on incompatible assumptions' (Bryman, 2016: 657). This came to be known as the 'paradigm wars' (Hammersley, 1992; Oakley, 1999) or the 'paradigm debate' (Creswell and Plano Clark, 2011). However, in more recent years the vociferousness of the debate has cooled somewhat, and it has been argued that the 'growing popularity of mixed methods research would seem to signal the end of the paradigm wars, as it is sometimes represented as having given way to **pragmatism**' (Bryman, 2016: 657). Nevertheless, in the wake of interpretivism's ascendancy, a number of additional epistemological stances have developed that in general tend to align with either interpretivist or positivist stances and so the basic opposition between the two is often reasserted. You might see references to post-positivist, realist, feminist, postmodern, poststructuralist,

Table 4.1 Key differences between positivism and interpretivism (adapted from Neuman, 2000: 85)

	Positivism	*Interpretivism*
Reason for research	To discover natural laws so people can predict and control events	To understand and describe meaningful social action
Nature of social reality	Stable pre-existing patterns or order that can be discovered	Fluid definitions of situations created by human interaction
Nature of human beings	Inescapably shaped by external forces	Social beings who create meaning and constantly try to make sense of their world
The way 'common sense' knowledge is thought of	Clearly distinct from and less valid than science	Powerful everyday theories used by ordinary people
Theory looks like . . .	a logical, deductive system of interconnected definitions, axioms, and laws	a description of how a group's meaning system is generated and sustained
An explanation that is true . . .	is logically connected to laws and based on facts	resonates or feels right to those who are being studied
Good evidence . . .	is based on precise observations that others can repeat	is embedded in the context of fluid social interactions
Role of values	Science is value free, and values have no place except perhaps when choosing a topic to study	Values are an integral part of social life, and are thus inherent in any research process

critical theory, and participatory epistemologies in your readings, and it is important to be aware of their existence. Table 4.1 highlights the key differences between the positivist and interpretivist epistemological positions and some of the points of seemingly unresolvable tension between them.

The main criticism of positivism and interpretivism from the point of view of a mixed methods researcher is that they do not acknowledge the reality that multiple epistemological stances can co-exist within the same project. Within a mixed methods strategy, parts of a research project (typically the data collection methods) might adopt a positivistic stance whilst others follow an interpretivist approach. As such, there are specific epistemologies that have been associated with mixed methods research. These include pragmatism (Denscombe, 2014), phenomenology (Mayoh and Onwuegbuzie, 2015), critical realism (Denscombe, 2014; Harrits, 2011; Layder, 1993, 1998; Lipscomb, 2008; Pawson and Tilley, 1997), constructionism (Denzin, 2012), and 'transformative' and 'emancipatory' epistemologies (Mertens, 2009; Onwuegbuzie and Frels, 2013). The most commonly adopted epistemology in mixed methods, and the one that we will focus on here, is pragmatism.

Pragmatism

Pragmatism tends to be the preferred epistemological standpoint in mixed methods research, what Denscombe (2014: 158) calls its 'epistemological partner'. For the pragmatist, knowledge 'is both constructed and based on the reality of the world we experience and live in' (Onwuegbuzie et al., 2009: 122). So although 'the "theory" might say that positivism and interpretivism are incompatible in terms of their basic beliefs about social reality, in practice social researchers have tended to pick and choose from the array of methods at their disposal' (Denscombe, 2002: 23).

Pragmatists prioritise getting the best from their research tools, recognising the strengths and weaknesses in different tools and combining them to best answer the central research question, and as such they 'consider the research question to be more important than either the method they use or the worldview that is supposed to underlie the method' (Tashakkori and Teddlie, 1998: 21). Pragmatists focus on 'not how well [research] sticks to its "positivistic" or "interpretivistic" epistemology, but how well it addresses the topic it is investigating' (Denscombe, 2002: 23). Pragmatism allows methodological decision-making to be driven by considerations of the most appropriate way to carry out the research in order to generate answers to the central research question, and takes the philosophical stance that 'good social research depends on . . . what it is practical to accomplish and what kind of data are required' (Denscombe, 2002: 24). Given all of this, pragmatism has assisted in moving us beyond the 'paradigm wars' (Hammersley, 1992; Oakley, 1999; Bryman, 2016) that pitched quantitative against qualitative and positivism against interpretivism, and therefore it creates an obvious epistemological home for mixed methods research.

As such, the four core principles of pragmatism are (from Denscombe, 2014: 158):

1   Knowledge is based upon practical outcomes and what works best for answering the central research question.
2   Research should test what works best through empirical investigation.
3   There is no single, best 'scientific' method that can lead the way to indisputable knowledge.
4   Knowledge is provisional and is the product of the historical era and the cultural context within which it is produced.

The central point for pragmatists is therefore not how well a piece of research adheres to 'its "positivistic" or "interpretivistic" epistemology, but how well it addresses the topic it is investigating' (Denscombe, 2002: 23). This is why pragmatism resonates so keenly with mixed methods research; it sees the research questions as being at the heart of the research process and this allows the researcher to move beyond the debate between the positivistic and the interpretivistic and the quantitative and the qualitative. Pragmatism focuses on using the best research tools for the problem at hand and on how to get the most from them. It recognises the strengths and weaknesses of different strategies and seeks to combine them in such a way as to accentuate their positives and compensate for their negatives, all the while being driven by a desire to provide an answer to the research questions.

The pragmatist epistemology is generally aligned with the ontology of **multiple realities** (see the next section on ontology), the mixed methods research strategy (see Chapter 1 – Introduction to mixed methods) and the abductive, problem-solving approach (see Table 4.2).

Ontology

Ontology is the study of the nature of reality. In the social sciences an ontological position provides us with a 'theory of the nature of social entities', social phenomena and their meanings (Bryman, 2016: 693). An ontological position addresses itself to questions of what constitutes reality and how we can understand existence (Raddon, n.d.). Within the social sciences, ontological attention has tended to focus upon the

> question of whether social entities can and should be considered objective entities that have a reality external to social actors, or whether they can and should be considered social constructions built up from the perceptions and actions of social actors.
>
> (Bryman, 2016: 28)

A focus on ontology raises the issue of whether we are able to objectively measure the social world in our capacity as researchers whilst remaining independent of it, or whether we actively help to create the social world in the process of learning about it from a position within it. Within criminology, for example, we may believe that we can objectively and impartially measure how people experience crime. Or, we may believe that as members of society likely to have had experience of crime ourselves, we are unable to act truly objectively and independently of the society that we are a part of; this will be reflected in the manner in which we carry out research, which in turn will influence others' perceptions of crime. These two ontological positions are known as **objectivism** and **constructionism**.

Objectivism

Objectivism is the

> ontological position that asserts that social phenomena and their meanings have an existence that is independent of social actors. It implies that social phenomena and the categories that we use in everyday discourse have an existence that is independent or separate from actors.
>
> (Bryman, 2016: 29)

For objectivism, reality exists 'out there', independent of our own existence in th[...]
Essentially, the social world goes on without us; it is indifferent to our existence o[...]
We can therefore understand social reality through the objective study and measure[...]
social phenomena. For example, utilising the Crime Survey for England and Wales (CS[...]
to carry out secondary analyses to test theories and hypotheses around crime and victimisatio[...]
might be considered a classic objectivist approach to research because the CSEW impartially
'measures' people's experiences of crime and victimisation through a quantitative questionnaire
(see Figure 4.5). The objective ontology aligns with positivist epistemology, the quantitative
research strategy and the deductive approach to research (theory testing). This is because they
all view research in a similar way: they assume that the social world can be objectively measured
and empirically tested.

Constructionism

The constructionist ontological position holds that social objects and categories are social
constructions created through interactions between people. Social actors, including researchers, create social reality through their exchanges and their attributions of meaning, in what is
an unending and unavoidable process. This applies to 'official' institutions such as courts and
prisons as much as it does to phenomena such as gangs. Indeed, the very notions of crime
and deviance themselves can be held to be social constructions. This ontological position
'asserts that social phenomena and their meanings are continually being accomplished by
social actors'; it follows that 'social phenomena are not only produced through social interaction but are in a constant state of revision' (Bryman, 2016: 29). An ethnographic study
of a gang and the experience of membership might be considered a classic example of the
constructionist approach to research. A study in this mould aims at building understanding
and recognises that knowledge is collectively created on the part of the researcher and the
researched (see Figure 4.5). Constructionism aligns with interpretivist epistemology, the
qualitative research strategy, and the inductive approach to research (theory generation).
This is because they all view research in a similar way: they assume that the social world is a
creation of human actors within it and is in a constant state of revision and re-construction.

Epistemology	Ontology	Method
Positivism	Objectivism	Quantitative, Deductive
Reality is external to the researcher	*Social phenomena are independent of social actors (humans)*	*Quest ionnaires, Official Statistics*
Interpretivism	Constructionism	Qualitative, Inductive
Reality is constructed by the researcher	*Social phenomena are produced by social interaction*	*Interviews, Focus groups, Ethnography*

Figure 4.5 Links between epistemology, ontology, and method.

alternative position on ontology that can support the adop-
...ggests that there is no single 'correct' ontological under-
...nd that instead there are multiple understandings of reality,
...his acknowledgement can influence our understanding and
...mena and the meanings we ascribe to them.

...oves us away from the 'paradigm wars' in the realm of epis-
...es moves us away from similar debates in the realm of ontol-
...ctivism and constructionism (Onwuegbuzie et al., 2009) and
...e in irrevocable opposition to one another. Ours is always a
partial perspective of the world, and the perspectives of others in different times, different
places and different social situations may be very different to ours but no less valid. Thus
'knowledge' is always inherently provisional and 'current truth, meaning and knowledge
are tentative and changing' (Onwuegbuzie et al., 2009: 122). In the absence of universally
valid truths, there is no 'magic bullet' of a method that can uncover that which is applicable to all. Instead, the best research tools to use in a given situation are those that offer
the best opportunity for a thorough investigation of the matter at hand. The similarity
between this stance and that of pragmatism is clear.

The adoption of the multiple realities ontology can help move research beyond the dualism of the objective and the subjective. Instead, the two can be combined within a single
research project. For instance, a project might combine an online questionnaire that seeks to
objectively measure and test theories about being a victim of burglary with an unstructured
interview to explore the subjective lived experience of being burgled. This, then, is a practical response to the difficulties of actually doing research in the real world and an acknowledgement of the validity of elements of both objectivist and constructionist ontologies.

Pragmatism, multiple realities, and mixed methods

As mixed methods is neither solely a quantitative nor qualitative approach to research,
the traditional (if contested) divisions between positivism and interpretivism and objectivism and constructionism are not especially useful in this setting. Instead, the focus is on
'pragmatism' (Denscombe, 2002; Tashakkori and Teddlie, 1998) as the most appropriate
epistemological approach and multiple realities (Onwuegbuzie et al., 2009) as constituting
the most appropriate ontological framework in mixed methods research.

When creating research proposals, it is vital to make sure there is a logical alignment
between the different philosophical and methodological aspects. In terms of the research
philosophy, it is important that the underlying epistemological and ontological position and
the chosen research strategy create a coherent whole which in turn underpins the actual
process of the research project. In this chapter we have looked at the relationship between
theory and research (deductive, inductive, abductive), epistemology (positivism, interpretivism, pragmatism), and ontology (objectivism, constructionism, multiple realities). The
links between positivism, objectivism, and a quantitative research strategy are clear and
much discussed, as are those between interpretivism, constructionism, and a qualitative
research strategy (see Figure 4.5). Similarly, for our purposes it is evident that pragmatism
links well with multiple realities and a mixed methods strategy. A 'what works' pragmatism
(Denscombe, 2014) that considers knowledge to be provisional and based upon practical
outcomes clearly fits together neatly with the sense that there are multiple realities and, in

turn, with a mixed methods strategy. Table 4.2 sketches the relationships betwe mology, ontology, strategy, and the role of theory as discussed in this chapter.

As Table 4.2 shows, the mixed methods strategy walks the line between qua and qualitative approaches. Mixed methods researchers look beyond the dualism 'paradigm wars' and instead focus on determining what would be the most appr methods to answer the research questions at hand; attention is turned to 'what works' given the circumstances of the project. In addition, the types of answers to central research questions that projects might produce are heavily dependent upon the underlying philo- sophical position adopted by the researcher or research team, as Figure 4.6 shows. Indeed, in an era where much criminological research is 'policy based' and funded by bodies who require easily digestible answers to very specific questions, there is a sense that the time has truly arrived for the mixed methods strategy in the discipline of criminology.

The example presented in Figure 4.6 shows how the same central research question – 'How successful are rehabilitative programmes at reducing reoffending?' – might be answered in different ways depending on the philosophical approach taken by the

Table 4.2 Summary of research philosophy

Strategy	Quantitative	Qualitative	Mixed Methods
Role of Theory	Deductive Testing of Theory	Inductive Generation of Theory	Abductive Problem Solving
Epistemology	Positivism	Interpretivism	Pragmatism
Ontology	Objectivism	Constructionism	Multiple Realities

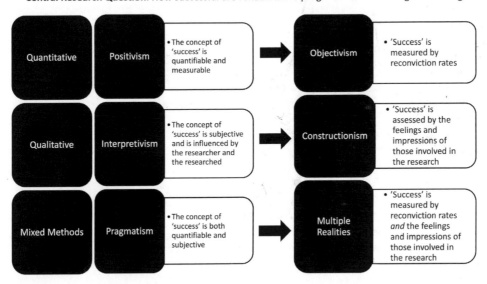

Figure 4.6 An example of the impact of philosophical approach on answering a central research question.

researcher. A researcher taking a positivist approach might look to objectively quantify and measure the success or otherwise of rehabilitative programmes and 'success' in this instance might be the lowering of reoffending rates, or some other proxy such as reconviction rates. A researcher taking an interpretivist approach and focusing upon the subjective lived experience might examine how offenders themselves experienced the rehabilitative programmes and how this affected their reoffending. 'Success' might be determined not by reoffending rates but by the feelings of the research subjects as to the impact of the programmes upon their lives. A researcher taking a pragmatic approach and willing to incorporate both objective measures and subjective experience might combine rates of reoffending and the subjective interpretations of the research subjects.

Summary

This chapter has discussed how social research can be founded upon different philosophical approaches, and how these approaches impact upon the manner in which we study and understand the social world. It should aid your understanding of the different research philosophies, how they inform research, and how they can justify methodological decisions. The chapter began by exploring the philosophies that underpin the creation of knowledge along with the relationship of research and theory. Then, the chapter went on to discuss epistemology and ontology before we argued for pragmatism (Denscombe, 2002; Tashakkori and Teddlie, 1998) as an appropriate epistemological approach and multiple realities (Onwuegbuzie et al., 2009) as an appropriate ontological position for those engaged in mixed methods. Ultimately, the arguments between positivism and interpretivism, and objectivism and constructionism, are rendered far less relevant in any mixed methods endeavour that utilises both the quantitative and the qualitative. Its resolute focus on answering the central research question by applying whatever tools and methods are best suited to the task at hand is surely mixed methods' biggest advantage over the more entrenched positions represented in the paradigm wars and across the ontological divide.

Learning questions

1   Which epistemological position is most often associated with mixed methods? Why?
2   Which ontological position is most often associated with mixed methods? Why?
3   Outline the nature of the compatibility between pragmatism, multiple realities, and mixed methods.

5   Mixed methods design

CHAPTER OVERVIEW

- Introduction
- The priority question
- The sequence question
- Priority, sequence, and overall mixed methods design
- Summary
- Learning questions

Introduction

This chapter discusses what to consider when deciding on your mixed methods design. You should note that the matters of mixed methods design covered in this chapter are distinct from what might be generally called research design, with the latter covered in Chapter 7 – Research design and sampling. This chapter will focus upon two key questions, namely the priority question and the sequence question (Bryman, 2016; Denscombe, 2014). The priority question is concerned with the weighting of the quantitative and qualitative components of the research. It asks whether the components are to be equally weighted, or whether one component is to be dominant. The sequence question focuses on the order in which the quantitative and qualitative components of the research are undertaken. It asks which component should come first, second, and so on, or whether each component is to be carried out at the same time. We then go on to consider how the answers to the priority question and the sequence question combine to create an overall mixed methods design for the research project. As we go through the chapter we introduce you to the **notation** that you will use to represent mixed methods designs in your written work. Notation is the shorthand, simplified version of how to express your mixed methods design. This notation is used throughout the rest of the book.

The priority question

Are the qualitative and the quantitative components in your research of equivalent priority or is one component of greater priority than the other?

The **priority question** demands that attention is given as to which component – the qualitative or the quantitative – is the most important or dominant component of the research project, or whether they are of equal importance. Your answer to the priority question will depend upon your central research question and the aims and objectives of your research. There are two possible answers to the priority question: Either the quantitative and qualitative components of the research are of equivalent priority, or else one is **dominant** and the other is **subordinate**.

Before we explore these two possible answers to the priority question, it is important to note that many different terms are used when scholars are discussing this topic. Some, as we do here, call this the 'priority' question (see also Bryman, 2016), whilst others refer to it as the 'status question' (Denscombe, 2014). Similarly, there is a range of terminology used when discussing the answers to this question, as Table 5.1 demonstrates. Remember that despite the different words used, the same ideas are being conveyed.

Equivalent priority

Equivalent priority is when both the quantitative and qualitative components in your research are of the same importance and neither component dominates the other. This is an appropriate route to take when the quantitative and qualitative components in your research will assist equally in answering your central research question, or when the central research question itself demands that one component should not or cannot dominate the research. It follows that if the quantitative and qualitative components in your research are of the same value because they will contribute to answering your central research question in the same measure, then the answer to the priority question is that the components are of equal priority. Equivalent priority can be shown through the use of notation. In this case it would be shown as 'QUANT QUAL', with both appearing in capital letters (see Table 5.2).

One example of a criminological research project where the quantitative and qualitative components were of equivalent priority is Best et al.'s (2016) evaluation of intuitive recovery. This research collected data about participants' substance use and recovery (QUANT) and carried out interviews (QUAL). Both data collection methods and the collected data were of equal importance to the overall research project and helped to answer the central research question in equal measure. Using notation, this would be shown as 'QUANT QUAL'.

Table 5.1 Synonyms for priority question terminology

When the question is termed . . .	*The answers tend to be termed . . .*
The priority question (e.g. Heap and Waters, in this textbook)	Equivalent or equal priority Non-equivalent priority; dominant and subordinate components
The priority question (e.g. Bryman, 2016)	Equivalent or equal priority Dominant and less dominant priority
The status question (e.g. Denscombe, 2014)	Equivalent or equal status Dominant and less dominant status
The importance question	Equivalent or equal importance More and less important
The weighting question	Equivalent or equal weighting Inequivalent and unequal weighting

Non-equivalent priority

There are many situations where one of the components, either quantitative or qualitative, is more important in providing an answer to your central research question, or dominates your research methodology and data analysis. In such situations it is not possible to describe the components as being of equal priority; they are of unequal status and one component is dominant whilst the other is subordinate. Reasons why one component might be dominant or subordinate could be one component being more integral to answering the central research question, or an inequivalent amount of or quality of data. A researcher should be able to justify why one component is dominant and why one is subordinate. Non-equivalent priority of this type can be shown through the use of notation. The dominant component is shown in capital letters, whilst the subordinate component features lower-case letters. Thus, if your research has a dominant quantitative component, the notation for this would be 'QUANT qual'. Alternatively, if the dominant component of your research is qualitative, the notation would be 'QUAL quant' (see Table 5.2).

One example of a criminological research project with non-equivalent priority is Waters' (2009) research into older illegal drug users. In this research the quantitative component (secondary data analysis of the British Crime Survey (now the Crime Survey for England and Wales)) took precedence over the qualitative component (interviews) because of the amount of available data. A large secondary dataset from the British Crime Survey was analysed, but the researcher was only able to conduct a handful of interviews for various reasons (Waters, 2015). This meant that the quantitative component dominated the research project and contributed in greater measure than the qualitative component to answering the central research question. Using notation, this would be shown as 'QUANT qual'.

More than two components

Thus far, our focus has been on those projects that have a single quantitative component and a single qualitative component. However, some research inquiries will demand a more intricate **mixed methods design** which incorporates more than one quantitative or more than one qualitative component, or more than one of both. In this instance, the priority question becomes more complex, but still needs to be addressed. It may be the case that all the components within the piece of research are of equivalent importance. When showing this through notation, follow the format shown above for equivalent priority and add as many components to the notation as is required (see Table 5.2).

Of course, it might also be the case that some components are dominant and some are subordinate. In such a situation you would need to identify each component as either dominant or subordinate and justify this decision in light of the overall research project. When showing this through notation, follow the format shown above for dominant and subordinate components (see Table 5.2). There is no requirement for how many dominant or subordinate components there should be; depending on the nature of the research, it is possible to have multiple dominant and multiple subordinate components, or there may be just a single dominant or a single subordinate component.

As part of the Cambridge University Public Opinion Project (CUPOP), King and Maruna studied the public perceptions of offender 'redeemability' (see, for example, King, 2008; King and Maruna, 2005, 2009, 2011; Maruna and King, 2004, 2009). Their study was made up of three components; two were quantitative and one was qualitative, and they were of equal priority (QUANT → QUAL → QUANT). The first component (QUANT) consisted of a postal questionnaire on punitiveness which was sent to a

Table 5.2 Priority notation

	Notation	Explanation
Equivalent priority	QUANT QUAL	This denotes that both the quantitative and qualitative component(s) are of equal priority
Dominant and subordinate priority	QUANT	This denotes that the quantitative component is dominant
	quant	This denotes that the quantitative component is subordinate
	QUAL	This denotes that the qualitative component is dominant
	qual	This denotes that the qualitative component is subordinate

random sample and completed by 941 British households. During the second component (QUAL), exploratory semi-structured interviews were carried out with a sub-sample made up of some of the respondents to the postal questionnaire; participants with the highest scores on punitiveness were interviewed along with those who had the lowest. The third component (QUANT) consisted of a series of random-allocation experiments that tested whether punitive attitudes could be manipulated through a variety of means. Note that this was a sequential study, hence the forward arrow between components (see section on the sequence question below).

Making decisions on priority

When thinking about the priority question for your own research, you need to think about your research project as a whole; the priority question cannot be addressed in isolation from the rest of your project. Crucially, you will need to think about any practical constraints you might have such as limitations of time, resources, and experience. For example, a large-scale probability quantitative questionnaire might not be practical in terms of the time and money at your disposal, so instead a small convenience sample questionnaire could be used (see Chapter 7 – Research design and sampling for more information on sampling). This smaller questionnaire might be less dominant than originally envisaged within the overall project. A different component might thus become dominant whilst the questionnaire takes a subordinate role. The priority of your components might also be linked to the data collection methods you use, with particular methods taking 'supporting' roles in your research and therefore ceding dominance to a different component. An example of this might be a project in which a small number of interviews supplement a large questionnaire by providing additional context and depth. Any decisions you make in this vein about priority should be justifiable in relation to the entirety of the project, the central research question, aims, objectives, the overall project methodology, and data collection, and you should be able to robustly defend them.

The sequence question

In what order do the quantitative and qualitative components occur: simultaneously or sequentially?

The **sequence question** is concerned with the sequential arrangement in which the components of the research are organised. It asks whether the different components of the research are to be carried out at approximately the same time, or whether there is some time-order to when the different components are to be undertaken. How you answer this question will depend on the overall nature of your research project and how you intend to address your central research question. There are three possible answers to the sequence question: Either the research can be carried out simultaneously, or else it can be carried out in sequential or multi-phase sequential fashion.

Simultaneous

In a simultaneous design the quantitative and qualitative components are carried out at roughly the same time. Sometimes this is also referred to as a 'concurrent' or 'parallel' design. With a simultaneous design, the two components resemble standalone 'silos' of work where the data from each are collected independently of the other, notwithstanding the fact that they ultimately remain part of a broader piece of research and are both directed towards providing an answer to the central research question (see Figure 5.1). Crucially, however, in a simultaneous study the components remain distinct and do not influence each other during the data collection phase. The two components are brought together and the inferences are combined at a later point (see Chapter 6 – Combining the data). It may be the case that in a simultaneous study the data collection for each component does not take place at exactly the same time, but there is generally no interaction between the two processes of data collection which are carried out as close in time as is practical.

The standard notation for a simultaneous design is illustrated in Table 5.3. However, as this can be difficult to incorporate into a block of text, it can be shown in a more informal manner if required. This involves the use of a so-called 'curly bracket' or 'brace' and a forward arrow. The priority of the components is also evident in the notation, as can be seen in the following examples of informal notation:

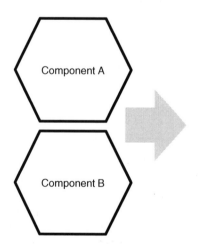

Figure 5.1 Simultaneous design.

Table 5.3 Sequence notation for simultaneous design

Simultaneous design	Component A (QUANT / quant) AND Component B (QUAL / qual)	→

- QUAL / QUANT } →
- qual / QUANT } →
- QUAL / quant } →

In practice, a simultaneous piece of research might involve carrying out secondary analysis of a dataset whilst working on a qualitative media analysis, or conducting qualitative interviews whilst at the same time carrying out a quantitative questionnaire. As noted above, in a simultaneous design, the simultaneous components take place concurrently and do not influence each other at the data collection phase; thus, in the latter example the questionnaire would not lead into or influence the makeup of the interviews or vice versa, unlike in a sequential design, as we will see shortly.

One example of a criminological research project with a simultaneous design is Waters' (2009) study of older illegal drug users, which we have already encountered in the section above on non-equivalent priority. This study involved a quantitative component (secondary data analysis of the British Crime Survey) being carried out at the same time as a qualitative component (semi-structured interviews with older drug users). This meant that the inferences from the secondary analysis did not influence the creation of the interview schedule in any way, and the themes that emerged from the interviews were not used to inform the statistical analysis. As we saw earlier, in this non-equivalent study the qualitative component was subordinate to the quantitative component. Therefore, using notation this would be shown as QUANT / qual } →.

It is important to note that a simultaneous design might have more than two components. When multiple quantitative and qualitative components are being utilised, provided that they are undertaken at around the same time and do not influence each other (remembering the 'silo' analogy above), then the study is a simultaneous one. A simultaneous study of this nature might involve a questionnaire, semi-structured interviews and focus groups, all carried out at the same time. As with a standard simultaneous study, inferences would only be combined at the end and the different 'silos' would not influence each other at the data collection phase. A simultaneous study with more than two components would be used in situations where your central research question, aims, and objectives warranted multiple instances of data collection at a single point in time.

Sequential

A sequential design involves two components, with one carried out after the other. This is sometimes also called a 'single-phase sequential' design. The experience of the data collection process, the data itself and the analysis of the data from the first component are then used to inform the design of the subsequent component. Either a quantitative or qualitative component can be used as the starting point depending on the central research question and the aims and objectives of the inquiry. The key to a sequential design is that the proceeding component feeds into the subsequent component; as such, the research 'builds' from one component to the next. The notation for a sequential design is shown in Table 5.4. Components are shown in order from first to last with a forward arrow in between each component (e.g. QUAL → QUANT).

In practice, a sequential design might begin with, for instance, a number of preliminary qualitative semi-structured interviews which would be analysed for themes. These themes could then be used to inform the subsequent component, which might be a large quantitative questionnaire that addresses the themes from the earlier interviews and becomes the focal point of the research. The notation for this would be qual → QUANT, with the latter quantitative component taking priority in this case.

Alternatively, there may be cases of sequentially designed research where the components share equivalent priority. For instance, a large-scale quantitative questionnaire could be used to inform a subsequent method of data collection such as qualitative interviews (QUANT → QUAL), as was the case in research by Best et al. (2016). Best et al. (2016) used their questionnaire (QUANT) not only to collect data, but as a precursor to the creation of their interview schedule and qualitative data collection (QUAL). The questionnaire was used to recruit interviewees through a question at its end asking if participants would be willing to be interviewed. Because of this, a sequential design was to an extent unavoidable as the quantitative component (questionnaire) had to come before the qualitative component (interviews), not only for analytical (theme development) reasons, but also for practical (participant recruitment) ones.

'Multi-phase' sequential

'Multi-phase' sequential design is where the research involves three or more components, with each component occurring successively rather than simultaneously, in a similar manner to the 'single-phase' sequential design described above which involves just two components. As with a 'single-phase' sequential design, the key with a multi-phase design is the way that the research builds over time, with earlier components informing subsequent components. In a multi-phase design it is especially important to be able to justify the order of the components and the way in which later components are derived from the earlier components. This justification needs to make sense in terms of the practicalities of the research process, the way the components build upon previous components in a logical manner, and the central research question and overall purpose of your project.

The notation for a multi-phase sequential design is shown in Table 5.4. Components are shown in order from first to last with a forward arrow in between each component (e.g. qual → QUANT → QUAL). Of course, the notation should include as many components as necessary, and some multi-phase sequential projects will involve more than the three components shown in this example.

In practice, a sequential design might begin with, for instance, a focus group (qual) intended to identify key issues. This is particularly useful if you are unsure about what the key issues are, for example in an exploratory-type study. The inferences of the focus group could then feed into a probability sampled questionnaire (QUANT) designed to measure some of the ideas to come out of the focus groups and begin to look for patterns of association between variables. This in turn could feed into a third component, a semi-structured interview (QUAL) that investigates in greater depth the inferences from the previous components, with a sample drawn from the questionnaire participants. The notation for the resulting sequence would be qual → QUANT → QUAL.

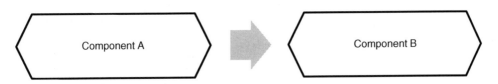

Figure 5.2 Sequential design.

Table 5.4 Sequence notation for sequential design

Single-phase design	Component A (QUANT / quant / QUAL / qual)	→	Component B (QUANT / quant / QUAL / qual)		
Multi-phase design	Component A (QUANT / quant / QUAL / qual)	→	Component B (QUANT / quant / QUAL / qual)	→	Component C (QUANT / quant / QUAL / qual)

One example of a criminological research project with a multi-phase sequential design is Platts-Fowler and Robinson's (2015) evaluation of the 'Gateway 9 Protection Programme', a refugee assistance scheme in the UK which provides 12 months of material and social support for refugees arriving into the country. Initially, refugees completed a questionnaire (QUANT), followed by a focus group (QUAL). Both of these components then fed into the next round of questionnaires (QUANT) and focus groups (QUAL) at 12 months, which in turn fed into the final round of questionnaires (QUANT) and focus groups (QUAL) at 18 months. The notation for this project would thus be QUANT → QUAL → QUANT → QUAL → QUANT → QUAL.

Making decisions on sequence

As with the priority question, when considering the sequence question for your own research, it is important to think about your project as a whole. The same issues need to be considered again when deciding on sequencing:

- What is the purpose of the study?
- What overall methodology are you adopting?
- What data collection methods are appropriate and feasible?
- What practical constraints do you face in terms of time, money, and skills?

You will need to order your components in a way that makes sense on its own terms and also in relation to your overall research project, providing the best 'fit' between your sequencing and the central research question, aims, objectives, overall project methodology, and data collection. The key is to have a clear decision-making process and to ensure that you can explicitly justify your answer to the sequence question in your planning and writing-up of the research project.

Priority, sequence, and overall mixed methods design

Priority and sequence can be combined in any number of ways in your mixed methods design. When deciding how to answer the priority and sequence questions, you should once again consider a number of things: What research questions are you seeking to answer? What are the aims and objectives of the research and what are you planning to achieve with your project? What is the purpose of and justification for the study? What data collection methods are being used and why? Are there any practical constraints on the research such as limits on time and resources? The way you answer these questions will have a big impact on the way that you combine priority and sequence into an overall design for your project. It is important to be able to justify the decisions that you make. You should have good reasons, for example, for having a dominant component or for giving your components equal priority. Similarly, you should have a clearly articulated rationale for your decision to adopt a simultaneous or sequential design. Ultimately, you should aim to bring together priority and sequence in such a way as to create a coherent piece of research that can be robustly defended. Your chosen mixed methods design should be explicitly justified within your work which should also include appropriate notation.

Although there is a multitude of potential mixed methods designs and no widely agreed-upon terminology to describe them, Bryman (2016: 639) outlines four basic designs that will likely cover most circumstances, themselves based on work by Creswell and Plano Clark (2011). Bryman calls these the '**convergent parallel design**', the '**exploratory sequential design**', the '**explanatory sequential design**', and the 'embedded design'. We will focus upon the first three as they are sufficient to cover the vast majority of projects and clearly demonstrate how your answers to the priority and sequence questions feed into the overall design of your mixed methods study (see Table 5.5 for details).

Table 5.5 Basic mixed methods designs (adapted from Bryman, 2016: 638–639)

Name	Description	Answer to priority question	Answer to sequence question	Example
Convergent parallel design	Simultaneous collection of quantitative and qualitative data typically of equal priority. The resulting analyses are then compared and/or merged to form an integrated whole. Typically associated with triangulation (see Chapter 6 – Combining the data)	Components can be of either equivalent or non-equivalent priority; decision on priority must be justifiable in the context of the project	Simultaneous	Bacchus et al. (2018)
Exploratory sequential design	Collection of qualitative data prior to the collection of quantitative data. Associated with the generation of qualitative-based hypotheses or hunches that are then tested quantitatively	Components can be of either equivalent or non-equivalent priority; decision on priority must be justifiable in the context of the project	Sequential, with qualitative preceding quantitative	Cabrera (2011)
Explanatory sequential design	Collection and analysis of quantitative data followed by the collection and analysis of qualitative data in order to elaborate upon or explain the quantitative inferences	Components can be of either equivalent or non-equivalent priority; decision on priority must be justifiable in the context of the project	Sequential, with quantitative preceding qualitative	Heap (2010)

Convergent parallel design

The convergent parallel design involves the roughly simultaneous collection of quantitative and qualitative data. Each component is effectively discrete and acts as a standalone 'silo', with each component not influencing the others during the data collection phase. In general, the components in a convergent parallel design tend to be of equal priority. Once both the quantitative and qualitative data collection and analysis has taken place, the inferences from each component are combined (see Chapter 6 – Combining the data), and the meta-inferences created. The convergent parallel design often employs triangulation as its method of integration (see Chapter 6 – Combining the data for a discussion of combining inferences into meta-inferences).

This design tends to be used when the aim of the research is to compare two sets of inferences, and generally in 'situations in which the research aims to offset the weakness of both quantitative and qualitative research by capitalizing on the strengths of both' (Bryman, 2016: 638).

An example of a criminological research project that utilised a convergent parallel mixed methods design is Bacchus et al.'s (2018) study of British gay and bisexual males' experiences of domestic violence. Data for the two components that made up the study were collected simultaneously and consisted of questionnaires (QUANT) and semi-structured interviews (QUAL). A convenience sample of 532 male participants who self-identified as gay or bisexual was constructed. Participants completed the quantitative questionnaires about their health and relationships at health clinics in London. They were given the opportunity to undertake an interview at the health clinics if

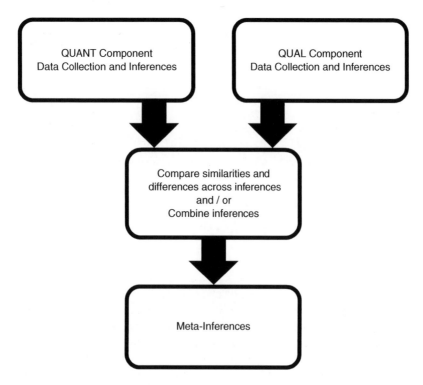

Figure 5.3 Convergent parallel design.

they provided their contact details on the questionnaire. Nineteen participants were interviewed as a result. Following the initial data collection phase, the quantitative and qualitative components were combined using triangulation.

Exploratory sequential design

The exploratory sequential design involves the collection and analysis of qualitative data prior to the collection and analysis of quantitative data. In this design either component can take priority over the other, although note that Creswell and Plano Clark (2011) suggest that typically the qualitative component takes priority, whereas Bryman (2016) argues that the quantitative component more often than not takes priority. Our view is simply that the priority of the components varies depending on the purpose of the research. The key to the exploratory sequential design is that the qualitative inferences help to prepare for the quantitative data collection, the former feeding into the latter, providing direction and sharpening focus (see Figure 5.4).

Bryman (2016) suggests three potential situations where an exploratory sequential design might be of value. The first is where the aim of the research is 'to generate hypothesis or hunches [using the qualitative component] which can then be tested [using the quantitative component]' (Bryman, 2016: 638–639). The second is where the aim of the research is to develop quantitative research instruments (such as questionnaires) out of the qualitative component, 'which can then be used in a quantitative investigation' (Bryman, 2016: 639). The third is where the aim is to 'follow up qualitative findings with quantitative research which allows the scope and generalizability of the qualitative findings to be assessed' (Bryman, 2016: 639).

An example of a criminological research project that utilised an exploratory mixed methods design is Cabrera's (2011) study on racial hyperprivilege and intersectionality in higher education. The initial phase of this study involved qualitative interviews with white male university students (QUAL). The inferences from the qualitative component informed the researcher's emerging understandings of the field and generated themes and concepts that fed into the subsequent quantitative phases of the study, which consisted of two successive waves of a questionnaire (QUANT). Specifically, the author wanted to 'examine whether the four frames of participants' racial ideologies are generalizable to a larger population' (Cabrera, 2011: 84). The notation for this project would be QUAL → QUANT → QUANT. This use of the initial qualitative inferences being used to inform the subsequent quantitative components is the essential feature of the exploratory sequential design.

Explanatory sequential design

The explanatory sequential design involves the collection and analysis of quantitative data prior to the collection and analysis of qualitative data. The qualitative data and analysis are used to elaborate upon, add depth to, or explain the earlier quantitative inferences (see Figure 5.5). Typically, this might involve a quantitative component such as a questionnaire followed by qualitative components such as interviews or focus groups. As with the exploratory sequential design, in this design either component can take priority over the other, although here again there are differences of opinion as to which component tends to be dominant (Creswell and Plano Clark, 2011; Bryman, 2016).

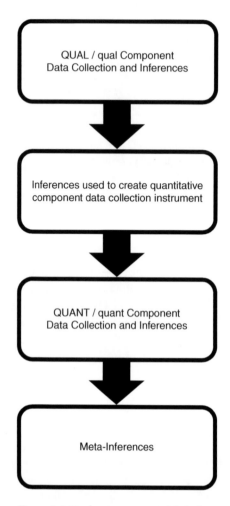

Figure 5.4 Exploratory sequential design.

An explanatory sequential design is advantageous in situations 'when the researcher feels that the broad patterns of relationships uncovered through quantitative research require an explanation which the quantitative data on their own are unable to supply or when further insight into the questionnaire findings is required' (Bryman, 2016: 640). Thus, explanatory sequential studies utilise the ability of qualitative methods to add depth and colour to the inferences provided by the initial quantitative components, therefore providing the type of 'thick', detailed, and nuanced inferences that are often of value in social science disciplines such as criminology and that quantitative methods can sometimes struggle to provide in isolation.

An example of a criminological research project that utilised an explanatory sequential mixed methods design is Heap's (2010) work on public perceptions of anti-social behaviour. Heap's study began with a public perception survey (quant) designed to identify important themes, before moving on to two qualitative components (QUAL / QUAL).

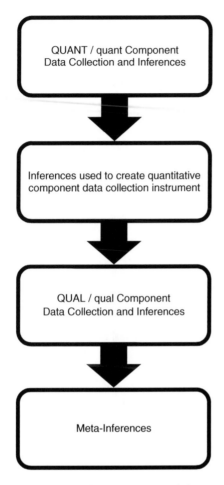

Figure 5.5 Explanatory sequential design.

These latter two components were designed to investigate in detail the themes that were generated in the initial quantitative phase and consisted of focus groups with members of the public and interviews with anti-social behaviour practitioners. The qualitative components were prioritised because of the depth and originality they provided, and the fact that a small-scale study conducted by a single individual with limited resources cannot hope to rival large-scale studies such as the Crime Survey for England and Wales (then the British Crime Survey) in terms of the amount of quantitative data that can be generated. Using notation, this would be shown as quant → QUAL / QUAL } →.

Summary

This chapter has focused upon the issue of mixed methods design, and the two key questions that all mixed methods researchers need to answer. We looked first at the priority question, which asks what the weighting of the different components in any piece of mixed methods research is to be. Equivalent priority is when the components are equally weighted and this might be appropriate for many projects. However, other projects might feature a component, or indeed more than one component, that is dominant over the other component or components. Then our attention turned to the sequence question, which asks in which order the mixed methods project is to be undertaken. Simultaneous projects consist of two or more components undertaken at the same time. Sequential projects consist of components that take place one after the other, either in a single-phase (two components) format or a multi-phase (more than two components) format.

The chapter concluded with a look at overall mixed methods design. This is the manner in which the answers to the priority question and the sequence question are brought together in order to create a complete schema for the work at hand. In theory there are an infinite number of ways in which priority and sequence can be combined; the key is to think about what works best for your project and how you can justify the decision that you make. When outlining your overall mixed methods design, you should use the appropriate notation to clearly illustrate the nature of your project. Our focus was on three mixed methods designs that between them cover most situations. The convergent parallel design involves components, typically of equal priority, carried out simultaneously. The exploratory sequential design involves carrying out the qualitative component before the quantitative component, in order to generate and test hypotheses and hunches. The explanatory sequential design involves carrying out the quantitative component before the qualitative component, in order to add depth and nuance to the quantitative inferences. In these sequential designs, there is some debate as to which component should take priority, but in principle there is no necessary reason for either the quantitative or the qualitative to always take priority in every case. This will depend upon the nature of the project at hand and what it is seeking to achieve.

Despite the wealth of terminology and the obvious potential for some very complex mixed methods designs to be developed, at root sequence and priority and overall mixed methods design are fairly simple and straightforward matters that should not daunt you unduly when you come to think about your own work. That said, as we have repeatedly stressed throughout the chapter, the answers to the questions posed in this chapter and the way your overall mixed methods design will look are at least partly contingent upon other factors, such as the nature of your central research question, the aims and objectives of the study, and the practical constraints you face. These issues will need to be considered when you are deciding upon your answers to the questions posed in this chapter. Thus, there is often much to think about when considering mixed methods design, even though the underlying questions might not appear to be particularly demanding.

As ever, when you are communicating your research, be it in a report, in a dissertation, or through a presentation, you must be able to explicitly discuss your mixed methods design. You should be able to clearly and robustly justify the decisions you have made on priority, sequence and your overall mixed methods design, and relate these decisions to the purpose of the study, the central research question and the aims and objectives of the research project, as well as any practical constraints you had to address.

Learning questions

1   What is the priority question?
2   What is the sequence question?
3   How is an overall mixed methods design created from the answer to the priority and sequence questions?

6   Combining the data

CHAPTER OVERVIEW

- Introduction
- The mixed methods minefield
- Triangulation
- Complementarity
- Development
- Initiation
- Expansion
- Evaluating attempts to combine the data
- Summary
- Learning questions

Introduction

Deciding on the way you are going to combine the data from the quantitative and qualitative components is one of the most challenging aspects of mixed methods research. This chapter introduces the process of combining the data from different components and explains five different ways to do this. Utilising these techniques will allow you to produce an overall set of meta-inferences for your mixed methods study. The first part of this chapter deals with one of the common problems in mixed methods: terminology issues. As the mixed methods strategy is relatively new, there are a number of terms in use which have the same meaning. Once the language of mixed methods has been clarified, the chapter moves on to outline five basic ways mixed methods data can be combined based on Greene et al.'s (1989) framework. This includes: triangulation, complementarity, development, initiation, and expansion. For each of the five different methods, an introduction to the technique is provided, followed by an example of it being employed in real-world criminological research. The section on each way to combine the data finishes with an overview of the things you need to think about to determine if that particular method is suitable for your research project, and how you should set about combining the data in practice. The final section of the chapter examines some of the strengths and weaknesses of combining the data, to help you make a range of justifiable decisions when planning your mixed methods research project.

The mixed methods minefield

Before examining the different ways your inferences can be combined, we discuss the context of 'mixing' in mixed methods. This includes an overview of the different terminology used by researchers, factors to consider when planning your mixed methods research project, and an introduction to the different ways that data can be combined.

Terminology

Mixed methods research is complex by nature. However, the discipline is often over-complicated by the lack of common terminology associated with some of the key processes undertaken in every study. To add to the confusion for novice mixed methods students, established researchers often use incorrect terminology when discussing their project. This chapter begins by exploring some of the often-confused and sometimes overlapping terms. Combining the inferences from the quantitative and qualitative components of your study to generate a set of meta-inferences that answer your central research question is the fundamental part of undertaking mixed methods research. However, in the literature, the actual business of doing the 'mixing' is talked about using a number of different terms, as demonstrated in Table 6.1. Creswell and Plano Clark (2011) simply use the term 'mixing', but Morse and Niehaus (2009) adopt a more technical phrase and refer to the 'point of interface'. Many mixed methods authors use the term 'integration', but we will use the broader term 'combining' to refer to how the data are brought together, as we feel it better reflects the five different ways of bringing together the data that we discuss in this chapter. 'Combining' is also used by Bryman (2016), but do be prepared to encounter the different terms in other textbooks, especially those published in the USA. To help you decode your wider reading, a summary of the different terms used by prominent mixed methods authors for combining the data can be found in Table 6.1.

Planning your 'mixing'

Once you have decided on your central research question, philosophical rationale, and mixed methods design (see Chapters 2, 4, and 5), it is time to consider how you will combine your data to allow you to answer your central research question as fully as possible (within any practical constraints you may face such as time and/or resources). It is a

Table 6.1 Terms used to describe the 'mixing' in mixed methods

Author	Term
Greene et al. (1989)	Purpose
Bryman (2006) Erzberger and Kelle (2003) Teddlie and Tashakkori (2009)	Integration
Morse and Niehaus (2009)	Point of interface
Creswell and Plano Clark (2011)	Mixing
Bryman (2016) Heap and Waters (2018)	Combining

useful starting point to think back to the reasons why you wish to use mixed methods in the first place and how you envisage the different components coming together to answer your central research question. For instance, what exactly do you want to find out about your chosen topic and how are you going to go about it? Let us consider a criminological example: a project investigating hate crime. Is the aim of the research for the inferences from one component to confirm, or validate, the other? If so, a quantitative questionnaire into perceptions of hate crime victims could be validated by qualitative interviews that address the same question. Or, is the central research question and subsequent project more flexible? Do you want to explore different aspects of hate crime in the questionnaire and interviews to build an overall picture of the phenomenon? Coming to a decision about combining the data involves asking yourself a lot of questions about the nature of the research project you intend to conduct, and to an extent, the types of answers you are looking for.

In practice, the process of combining the data from the quantitative and qualitative components is about examining the different sets of inferences and discerning how they can contribute to answering your central research question. Until the point in time when you deliberately bring the data together, the quantitative and qualitative components should be kept separate (unless you are using development to combine your data, which features a sequential design. We explain what this involves later in the chapter). Each component should be analysed according to the relevant underpinning epistemological and ontological assumptions and should remain a discrete entity until a full set of inferences for that component is finalised. Once the inferences for each component are complete, you can begin to combine your results. Some authors, such as Morse and Niehaus (2009), suggest that combining the data can take place in some circumstances before the results of each component are finalised. This is a more complex approach to conducting mixed methods research. Whilst this approach has merit, we suggest that those new to undertaking a mixed methods study combine the results at the end when writing-up the discussion section of your piece of work (see Chapter 12 – Writing-up for more information).

When discussing your inferences, Morse and Niehaus (2009) state that it should be made clear which inferences come from which component, for instance which ones are quantitative and which ones are qualitative. This approach makes your research process clear to the reader and demonstrates a thorough and systematic approach. When writing about your meta-inferences you will incorporate the inferences from each component within a discussion about what you have found. To continue with the example of a mixed methods project about hate crime, you would discuss your quantitative inferences from the questionnaire and your qualitative inferences from the interviews (the order in which these are presented being dependent on the priority of the components; see Chapter 5 – Mixed methods design), before writing about what meta-inferences can be drawn from both components that answer the central research question.

Different ways to combine the data

How you go about combining the inferences to create a set of meta-inferences is the focus of this chapter. As mixed methods has developed as a research strategy over time, the ways in which meta-inferences are generated have evolved. With the discipline of mixed methods research growing quickly, this is contested terrain and several scholars have offered different perspectives about the underlying purpose of combining quantitative and qualitative inferences (see Bryman, 2016). To determine the number of different ways being used to combine the data in practice, Bryman (2006) undertook a content analysis of mixed methods research studies. He found that *16* different ways of combining quantitative and qualitative components had been utilised. A more manageable starting point for student researchers using mixed methods for the first time is to consider the framework developed by Greene et al. (1989). To create this, they assessed the purpose and design characteristics of 57 mixed methods studies in their sample. They found the studies used five principal ways to combine the data (which they call purposes): **triangulation**, **complementarity**, **development**, **initiation**, and **expansion**. These five different techniques are a useful starting point to consider when planning your mixed methods research project.

Determining how you will combine your data is a pivotal decision that will impact upon the type of mixed methods design, research design and data collection methods you adopt. For example, the research design and data collection methods you use to combine your data by triangulation would be very different to those you would employ if you wanted to combine the data using development. These planning decisions will influence how your project develops in practice. However, mixed methods does afford some flexibility should your data collection plans not come to fruition. Although these decisions are important to make at the outset, they can be adapted later if necessary, so avoid putting too much pressure on this part of the decision-making process. Chapter 11 – Troubleshooting explores a range of issues that arise in the field and how to overcome them.

The remainder of the chapter is dedicated to explaining the five techniques for combining the data proposed by Greene et al. (1989), namely: triangulation, complementarity, development, initiation, and expansion. An overview and explanation are provided for each technique, illustrated by an example from criminological research. This is followed by an indication of the types of methodological decisions you will need to make at the planning stage to help you develop your own mixed methods research project. Reference will be made to the type of central research question you have created (see Chapter 2 – Creating a mixed methods question and project planning). This is because your central research question is the driving force behind the decisions you will need to make about how to combine your data. According to Onwuegbuzie and Leech (2006), the central research question is the factor that determines whether a research project will be mixed methods or not, and in turn this influences the decisions that follow. The method you select to combine the data will subsequently determine the choices you have surrounding the priority question and the sequence question (see Chapter 5 – Mixed methods design). Furthermore, philosophical perspectives underpin the rationale for conducting mixed methods research. Consequently it is important to acknowledge that the following discussions about combining the data reflect a pragmatic epistemology, multiple realities ontology and an abductive relationship between theory and research (see Chapter 4 – Philosophy). As your chosen methods of combining the data are central to many other decisions you will need to make, this chapter creates a framework for you to follow when deciding upon the best option to utilise when combining your data in practice.

Triangulation

Triangulation is where two or more methods are used to investigate the same phenomenon. The aim is to seek a convergence and corroboration of the inferences generated from each research component to create meta-inferences.

Understanding triangulation

If you type 'triangulation' into Google, the dictionary definition that appears at the top of the page has nothing to do with research methods. In the non-research world, the term primarily relates to surveying, namely

> the tracing and measurement of a series or network of triangles in order to determine the distances and relative positions of points spread over an area, especially by measuring the length of one side of each triangle and deducing its angles and the length of the other two sides by observation from this baseline.
>
> (Google Dictionary, 2017)

This description demonstrates the linguistic roots of the word, which bears some semblance to the context within which we use it, but it also highlights how 'triangulation' has multiple meanings. See Erzberger and Kelle (2003) for a more in-depth discussion about the roots of this 'fuzzy' concept and evolution of its use within research methodology. The term was first used in a research methods context by Webb et al. (1966), following Campbell and Fiske's first conception and discussion of mixed methods in 1959. It is the way to combine the data most written about by mixed methods scholars, hence you will find this to be the largest section of the five different techniques outlined in this chapter.

Unfortunately for the new mixed methods researcher, there is no universally accepted definition of triangulation used within the mixed methods discipline. This is partly because the mixed methods research strategy is still being developed and refined. For instance, in some textbooks triangulation is employed as the umbrella term for describing mixed methods; it is used to portray the combination of different components, rather than reflecting the combining technique itself. Furthermore, triangulation is often cited by researchers as the method used to mix the inferences, when in fact one of the other ways of combining the data defined by either Greene et al. (1989) or Bryman (2006) has been utilised. Some authors have even described triangulation as a strategy in its own right (Mathison, 1988). Hammersley (2008) has identified six scholars that have contested the interpretation and value of the term triangulation. When you are conducting wider reading about mixed methods research, and triangulation in particular, it is vitally important to bear these issues in mind. The aim of this chapter is to help you navigate through this terminological minefield.

Basic triangulation

A useful straightforward definition of triangulation, which appears to be used most often by mixed methods scholars and is how we apply the term throughout this book, is where two or more methods are used to investigate the same phenomenon and answer the same central research question. The aim is to seek a convergence and corroboration of the inferences generated from each research component to create the meta-inferences. For example, does the quantitative component substantiate the qualitative component or vice versa? This is referred to elsewhere as: *between method/methodological triangulation* (Denzin, 1970), *data triangulation* (Crowther-Dowey and Fussey, 2013), and *triangulation as validity checking* (Hammersley, 2008). The central proposition is that threats to validity are cancelled out by using data from different components, making it possible that the conclusions drawn from the inferences are less likely to be false because of errors and/or bias within the data. Thinking about a mixed methods project researching hate crime, a quantitative component utilising a questionnaire to collect data about student perceptions of hate crime could be validated by qualitative semi-structured interviews that ask participants about the same topics featured on the questionnaire. The limitations of a questionnaire (e.g. respondents being forced to answer a closed question) could be offset by the strengths of an interview (e.g. allowing respondents to provide their own account of their perceptions). Scholars sometimes refer to validity checking as the *offset method* (Bryman, 2016). The convergence and corroboration rationale aligns with the epistemological position of pragmatism, where a practical approach is taken to the research. When Greene et al. (1989) constructed their framework of different ways to combine the data, they referred to the type of triangulation outlined above. However, there are further interpretations of triangulation that you might find useful, which are outlined below:

Indefinite triangulation

Indefinite triangulation adopts a more flexible approach; the same basic principle of using one or more methods to answer the same question is applied, but its purpose is not to check the validity of the inferences from each component. Conceived by Cicourel (1974), this technique collects accounts from different people who witnessed the same event (which could be the commission of a crime, or the policing of street disorder) using mixed methods. The researcher then documents their perspectives with a view to developing and creating knowledge, rather than using them to check the validity of each component. For example, a researcher may investigate a racist hate crime that has taken place on public transport by surveying all the witnesses, and conducting in-depth interviews with a selection of key actors such as the victim, the offender and the person who reported the crime. This approach neatly reflects the multiple realities ontological position.

Within-method triangulation

Within-method triangulation is where quantitative and qualitative data are collected through the same data collection method (Denzin, 1970). To illustrate, a questionnaire about hate crime victimisation may have closed and open-ended questions that generate both quantitative and qualitative data. By nature, this approach is not mixed methods because only one method is being used. However, the inferences from the data collection still need to be combined and can be triangulated in any of the ways mentioned above. Using this type of triangulation may be a useful starting point when using initiation to combine the data, outlined later in this chapter, as it can be used as a cross-checking tool to determine the reliability of the emerging inferences.

Triangulation as epistemological dialogue or juxtaposition

Confident mixed methods researchers may also be interested in **triangulation as epistemological dialogue or juxtaposition**, where the use of mixed methods is not as simple as providing different kinds of information about the same phenomenon, but is about constituting the world in different ways (Flick, 2004). For instance, a hate crime researcher may use a qualitative component that adopts grounded theory (which is a heavily inductive process; see Bryant and Charmaz (2007) for further information) as the analytical framework to explore semi-structured interviews about perceptions of hate crime offenders. In contrast, this could inform and be juxtaposed by a quantitative component that uses a questionnaire to examine the same topic. This approach relates to the theoretical influences of constructionism and postmodernism and is an area that advanced researchers are encouraged to explore. See Flick (2004) and/or Hammersley (2008) for more detailed discussions.

The overview provided about the different types of triangulation highlights how planning a mixed methods research project can sometimes be confusing, particularly when philosophical arguments are involved. However, the key to addressing these issues is to decide upon the triangulation method you intend to employ and communicate this clearly to your audience (be that a research ethics committee, your research participants, your research supervisor, or in your written work). Developing and executing a mixed methods research project is a systematic process where you should be clear about the justifications for your methodological decision-making. To model that sentiment, when we talk about triangulation in this book, we refer to two or more components being used to investigate the same phenomenon and answer the same central research question. The aim is to seek a convergence and corroboration of the inferences generated from each research component.

An example of triangulation from criminological research

Phillips and Lindsay (2011) Prison to Society: A Mixed Methods Analysis of Coping with Re-Entry

The focus of this research is how individuals use coping mechanisms when they re-enter society following release from prison. Drawing on coping theory, participants who returned to prison following release were asked about the coping strategies they employed and the barriers they faced on the outside. The aim was to investigate how offenders manage when released from prison, with a view to better understanding coping deficits and how this impacts upon prisoners on their release. Set in the USA, Phillips and Lindsay (2011) used one qualitative and two quantitative components. The qualitative component was prioritised and comprised in-depth exploratory interviews with 20 male participants who had been in prison on at least one previous occasion. The interviews were supplemented by the simultaneous completion of a quantitative Coping Inventory for Stressful Situations (CISS), as well as a demographic questionnaire (QUAL / quant / quant } →). The data from the CISS were triangulated with the interview data to validate the qualitative questions about coping strategies. The researchers found that avoidance was the most common coping strategy employed. The meta-inferences suggest that although the participants endorsed emotion-focused mechanisms (identified by the quantitative CISS), they may not have been able to utilise these strategies when faced with barriers in the outside world (qualitative interviews).

Is triangulation appropriate for my project?

Triangulation is talked about a lot in the mixed methods literature. However, Greene et al.'s (1989) research found it to be utilised in only 7% of the studies in their sample, which is probably because it is a demanding (and difficult) type of project to undertake. This illustrates that despite the volume of information about triangulation, it might not be the most appropriate way to combine the data in your research. The ultimate determining factor as to whether triangulation is appropriate for your project is your central research question – what do you want to find out? Think about your central research question. Is it one set question that is quite fixed, such as: *Do the public perceive hate crime perpetrators more negatively than the perpetrators of other crimes?* Or, is it an overarching general question or topic area with a range of different research objectives, such as: *What are the public's perceptions of hate crime perpetrators?* If it is the former, and you have a question that is focused, then triangulation might be the best method of combining the data for you. This is because triangulation is rigid in its approach; there is one question to answer and two methods being used to answer it. There is no room for flexibility because as soon as different elements of the question are added, the research can be defined by a different combination technique. Of the five methods to combine data discussed in this chapter, triangulation is the least flexible. Consequently, before selecting it as the means of combining data for your research project, you should read through all the other different methods to see if they better reflect the aims of your central research question.

Combining the data using triangulation

When the mixed methods discipline was beginning to develop throughout the 1970s, Jick (1979) wrote a seminal paper about how to combine quantitative and qualitative methods when triangulating, citing a lack of previous guidelines about how to undertake the process. His article provides some useful pointers about how to go about combining the data, but (unfortunately for the novice mixed methods researcher) there is no one 'way' to do this. Fast-forward 24 years and Erzberger and Kelle (2003) reiterate the difficulty in finding advice about how to best combine quantitative and qualitative data and inferences. This is because of the vast array of different mixed methods projects that can be created, as well as the subjectivity and personal epistemological and ontological perspectives held by individual researchers.

Jick (1979) suggests that combining the data through triangulation is a delicate process. Ultimately you are trying to determine whether the inferences from the quantitative and qualitative components:

- *converge* – are the same/consistent/corroborate; or
- *diverge* – contradict each other

Erzberger and Prein (1997) extend this dichotomy to include a middle-ground option, which suggests the results may:

- *supplement* each other (they are relatable and complementary)

When you undertake your analyses, you are checking to see if the different measures of the same phenomenon, using two (or more) methods, produce consistent/similar inferences, from which you can finalise your meta-inferences. As you are using different methods to answer the same question, it is advisable to undertake this combining exercise using a systematic process. For example, if you have used a questionnaire and semi-structured interviews, you should be able to check to see if the same questions from the questionnaire and the interview have been answered in a similar way. The exact process, or order in which you do things, will be determined by your central research question and the nature of the data you collected, but it seems logical to compare the similar quantitative and qualitative elements one by one to try to identify convergence. For instance, if the quantitative component of a study about hate crime asks about the perceived characteristics of hate crime perpetrators, the answers can be compared to the inferences from the qualitative component that asks the same questions in a semi-structured interview setting. If the responses are similar, then the inferences are deemed to converge and can be reported as a meta-inference.

What counts as a convergent or consistent inference is another one of those frustratingly subjective elements of social research. However, you should be able to identify your own boundaries of reasonable consistency based on the type(s) of inferences generated and the central research question you have employed. Let us continue to explore the example above about the quantitative and qualitative components relating to the perceived characteristics of hate crime perpetrators. If the responses are similar, you can justify convergence; for instance, if the questionnaire has a nominal variable that lists a characteristic such as being 'thoughtless'. A convergent qualitative response might include something like, 'they don't think before they act'. Consequently, it should be quite apparent if the inferences are not consistent and you cannot achieve convergence, such as if the qualitative response suggested that perpetrators were 'thoughtful'. If this is the case in your research, and the inferences from the two components do not match up and are not consistent, and/or produce unexpected inferences, then your meta-inferences are *divergent*. It is very important for you to know that this is not a bad thing. Producing divergent results does not mean your attempt at conducting mixed methods research has failed. It simply means that something else is going on in the phenomenon you studied. Jick (1979) indicates that divergent inferences are often an opportunity to enrich and develop our understanding about a topic; it just might not be as part of the specific research project being undertaken at that time. If the meta-inferences produced by your dissertation or thesis are divergent, do not panic! The most important thing is that you have justified your methodological decision-making throughout your research and that you have reported your results in a manner that is representative of the data. Speak to your research supervisor about this further as they will be able to reassure you.

Complementarity

Complementarity is where two or more methods are used to investigate distinct, albeit often overlapping, aspects of a phenomenon in order to produce rich, deep understanding.

Understanding complementarity

Complementarity is similar to triangulation, but allows for a more flexible project that reflects a broader central research question. In fact, to (un)helpfully add to the range of overlapping terms, it is sometimes known as *triangulation as complementary information* (Hammersley, 2008). Complementarity is where two or more methods are used to investigate distinct, albeit often overlapping, aspects of a topic. To illustrate, a mixed methods research project about hate crime that utilises complementarity will have an overarching central research question that aims to explore public perceptions of hate crime perpetrators, with subsidiary questions for each component that explore different elements of the subject area. One component might investigate the perceptions of victims, with another examining the portrayals of hate crime perpetrators by the print media. Therefore, complementarity allows the scope of a project to be much broader and exploratory in nature.

This way of combining the data focuses on improving the meaningfulness of the meta-inferences generated. Greene et al. (1989: 258) suggest that complementarity provides an 'enriched, elaborated understanding of the phenomenon'. Erzberger and Kelle (2003: 461) use a helpful analogy of a jigsaw puzzle to help explain how this integration technique works to 'provide a full image of a certain object if put together in the correct way'. Greene et al. (1989: 258) also use an analogy but envisage complementarity slightly differently, by seeing it as akin to 'peeling the layers of an onion'. Whether your understanding is enhanced by the jigsaw or onion analogies, the central tenet of this way of combining the data is that different aspects of a phenomenon can be investigated to provide a more complete understanding.

Complementarity, alongside the three remaining ways to combine the data outlined in this chapter, does not have the same coverage in textbooks as triangulation. This is because different terms are used in different disciplines and no one term has been agreed on. As mentioned previously, not all scholars accurately indicate when they are using a specific method to combine the data, so you may not see complementarity mentioned explicitly in a journal article. As a result, you will often have to deduce the combination method for yourself. When reading a journal article, an easy way to spot the difference between triangulation and complementarity is to look at the focus of the study. This information is likely to be found in either the introduction or the methodology section of the article. Triangulation is where mixed methods is used to answer a single research question, whereas complementarity investigates overlapping aspects of a broader topic. Remember: not all scholars identify how they have combined their data, and even then some misclassify. The most similar alternative term for complementarity is *completeness*, which is used by Bryman (2016). He suggests that using mixed methods allows for a more complete view of the object of study because the gaps left by one component can be filled by another. This is not as broad as the definition of complementarity, which focuses on how this way of combining the data enhances knowledge rather than simply filling gaps. Bryman (2016) suggests that completeness is often used by ethnographers to fill the gaps that remain following a qualitative participant observation, by using a quantitative questionnaire, structured interview or secondary statistical data. Ethnography, where a researcher immerses themselves for a period of time in a social setting to observe behaviour, is becoming increasingly common in criminology. To illustrate, a hate crime researcher might undertake an ethnography within the Muslim community to observe the extent and type(s) of hate crimes being experienced. They may supplement their data by undertaking a secondary analysis of quantitative police data, or third-party hate crime reporting centre data, to build a greater understanding of hate crime within that community. Under Greene et al.'s (1989) definition, completeness, as described by the example above, could also be considered as complementarity. When undertaking your wider reading, be aware of the overlapping nature of the terms complementarity and completeness. Overall, the key message is to be mindful of the differences between triangulation and complementarity and be prepared (and confident enough) to identify the way the components are being combined.

An example of complementarity from criminological research

Waters (2009) Illegal Drug Use Among Older Adults

This work was triggered by a dearth of research on illegal drug use in the over 40s. As there was little knowledge of this particular population at the time, the study had exploratory intentions. The aim was to try and show the extent of illegal drug use among older adults, and also paint a picture of the older illegal drug user and the reasons behind their drug use. The research adopted a mixed methods strategy by having a quantitative component, which encompassed a secondary data analysis of the British Crime Survey (now known as the Crime Survey for England and Wales), and a qualitative component comprising semi-structured interviews with members of the target population. The study was created so that each component supported the other in order to provide a robust overall picture of the field, demonstrating that complementarity was used to combine the data. A simultaneous design was utilised, where both the quantitative and qualitative components were carried out at approximately the same time, with greater priority afforded to the quantitative component because of difficulties recruiting interview participants: QUANT / qual } →. Inferences from the quantitative component found the demographic and criminological characteristics of older illegal drug users were that the majority were male, white, in good health, alcohol drinkers, and tobacco smokers. The key themes that were extracted and examined from the qualitative component were: changes in drug use over time, reasons behind drug use, the effects of drug use on life, and the legal and deviant implications of drug use. When bringing together the two components, the meta-inferences of the research identified the existence of this poorly researched, 'hidden' population and outlined some of its key characteristics including demographics, reasons for using illegal drugs and its effects over the lifecourse.

Is complementarity appropriate for my project?

Complementarity can work particularly well in student projects because it allows for a good degree of flexibility, especially when compared to triangulation. Nevertheless, it retains enough structure to create a project that can answer a very clearly defined central research question and subsidiary questions. For instance, an undergraduate dissertation may have the central research question of 'how is hate crime understood by students?' The overall aim is to examine student perceptions of hate crime, and the project could have three subsidiary questions allied to different components:

  i)   What is the prevalence and awareness of hate crime? (Quantitative questionnaire);
 ii)   How have students experienced hate crime? (Qualitative focus groups); and
iii)   How do the print media represent hate crime? (Qualitative media analysis).

If one component was to suddenly become unfeasible – for example, subsidiary question ii) might not receive ethical approval because of the potential harm that could be caused to victims, since the research is being undertaken by a novice researcher – the project could still proceed. The subsidiary question could be changed, or a new one created. The central research question will still be answered, and so long as the subsidiary question remains relevant to the central research question, an in-depth and elaborated understanding of the phenomenon will be pursued.

Complementarity is also a helpful way to combine the data when practical limitations dictate the nature of the project. For example, the time constraints associated with an undergraduate dissertation may not allow for triangulation to take place because not enough data can be gathered or analysed for each component to validate the inferences of the other. Complementarity permits smaller data components to be used together to build a better picture of a phenomenon. Similarly, when ethical guidelines prevent access – such as student researchers being prevented from talking to perpetrators of hate-related murder in prison because of their lack of research experience – complementarity can offer the chance to build up knowledge relating to this area by incorporating a range of related components, such as exploring student perceptions of hate crime perpetrators (quant) alongside a media analysis of newspaper articles about hate crime perpetrators (qual). For these reasons, it is likely that most student mixed methods projects will use complementarity to combine the data.

Combining the data using complementarity

There is no specified method to combine the inferences produced with the intention of complementarity. Like most aspects of mixed methods research practice, it depends on your central research question. To an extent, it is possible to see whether the inferences converge, diverge or supplement each other in a similar way to that outlined when discussing triangulation. For example, there might be certain overlapping elements within each of your components which you can compare to determine their relationship. As complementarity is about producing a rich, deep understanding, a systematic way to approach generating your meta-inferences would be to assess the extent to which the inferences from each of your components answer your central research question, or more likely when employing complementarity, your numerous subsidiary questions. Consider how the inferences from each component build on one another to produce a set of over-arching meta-inferences about the topic you are studying. Explain and explore the links between the objectives and highlight any areas where there are data missing (which could lead to further research). Think about your contribution to the field and state how your inferences/meta-inferences have enriched your understanding.

When using complementarity, divergence is less of a concern because you are building a picture of the phenomenon being studied. Consequently, there should be less anxiety surrounding whether your inferences and meta-inferences are 'right'. This prospect is often quite liberating for the student researcher as it removes some of the peril from the dissertation/thesis/research project process.

Development

Development is a technique of mixed methods research involving the employment of a sequential design, with the inferences drawn from the first component used to help inform the development of the second component.

Understanding development

A slightly different approach to combining the data is offered by the development technique. It involves the employment of a sequential design, with the inferences generated by the first component used to help inform the development of the second component (see Chapter 5 – Mixed methods design). The purpose of this practice is to 'increase the validity of constructs and inquiry results by capitalizing on inherent methods strengths' (Greene et al., 1989: 259). This practice is used to increase the robustness of the inferences and any concepts generated as a result. To illustrate, if you were conducting a mixed methods project researching public perceptions of hate crime, you could conduct an initial quantitative component, utilising a questionnaire to collect a large amount of data to gather inferences about a perceptions-based hate crime topic (the questionnaire could also be used as a mechanism to generate the qualitative sample by collecting the contact details of willing participants). These inferences are then used to inform the questions in a second qualitative component that employs an interview-based data collection method, with a smaller sample to explore the inferences from the first component in greater depth. For instance, the questionnaire could have highlighted concerns about the sentencing of hate crime perpetrators, which could be explored further in the interviews.

An example of development from criminological research

Best et al. (2016) An Evaluation of Intuitive Recovery

When evaluating the Intuitive Recovery programme, Best et al. (2016) employed development (as well as complementarity). Intuitive Recovery (IR) is an educational programme that offers a toolkit to individuals to help them address their addictive behaviour, based on the promotion of a mind-set of independence and self-control. It claims to offer solutions to any type of addiction, be that substance use, alcohol or gambling disorders, and Best et al. (2016) set out to test this assertion. The research evaluated the outcomes of up to 50 individuals that completed the programme, examining the programme's effectiveness and any changes individuals had made since completing the programme. The project started with a quantitative questionnaire that collected data about participants' substance use and recovery outcomes. The baseline inferences generated from the quantitative component were utilised to inform the development of the qualitative interviews with participants, to better understand how IR has benefited them in comparison to previous treatment interventions (QUANT → QUAL). The inferences from the quantitative component suggested IR had positive results for those with opiate addictions, and across a range of well-being measures. The qualitative inferences provided greater insight into the more positive effects of IR around empowerment and self-control. Overall, the meta-inferences suggest that the participants enjoyed the IR programme, with a desire to engage further with the approach.

Is development appropriate for my project?

A key concern for student researchers considering whether to employ development is whether you will have time to employ a sequential mixed methods design. This is because the inferences for the first component must be generated before any subsequent component can be created, which means all the data analysis must be completed before the second component can begin. This approach could be problematic for undergraduate dissertation students who may need to collect their data simultaneously to save time, so think carefully before using it. It does, however, provide a useful starting point to explore a topic that is relatively unknown. So, like all the combination methods discussed here, it will depend on the nature of your central research question. Furthermore, development does not have to be used in isolation; it can be employed alongside complementarity, initiation, and expansion as part of a larger project (as demonstrated in a number of criminological examples in this chapter, such as Heap (2010)).

Combining the data using development

The combination of the data from the different components of a development mixed methods study is unlike the other techniques described in this chapter. This is because the inferences from the first component are used to inform the development of the subsequent components. In that sense, there is no big combination moment at the end of the project. However, the inferences generated by the first component, which are used to inform additional components, can also be used to inform the overall meta-inferences for the project when relevant to your central research question. If it is appropriate to consider the inferences from the first component, they should be examined alongside the inferences from the other components in a similar way to complementarity; for example, by using a systematic strategy to determine if there is any convergence, divergence, or supplementary meta-inferences that can be drawn.

Initiation

Initiation is where new perspectives or paradoxes emerge. This may not be the purpose of the mixed methods design, but the inferences generated from each component of the research allow for further analysis to be undertaken to create new knowledge and ideas.

Understanding initiation

According to Greene et al. (1989), the deployment of initiation may occur serendipitously, rather than as a result of careful planning. This is because initiation transpires when new perspectives or paradoxes emerge; and this can happen by accident. It allows the inferences generated from each component of the research to be re-analysed to develop new ideas and create new knowledge. For instance, as part of the analysis process it might become clear that the inferences could be assessed using a different criminological theory as the analytical framework. As initiation may be undertaken as an 'extra', it is often used alongside one or more of the other ways to combine the data. It is also flexible enough to be employed should the inferences from individual components warrant further exploration.

An example of initiation from criminological research

Large (2015) 'Get Real, Don't Buy Fakes': Fashion Fakes and Flawed Policy – The Problem with Taking a Consumer-Responsibility Approach to Reducing the 'Problem' of Counterfeiting

Counterfeiting goods comes under the banner of intellectual property crime and this exploratory mixed methods project investigated attitudes towards, and the consumption of, counterfeit (fake) fashion goods. Enforcement agencies adopt a consumer-responsibility tactic to prevent counterfeiting, which assumes that the public are aware of the 'danger' of buying counterfeit goods. As a consequence, the public will supposedly not buy fakes and the drop in demand will equate to a drop in supply. This study used a quantitative component and two qualitative components to assess public attitudes towards counterfeiting, with a view to problematising the use of the consumer-responsibility approach (QUANT → QUAL / QUAL } →). Large (2015) explains how the approach she took allowed for movement between collecting and analysing the data between the components, which enabled emerging perspectives to be utilised in the research. This way of combining the data could therefore be classed as initiation (as well as complementarity and development). The quantitative component utilised a questionnaire as a context-setting device, which informed the qualitative components that constituted 27 semi-structured interviews and two focus groups. The qualitative components examined three groups of consumers: those that bought counterfeit fashion, those that had not bought counterfeit fashion, and those that consciously do not buy fashion goods. The meta-inferences suggest that consumers did not think it fair that the responsibility to recognise counterfeit goods was placed on them, although they were concerned about the social harms associated with counterfeiting. Further, the meta-inferences question the utility of a consumer-responsibility approach.

Is initiation appropriate for my project?

Initiation could add a very useful dimension to your research project, but it will depend on your central research question and the types of inferences generated. It might be that when you plan your research project, you start off with the intention of combining the data using complementarity and initiation. Depending on how the inferences develop and relate to the central research question, you may, or may not, be able to claim the initiation element. In terms of research practice, changing your mind about using a method or undertaking a process is okay – so long as that decision is justified, using methodological theories (from textbooks) and/or practical evidence (a reflection on time constraints).

Combining the data using initiation

As initiation is concerned with generating 'fresh insights' (Greene et al., 1989), the important part about combining the data is making sure that the inferences are examined for new evidence of convergence or divergence. To illustrate, a mixed methods project examining public perceptions of hate crime may have been considered using a victimological analytical framework. However, to create initiation the data may be re-examined using a Marxist perspective to discern if this would add a new perspective to the inferences. Any new analysis would need to be justified, so in this example, the decision to adopt Marxist theories may have been because some of the inferences reflected issues relating to class and socioeconomic status. This is an example of a defensible decision, as it is based on tangible evidence from the data. If the new analytical tool had no relation to the original inferences, say a theoretical framework that related to drug use, this methodological decision would not be justifiable. Once you have re-analysed the data, a similar process of determining convergence and divergence can be undertaken to that discussed previously. Again, the important aspects are answering the central research question and undertaking a systematic process of generating meta-inferences.

Expansion

Expansion refers to a way of combining the data that provides breadth and depth to the exploration of a particular phenomenon.

Understanding expansion

The final way of combining the data that we explore is perhaps the most wide-ranging and flexible. To add breadth and depth to a mixed methods study, expansion can be employed; for example, selecting the data collection methods that will allow for the broadest possible project. This could be through combining a range of very different quantitative and qualitative data collection methods across a number of components. This type of project is particularly useful if your central research question has multiple subsidiary questions. Expansion can also be used alongside complementarity and initiation to add clarification and innovation to a project (see Large, 2015). For instance, consider again a mixed methods project that seeks to explore public perceptions of hate crime. The project could have four components, all of equal priority, which examine different aspects of the phenomenon. Components one and two could be quantitative and comprise a questionnaire about public perceptions of hate crime, and a structured observation of hate crime at a football match. This could be combined with two qualitative components, namely a focus group with victims of hate crime, and semi-structured interviews with specialist hate crime police officers about their interactions with the public, hate crime perpetrators, and offenders. In combination, the inferences generated from these components would allow for a range of meta-inferences to be drawn about a variety of aspects relating to the central research question.

An example of expansion from criminological research

Heap (2010) Understanding Public Perceptions of Anti-Social Behaviour

This PhD study was undertaken as part of an ESRC Collaborative Award Studentship that was part-funded by the Home Office. As sponsors, the Home Office wanted to develop a better understanding about the drivers of public perceptions of anti-social behaviour (ASB), as perceptions were used at that time as the proxy measure to determine the extent of ASB (the police now also record incidents of ASB). The research also explored variations in perceptions of ASB between different localities and investigated the different methods used by practitioners to reduce public perceptions of high levels of ASB in local areas. Therefore, the answers to three different research questions were pursued and expansion was used to combine the data (as well as complementarity, development, and initiation). An explanatory sequential design was used, starting with a quantitative component to identity important themes (a public perception questionnaire), followed by two simultaneous qualitative components to investigate the inferences from the questionnaire in greater detail (focus groups with members of the public and interviews with ASB practitioners). The qualitative components were prioritised because of the depth and originality they provided (quant → QUAL / QUAL } →). The quantitative inferences generated from this study uncovered new attitudinal factors that are statistically and independently associated with public perceptions of ASB. Furthermore, the qualitative inferences uncovered primary and secondary drivers of public perceptions of ASB, with new insight also gained into the relationship that exists between ASB practitioners and members of the public. The meta-inferences suggest that public perceptions of ASB are complex, with the factors influencing perceptions often interconnected. This depth of understanding would not have been achieved without adopting a mixed methods strategy and expansion as a way of combining the data.

Is expansion appropriate for my project?

Expansion could be a very useful technique to employ in your project. Before doing so, however, consider the amount of time you have to undertake the project; will you have enough time to complete a number of different components, with diverse data collection demands? It would be useful at the outset to consider the priority of each of the components, so if for some reason you had to drop one of them, you can retain the ones that are most pertinent to answering your central research question. The other aspect to think about is whether you have the appropriate research skills to undertake a variety of different data collection methods. For example, if you are inexperienced at facilitating focus groups, you will need to weigh up the advantages and disadvantages of doing so, and what impact this might have on the quality of the inferences you generate. It is not expected that you will be good at every data collection method immediately, and some will take more practice before you become proficient and confident. However, in relation to planning a mixed methods project, you need to consider what impact one or two weaker components might have on the production of your meta-inferences, and whether choosing certain data collection methods will hinder your ability to answer your central research question. This is a particular concern for expansion because of the number of different components involved. If there is time available, one way to mitigate proficiency problems is to undertake a pilot study to test out and refine your skills.

Combining the data using expansion

As a project using expansion is likely to have a high volume of data, as well as a wide range of inferences generated from each component, undertaking a systematic review to generate the meta-inferences is more important than ever. Following Morse and Niehaus's (2009) advice about reporting which inferences are from which component would be a good starting point here. Furthermore, as has been suggested in previous 'combination' sections, try to align the inferences from each of the components where similar or overlapping topics are represented. As expansion, initiation, and complementarity often go hand in hand, use any novel or innovative inferences to build a better picture of the phenomenon being studied.

Evaluating attempts to combine the data

As justifying your methodological decision-making is such a big part of the research process, especially for mixed methods, this final section reflects on some of the strengths and weakness of the ways to combine the data described above. Due to the prominence of triangulation in the mixed methods literature, the points listed below were written about this way of combining the data. However, the basic tenet can be applied more broadly to encompass combining the inferences in general. A range of authors have outlined the numerous reasons why triangulation is perceived as a useful way to combine the data.

Strengths (Jick, 1979)

- Allows the researcher to be more confident in their results
- It can stimulate the creation of inventive methods
- Unknown dimensions of a phenomenon can be revealed

However, the use of triangulation (and combining the data in general) has also been criticised in addition to the general philosophical and mixed methods design-based criticisms of mixed methods as a research strategy (see Chapters 1 – Introduction to mixed methods, 4 – Philosophy and 5 – Mixed methods design for further details).

Weaknesses

- 'Pure' replication is difficult and 'nearly impossible' (Jick, 1979: 609)
- Triangulation is no use if the 'wrong' central research question is employed (Jick, 1979: 609)
- It can be time consuming (Jick, 1979)
- 'Distinctions are not drawn between combining the data from different sources, using different methods and integrating different methodological approaches' (Hammersley, 2008: 29)
- There is an assumption that using triangulation to validate inferences can provide certainty about a phenomenon, but is complete knowledge ever possible? (Hammersley, 2008)
- At the planning stage, how can we be sure which data sources will provide the most useful type of validity information? (Hammersley, 2008)
- It assumes there is one 'reality' (Hammersley, 2008)
- Convergence of results does not equal validity (Bryman, 1988) because integrity could be lacking in both components

It is evident that there is more than double the number of weaknesses listed compared to strengths. This does not mean that triangulation or combining data is a weak methodological approach to adopt. It is simply important to know, understand and acknowledge these factors when planning your mixed methods project to create the best possible research. Those that adopt a pragmatic epistemology and multiple realities ontology would argue that despite the criticisms outlined above, using mixed methods allows for the best tools to be used for the job of answering your central research question, with the supremacy of the central research question having been highlighted throughout this chapter.

Summary

The aim of this chapter is to unpick some of the difficult and often misunderstood debates about combining the data in a mixed methods research project. From the outset, the deployment of the correct terminology has been emphasised, or in the absence of a 'correct' or ubiquitous term, the consistent use of terminology within your research project. Thinking about, and subsequently deciding upon, the method you are going to use to combine your mixed methods data should be considered as soon as a central research question has been decided upon. The question is the driving force of mixed methods research, and will impact significantly on the type of combination method you decide to adopt. Five basic combination methods, first discussed by Greene et al. (1989), were outlined in this chapter, namely: triangulation, complementarity, development, initiation, and expansion. They range from rigid to very flexible and will produce incredibly different mixed methods projects. An important factor that transcends the different techniques available to combine the data is that adopting a well-justified and systematic approach to your analysis is vital. Inferences from each component should be identified as such, with a logical process put in place to identify convergent, divergent and supplementary meta-inferences. It is imperative to remember that a mixed methods study which produces a divergent meta-inference is okay (and definitely not 'wrong'); it is part of the knowledge-creation process and provides fuel for future research.

Learning questions

1 Which of the five methods of combining data offers the least flexibility to researchers? Why?
2 Provide an example of how complementarity and development could be used in the same mixed methods research project.
3 Outline how the different ways of combining the data relate to the underpinning research philosophy of mixed methods.

7   Research design and sampling

Introduction

This chapter provides the theoretical foundations for two core aspects of the project design process, namely: research design and sampling. The purpose of the chapter is to assist you in making informed decisions about how you collect and analyse data in your mixed methods research project. The first section explores five different research designs: cross-sectional, case study, longitudinal, experimental, and comparative. We provide an overview of each research design, their inherent methodological strengths and weaknesses, as well as examples of their use in a mixed methods context. The second section of the chapter focuses on sampling, detailing: probability sampling, non-probability sampling and sampling that can be both probability and non-probability depending on the context. We discuss the strengths and weaknesses of each technique and relate them to mixed methods examples.

Research design

Research design is different to mixed methods design, which is detailed in Chapter 5 – Mixed methods design. Bryman (2016: 40) states that a research design 'provides a framework for the collection and analysis of data'. The framework you choose will impact on the decisions you make about sampling and data collection methods, so it is important that you understand a range of research designs and the implications they could have on your mixed methods project.

The research designs are different to the research strategies, in the sense that they are not considered to be inherently quantitative, qualitative, or mixed methods. The five research designs we discuss in this chapter were developed before mixed methods research came to prominence, therefore careful consideration is required to determine how they might work best in your mixed methods project. Some research designs, namely cross-sectional, experimental, and longitudinal, can be employed on a component-by-component basis or as an overarching design for the entire project. A component-by-component design means the quantitative and qualitative components in your research project can share the same design, or they can be different. For instance, all components could use the cross-sectional design. Or, if there are two components, the quantitative component could be experimental and the qualitative component cross-sectional. An overarching design is where one design is applied to the whole project. The case study and comparative designs, because of their intrinsic characteristics, only operate as an overarching design. As such, adopting a case study design will determine the data collection methods employed in each component because one of the features of a case study is that both quantitative and qualitative methods can be used.

Ultimately, it is your central research question that will initially guide your research design selection. It is often the case that more than one of the research designs could be used. However, as a student researcher you will also need to balance the requirements of your central research question with the feasibility of the different options in relation to time and resources, as well as considering any ethical constraints. This section of the chapter will discuss five different research designs in turn, namely: **cross-sectional**, **case study**, **longitudinal**, **experimental**, and **comparative**. The order and depth in which they are presented reflect their suitability for use in a student mixed methods project. Based on our experience of supervising undergraduate and postgraduate research projects, the cross-sectional research design is likely to be your best option in an undergraduate mixed methods study. It is the most practical choice in terms of the time required and expertise needed. Other research designs can be used for mixed methods studies, but beware of pursuing these options if you are not proficient or confident in these designs. It is better to execute a simple research design well than a complicated research design poorly. Table 7.1 provides our suggestions on the most appropriate research designs to use in an undergraduate mixed methods research project from our supervisory experience. Postgraduates have much greater flexibility in their choice of research design because of their prior research experience and the likelihood that they will have more time to complete their research. As such, the full range of different possibilities should be considered.

In addition to outlining each design, we present their strengths and weaknesses so you can craft a strong justification for your selections. This includes the associated evaluative terms relating to reliability and validity, and trustworthiness and authenticity, which are explained in detail in Chapter 10 – Critique.

Cross-sectional

The cross-sectional research design is popular with experienced and student researchers alike, since it offers a straightforward approach to collecting and analysing both

Table 7.1 Research designs rated on their appropriateness for undergraduate students' mixed methods research projects

Research design	Rating/5*
Cross-sectional	*****
Case study	****
Longitudinal	***
Experimental	**
Comparative	*

quantitative and qualitative data. It is particularly attractive because cross-sectional research can be undertaken within a limited timescale, and can be employed on a component-by-component basis or as an overarching design. The core features of a cross-sectional research design are that: you collect data at a single point in time, and there is more than one case (one participant). This means there is one data collection stage in your research project. For example, your data could be collected over a four-week period when you conduct interviews; the data do not need to be collected all on the same day. The key principle is that the point in time is distinct, in the sense that it will have a start and end point. As the data collection period takes place at a single point in time, participants will only take part in your research once. Therefore, cross-sectional design allows the researcher to obtain a snapshot of the topic being studied, such as interviews gathering student opinions about the perpetrators of anti-social behaviour over a six-week period. Secondly, the data collection involves more than one case. A case is simply a research participant in people-based research, but could also include documents or media articles in non-people-based research. Therefore, to utilise a cross-sectional design you need to have more than one participant for research involving people, and more than one document or unit of analysis when analysing data such as media articles.

There are two further features of a cross-sectional design that specifically relate to the quantitative strategy, namely: you can collect quantifiable data, and patterns of association can be assessed. Collecting quantifiable data allows for a standardised data collection procedure. A quantitative component could comprise an online questionnaire containing 25 closed questions about anti-social behaviour victimisation, which is completed by 100 people. Having more than one case allows the researcher to establish patterns of association between two or more variables (questions from the questionnaire). Therefore the researcher can assess if, say, gender is associated with anti-social behaviour victimisation.

Cross-sectional designs are commonly used in mixed methods research. All five research projects reported in Chapter 13 – Case studies use a cross-sectional research design. Banks et al. (2018) utilised a cross-sectional design in both the quantitative and qualitative components of their study on families living with problem gambling. Visit this chapter to see how the cross-sectional design has been employed in practice. As a student, it is very likely that you will use a cross-sectional research design in at least one of your components because of its many advantages. Table 7.2 contains a summary of the inherent methodological strengths and weaknesses associated with this research design.

Table 7.2 Strengths and weaknesses of the cross-sectional research design

Strengths	*Weaknesses*
• Quick, simple and cheap (Bryman, 2016) • Large sample sizes can be used	• Limited to a snapshot in time • Does not show causality (low internal validity)
• Can be replicated (especially in a quantitative component) • Can allow for generalisation in quantitative components (high external validity) and transferability in qualitative components (high transferability) depending on the sampling • QUANT ONLY: Patterns of association between the variables can be assessed	• Does not reflect a real-world setting (low ecological validity)

Case study

A case study research design allows a researcher to focus in-depth on one phenomenon, such as a person, setting, or institution. Denscombe (2017) suggests six characteristics of a case study approach, which can be seen in Box 7.1.

Box 7.1 Denscombe's (2017: 57) characteristics of a case study research design in mixed methods

One setting	rather than	Many instances
Depth of study	rather than	Breadth of study
The particular	rather than	The general
Relationships/process	rather than	Outcomes and end products
Holistic view	rather than	Isolated factors
Multiple sources of data	rather than	One research method

As Denscombe (2017) notes, the case study design involves building a thorough understanding of a phenomenon, which can incorporate multiple sources of data. This can be achieved using multiple data collection methods (see Chapter 8 – Data collection methods) that can be employed in the quantitative or qualitative component(s). As such, the case study research design can only be used as an overarching design across your entire mixed methods project. For example, a mixed methods project could use a case study design to investigate the phenomenon of online vigilante paedophile hunters. There could be a qualitative component that analyses one particular group of active paedophile hunters in-depth, using documentary and media analyses. The quantitative component could use a questionnaire to collect data on public opinions towards vigilante paedophile hunters. When the inferences from each component are combined, an in-depth insight into the phenomenon will be achieved. Table 7.3 provides an overview of the strengths and weaknesses of the case study research design.

Table 7.3 Strengths and weaknesses of the case study research design in mixed methods

Strengths	Weaknesses
• Applicable to the real world (high ecological validity/high credibility)	• Inability to generalise inferences (low external validity/low transferability)
• One research site	• Difficult to replicate (low reliability/low dependability)
• Can inherently be mixed methods – theory building and testing	• Access to data/participants can be difficult
• Rigorous	• Difficult to ascertain the scope of the case and how much data to include/exclude
	• Potentially time consuming

Longitudinal

The longitudinal research design is concerned with the collection and analysis of data over time. Data collection takes place with the same (or a comparable) sample of participants on two or more distinct occasions. The responses from the participants are then compared to assess change over time. This type of research is particularly useful for observing shifts in public opinion based on seminal events; for instance, attitudes towards drug use pre- and post-legalisation. In mixed methods research, a longitudinal design can be employed either on a component-by-component basis, or as an overarching design. We will outline what both of these types of longitudinal designs would look in a mixed methods project, using an example based on a project about student perceptions of safety on campus.

The simplest way to employ a longitudinal design on a component-by-component basis is to have one component in your mixed methods project that adopts the longitudinal design. To illustrate, your qualitative component may comprise an exploratory focus group to explore student safety concerns, which informs the development of a questionnaire that measures perceptions of student safety that will be used in your quantitative component (QUAL → QUANT). The quantitative component could adopt a longitudinal design to collect questionnaire data on two or more occasions with the same students, to assess any changes in perceptions of safety over time. The first data collection period could take place in November when there are dark nights, and the second could take place when lighter nights arrive in April (in the UK).

Alternatively, you could utilise a longitudinal design as the overarching research design for your mixed methods project. This means that all of your components will use a longitudinal design. This could be achieved by undertaking a quantitative questionnaire to measure perceptions of student safety on campus, which is followed up by qualitative interviews to gain greater insight into students' feelings. The quantitative and qualitative data collection processes would then be repeated in 12–18 months' time with the same students, to assess if and how perceptions of safety had changed during that period.

One of the biggest challenges of conducting longitudinal research is that it can be very difficult to retain the same participants over two or more data collection points. When retention is difficult, topping up your sample with comparable participants is acceptable, but this approach must be acknowledged and justified in your methodology. The feasibility of using a longitudinal design should also be carefully considered because of the additional data collection and analysis points required. This approach may be more suitable for postgraduate projects where there is generally more time available to undertake the research. Further strengths and weaknesses of the longitudinal design can be found in Table 7.4.

Table 7.4 Strengths and weaknesses of the longitudinal research design in mixed methods

Strengths	Weaknesses
• Assess changes over time	• Difficult to replicate
• Causation can be inferred when probability sampling has been used (high internal validity)	• Retaining participants can be challenging
• Large sample sizes can be used	• There can be issues with comparability across time and context
• QUANT ONLY: Patterns of association between the variables can be assessed	• Can be very labour intensive

Experimental

The experimental research design 'is an empirical investigation under controlled conditions designed to examine the relationship between specific factors' (Denscombe, 2017: 69); consequently it is most aligned with the quantitative strategy. The nature of the experimental design means that it can be employed on a component-by-component basis and as an overarching design. According to Denscombe (2017), there are three foundational principles of experiments:

1   Controls – where variables are manipulated so their effects can be seen
2   Empirical observation and measurement – monitoring and measuring changes that occur
3   The identification of causal factors – to distinguish the factor(s) causing the outcome(s)

In criminology, experiments are generally used to evaluate the success of an initiative. Painter and Farrington (1999) used the experimental design to assess whether improved street lighting reduced crime rates; see Box 7.2 for an overview.

Box 7.2   Overview of Painter and Farrington's (1999) experiment investigating the effects of improved street lighting on crime

Painter and Farrington (1999) undertook an experiment to determine if improved street lighting had an effect on the prevalence and incidence of crime in three areas: i) an experimental area where street lighting was improved, ii) an adjacent area where the lighting remained unchanged, and iii) a control area where the lighting also remained unchanged. They administered victimisation questionnaires in all three areas to measure crime 12 months before and 12 months after the installation of improved street lighting in the experimental area. The surveys found that the prevalence of crime reduced by 26% and the incidence of crime by 43% in the experimental area. They also found that the prevalence of crime dropped by 21% and the incidence of crime by 45% in the adjacent area. In contrast, the prevalence of crime increased by 12% in the control area, with the incidence of crime reducing by 2%. Overall, Painter and Farrington (1999) concluded that improved street lighting had a considerable impact on the reduction of crime in the experimental area, with these gains also witnessed in the adjacent area, suggesting the diffusion of benefits.

Conducting an experiment in any social research project is complex, but in a mixed methods context it is even more demanding because of the precise controls required to execute experimental research, whilst at the same time planning or delivering an additional data collection component(s). Resultantly, an experimental design is especially challenging for student researchers or those new to undertaking mixed methods research. Furthermore, it does not lend itself to research projects that need to be completed quickly. We have provided the strengths and weaknesses of the experimental design in Table 7.5.

Table 7.5 Strengths and weaknesses of the experimental research design in mixed methods

Strengths	Weaknesses
• Lab experiments can be: replicated, precise, and conveniently situated on campus • Causality can be determined (high internal validity)	• Lab experiments can be artificial (low ecological validity) and participants may not be representative • It can be difficult to control the variables • Conducting an experiment may involve deceiving participants, which may not be approved by a research ethics committee • May be difficult to manage alongside another component(s) in a mixed methods project • Time consuming and organisationally challenging

If you are not using this research design, the limitations can help you to justify why you have not adopted this research design in your mixed methods study.

Comparative

The focus of comparative research is the examination of similar phenomena in two or more contrasting cases, and as a result should be applied as an overarching design for a whole mixed methods project. This design is most regularly employed in cross-cultural studies to assess the criminological similarities and differences between different countries; for instance, to investigate the different policing practices used to tackle anti-social behaviour in the UK and Australia. To use a comparative design in mixed methods research, the same data collection components need to be undertaken in each country being studied. As such, if you were investigating the policing practices used to tackle anti-social behaviour in the UK and Australia, you could use a QUANT → QUAL (explanatory sequential) design. The same quantitative and qualitative components would be undertaken in each country, such as a quantitative questionnaire followed by qualitative focus groups. Essentially, this equates to running two mixed methods projects side by side, one in the UK and one in Australia, with the added mixed methods bonus of being able to compare the inferences from both countries to generate a set of meta-inferences. An overview of the strengths and weaknesses of this design can be found in Table 7.6.

Table 7.6 Strengths and weaknesses of the comparative research design in mixed methods

Strengths	Weaknesses
• Comparisons can be made across groups • Cross-cultural/cross-national comparisons • Theory building	• Difficult to replicate (low reliability/low dependability) • Access to data/participants can be difficult • Managing cross-national projects can be complicated (e.g. different time zones) • Time consuming and organisationally challenging

Sampling

Whether undertaking primary or secondary data collection, you will need to decide which people or data you intend to study. This is known as sampling and is defined as the process of selecting participants or data that will be studied in your research. Sampling is used when the research **population** is too large to study everyone, or you are unable to analyse every document available. In social research, the term population has a different meaning to how we use it in everyday life; it is the entire number of units (people or data) from which a **sample** is selected. To illustrate, if we wanted to research the opinions of students at Sheffield Hallam University about the death penalty by using a questionnaire in a quantitative component, we would need to generate a sample of the population to study because we would not be able to engage with all 30,000+ students that attend the university.

In mixed methods research you will need to decide the sampling technique you will use in each of your components. Morse and Niehaus (2009) suggest that the sampling technique must fit with the strategy of the component it serves. For example, **probability sampling** requires a known population and aligns more with the quantitative strategy, and **non-probability sampling** operates where there is no known population and is mainly associated with the qualitative strategy, which we explain further below. However, student researchers must balance these philosophical demands alongside the feasibility of generating an adequate sample. We outline the purpose of each sampling type, as well as the main strengths and weaknesses, to help you justify your selections. For undergraduate students it is most likely that a non-probability sampling technique will be employed, chiefly because of time constraints and the inaccessibility of a known population, regardless of your central research question or the strategy of each component. Postgraduate students with more time to undertake their research will have more scope to pursue a probability sample. It does not matter which type of sampling you use in your mixed methods research project. The most important thing is that your sampling technique is well justified, aligns with your central research question, and allows you to successfully complete your data collection in a timely fashion, and that the strengths and weaknesses are considered in the write-up.

Probability sampling

The purpose of probability sampling is to obtain a **representative** sample where the inferences can be generalised from the sample to the population. If the inferences can be generalised, then they will be considered to have high external validity or high transferability, which is explained further in Chapter 10 – Critique. We outline three types of probability sampling in this chapter: random, systematic, and stratified.

The premise of probability sampling is that participants are randomly selected from the population, where each person in the population has a known chance (probability) of being selected to take part. Probability sampling is generally associated with the quantitative strategy because it is regularly deployed in large-scale studies, such as the Crime Survey for England and Wales. Probability sampling can be used with the qualitative strategy where there is a known population, but this will likely be on a smaller scale because of the time-consuming nature of qualitative data collection and analysis. See Chapter 8 – Data collection methods for more information.

To be able to utilise probability sampling, the researcher must be able to define the population they intend to research. This is easier in some cases than others. For instance, if you plan to undertake research in a university or prison, the number of people within that population is defined by membership of the institution. In contrast, if you are seeking to study victims' experiences of hate crime, it is much more difficult to define your population. For instance, is the population: all hate crime victims in the country, city, university, or on a university criminology course? In such instances, try to define a population that is practicable to research. Once the population has been defined, access to that population is required so you can contact them about taking part in your research. This list of people is known as the **sampling frame**, but it can be difficult to obtain for a probability sample, so consider the access requirements carefully when considering your sampling options. For example, if your population is everyone studying your criminology course, you will need to think about how you can obtain their contact details and whether this needs to form part of your application for ethical approval. Obtaining contact details for your population may mean relying on other people to supply information, which may delay your data collection, so try to plan ahead as much as possible. Overall, developing a probability sample can be very time consuming. The aforementioned issues should be taken into consideration alongside all your other planning decisions to ensure you are able to complete the project within the given timescale.

Random

Random sampling is the most simplistic form of probability sample, where every person in the population has the same and equal chance of being selected to take part. A useful analogy to consider is: if the population of your cohort on your criminology course was 100 and you wanted to select 50 people to participate in your research, you could put everyone's name into a hat and draw out 50 names. Every name has the same and equal chance of being drawn. In practice, you can generate your random sample more easily by numbering your sampling frame and using a random number generator from the internet to select the sample (e.g. http://stattrek.com/statistics/random-number-generator.aspx). The website will ask for your population size and the number of random numbers required, and will produce the required list of numbers at the touch of a button.

Systematic

Systematic sampling is where a sample is selected through a systematic method, usually by picking the 'nth' case. To illustrate, if your sampling frame contains 100 names and you would like a sample of 20 participants, you would select every fifth name from the list. The number of the 'nth' case will be dependent on the number of people you wish to sample from the population. When using systematic sampling, care must be taken to ensure that the selection of the 'nth' case does not bias the sample. If the list of names was in alphabetical order, the systematic sample could be biased because surnames are more likely to start with certain letters. Therefore, ensure the names are not ordered in any way to create a true probability sample.

Stratified

Stratified sampling is where the researcher ensures different sub-groups of the population are adequately represented in the sample, when it is important to the central research question. This is achieved by selecting sub-groups (strata) and then randomly sampling

from these strata. To illustrate, if the population of the criminology cohort you are sampling contains 100 students, with 10% of those studying part-time, you would need to
stratify the sample to ensure the part-time students are fairly represented in the research.
If you wanted to sample 50 out of 100 students in total, i.e. half of the population, you
would need to ensure that half of the population of part-time students were randomly
sampled once you had separated them as a stratum. Therefore if 10% of 100 students
study part-time, the stratum would contain 10 students. Of these 10 students, half would
need to be randomly sampled, giving you a total of five part-time students in the sample.
This would leave 45 students to be randomly sampled from the remaining 90 full-time
students in the cohort. Adopting this approach adds an element of researcher intervention, meaning that the sampling is not completely random even though it is based on
random sampling principles. When considering whether to use stratified sampling, think
about whether strata are required to answer your central research question. As such, if
your central research question relates to gendered aspects of criminology, you will need to
make provisions to ensure different genders are represented in your sample, which could
be achieved through stratified sampling.

Non-probability sampling

Non-probability sampling is used when there is an unknown population. For example,
in criminological research this includes drug users and street sex workers. As a result,
each person within the population does not have an equal chance (probability) of being
included in the sample. Therefore the representativeness of the sample is not known. An
advantage of non-probability sampling is that a known population is not required. This
allows the researcher to target specific groups of people for inclusion in their research,
which includes colleagues, friends, and family, which makes it popular with student
researchers. The main disadvantage of non-probability sampling is that any inferences
generated cannot be generalised and will be low in external validity because the representativeness of the sample is not known. From a student perspective, this is not too problematic because it would be unrealistic to always expect generalisability in a student research
project. The most important thing is that central research question can be answered by
the type of sampling selected. We outline five different types of non-probability sampling:
convenience, purposive, snowball, theoretical, and quota.

Convenience

Convenience sampling reflects its name, with the sample being selected as a result
of its convenience to the researcher. All non-probability sampling contains an element
of convenience, but convenience sampling itself takes this to the extreme by being the
main reason why a sample is selected. In many circumstances, this approach is justifiable
because of the unfeasibility of using a different type of sampling, which makes it common
in student research projects. For instance, a mixed methods project may be exploring
students' perceptions of alcohol consumption and violence in the night time economy.
For convenience, the researcher may post the link to their online questionnaire on their
Facebook page for any of their student contacts to complete. If you decide to use convenience sampling, it is important to stress why other types of sampling are impractical,
hence their rejection, to avoid the appearance of using a convenience sample for the sake
of it being the least amount of effort.

Purposive

Purposive sampling is where a researcher locates a sample 'based on the researcher's skill, judgement and needs' (Hagan, 2005: 139). The researcher purposely selects participants or a dataset based on the known characteristics of the people/data involved. Heap (2010) used purposive sampling in a mixed methods study about perceptions of anti-social behaviour to recruit practitioners to interview in a qualitative component. The participants were selected because of their knowledge of the location being studied and their ability to contribute to answering the central research question. Hand-picking participants also provides the researcher with the opportunity to create the most relevant sample possible, because of the prior knowledge held about the people being selected. This can be beneficial in small research projects when limited numbers of participants are involved because the most relevant people can be approached to take part. It is also particularly beneficial for students because they can identify who they need to collect data from to answer their central research question.

Snowball

Snowball sampling begins by engaging a small number of participants, who then inform the researcher about other participants that may be willing to participate in the research. This process is repeated again and again to build up a sample in a snowball-like fashion. Snowball sampling is particularly useful when studying hard to reach groups (Atkinson and Flint, 2001) or sensitive topics (Biernacki and Waldorf, 1981) as recruitment can continue until a sufficient sample size is reached. Waters (2009) used this technique in a mixed methods project about illegal drug use among older adults. Participants were recruited from this hidden population to participate in interviews as part of the qualitative component, with participants passing on the names of additional people to speak to. Snowball sampling can be time consuming and labour intensive, with it being heavily reliant on the researcher (Waters, 2015). Furthermore, adopting this approach does not automatically guarantee that a sufficient sample will be generated, as discussed in Waters (2015).

Theoretical

Theoretical sampling works by selecting participants or data that help to aid theoretical understanding by answering the central research question. Decisions about what to include in the sample are based on evidence derived from existing theory and/or previous research studies. The sample continues to be generated until the researcher decides they have sufficient information to answer the central research question. For example, this technique can be employed in a qualitative component that uses a media analysis data collection method. The media articles can be sampled theoretically based on important characteristics from the theory, using inclusion and exclusion criteria to narrow down the number of articles to a manageable sample size (see Chapter 9 – Data analysis for more information).

Quota

Quota sampling is similar to stratified sampling, in the sense that specific quotas (strata) are selected for inclusion based on their proportion of the population. However, quota sampling is not random as the researcher decides who is selected for inclusion. We can adapt the example provided to explain stratified sampling to illustrate the differences when quota sampling is employed. To illustrate, if the population of the criminology cohort you are sampling contains 100 students, with 10% of those studying part-time, you would need a quota of the sample to be made up of part-time students. If you wanted to sample 50 out of 100 students in total, i.e. half of the population, you would need to ensure that half of the population of part-time students were sampled once you had separated them out as a quota. Therefore if 10% of 100 students study part-time, the quota would contain 10 students, with five needing to be selected for your research. These five people would be chosen by the researcher, for either convenience or purposive reasons. This approach allows relevant groups to be represented in the sample without the difficulties associated with creating a sampling frame.

Probability and non-probability

Some types of sampling can be employed as either a probability or non-probability sample, depending on the context within which they are used. We outline two types: cluster and multi-stage.

Cluster

Cluster sampling involves using naturally occurring pre-existing groups as the sample population. For instance, if you wanted to recruit 1,000 prisoners for a questionnaire, the participants could be drawn from 10 different prisons, with each prison representing a cluster. The caveat to this approach is that the cluster must reflect the composition of the population being studied, i.e. prisoners. Once the clusters have been identified, probability or non-probability sampling techniques can be employed to generate the sample of the participants.

Multi-stage

Multi-stage sampling occurs when more than one stage of sampling is required, with each new sample being drawn from the existing sample. Heap (2010) used a multi-stage sample when selecting areas to study public perceptions of anti-social behaviour. Figure 7.1 visualises this process and shows how the initial decision was made to sample 'Respect' and 'Non-Respect' areas, a policy distinction, at the top level, followed by

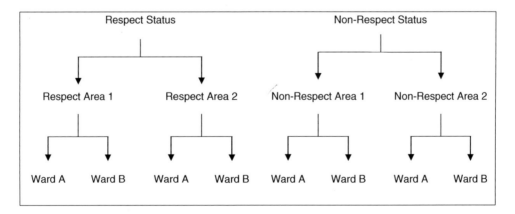

Figure 7.1 Example of multi-stage sampling used by Heap (2010: 82) when examining public perceptions of anti-social behaviour.

different areas (towns), and eventually electoral wards (local communities). The sampling was undertaken on a non-probability basis, but a probability sample could have been generated with the right resources and sampling frame.

Sample size

Students always ask what their sample size needs to be when planning a research project. This is a particular concern when planning a mixed methods study because a sample needs to be generated for each of the components. Unfortunately, there is no magic number. In reality, the sample size will depend on the central research question, as well as the time and resource available to the researcher.

For quantitative components in a student mixed methods research project, the sample you generate must be enough to undertake a worthwhile statistical analysis. This will depend, to an extent, on the types of statistical tests you wish to carry out. Denscombe (2017) suggests that at least 30 responses are required to undertake statistical analysis. If you plan to run the range of basic tests outlined in Chapter 9 – Data analysis, 30 cases will be sufficient. From both undergraduate and postgraduate student perspectives, this is a very feasible baseline to aim for, particularly if non-probability methods are used. A very good size would be nearer 100–125 and an excellent one above 200. The size, representativeness, and type of sampling employed will need to be considered when determining whether the quantitative inferences have high or low levels of external validity; see Chapter 10 – Critique for more information.

Smaller sample sizes are much more common in qualitative components because of the time and resources required to collect and analyse qualitative data. There is little consensus about the number of participants required, which is due to the more flexible nature of qualitative research. One principle that qualitative researchers adopt is known as **theoretical saturation**, with the sample being complete once all the emerging and relevant concepts have been fully investigated, with no new material generated by including additional participants. Theoretical saturation is difficult to gauge, especially for novice researchers, but is aided by a clear central research question where the concepts are distinctly defined. A feasible starting point for a qualitative sample would be no fewer than five research interviews, two to three focus groups and at least 10 media articles. In qualitative research it is very important to justify why your sample is the size it is, in relation to the project planning decisions you have made and your central research question. This will affect the transferability of your research: see Chapter 10 – Critique for more information.

Sampling and mixed methods

Mixed methods researchers should consider how the samples from each of their components might work together. It is worth examining the methodology of the studies you discuss in your literature review to assess the different sampling techniques used by others researching your chosen topic. This will give you an indication of successful, and possibly unsuccessful, approaches. Think about whether the same population can be sampled by both the quantitative and qualitative components and if this is possible, because it could save you resources, time, and money. For example, if the mixed methods project has an explanatory sequential design, with a quantitative component followed by a qualitative component, the participants from the quantitative component could be recruited to take part in the qualitative component. If you do not intend to use one component to assist the recruitment for another, be mindful that every sample you are required to create will take time.

To ensure that your samples are appropriate for your mixed methods project, Teddlie and Yu (2007: 96–97) have created a useful checklist that contains the principles for conducting mixed methods sampling; see Box 7.3.

Box 7.3   Teddlie and Yu's (2007: 96–97) checklist of principles for conducting mixed methods sampling

✓ The sampling strategy should stem logically from the research questions and hypotheses that are being addressed by the study
✓ Researchers should be sure to follow the assumptions of the probability and non-probability sampling techniques that they are using
✓ The sampling strategy should generate thorough qualitative and quantitative databases on the research questions under study
✓ The sampling strategy should allow the researchers to draw clear inferences from both the qualitative and quantitative data
✓ The sampling strategy must be ethical
✓ The sampling strategy should be feasible and efficient
✓ The sampling strategy should allow the research team to transfer or generalize the conclusions of their study to other individuals, groups, contexts, and so forth if that is a purpose of the mixed methods research
✓ The researchers should describe their sampling strategy in enough detail so that other investigators can understand what they actually did and perhaps use those strategies (or variants thereof) in future studies

---

Summary

This chapter has focused upon the theoretical foundations of research design and sampling. First we examined five different types of research design, namely: cross-sectional, case study, longitudinal, experimental, and comparative. Some research designs, notably cross-sectional and experimental longitudinal designs, operate on a component-by-component basis or as an overarching design for the whole project. In contrast, the case study and comparative designs can only be employed as an overarching design. Being able to answer the central research question, coupled with feasibility, is considered to be the key constituent of the research design decision-making process, with cross-sectional designs highlighted as being the most practicable approach for undergraduate students. The second half of the chapter concentrated on sampling, first outlining probability sampling, before considering non-probability sampling, and sampling that can be both probability and non-probability depending on the context in which it is employed. When deciding which type of sampling to use, you will need to consider practical constraints, such as time and access, alongside the inherent methodological strengths and weaknesses. As ever, the demands of your central research question are integral to all of these decisions.

Learning questions

1   Which research designs can only be used as an overarching design in mixed methods research?
2   Why is non-probability sampling useful for student researchers?
3   What factors do you need to take into consideration when deciding which sampling technique to employ?

8   Data collection methods

Introduction

This chapter discusses the process of data collection in mixed methods research. There are two different basic strategies that can be used when gathering data for your project. On the one hand, you may wish to collect your own data; this is called primary data collection. On the other hand, you may wish to utilise data that already exist and use them for your own needs; this is called secondary data collection. Secondary data are data that have been collected by another researcher for a different piece of research and then made available to you and others, often through a data repository. Your decisions around which data collection methods to use should be based upon your central research question; what data do you need in order to provide the fullest answer possible to that question?

As well as considering whether primary or secondary data, or some combination of the two, is most appropriate for your project, it is also important to bear in mind that because mixed methods projects require at least one quantitative and at least one qualitative component, the data collection phase can be particularly challenging. This is because it requires you to have knowledge of both quantitative and qualitative strategies to gathering data, as well as the processes by which such data are analysed (which will be covered in Chapter 9 – Data analysis). As a result, data collection in mixed methods research requires careful thought and planning before the actual gathering of data commences.

In addition, before carrying out any data collection, it is vital to consider whether your plans raise any ethical issues. It is likely that you will require ethical approval from a relevant governing body (most probably your university) and this must be done prior to the gathering of any data. Chapter 3 – Ethics provides guidance on the potential ethical implications of your research and the process of gaining ethical approval.

This chapter begins by discussing five common primary data collection methods that can be gainfully utilised in mixed methods projects: questionnaires, interviews, focus groups, observations, and media analysis. These are the primary data collection methods that, in our experience, are most commonly used in undergraduate work. The chapter will then go on to look at secondary data collection. Following this, we will discuss the way that the data collection methods introduced in this chapter can be deployed within projects that adopt the basic mixed methods designs that were introduced in Chapter 5 – Mixed methods design and ways of combining the data outlined in Chapter 6 – Combining the data.

Note that there are other data collection methods in addition to the ones covered in this chapter. Some of these are rather more complex and time consuming, or else novel and still in the process of rapid development. For example, ethnography (see Treadwell and Wakeman (forthcoming)) covers a range of techniques designed to explore cultural phenomena from the point of view of those being studied. Some ethnographers immerse themselves in the group under study for a prolonged period of time. Social identity mapping (see Cruwys et al., 2016; Best et al., 2014; Haslam et al., 2017) is a new method of data collection which allows for the investigation of social identity through social network groups. Social media analysis (see Best et al., 2018; Bliuc et al., 2017; Pennebaker et al., 2015) is a term that covers a number of emerging data collection methods, each of which involve drawing on data from online social media sources such as Twitter and Facebook. Chief among these techniques are social network analysis (SNA) and Linguistic Inquiry Word Count (LIWC). Photovoice (see Chonody et al., 2013) allows for participants to explore and document their experiences with photos, followed by group discussions. Photovoice has been used in the criminological field in projects on, for instance, youth violence in the USA (Chonody et al., 2013), recovery from intimate partner violence (Duffy, 2015), marginalised women in the criminal justice system in Hungary and England (Fitzgibbon and Stengel, 2017), and the prison re-entry process of Roma and Romanian participants (Durnescu, 2017). If you intend to use these or other data collection methods, then you must ensure you fully understand their nature and how to operationalise them. Read widely and seek advice from your research supervisor.

Primary data collection methods

Primary data collection involves the collection of your own data. 'Data' in this context is a broad category that encompasses a wide variety of things; indeed, as Walliman (2016) suggests, our senses deal with a wealth of primary data that surrounds us throughout our waking lives, including sounds, visual stimuli, tastes, tactile stimuli, and so on. When conducting a research study, you will be seeking out very specific kinds of data that will allow you to address your central research question as effectively as possible.

Primary data collection's main advantage is that it can be tailored to your research project and the specifics of your central research question. You can collect precisely that data which will give you the best chance of providing a robust, defensible answer to your central research question, because you are in control of the process. As well as this, primary data collection also ensures that your work has originality and novelty; if the data you use for your study has been collected by you for the specific purposes of answering your central research question, then you have created something that is unique and have explicitly engaged in the production of new knowledge. A further incidental advantage of primary data collection is that it offers you the opportunity to gain some first-hand experience of one of the key facets of research; it helps you to develop a range of practical skills that might be of use in a variety of careers, as well as providing a handy boost to your CV.

There are also some disadvantages associated with primary data collection, and these chiefly revolve around the practicalities of going 'into the field'. For one thing, collecting primary data can be an enormously time-consuming process. It might involve locating potential participants, persuading them to take part and then actually conducting the data collection itself, be it through a questionnaire, an **interview**, a **focus group**, and so on. A mutually convenient time to carry out data collection needs to be arranged if you need to meet or speak in person with your participants, and this is not always easy. Thus, primary data collection can take a great deal of time and effort, and is often incredibly frustrating; imagine, for instance, if a participant cancels your meeting at the last minute. If you are working to a non-negotiable deadline, these difficulties are magnified. Secondly, primary data collection usually incurs some kind of financial cost. This might simply be the cost of travel to the site where the data collection will take place, but some studies also offer research subjects a small cash reward for their participation. These things need to be borne in mind if you are working on a limited budget, or even no budget at all. Thirdly, primary data collection requires knowledge and skill on the part of the researcher. Conducting, for example, a semi-structured interview is a feat of planning, concentration and active listening; indeed, each and every data collection tool is demanding on the researcher in different ways, and the difficulty of primary data collection should not be underestimated.

Yet the advantages of primary data collection, in particular the manner in which it allows you to directly address your central research question, usually outweigh these difficulties. Collecting your own data can be an incredibly rewarding experience and, provided the process is planned and prepared for in detail, you should be able to avoid the worst of the problems. The remainder of this section will cover five of the most common primary data collection methods in greater detail.

Questionnaires

A **questionnaire** is composed of a series of questions or other prompts designed to gather data from the respondents. According to Denscombe (2014), a research instrument qualifies as a questionnaire only if it is designed to collect information which can be subsequently analysed, if it consists of a written list of questions, and if it gathers information by asking people directly about points concerned with the research. Questionnaires are predominantly used for the collection of quantitative data, and tend to consist of closed questions which invite the respondent to select from a list of possible answers. However, this is not always the case and questionnaires can also be made up of open-ended qualitative questions. Questionnaires can be conducted face-to-face, by post in hard copy, online, or with the assistance of a computer using so-called CAPI (computer-assisted personal interviewing) or CASI (computer-assisted self-interviewing) techniques. The Crime Survey for England and Wales utilises CAPI, with some of its self-completion modules on more sensitive topics utilising CASI.

The terms 'questionnaire' and 'survey' are often used interchangeably, although they in fact have slightly different technical meanings. A 'questionnaire' is a set of questions used in order to gather data from a participant, whilst the term 'survey' refers to the process of collating and analysing the data from individual questionnaires. So, surveys aggregate the data collected through questionnaires, but not all questionnaires are necessarily part of a wider survey (for example, questionnaires that are completed as part of the process of applying for a job or applying for credit). The two terms have been increasingly conflated in recent years with the rise of online tools that allow questionnaires to be administered and data to be gathered whilst simultaneously performing the required survey analysis. However, the distinction between the two remains relevant because it is important to properly inform participants what will happen to the data they provide through a questionnaire, including whether it will be aggregated as part of a wider survey.

Things to consider when preparing a questionnaire

Questionnaires can be tricky to construct properly and there are several issues to consider. Perhaps above all, questions should be clear and concise, and relevant to the topic; the questionnaire as a whole should be as short as possible whilst covering all the necessary issues, so as not to deter respondents. Beyond this, Neuman (2000) provides a useful checklist of things to bear in mind when designing a questionnaire. He suggests that you should:

1   Avoid jargon, slang, and abbreviations
2   Avoid ambiguity, confusing language, and vagueness
3   Avoid emotional language and prestige bias (that is, questions that encourage socially desirable answers rather than truthful ones)
4   Avoid double-barrelled questions (questions that touch upon more than one issue but allow for only one answer)
5   Avoid leading questions (questions that encourage a particular answer)
6   Avoid questions that are beyond the respondents' capabilities
7   Avoid false premises (assuming something, for example about your respondents, that might not be true)
8   Avoid asking about future intentions
9   Avoid double negatives as they can confuse
10 Make response categories mutually exclusive (so categories do not overlap), exhaustive (so all respondents have a choice that applies to them), and balanced (so each end of the spectrum is covered; from good to bad, for example)

As useful as this checklist is, it is still not exhaustive. It is also important to consider the order of your questions; questionnaires should not start with complex questions, or questions of a personal or sensitive nature, as this can discourage respondents from completing the questionnaire. In addition, the sequencing of the questions should not lead respondents towards answering in a particular way; that is, the answers to later questions should not be predicated on the answers to earlier ones (Denscombe, 2014). You should also consider whether you wish to have consistency in the manner in which each question is constructed (yes/no questions, a list of options, agree/disagree questions and so on) so as to reduce the chances of confusion, or whether you favour a variety of question types so as to guard against boredom. And it is vital that each and every question addresses something that you actually need to find out about; superfluous questions are a waste of your and your participants' time, and will add nothing when you are conducting your analysis and trying to answer your central research question. Bear in mind that you will also require an information section where you briefly explain the nature and purpose of your work and the institution, if any, with which you are affiliated. Details of the ethical precautions you have taken should be outlined and a statement of consent included (see Chapter 3 – Ethics for further details on ethical procedures). Return addresses and dates should also be made clear if necessary.

Both Brace (2013) and Denscombe (2014) offer detailed advice on all these issues and more. It is also worth noting that, depending on the nature of your study, it is sometimes possible to use pre-existing questionnaires and scales which have been tested on different samples in order to ensure they are reliable and valid (see Chapter 10 – Critique for information on reliability and validity). If you plan to use a pre-existing questionnaire or scale, then it is often necessary to gain permission for this from the author or the institution responsible for it.

Advantages and disadvantages of questionnaires

Questionnaires offer a number of significant advantages to researchers. They can be a very efficient way of gathering a large amount of data for relatively little cost and in a relatively short time. They tend to reduce the number of arrangements and communications that need to be made when compared to other research instruments, with the respondent free to choose a convenient time and place to complete the questionnaire, and they usually do not take up too much of the respondent's time. Questionnaires are also standardised, so all respondents are presented with the same questions and there is little opportunity for the researcher to influence the nature of those answers.

On the other hand, questionnaires can sometimes suffer from low response rates, particularly where respondents are required to return completed questionnaires by post. Poorly drafted questionnaire questions can also sometimes shape the respondents' answers, and even the best-drafted questions can still feel restrictive and limiting (Denscombe, 2014). This is because questionnaires offer no scope for the researcher to probe more deeply into the answers given to particular questions, and given that the questions tend to be fairly simple and straightforward, this can lead to a lack of depth in the resultant data. Questionnaires are also dependent upon a certain level of literacy or familiarity with a particular language among the respondents, which may not be evident in every target population.

Over recent years the rise of online questionnaires has been a particularly important advance. Email and social media allow for the efficient and free distribution of questionnaires to potentially massive numbers of respondents. Cloud software such as that provided by SurveyMonkey and Qualtrics allows for the creation and distribution of questionnaires for little cost or even for free. This has been a real benefit for those working on tight budgets, including students and unfunded researchers.

However, it should be remembered that online questionnaires are not appropriate in every situation. If the research demands a sample with particular characteristics rather than a convenience sample, then online methods of distribution might not always be feasible. In addition, some groups might be less likely to be comfortable with computers and might prefer more traditional paper-based methods, or internet access itself might be problematic among certain demographics or in certain geographical regions. Even in situations where the advantages of online questionnaires can be harnessed, it is important to remember that the design of the questionnaire itself remains paramount. Whilst the internet might have revolutionised the questionnaire in terms of the ease of its distribution, careful and considered questionnaire design is as vital as it ever was.

Example of a questionnaire

Box 8.1 is an example of a quantitative online questionnaire. It was designed for under-graduate criminological research methods students, and was inputted into Qualtrics to enable it to be completed easily. The researcher's copy is shown here, and it includes the applicable response categories, the **level of measurement** (see Chapter 9 – Data analysis for details on this) and the variable name for each question. This information would not be included on the participant-facing version of the questionnaire, but it can be useful to include on the researcher's copy.

Box 8.1   Example questionnaire

Quantitative subsidiary question = What is the relationship between personal char-acteristics and attitudes towards the police?

Independent variable questions

1   What was your age, in years, at your last birthday? _____ (scale) AGE
2   How would you self-identify your gender? Female/Male/Different to Female or Male/Prefer Not to Say (nominal) GENDER
3   Do you self-identify as black, Asian, or minority ethnic? Yes/No/Prefer Not to Say (nominal) ETHNICITY
4   How often do you read a newspaper? Daily/Weekly/Monthly/Yearly/Never (ordinal) NEWSPAPER

Dependent variable questions

5   On a scale of 1–10, with 1 being 'not at all' and 10 being 'extremely', how confi-dent are you that the police are effective at catching criminals? (scale) CATCH
6   On a scale of 1–10, with 1 being 'not at all' and 10 being 'extremely', how con-fident are you that the police are effective at keeping people safe? (scale) SAFE
7   On a scale of 1–10, with 1 being 'strongly disagree' and 10 being 'strongly agree', how much do you agree with the following statement? 'The police do a good job'. (scale) GDJOB
8   On a scale of 1–10, with 1 being 'strongly disagree' and 10 being 'strongly agree', how much do you agree with the following statement? 'The police treat everyone fairly regardless of who they are'. (scale) FAIRLY
9   On a scale of 1–10, with 1 being 'strongly disagree' and 10 being 'strongly agree', how much do you agree with the following statement? 'The police would treat me with respect if I had contact with them for any reason'. (scale) RESPECT

Interviews

Put simply, 'research interviews are a method of data collection that uses people's answers to researchers' questions as their source of data' (Denscombe, 2014: 184). Interviews are an appropriate choice of data collection tool when the research requires complex and subtle phenomena to be investigated. This might include opinions, attitudes, feelings, emotions, and experiences. Interviews also represent a good option when you have the opportunity to involve people with privileged information in your research, such as senior figures in a particular field or those with special expertise and experience.

Like questionnaires, interviews rely on the participants telling the researcher about their experiences or their feelings on a particular topic. However, they tend to be more open-ended than tightly focused questionnaires, and resemble more closely ordinary, everyday conversation. Nevertheless, interviews can and must be distinguished from mere conversation (Denscombe, 1983): Research interviewees accept and give consent to the fact that they are taking part in research, that their words can be used as research data, and that the agenda for the discussion is set by the researcher.

Interviews are a very common means of data collection in qualitative criminological research and have been used in studies on a wide range of issues. To give just a few examples, in recent years interviews have been used in research on older drug users in the UK and Canada (Moxon and Waters, 2017), police interviews with crime suspects (Leahy-Harland and Bull, 2017), collective efficacy, deprivation and violence in London (Sutherland et al., 2013), those incarcerated in the Netherlands for organised crime (Van Koppen and De Poot, 2013), and graffiti writers and their graffiti sites in Los Angeles (Bloch, 2018). Note that interviews are occasionally used to gather quantitative data as well as qualitative data; Moxon and Waters' (2017) research on older drug users collected basic demographic information as part of the interview, before moving on to a qualitative exploration of drug use through the participants' lifecourse.

A number of different interview formats are available, and the decision as to which one you use depends upon various factors such as who you are going to be interviewing and what type of data you are hoping to collect. At one end of the scale, structured interviews involve a predetermined list of questions, rather like a questionnaire 'administered face-to-face with a respondent' (Denscombe, 2014: 186). Whilst this offers no flexibility to develop interesting points, it does allow for standardised data collection which facilitates analysis and comparison of **inferences**. Structured interviews are also a good place to start for students and novice researchers as they do not rely upon the ability of the interviewer to react to what has been said during the interview itself. At the opposite end are unstructured interviews, which do not follow a particular set of questions but instead allow the interviewee and interviewer to pursue their thoughts and go in whichever direction feels appropriate. As a starting point the interviewer may introduce a theme or topic to be discussed, but beyond this complete flexibility is permitted. Somewhere in between these two poles are semi-structured interviews. As the name suggests, these interviews are relatively open-ended and permit the development of themes and some flexibility, but there will still be a list of topics or questions that the interviewer wishes to cover.

Interviews can be conducted face-to-face, which can allow for a rapport to be built between researcher and participant, but they can also be difficult to organise at a mutually convenient time and location. Interviews by telephone are generally more convenient, but the researcher will be unable to pick up on body language and other non-verbal communication and cues (O'Leary, 2017) which can make for a more difficult interviewing experience. In recent years online tools have emerged to provide a viable set of additional options. Interviews carried out using email or 'chat' applications have largely the same advantages and disadvantages as telephone interviews, although with the additional hindrance that meaning communicated through intonation of the voice is also lost as well as the non-verbal signals. The development of online videotelephony using applications such as Skype and FaceTime has been especially good news for interviewers; they feature all the convenience of telephone interviews but allow the researcher and the researched to see each other.

One-to-one interviews are the most common type of interview. They are relatively easy to arrange and conduct and ensure that the participant gets a good chance to air their views. However, group interviews have the advantage of capturing the views of several people at once and are therefore a good option to consider if time is tight. The dynamics involved in a group interview must be considered; in some situations they can encourage participants to reflect on their views, but there is also a danger that some voices will be dominant and there is a risk of 'groupthink': making flawed decisions as a result of group pressures, leading to a weakening of 'mental efficiency, reality testing, and moral judgment' (Janis, 1972: 9). Note also that the line between group interviews and focus groups is sometimes a blurred one: they are very similar in many ways, but there is less of a focus on social interaction as data with group interviews.

Things to consider when preparing an interview

There are three steps involved in a successful research interview: the construction of an appropriate and effective **interview schedule**, the proficient conducting of the interview, and the transcription of the interview.

All interviews require an interview schedule, but the level of detail involved will depend on the type of interview you are planning on carrying out. Structured interviews require the most detailed schedules and unstructured interviews the least. Regardless of type, it is important to think carefully about the questions that you want to ask, how you will ask them, and the order they will be presented in. The interview schedule should include information about location and date, instructions to the interviewer, and the interview questions (Creswell, 2015). O'Leary (2017: 244) suggests six steps that should be followed when creating your interview schedule; we have added a seventh:

1   Write a draft of the questions or themes that you want to ask about or explore with your research. It should be clear how these will help you answer your central research question.
2   Review the themes and questions. As part of this review you could look at the existing literature, and ask for feedback from peers and/or research supervisors.
3   Rewrite the questions in light of the feedback. All themes should now be written up as questions.
4   Order the questions (logically and/or in order of difficulty). Your interview schedule should have a beginning, middle and end.
5   Prepare additional information (such as instructions, prompts, and follow-up questions).
6   Decide on recording methods. It is good practice to audio record your interview for accuracy of data, and ideally you would use a voice recorder to do this.
7   Pilot your interview schedule. The best way to find out if your schedule is effective and is going to give you the information you need is to do a practice run. Ideally your pilot would be with someone from your sample group, but you could also use your peers or family members.

When drafting your questions, the first step in O'Leary's (2017) list, it is vital to consider the types of question you need to ask. Berg (2001) identifies four types of questions:

- Essential questions 'exclusively concern the central focus of the study' and can be placed closely together or scattered throughout the interview (Berg, 2001: 75). As the name suggests, every interview schedule should include essential questions.
- Extra questions are questions that are similar to essential questions but are slightly differently worded in order to act as a check on the reliability of the responses.
- Throw-away questions, often found at the start of interviews but also sometimes scattered throughout, are used to develop rapport, control the pace of the interview or allow for a change in focus.
- Finally, probing questions 'provide interviewers with a way to draw out more complete stories from subjects . . . their central purpose is to elicit more information about whatever the respondent has already said in response to a question' (Berg, 2001: 76).

Extra questions, throw-away questions and probing questions can be included or not depending on the requirements of the research project. Every interview question, regardless of its type, should be clear and allow participants to effectively communicate their ideas.

Interview schedules should not include your central research question or subsidiary questions. You should also avoid affectively worded questions that have the potential to arouse an emotional or antagonistic response from participants (for example, 'how many laws have you broken?'). Double-barrelled questions which ask the interviewee to respond to two issues simultaneously should also be avoided (for example, 'how many times have you tried ecstasy, or have you only smoked cannabis?'), as should long, complex questions which preclude concise, clear responses (Berg, 2001: 78–79).

When you are ready to conduct your interviews, you should remember that as with any skill, you will become better and more effective with experience. There is a good chance your first interview will feel awkward and a little uncomfortable. However, as you conduct more interviews and reflect on your practice, you will begin to feel more at ease with this form of data collection. Piloting your interview schedule can be a valuable method of honing your questions, practising your technique, and getting over the nerves of interviewing. The key is to make the interview conversational, and not inquisitorial. Berg (2001: 99-100) suggests the following tips:

- Never begin an interview cold. It is a good idea to start with a bit of 'small talk' (for instance, 'how are you doing today?').
- Remember your purpose. You are conducting an interview rather than a chat, and you have specific aims to achieve.
- Present a natural front.
- Demonstrate aware hearing. Be 'present' in the interview and show that you are listening.
- Think about your appearance. Wear something appropriate for the situation.
- Interview in a place that is comfortable (and safe) for both interviewee and interviewer.
- Do not be satisfied with monosyllabic answers. Gently prompt your participants to say more than 'yes' and 'no'.
- Be respectful.
- Practise, practise, and practise some more.
- Be cordial and appreciative. Remember to thank your participant for their time.

Completed interviews need to be transcribed. Transcription is the process of turning an audio recording into written text to facilitate its analysis. This process needs to be done manually by the researcher and involves listening to the interview and typing out what is being said. It is likely that you will find a way to transcribe that suits you, but a typical process of transcription might involve listening to a short extract of audio recording (for instance for 10 seconds) and then typing out the content. Non–audio content (such as body language and gestures if these were noted at the time) and non-verbal noises (such as laughing) can also be noted. Sections of audio that are unintelligible can be marked in the transcription using the notation '[. . .]'. After you have typed up the 10 seconds of interview, the audio is rewound and the short extract is listened to again, and the transcription is checked for errors. This process is repeated for the whole audio file until the entire interview has been transcribed. It is also a good idea to listen to the entire recording once the transcription is complete, again checking for errors. During the process of transcription, names and other identifying features should be removed in order to anonymise your data. A blank line ('_____') can be used in their place. Initials or a pseudonym should be assigned to respondents in order to ensure anonymity. You should also download audio files from the voice recorder onto a computer and back them up to ensure that you do not lose your valuable data. Transcription can be an incredibly time-consuming process. It can take six to eight times longer to transcribe the interview than it did to conduct it (so a one-hour interview can take six to eight hours to transcribe). This needs to be factored in when you are planning your project.

Advantages and disadvantages of interviews

Interviews offer a relatively straightforward means of acquiring in–depth data. The ability of interviewers to probe their interviewees and to encourage them to develop themes and ideas can lead to a wealth of 'thick', complex, and multi-layered data that ultimately allows for sophisticated answers to your research questions to be developed. Interviews allow research subjects to discuss what is important to them and, if access to key figures can be attained, then researchers can also benefit from the special insights and expertise that only privileged insiders can provide. There is also the prospect of flexibility both within a single interview and over a series of interviews if a particular theme or idea that was not initially felt to be of any importance proves to be so. All of this stands in contrast to the more fixed and inflexible nature of the typical questionnaire. On a more practical level, interviews have the advantage of requiring little in the way of equipment. Often, a simple voice recorder is all that is required for a face-to-face interview. Interviews can also prove to be rewarding and even therapeutic for the participants, who are provided with a rare chance to speak at length about their ideas and feelings (Denscombe, 2014).

Nevertheless, there are a number of disadvantages to interviews as a method of data collection. As with questionnaires, interviews rely on respondents being truthful and there is often no way of checking this. As a result, the integrity of the data can never be totally guaranteed. Dependability is also an issue, as the specific circumstances and context of one interview can never be fully replicated in another; an interviewer may enjoy a very good rapport with one participant but not with another, for instance. This also calls to mind the problem of interviewer effect, and the extent to which participants tailor their answers according to what they feel is socially desirable or what the interviewer wants to hear. Similarly, the presence of an interviewer and a voice recorder might inhibit the participant, particularly where sensitive matters are being discussed, and interviews may even cause distress to the participant. In terms of the practicalities of interviews, it can be costly in terms of time and finances to actually conduct the interviews, especially if interviewees are spread across a wide geographical area. As already noted, interviews can also be extremely time consuming to transcribe, to code and to analyse, notably when participants have been allowed freedom to develop their thoughts on an issue during the interview itself.

Example of an interview schedule

Box 8.2 is an example of a qualitative semi-structured interview schedule. This was the interview schedule used in Moxon and Waters' (2017) study on illegal drug users over the age of 40 years, which investigated people's experiences of drug use over their lifecourse.

Box 8.2 Example interview schedule

Qualitative subsidiary question = What is the nature of older people's illegal drug use?

Introductions

Statement about research:

As you are already aware the project focuses on illegal drug use in the over 40s. We are particularly interested in people who have used illegal drugs at various points in their lives and who are not 'problem users'. The interview itself consists of questions about drug use over time. It should take approximately one hour. In order to protect your identity, all identifying factors will be omitted from the transcription, the recording will be erased at the end of the research project and any publications based upon the research will be wholly anonymised. You do not have to answer any questions that you feel uncomfortable with.

Do you mind if the interview is audio recorded?

1) Thinking back, what was your first experience with illegal drug use?

When did you start using drugs?

What drugs were you using?

Why did you start using?

Who did you start using drugs with?

Where did you use drugs? *Home/street/party/club etc.?*

Where did you get drugs from?

How did you feel about your drug use? *Did you intend to continue?*

2) After this first experience, what happened next?

Did you continue using?

Did your patterns of use change? *Type of drugs used/people used with/where/sources?*

Why do you think this happened?

Changed preferences/studying/work/partner/children/change in location?

[REPEAT AS NECESSARY]

(continued)

(continued)

3) How would you describe your current drug use?

    What drugs do you use currently?

    How often are you currently using?

    Who do you tend to use drugs with?

    Where do you use?

    Where do you get your drugs from?

    What are your reasons for use?

4) How do you think illegal drug use has affected your life?

    career, family, parenthood, relationships, health

5) Why do you think that you have continued using drugs throughout your life?
6) What are your future intentions – Do you plan to continue using drugs?
7) Is there anything else that you would like to tell me?

    About your past, present or future? Is there anything I have missed?

8) Would it be possible to contact you again?

Thank you for your time.

Focus groups

Focus groups are a variation on interviews that can provide an efficient means of col-lecting large amounts of in-depth qualitative data. Focus groups generally consist of a handful of people (four to 12 according to O'Leary (2017), and six to nine according to Denscombe (2014)) partaking in a guided group discussion about a particular topic or issue. Focus groups are often used profitably in tandem with another data collection tool. They can be useful at the outset of a study in order to gain something of an overview of people's views on a particular topic, which can then be further investigated and explored using a different method. Alternatively they can be adopted towards the end of a study to gather people's opinions on what has been found thus far in the research process.

Focus groups rely on the processes of discussion and debate within the group to elicit information and data. As Morgan (2006: 121) suggests, group members 'share their expe-riences and thoughts, while also comparing their own contributions to what others have said'. Ideally, a focus group will reveal not only what group members think about a particular subject, but also why they think what they do. This is because over the course of a discussion participants will hopefully be required to, among other things, make the case for their viewpoint, support their assertions, and respond to challenges from other members of the group. The focus group also has potential to reveal consensus or dissensus among the group, or any particularly staunchly held opinions.

The role of the researcher or moderator in a focus group is to facilitate the group interaction (Denscombe, 2014) and the group dynamics that are vital in revealing people's thoughts and attitudes. For a focus group to be successful, the moderator must foster a trusting relationship between the participants, with confidentiality often vital if sensitive subjects are to be discussed. The moderator must also ensure that the discussion stays on track, although this is dependent upon the level of freedom afforded to the group; like interviews, some focus groups might be unstructured and some semi-structured depending on the needs of the research.

Things to consider when preparing a focus group

In many respects, the preparation required for a focus group is similar to that required for interviews, particularly when it comes to developing a script of questions or topics to be covered (see, for example, Berg, 2001: 121). The script should include:

1 An introduction to the focus group (including, for example, a reminder of the nature of the research study)
2 A statement of ethics and ground rules (particularly covering the issue of confidentiality)
3 Introductory activities if required (for instance, introductions to other members of the group)
4 The **focus group script** itself (the main part of the focus group, including questions, topics to be discussed, and activities if required)
5 Concluding remarks and reminder of confidentiality
6 Guidance for dealing with sensitive issues if required

However, there are a number of issues specific to focus groups that need to be considered both at the planning and preparation stage and during the conduct of the focus group itself. Berg (2001) outlines some of the most important:

- Focus groups require a 'clearly defined objective' (Berg, 2001: 123). A focus group must address the central research question and/or subsidiary question and it is vital that the moderator is clear on this because once the focus group begins, much of their attention will be on managing the group dynamics and developing the discussion.
- It is vital to consider 'the nature of the group' (Berg, 2001: 123). What are their characteristics? Is it largely homogenous or not? Is it an appropriate group given what is being asked? For example, if you want to know about what it is like living in a prison, you need to speak to prisoners or ex-prisoners.
- The atmosphere and rapport in the room is critical. Group members must feel comfortable. Ensuring the confidentiality of what is discussed can be vital in creating this.
- The moderator must be very well organised and have a clear idea about the schedule and what the discussion should cover.
- The moderator must be an aware listener. The schedule should not be so inflexible that 'interesting topics that spontaneously arise during the group discussion' (Berg, 2001: 124) are ignored or bypassed. A good facilitator will recognise when something important has been raised even if this is 'off-script', and allow it to be developed.
- The moderator should be 'restrained' (Berg, 2001: 124). They should guide the discussion and provide structure and direction, but avoid offering opinions and substantive comments.
- Ideally, a second researcher should be used in order to sit and observe the group, taking notes on group dynamics. They can also assist in identifying voices at the transcription stage. Of course, this might not always be possible given limitations of time and cost, especially in student projects.

Advantages and disadvantages of focus groups

The obvious advantage of focus groups is the fact that they allow a large amount of data to be collected with few resources in a short space of time, as mentioned above. A focus group with, say, eight participants can be akin to conducting eight interviews simultaneously in terms of the amount of useful data it might yield. Focus groups are also superior to interviews in the manner that they allow views and opinions to be compared and contrasted, and in their ability to reveal consensus or discord.

Focus groups suffer from many of the same disadvantages as interviews, expressly group interviews. In particular, there is a risk that one or two individuals might dominate the proceedings, and it takes tact and skill on the part of the moderator to successfully guard against this. Indeed, moderators of focus groups need to be prepared to handle group dynamics that will differ to some degree in every single focus group that is undertaken. There is also a risk of 'groupthink' and, on the other hand, the potential for things to become too heated in the case of serious disagreement. Again, it is the moderator's responsibility to deal with this and try to ensure that the focus group proceeds smoothly. In more practical terms, the sheer amount of data from a number of respondents that a focus group produces, and the fact that it is likely to be very conversational in nature, can make transcription and analysis an extremely laborious and time-consuming process.

The issue of confidentiality is also a vital one. In a focus group, anonymity is not possible as there are several people partaking in the group at the same time. Therefore, moderators must stress the importance of confidentiality and request that the identities of the individuals involved in the focus group are not divulged elsewhere. This is particularly important when sensitive or personal matters are being discussed. Assurances of confidentiality can also assist in creating a trusting, relaxed atmosphere, thus helping to generate better data.

Example of a focus group script

Box 8.3 is an example of a focus group script. This script was used in Heap's (2010) PhD research on anti-social behaviour. Heap carried out focus groups with community and volunteer groups within specific geographical areas with the aim of eliciting people's thoughts and feelings about such behaviour.

Box 8.3   Example focus group script

Qualitative subsidiary question = What do residents think about anti-social behaviour in their neighbourhood?

Introduction

Hello, my name is Vicky Heap and I'm a PhD research student at the University of Huddersfield. My research is on the topic of anti-social behaviour. I'm investigating what sorts of things affect how people form their views about anti-social behaviour in their local area and how it affects their lives.

Your opinions are very important to my research.

The focus group involves having a discussion with me for about one hour about your thoughts on anti-social behaviour. Our discussion will be recorded by a Dictaphone. This is just to help me take part in the discussion instead of having to take written notes. I will be the only person with access to the recording and the content of the discussion will be kept confidential, with it only being used for research purposes. Taking part in the focus group is entirely voluntary and if you decide that you no longer want to take part, or don't want to discuss some of the questions, that is absolutely fine. You won't even have to give a reason.

When I have completed my research I will have to write a report. As your opinions are so important to my research, some of what you tell me will be written in this report. I will not name you. Your identity will be protected by using a pseudonym (E.g. 'Person 1'). You will remain completely anonymous and there will be no way of tracing your responses to you. As this research is being conducted for a PhD, a copy of the final report (thesis) will be held in the library at the University of Huddersfield. Reports will also be written for academic audiences, such as journals and conference presentations.

1) Definition

    a   What does anti-social behaviour mean to you?

2) Extent of problems

    a   Is anti-social behaviour a problem in your local area?
    b   What is it that informs your view about this?

3) Concerns about ASB

    a   Do you worry about anti-social behaviour?

       YES

       Why do you worry about it?

       What is it that makes you worried?

       Does the extent to which you're worried change very easily?

       NO

       Why don't you worry about it?

       What would it take for you to worry about it?

4) Motivation

    a   Do you think that anti-social behaviour is something that is committed deliberately or is it something that's done without thinking?
    b   Why do you think people commit anti-social behaviour?

5) The authorities

    [RESPECT ONLY] Do you know if this is a Respect area?

    a   Do you think the authorities (police/council/housing association) do enough to stop anti-social behaviour? (*Do they meet your expectations?*)
    b   Do you think enough money is being spent to tackle anti-social behaviour in your area?
    c   Do you think the punishment for committing anti-social behaviour is fair?
    d   Does this affect how you view people who commit anti-social behaviour?

(continued)

(continued)

6) Communication

   a   Do you feel you're kept informed about what is being done to tackle anti-social behaviour?

   b   Does this make you more or less worried about anti-social behaviour?

7) And finally . . .

   a   What would you like to see happen in your area in the next five years?

8) Anything else?

Thank you for your time.

Observations

An **observation** takes place when a researcher goes out into the field in order to directly witness events. In this respect they differ from questionnaires, interviews and focus groups which rely on the participants telling the researcher about their experiences or opinions. Observations can be qualitative (for example, where a participant's behaviour is observed) or quantitative (systematic observations which, for example, measure the number of times a particular action occurs in a given setting over a set period of time).

In general, observations are held to be useful in situations where it is necessary to observe people or phenomena in their 'natural' social environment. Increasingly this also encompasses the online environment and observations of behaviour in chatrooms, virtual worlds, and so on. The aim is usually to observe what happens in normal, everyday situations, rather than asking participants to explain their feelings or describe their experiences, which can sometimes be difficult and leads to the possibility of socially desirable or untruthful answers being given. In addition, in situations where interviews, questionnaires and the like would not be feasible, for instance when the object of study is a particular artefact or phenomenon, observations can be a useful way in which to collect data and can also tap into other senses than vision (e.g. sound, smell, etc.) (Walliman, 2016).

On the whole, observations are not as common a mechanism for data collection as interviews and questionnaires. Nevertheless, there are some examples of criminology studies that rely on observation. For example, Hollis-Peel and Welsh (2014) conducted direct observations of residents of a town in the USA to test a so-called 'guardianship in action' tool.

Things to consider when preparing an observation

One of the key decisions to make when planning an observation is the level of involvement you will have in the situation that you are observing. At one end of the scale, the 'participant as observer' approach sees the researcher actively participating in the goings-on at the research site, to the extent that their role as an observer might well be secondary to their role as a participant. This can make note-taking particularly difficult, and of course raises questions about the effect of the researcher's participation on the research subjects. At the other end of the scale, 'complete observation' occurs when the researcher conducts their observation without engaging in any participation whatsoever (Creswell, 2015), and simply aims to 'try and see things as they happen' (Bachman and Schutt, 2011: 253) without any interference, although the very presence of the researcher may affect the events that are playing out in front of them.

Whether the researcher is acting as a complete observer or as a participant, it also needs to be decided whether the observation is to be covert. A covert observation should in theory minimise the effects the researcher has on the events at hand, but it leads to a host of other problems such as the fact that the researcher cannot take notes or record the events openly. As a result, this type of data collection often relies on the researcher's own recall of events, and of course it is fraught with ethical difficulties that must be satisfactorily addressed before the study can commence (see Chapter 3 – Ethics). In certain situations it also runs the risk of placing the researcher in danger if they are exposed partway through the observation.

Prior to the observation, the researcher should create an **observation schedule** that will allow them to record what they witness when in the field. Schedules should be designed specifically for the type of observation that is to take place, and there is no single correct format that can be adopted. Typically, the schedule might have space for the researcher to take notes and add their reflections. It is also likely to include space to record information about the research site (Creswell, 2015). Beyond this, particularly for qualitative observations, the field notes can be taken in different ways, either in a structured, semi-structured, or unstructured manner, depending on the preferences of the researcher and the nature of the thing being observed (see Bryman, 2016). For more systematic, quantitative observations, schedules are likely to be more structured and require the researcher to capture specific pieces of information. Denscombe (2014) provides a good example of a simple observation schedule for a systematic, quantitative observation (see also Bryman, 2016). Whether the observation is qualitative or quantitative, it is vital that there is complete clarity about who or what is to be observed. And, as Bryman (2016: 441) puts it, 'if in doubt, write it down'.

Advantages and disadvantages of observations

Observations can be an enormously powerful tool for researchers. They offer the opportunity to observe events as they happen in their 'natural' social setting in a manner that potentially reduces the effect of the researcher themselves. As a result, observations can provide great insight into the research subject's behaviour or point of view that would not otherwise be available. A well-thought-through and successfully carried-out observation can provide rich, detailed and nuanced data that is difficult to gather in any other way. In addition, observations are largely reliant on the researcher themselves; little equipment or technical support is needed and this can make them cheap to conduct and an efficient way of gathering a great deal of high-quality data.

However, that reliance on the researcher is also problematic in several regards. For one thing, the researcher must observe, interpret and come to an understanding of the events that play out under their gaze. It is possible that they may misconstrue what they have witnessed and this would clearly have massive implications for the soundness of their inferences. As observations of the same events cannot be repeated, there are also questions of reliability and dependability. Observations can also be time consuming and the process of making sense of the mass of data that can potentially be gathered can also be a lengthy one. Gaining access to conduct an observation can also be difficult, and there are often ethical problems involved, particularly if the researcher intends to carry out the observation covertly without the knowledge and prior agreement of the participants. Finally, as noted above, it is worth bearing in mind that observations have the potential to place the researcher in situations where their personal safety might be at risk, or where they might be witness to or even partaking in illegal activities, or where their psychological well-being is threatened (Denscombe, 2014). The risk of exposing oneself to these dangers must be carefully considered prior to commencing any programme of observations.

Example of a structured observation schedule

Box 8.4 shows an example of a structured observation schedule, although note that Armitage refers to it as a visual audit schedule. This schedule was developed and used in Armitage's (2011) evaluation of the effectiveness of the Secured by Design (SBD) scheme.

Box 8.4   Example structured observation schedule

Research question – How effective is the Secured by Design (SBD) scheme?
Visual Audit Schedule
Name of estate/development: ————————————————————
Date and time of day: ————————————————————————

Factor	Rater 1: ——	Rater 2: ——	Mean score and comment
People			
Presence of homeless/people begging			
Groups of people (youths) hanging around			
Pedestrian movement			
People under the influence of drink/drugs			
Buildings			
Derelict/empty properties			
Evidence of short-term desertion (e.g. milk bottles left outside)			
Evidence of long-term desertion (e.g. untended garden/piles of letters, newspapers)			
Broken/boarded-up windows			
Bars on windows			
Graffiti to buildings			
Vandalism to buildings			
Signs of neglect			
Graffiti within development			
Vandalism within development			
Litter/rubbish on streets			
Litter/rubbish in gardens			

Dog dirt			
Evidence of drug, alcohol, solvent abuse			
Abandoned/burnt-out vehicles			
Stray dogs			
Damaged/missing street signs/ lights			
Broken glass on pavements			
General environmental features			
Level of lighting (0 = highest level of lighting, 5 = lowest)			
Overgrown shrubs/trees (places to hide)			
Other potential places to hide (e.g. alleyways)			
Noise level			
Control signals			
Evidence of police on foot/ cycle*			
Evidence of police in patrol cars*			
Other authority figures (e.g. street wardens/concierge)*			
Neighbourhood Watch signs (0 = high level of signage, 5 = low level)			
Fieldworkers observed by residents (0 = high level of observation, 5 = low level)			
Fieldworkers questioned/ confronted by residents (0 = high level of confrontation, 5 = low level)			

All developments to be scored by two fieldworkers and mean score assigned.

Except where stated otherwise (i.e. lighting, Neighbourhood Watch, observed/confronted by residents), scores are from 0–5 (0 being lowest presence of factor, 5 being highest presence of factor).

* For factors highlighted with a *, score 0 as no patrols and 5 as high patrols; however, do not include numbers in analysis as it is not clear whether a high level of patrols would indicate a good or a bad sign. For these factors, analysis should be qualitative.

Example of an ethnographic observation

Box 8.5 provides an example of an ethnographic observation carried out by Phillips (2013). For his doctoral research he conducted an ethnography into probation practice to understand how probation practice could be understood in the context of David Garland's 'culture of control'.

Box 8.5   Example ethnographic observation

My central research question was: 'How are probation workers' practices and values shaped by the policy changes associated with Garland's "culture of control"?'. Through relatively unstructured observations of probation workers' daily lives, I was trying to get to the heart of the lived experience of probation workers by watching what they did and asking them about their work. Rather than having a structured observation checklist, my day-to-day observations were guided by finding out what probation workers did and why. I observed supervision sessions with offenders, sat in on staff meetings, went on home and prison visits, chatted to people in the staff kitchen and smoking area, and hung about in the waiting area of the probation office. I made notes during the day in a notebook and then typed them up at the end of each day. Alongside the field notes I kept a research diary in which I recorded my thoughts and feelings about the research and wrote down ideas to follow up in subsequent observations.

In this edited extract from my field notes, I was able to see what happens in terms of supporting people who have been convicted of sex offences. The probation officer [Dan] was both supportive and challenging – he was trying to assess and manage risk whilst also maintaining a positive, open and trusting relationship with the offender. In particular in this example, I was able to find out how probation workers deal with new risks that arise unexpectedly and what their strategies are for dealing with them in a real-life setting – this is very different to the data generated in a semi-structured interview. I also got some insight into what Dan thought about the programme and why which helped me understand how probation workers work with criminological concepts such as risk, 'what works', techniques of neutralisation, and compliance on a daily basis.

15 November 2009

11.15am

Observed meeting between Dan and an offender who had just finished a module on the sex offender programme. The programme tutor was also present. I was introduced, verbal consent gained from offender, and then I sat at the back of the room. They started by going through the report written by the tutor, mainly talking about attitudes to women. Offender was challenged very strongly by Dan, less so by tutor. Discussion then moved on to children and access to children. New concerns arose when offender disclosed that he had just entered a relationship with a woman. Again – challenged very strongly and offender appeared to be struggling to explain himself. Dan and tutor discussed strategies of coping – how will he deal with his triggers for offending, how will he ensure he won't reoffend. Offender talked about how he had met woman through local church which had been very supportive in recent months. He said he'd found some solace in religion. Generally supportive of progress on programme though. Tutor then left. [45 minutes]. Discussion between Dan and offender – much more focused on the future, getting though next module and general lifestyle issues including alcohol use, accommodation, and other issues. [15 minutes]. After the meeting Dan I chatted – he said he had found it hard to challenge the offender because his views, especially towards women, are so ingrained. He disclosed he was worried about offender's references to church/religion as he has used religion in the past to justify offending – this was clearly a considerable risk factor in Dan's eyes [which I hadn't picked up on in observation itself]. Dan also discussed issues with the programme itself and how there were, in his view, insufficient consequences for not engaging in the programme.

Media analysis

At its broadest, **media analysis** involves 'the examination, interpretation and critique of both the material content of the channels of media communication and the structure, composition and operations of corporations that either own or control those media' (Cashmore, 2006: 169). It has a long history in the discipline of criminology (Wincup, 2017), where the output of newspapers in particular has come under great scrutiny over many decades. This body of work has tended to focus upon the media's reaction to crime and includes famous studies such as those by Cohen (1972) and Hall et al. (1978). In general, such studies have consistently found that the media is inclined to amplify crime and deviance, and that it lends support to harsher, more punitive policies.

Although newspapers have commanded a great deal of attention, other traditional forms of media such as television have also come under examination from media analysts. Increasing attention is now being paid to newer online forms of media such as blogs and social media outputs. Caulfield and Hill (2014: 141) suggest a range of 'media and contemporary entertainment' is amenable to study, such as websites, newspapers, magazines, YouTube, news and current affairs programmes, TV dramas, sitcoms and reality shows, commercials, and music videos. Furthermore, the rise of the internet has also made the study of traditional forms of media more straightforward; newspapers, for example, are increasingly accessed online, and databases such as Nexis contain archived issues going back over many years.

Media analysis can be quantitative or qualitative in nature. Quantitatively this tends to take the form of a content analysis; the systematic quantifying and categorising of the contents of the text. This allows for observations to be made about the types of crimes, offenders and victims that are typically covered in the media (Wincup, 2017). It also supports the exploration of deep-rooted and possibly unintentional messages that might be implicit in the text; the frequency with which particular words or ideas are repeated can betray a text's real priorities and underlying values (Denscombe, 2014). Qualitative media analysis focuses on thematic analyses, assessing the narratives or discourses present in the text:

> this requires researchers to look in detail at the structure of the text and identify patterns within it, for example the repeated use of terms or metaphors. [This can expose] dominant narratives by deconstructing the text and revealing the underpinning social values and assumptions.
>
> (Wincup, 2017: 87)

Things to consider when preparing a media analysis

Unlike the data collection methods discussed above which involve the creation of new data gleaned in some way from individuals, media analysis entails the collection of data from existing sources. Therefore the process of data collection requires the creation of a framework for identifying and working with the sources that will yield your data. This process can be divided into three steps:

1   Initial decisions on the type of media sources that you are going to use. This will be dictated by the needs of your central research question; what type of data and analysis is required to provide an answer to that question?
2   Finding the data. This might involve searching for actual physical documents, although increasingly searches are made easier using online methods. You might use a specific database (e.g. Nexis) or a search engine, for example. A range of search terms linked to your central research question can be created. You need to plan carefully how you will collect and record your data, remembering to systematically record what you have gathered. Keep full references and, for online sources, URLs.

You can boost your search by adding more search terms (but not too many), using synonyms (for instance, using the terms nuisance and disorder as well as anti-social behaviour), and using your terms in different combinations. Once you have established what your search terms are going to be, you can carry out a Boolean search (see Figures 8.4 and 8.5 for examples of a Boolean search box). Boolean searches are based on so-called Boolean logic (named after the mathematician George Boole (d.1864) who developed this method of notation) which is a means of combining your search terms in 'a meaningful way [that] allows the searcher to be specific about what they wish to retrieve from the database. When executed properly, this means that the results should contain relevant records and ignore others' (Rumsey, 2008: 68). Boolean searches utilise three 'Boolean connectors' that are used between the search terms. They are as follows.

AND: 'Combining two (or more) terms with the AND connector means that the results must contain both (or all) of the words. This means that records that include fewer than all of the terms will be ignored. Using an AND search term will narrow down the number of results' (Rumsey, 2008: 69). For example, if you were to search for 'fish' AND 'chips', only those records that contain both fish and chips would be returned (see darker-grey area in Figure 8.1). Records that only look at fish or only look at chips will not be returned.

OR: 'The OR connector is generally used when there are two or more alternative terms and the searcher requires that records containing both (or all) are included in the search. Consequently, an OR connector broadens the search' (Rumsey, 2008: 70). For example, if you were to search for 'fish' OR 'chips', records that contain fish and records that contain chips would both be returned, as per Figure 8.2.

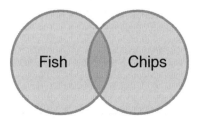

Figure 8.1 Fish AND chips.

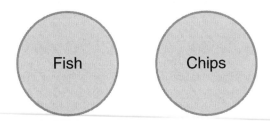

Figure 8.2 Fish OR chips.

NOT: 'The NOT connector is used when a particular term is to be excluded from the search. This may be either to limit the search or to clarify meaning . . . This is a useful means of disregarding irrelevant records, but the area of overlap where both terms appear will not be retrieved' (Rumsey, 2008: 70). For example, if you were to search for 'fish' NOT 'chips', this will return records that contain fish, but will exclude any records where there is also a mention of chips, even if those records also mention fish, as per Figure 8.3.

To complete your search, combine your key terms with Boolean search logic. Use Figure 8.4 to support you in this. In the box, start by placing OR between the synonyms for your key terms. Then combine your key terms together using AND or exclude terms using NOT. Continuing with the fish and chips from above, Figure 8.5 shows how you might search for articles on fish and chips.

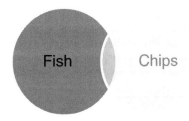

Figure 8.3 Fish NOT chips.

(	OR		OR		)
AND					
(	OR		OR		)
NOT					
(	OR		OR		)

Figure 8.4 Boolean search box.

(fish	OR	cod	OR	haddock)
AND				
(chips	OR	fries	OR	wedges)
NOT				
(restaurant	OR	takeaway	OR	location)

Figure 8.5 Completed Boolean search box for fish and chips example.

Inclusion and exclusion criteria can also be used to aid your search for data. Inclusion criteria 'describe the specific attributes that a [source] must have to be included in the [sample]' (Cherry and Dickson, 2017: 50). For example, you may only wish to search for sources published within a particular date range. Exclusion criteria 'describe the specific attributes that disqualify a [source] from inclusion in your [sample]' (Cherry and Dickson, 2017: 50). For example, you may wish to discount sources not published in the UK or that are not in English. Remember that the needs of your central research question should guide what you include and exclude, and you should be able to justify every decision you make.

You may need to narrow your search if you are faced with too much data. This might involve reducing the number of initial search terms, using exclusion criteria or identifying more specific sources (such as looking at just one or two newspapers). A typical undergraduate project might have a sample of between 20 and 40 sources.

3   Refining the data and creating your sample. Once you have 20–40 sources you can use the process of theoretical sampling (see Chapter 7 – Research design and sampling) to further narrow down your sources to a manageable number. Theoretical sampling is a type of non-probability sampling that emphasises careful selection of cases (in this case, media sources) in order to allow the construction of a theoretical understanding. This is carried out by reading the sources and assessing their relevance to your central research question. Those articles that are the most theoretically relevant to the central research question remain in the sample, whilst others can be discarded. This ensures that the quality of the sample is high and can assist in the development of a theoretical understanding, ultimately providing an answer to the central research question. More details on theoretical sampling can be found in Chapter 7 – Research design and sampling.

Advantages and disadvantages of media analysis

Media analysis can take a variety of forms, each with their own specific strengths. Nevertheless, there are a number of advantages that all forms of media analysis share. Firstly, it tends to be relatively efficient in terms of time. Compared to most other forms of primary data collection, if you enjoy access to texts, then you can collect large of amounts of data very quickly and begin the process of analysis almost immediately. This can be particularly advantageous if you are faced with a strict deadline. Media analysis is also cost effective. Many media sources can be accessed at little or no expense to the researcher, and there are vast amounts of data now held online that are relatively easy to access and search. Many of these data are held permanently and in a form that is open to public scrutiny and can be checked by others (Denscombe, 2007). For students and those working on tight budgets, this ease of access is an important consideration. Furthermore, as media analysis is a purely 'desk-based' form of research, there is no need to make arrangements to meet with participants, create questionnaire or interview schedules, and so on. This means your project is not reliant on the cooperation of others with no real stake in the process, and it is logistically far more straightforward. Media analysis also offers you the opportunity to assess how phenomena were considered in the past if you analyse older, archive material, in a way that other forms of primary research do not. Yet it simultaneously allows for extremely up-to-date studies focusing on present-day attitudes and concerns.

There are also a number of disadvantages associated with media analysis. Many of these relate to the nature of the sources. Great care must be taken to ensure the credibility of the sources used in media analysis. Researchers need to evaluate the authority of the source and the procedures used to produce it in order to gauge the credibility of the documents (Denscombe, 2007). Consideration also needs to be given to whether the source is authentic; is it what it says it is and from where it claims to be from? These issues are of particular concern when dealing with online sources, which require special scrutiny. It is also important to bear in mind that some sources may be unavailable because, for instance, the database you are using is not comprehensive. This might mean that useful and pertinent documents are missed during your search process. Perhaps even more gravely, it might prove to be the case that very little useful data exists on your particular area of study. Therefore it can be worth spending a little time researching the amount of data available before you finalise your central research question or subsidiary questions to ensure that you will be able to provide a robust answer to them. Finally, you should always bear in mind that most media content is produced with a purpose in mind. It does not provide an objective picture of reality but a socially constructed view of the world (Denscombe, 2007) that is shot through with particular interests and agendas. This should be remembered when you are collecting and then analysing your data so that you are clear on what it is that you are actually looking at.

Secondary data collection methods

Secondary data are data that have already been collected by someone else for another purpose. These data can be subsequently reanalysed by other researchers who are working on different projects with different purposes. As Bryman (2016: 309) puts it, 'secondary analysis is the analysis of data by researchers who will probably not have been involved in the collection of those data, for purposes that may not have been envisaged by those responsible for the data collection'. This distinguishes it from primary data, which are collected by the researcher for the research project at hand, although the difference between primary and secondary data is not always clear-cut (Bryman, 2016).

Collecting data tends to be the most costly and time-consuming part of a research project. The use of secondary data effectively allows much of this aspect of a research project to be avoided. Many research projects collect a large amount of data, sometimes more than what can actually be used in the initial project, and therefore the use of secondary data represents a good way to get more out of data that have already been collected. Secondary data can be either quantitative or qualitative in nature, and sometimes a database will contain both types of data. Secondary data include, among other things, documents, official data and records (such as data collected by the police, the courts, the probation service and so on), organisational data and records, personal communications (letters, emails, and others), or questionnaire and interview data (such as the Crime Survey for England and Wales).

It might be appropriate to use secondary data collection methods if you do not have the time or resources to collect your own data. You might also decide to use secondary data if you are working on a research project that covers highly sensitive topics, involves a vulnerable or difficult to access population, or where primary research might place you in an unsafe situation. Before committing to the use of secondary data in your own research, a number of important questions need to be asked (Neuman, 2000: 305):

- Are the secondary data appropriate for the research question?
- What theory and hypothesis can a researcher use with the data?
- Is the researcher already familiar with the substantive area?
- Does the researcher understand how the data were originally gathered and coded?

Only if there are satisfactory answers to these questions should the use of secondary data be considered a viable option for your research project.

In criminology and criminal justice research, relying on secondary data sources is an extremely common practice, particularly in the USA. About two-thirds of articles published in the top American criminology and criminal justice journals between 2000 and 2010 relied on secondary data for their analyses (Nelson et al., 2014). Of course, as Nelson et al. (2014: 16) go on to point out, 'as with all disciplines, the research produced in criminology and criminal justice (CCJ) literature is only as credible as the data used'. Secondary data collection might be an accepted part of the criminological landscape, but it must always be carried out with caution and rigour.

Sources of secondary data

There are many different sources of good quality secondary datasets. Some will require you to create an account and sign in, some will require you to sign a user agreement, and others will charge you to use their data. Sometimes academics at your university will upload their data to an institutional repository, which tend to be free to use for students at that institution. Table 8.1 below provides details of some of the more reputable sources of secondary data. It is not comprehensive or exhaustive, but provides a flavour of the mass of data that is already available to the criminological researcher.

Advantages and disadvantages of secondary data collection

Secondary data collection comes with a range of advantages. In the first place, as Table 8.1 shows, there are a great number of extremely comprehensive datasets available,

Table 8.1 Sources of secondary data for criminologists

Dataset	Region/coverage	Type	Access	Cost
UK Data Archive	United Kingdom	quantitative and qualitative	www.data-archive.ac.uk/find	Free
Crime Survey for England and Wales	United Kingdom	quantitative	www.crimesurvey.co.uk/SurveyResults.html	Free
Inter-Consortium for Political and Social Research (ICPSR)	United States	quantitative and qualitative	www.icpsr.umich.edu/icpsrweb/ICPSR	Mostly free
Uniform Crime Report (UCR)	United States	quantitative	https://ucr.fbi.gov	Free
National Crime and Victimization Survey (NCVS)	United States	quantitative	www.bjs.gov/index.cfm?ty=dcdetail&iid=245	Free
United Nations Surveys on Crime Trends and the Operations of Criminal Justice Systems (UN–CTS)	International	quantitative	www.unodc.org/unodc/en/data-and-analysis/United-Nations-Surveys-on-Crime-Trends-and-the-Operations-of-Criminal-Justice-Systems.html	Free
World Health Organization (WHO) Mortality Database	International	quantitative	www.who.int/violence_injury_prevention/surveillance/databases/mortality/en	Free
International Crime Victimization Survey (ICVS)	International	quantitative	http://wp.unil.ch/icvs/statistics	Free

containing a wealth of data that a single researcher could not hope to replicate. Using secondary data helps to avoid the risks associated with collecting primary data, such as placing oneself in danger of personal harm. It also reduces the chances of bias in your research and might allow for a better representation of the 'real' world when compared to the use of, for instance, a small convenience sample (Caulfield and Hill, 2014). Secondary data collection is also relatively inexpensive, with many reputable datasets being freely available online. It also saves time, as there is no need to go out into the field and collect data; the researcher can simply download an appropriate dataset and commence their analysis. Indeed, Bryman (2011) suggests that students using secondary data should have more time for analysis and interpretation than students who spend time collecting their own primary data, and this can contribute to the fuller exploration of existing data, much of which is often under-utilised in the original study that it was collected for. The use of secondary data allows for the independent replication of inferences by others, a factor that has led to calls for the increased use of secondary data in criminological research (Cullen, 2013). Finally, there are few ethical concerns associated with the use of secondary data. You must ensure you have the appropriate permissions, and you should store any data in the required manner, but beyond this you are largely free from any ethical worries.

The use of secondary data is not without its disadvantages. Perhaps the most significant is the fact that the data were not collected with your own central research question, aims, and objectives in mind. It is therefore not specific to your study and must be used very carefully. You need to consider how the data were originally collected, what sampling techniques were used, how the data have been cleaned and processed (usually explained in the code book that accompanies the data), and why they were collected. Ask yourself the following questions to help you with this process (Neuman, 2000: 306):

- Are the categories used too broad or do they not match your needs?
- Do the definitions used in the data not tally with your own?
- Is there evidence of any mistakes in the original data collection process?

It is necessary to come to an overall view on both the quality of the data and their appropriateness for the task at hand, a process that is not required when using your own primary data. Above all, you need to ask whether the data are appropriate for your study; will they properly assist you in creating an answer to your central research question? In addition, not all data are collected ethically and for benign purposes, and this needs to be considered.

'Doing' mixed methods data collection

This section offers a visual guide as to how some of the data collection methods discussed in this chapter can be brought together with mixed methods designs (Chapter 5 – Mixed methods design) and data combining (Chapter 6 – Combining the data). The aim is to show what a mixed methods project might look like in practice, and the place of data collection within that. The designs, data collection methods, and combining techniques that are represented in Figures 8.6–8.14 below have been chosen because they have proven to be some of the most common approaches adopted by our undergraduate students. They offer feasible and robust solutions for students and researchers who are seeking to put together a mixed methods project but who are faced with severe limitations of time and resources.

Data collection in a convergent parallel project

Example A

Figure 8.6 shows a convergent parallel design with data collection via an online questionnaire (QUANT) and semi-structured interviews (QUAL). The online questionnaire and semi-structured interviews are carried out simultaneously and with equal priority. The inferences for each component are then combined using triangulation to create the meta-inferences.

Example B

Figure 8.7 shows a convergent parallel design with data collection via a questionnaire (QUANT) and media analysis (QUAL). The questionnaire and media analysis are carried out simultaneously and with equal priority. The inferences for each component are then combined using complementarity to create the meta-inferences.

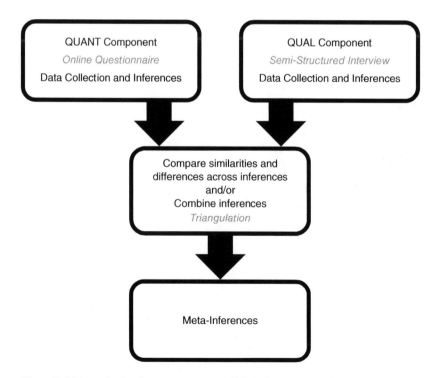

Figure 8.6 Example A of a convergent parallel project.

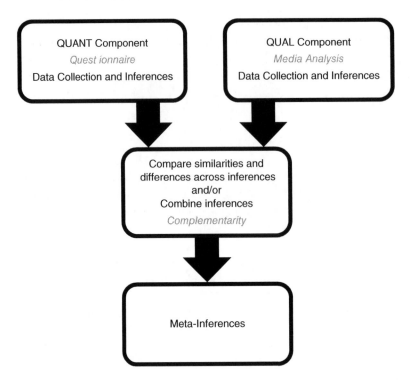

Figure 8.7 Example B of a convergent parallel project.

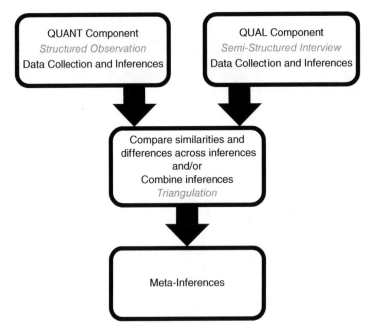

Figure 8.8 Example C of a convergent parallel project.

Example C

Figure 8.8 shows a convergent parallel design with data collection via a structured observation (QUANT) and a semi-structured interview (QUAL). The questionnaire and media analysis are carried out simultaneously and with equal priority. The inferences for each component are then combined using triangulation to create the meta–inferences.

Data collection in an exploratory sequential project

Example D

Figure 8.9 shows an exploratory sequential design with data collection via interviews (qual), the inferences of which feed into the design of a questionnaire (QUANT).

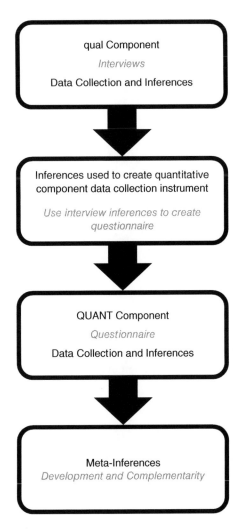

Figure 8.9 Example D of an exploratory sequential project.

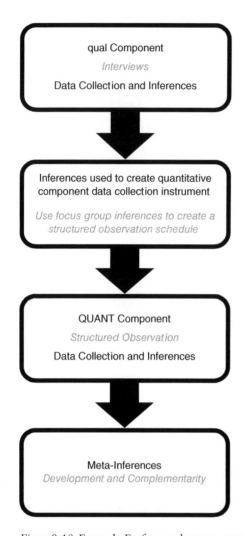

Figure 8.10 Example E of an exploratory sequential project.

The meta-inferences are created following the completion of this latter, dominant component. Ways of combining the data might include development and complementarity.

Example E

Figure 8.10 shows an exploratory sequential design with data collection via focus groups (qual), the inferences of which feed into the design of a structured observation (QUANT). The meta-inferences are created using development and complementarity.

Example F

Figure 8.11 shows an exploratory sequential design with data collection via media analysis (QUAL), the inferences of which feed into the design of an online questionnaire

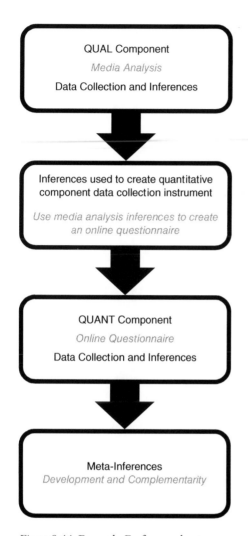

Figure 8.11 Example F of an exploratory sequential project.

(QUANT). The meta-inferences are created following the completion of this latter component using development and complementarity.

Data collection in an explanatory sequential project

Example G

Figure 8.12 shows an explanatory sequential design with data collection via an online questionnaire (QUANT), the inferences of which feed into the design of the interview schedule (QUAL). The meta-inferences are created following the completion of this latter component. You could use development, complementarity, and initiation for combining the data.

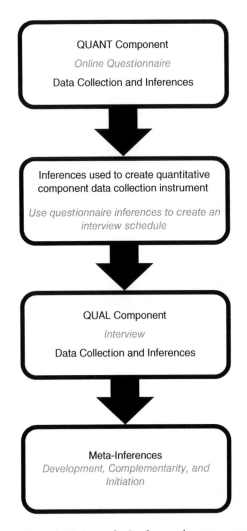

Figure 8.12 Example G of an explanatory sequential project.

Example H

Figure 8.13 shows an explanatory sequential design with data collection via a structured observation (QUANT), the inferences of which feed into the design of the focus group script (QUAL). The meta-inferences are created following the completion of this latter component using development, complementarity, and expansion.

Example I

Figure 8.14 shows an explanatory sequential design with data collection via an online questionnaire (QUANT), the inferences of which feed into the design of the focus group

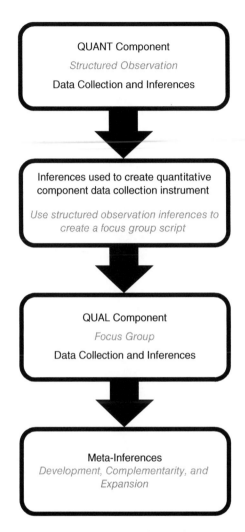

Figure 8.13 Example H of an explanatory sequential project.

script (qual). The meta-inferences are produced using development and following the completion of this latter component complementarity.

Summary

This chapter has looked at some of the different ways that data can be collected for your criminological mixed methods project. It began by looking at some of the most common primary data collection tools, with primary data being data that the researcher has collected themselves. Questionnaires, interviews, focus groups, observations, and media analysis were discussed. The chapter then went on to discuss secondary data collection, where data that has already been collected by someone else for another purpose is utilised.

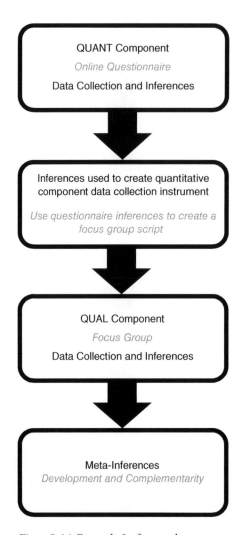

Figure 8.14 Example I of an explanatory sequential project.

Finally, we outlined the manner that these data collection methods can be integrated with basic mixed methods designs (Chapter 5 – Mixed methods design) and combining techniques (Chapter 6 – Combining the data), thereby mapping out the structure of a mixed methods study.

Learning questions

1   Which data collection methods could you use to collect quantitative and qualitative data respectively?
2   In your research, when might you use primary data collection and when might you use secondary data collection?
3   How might you amalgamate your data collection methods, mixed methods design, and combining techniques into one overall research structure?

9   Data analysis

Introduction

As a mixed methods researcher you must have the requisite skills to competently analyse both quantitative and qualitative data. The purpose of this chapter is to offer easy-to-follow guidance on how to conduct a basic range of quantitative and qualitative data analyses, which can be used in conjunction with the data collection methods outlined in Chapter 8 – Data collection methods. We focus here on providing clear information about foundational analysis techniques. This is because executing a simple method of analysis correctly can provide more convincing inferences than using a complicated technique poorly. Although the size and scope of this chapter do not allow for advanced techniques to be introduced, we do signpost you to other textbooks that are solely dedicated to data analysis.

The chapter is split into two parts. First, we consider quantitative data analysis and outline how to undertake a range of statistical tests using SPSS. We start by explaining a range of core terms associated with quantitative data, including: levels of measurement, independent and dependent variables, and hypotheses. We then move on to detail how to conduct univariate and bivariate analyses, providing step-by-step SPSS instructions. Secondly, we focus on qualitative data analysis by providing an introduction to thematic analysis. We illustrate how the systematic process of searching for themes in the data can be undertaken by following five basic steps: authenticating the data, creating sensitising concepts, coding, moving from codes to themes, and generating themes. Overall, the analysis techniques outlined in this chapter will provide you with enough information to be able to generate quantitative and qualitative inferences from your data that can be used to create a set of meta-inferences for your mixed methods research project.

Quantitative data analysis

This section explores various ways in which you can analyse your quantitative data and produce your quantitative inferences. It will cover levels of measurement, independent and **dependent variables**, hypotheses, **univariate** analysis, and **bivariate** analysis. Please note that you must select statistical tests that will allow you to answer your central research question/quantitative subsidiary question. Like many other aspects of this book, the analysis that you will carry out is driven by your research questions. In this section, all instructions for carrying out your statistical tests are based on the IBM SPSS Statistics 24 software. A number of texts are dedicated to the analysis of data using SPSS, such as the comprehensive Field (2018).

Structuring your analysis

Before looking at the manner in which you can analyse your quantitative data, it is worth bearing in mind that it is good practice for your analysis to follow a consistent structure. This ensures that you cover all the necessary elements in your analysis, and that it follows a coherent, logical order. In this section, we have adopted the following structure:

- State the statistical test being used.
- Identify the variable(s).
- State the **hypothesis**.
- Results table (can be copied and pasted from SPSS).
- Interpret the table (include numerical values and percentages as appropriate): Clearly state what the table is saying and what it means in relation to the variables used. What is included in this section will depend on the type of statistical test being used.
- State whether you have proven or disproven your hypothesis.
- State how your inferences relate to previous research findings from your literature review.
- State how your inferences help you answer your research questions.

In the sections below you will see this structure being used with the various statistical tests.

Level of measurement

Level of measurement, which refers to 'the relationship between what is being measured and the numbers that represent what is being measured' (Field 2009: 8), is vital to understand when devising and carrying out your quantitative data collection and analysis. It is associated with variables and their outcomes. Variables are used to quantify your research concepts and can be anything that is measurable and that varies (e.g. the questions on your questionnaire). Every variable has a level of measurement based on the nature of the outcome data. Outcomes are the possible response categories, answers, choices, options, or numbers that represent the data of the variable and can be either categorical (data composed of categories) or continuous (data composed of numbers).

Levels of measurement are important for three reasons. Firstly, they give an indication of how precise the variable response categories are, and therefore also the associated data. For example, if you ask someone their age, the answer 'young' is less precise than the answer '18 years'. Figure 9.1 shows the relationship between the levels of measurement. Secondly, a variable's level of measurement often determines what statistical tests to run. Different tests are required to answer the same question depending on the levels of measurement of your variables. For example, if you want to find out about the nature of a relationship between two variables, depending on the levels of measurement of the two variables you might run a **Cramer's V**, a **Spearman's rho**, or a **Pearson's r** test (see below for further details on these statistical tests). Thirdly, the levels of measurement of your variables affect how you analyse, interpret and understand your data. There are three levels of measurement: Nominal, **ordinal** and **interval/ratio** (**scale**). Nominal is the least precise level of measurement (e.g. 'young'), and interval/ratio is the most precise ('18 years'), with ordinal falling in the middle (see Figure 9.1).

Nominal variables are the lowest level of measurement as they are the least precise. They are categorical, consisting of two or more categories with no ordering of values or relationship between the categories. The values/categories cannot be numerical. Examples of **nominal** level variables are gender (female, male, different to female or male), eye colour (green, blue, brown, hazel), or security features installed in the home (prickly hedges, burglar alarms, sash locks, guard dog).

Ordinal variables fall between the nominal variables and interval/ratio (scale) variables. They provide more precision in their response categories than nominal variables, but not as much as interval/ratio (scale) variables. They are categorical, but unlike nominal variables, there is a logical order or a relationship between the categories. However, the spacing between the categories can be uneven and is not meaningful. For example, consider a question that asks how much respondents like fish and chips. They can answer 'not a lot', 'it's OK', and 'a lot'. These ordinal variables can be ranked, but they cannot be assigned a value, so it is not possible to say that 'a lot' is twice or three times as much as 'it's OK', for example. Other examples of ordinal level variables are degree classifications (e.g. first, upper second, lower second, third) and clothing sizes (e.g. xs through to xxxxl). The classic Likert scale (strongly agree, agree, neither agree nor disagree, disagree, strongly disagree) also creates ordinal level data.

Interval/ratio (scale) variables offer the greatest amount of precision. They are continuous, and the response categories are of numerical value, with equal distance between the values (e.g. 10 is twice as much as 5). Interval and ratio variables do have slight differences,

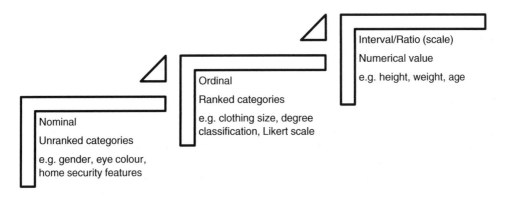

Figure 9.1 Levels of measurement.

as ratio variables can have a measurement of absolute zero (for example, the variable of height or distance) and interval variables cannot. However, we deal with interval and ratio variables together in this book, and refer to them as scale to remain consistent with the way they are treated in the SPSS software.

Independent and dependent variables

Independent and dependent variables are vital to understand when you are planning your quantitative data collection and analysis. This is because if you do not plan your data collection properly, then you might not have the data you require in order to answer your central research question when you come to conduct your analysis. The majority of bivariate analyses (analysis of two variables) need clearly identified independent and dependent variables. A variable is any factor, trait, or condition that exists in differing amounts (that is, it *varies*) that you attempt to measure.

An *Independent Variable* (IV) is one that is not changed by other variables, hence it is independent. Independent variables are 'thought to be the cause of some effect' (Field, 2009: 7); researchers can look for the effect (or prediction) of **independent variables** on dependent variables. This is sometimes referred to as the 'influencing' variable. Examples of possible independent variables include personal characteristics (gender, age, ethnicity, nationality, education, etc.) or location (e.g. urban/rural).

A *Dependent Variable* (DV) is one that is 'thought to be affected by changes in the independent variable' (Field, 2009: 7). Changes in the dependent variable are caused or influenced by the changes in the values of other variables. This means that dependent variables, which are sometimes also known as 'outcome variables', are the variables of interest in many research studies which try to ascertain precisely what the relationship is between independent and dependent variables; what changes in the dependent variable does the independent variable cause? The dependent variable is often thought about as the 'thing' (concept) you want to find out about and is often a criminological concept (e.g. crime, fear of crime, victimisation, illegal drug use, anti-social behaviour, etc.). An example of an independent variable affecting a dependent variable might be age influencing illegal drug use, or poverty causing crime.

Hypotheses

In its everyday meaning, a hypothesis is simply 'a prediction about the state of the world' (Field, 2009: 787). In research studies it generally refers to something a little more specific, namely 'an informed speculation, which is set up to be tested, about the possible relationship between two or more variables' (Bryman, 2016: 691). It is informed because it is based upon the existing research literature (i.e. your literature review) in the particular field that the research is taking place in, rather than on mere idle speculation or guesswork.

All of your quantitative analyses should begin with a hypothesis. For example, you might hypothesise that 'there will be a strong relationship between gender and fear of crime'. In this hypothesis you are predicting, firstly, there will be a relationship between the two variables and, secondly, that this relationship will be strong. This purpose of the analysis is to test this hypothesis.

Univariate analysis

Univariate analysis is 'the analysis of a single variable at a time' (Bryman, 2016: 697). This means that univariate analysis focuses on the description of one variable. It summarises and finds patterns in the data of that single variable. For example, univariate analysis will tell you about the nature of one (and only one) question on your questionnaire (you need to repeat the analysis with each question individually as needed). Univariate analysis does not look at the relationship between two variables.

Two statistical tests are used when conducting a univariate analysis. They are '**measures of central tendency**' and 'frequencies'.

Measures of central tendency

Measures of central tendency are a trio of statistical tests that provide ways of describing the typical or central value in the distribution of values, where the 'distribution of values' is 'a term used to refer to the entire data relating to a variable' (Bryman, 2016: 690). In effect, they help you to identify the middle point of the data in various ways.

Different statistical tests are used depending upon the level of measurement of the variables being used.

1   For interval/ratio (scale) variables, the mean is used: 'This is the everyday average – namely, the total of a distribution of values divided by the number of values' (Bryman, 2016: 688). You can also use median and mode.
2   For ordinal variables, the median is used: This is 'the mid-point in a distribution of values' (Bryman, 2016: 692). You can also use mode.
3   For nominal values, the mode is used: This is 'the value that occurs most frequently in a distribution of values' (Bryman, 2016: 693). You can only use mode.

Box 9.1   SPSS instructions for measures of central tendency

1   Click on the 'Analyze' tab located at the top of the screen (you can be in either data view or variable view).
2   Click on 'Descriptive Statistics' and then 'Frequencies'.
3   All your variables (questionnaire questions) appear in the list on the left-hand side. Pick your independent variable(s) and dependent variable(s), one at a time, and move to the 'variable(s):' list on the right using the arrow button (located between the variable list and the variable box).
4   Click 'Statistics' (buttons down the right-hand side).
5   From the 'Central Tendency' section on the right-hand side, select 'Mean', 'Median', or 'Mode' as appropriate.
6   Click 'Continue'.
7   Click 'OK'.
8   The output window now opens and you will see the results of your analysis.
9   Copy and paste the 'Statistics' table into a text (Microsoft Word/Pages) document.

Structuring your measures of central tendency analysis

You can see how this might work by considering an example. Imagine that your variable is the age that people first tried the illegal drug cocaine. You have asked 15 cocaine users (valid N) how old they were when they first tried cocaine and you have collected the following data:

AGE (in years) – 17, 18, 18, 19, 19, 19, 19, 20, 20, 20, 21, 21, 23, 26, 28

Following the structure outlined above in the introduction to this section, your measures of central tendency analysis would look as follows:

State the statistical test being used: Measures of central tendency

Identify the variable: Select one variable only; in this case – AGE

State the hypothesis

Based on previous research literature, what do you think the measures of central tendency will be for your variable? If the research literature has suggested that most people's first experience with cocaine was whilst they were still teenagers, then your hypothesis might be that 'people who use cocaine are likely to have first tried the drug before they reach the age of 20'.

RESULTS TABLE

AGE (in years)	
Valid N	15
Mean	20.53
Median	20
Mode	19

INTERPRET THE TABLE

State the mean, median, or mode as appropriate for your variable, and what this means in relation to your variable. In this example, for the AGE variable, there is a mean of 20.53 years, median of 20 years, and mode of 19 years. This means that the average age at which those in the sample first tried cocaine was at 20.53 years old. The middle age for this occurrence was 20 years old. The most common age was 19 years old (see Table 9.1). Note that because AGE is an interval/ratio (scale) variable, it is possible to use all three measures of central tendency. If your variable is ordinal, you can only use median and mode. If your variable is nominal then you can only use mode.

STATE WHETHER YOU HAVE PROVEN OR DISPROVEN YOUR HYPOTHESIS

In this case, there is only partial support for the hypothesis; the mode offers support for it as it suggests that people first try cocaine whilst they are still teenagers, but the mean and the median suggest people first try cocaine once they are slightly over the age of 20.

Table 9.1 Interpreting measures of central tendency

AGE (in years)

	Outcome	How to interpret outcome
Valid N	15	This is the number of people who answered your question (your sample)
Mean	20.53	This is the average age at which those in your sample first tried cocaine
Median	20	This is the middle age at which those in your sample first tried cocaine
Mode	19	This is the most common age at which those in your sample first tried cocaine

STATE HOW YOUR INFERENCES RELATE TO PREVIOUS RESEARCH
FINDINGS FROM YOUR LITERATURE REVIEW

This involves identifying similarities and differences between your inferences and the existing literature. The research literature had suggested that most people's first experience with cocaine was whilst they were still teenagers; these inferences suggest that people's first experience with cocaine is sometimes whilst they are still teenagers, but for many it tends to be slightly older than this, in the very early 20s. Thus this research might offer a slight refinement to the existing knowledge on the topic.

STATE HOW YOUR INFERENCES HELP YOU ANSWER YOUR
RESEARCH QUESTIONS

This depends entirely on the nature of the research questions which we have not covered in this example.

Frequency

A **frequency** is the number of times a value or category occurs in one variable. A frequency table clearly illustrates this and tends to be the starting point for most analyses. Frequency tables can also be used to ascertain the level of measurement for a variable as they make clear the response categories of each variable.

The columns in a frequency table are as follows, and can be seen in the example below in the 'structuring your frequency analysis' section:

- Frequency: This shows the number of times that the response category occurs in the variable.
- Percent: This gives the frequency as a percentage of the entire data for the variable (thus it shows the proportion of respondents in each category).
- Valid percent: This gives the frequency as a percentage of the *valid* data only (it excludes missing data).
- Cumulative percent: This gives a running total of the valid percentage (it excludes missing data).

Box 9.2   SPSS instructions for frequencies

1   Click on the 'Analyze' tab located at the top of the screen (you can be in either data view or variable view).
2   Click on 'Descriptive Statistics' and then 'Frequencies'.
3   All your variables (survey questions) appear in the list on the left-hand side. Pick your independent variable(s) and dependent variable(s), one at a time, and move to the 'variable(s):' list on the right using the arrow button (located between the variable list and the variable box).
4   Click 'OK'.
5   The output window now opens and you will see the results of your analysis.
6   Copy and paste the frequencies table into a text (Microsoft Word/Pages) document.

Structuring your frequency analysis

Once again, it is useful to see how this might work by considering an example. In this case, imagine a study that looks at rates of participation in graffiti. Following the structure outlined above in the introduction to this section, your frequency analysis would look as follows:

State statistical test: Frequency

Identify the variable: Select one variable only; in this case – HAVE YOU EVER ENGAGED IN GRAFFITI?

State the hypothesis

How much of your data will fall into each response category? Based on the research literature, it could be hypothesised that fewer people will have engaged in graffiti than those who have.

RESULTS TABLE

HAVE YOU EVER ENGAGED IN GRAFFITI?		Frequency	Percent	Valid percent	Cumulative percent
Valid	Yes	25	25	32.5	32.5
	No	52	52	67.5	100
	Total	77	77	100	
Missing	Missing	23	23		
Total		100	100		

INTERPRET THE TABLE

In a frequency analysis there are a number of things to include as follows:

•   The total number of respondents in the sample (overall total): In our example, there are 100 respondents.

- The number and percentage of people who answered the question (valid cases): In our example, there are 77 valid cases; 77 people (77%) answered the question.
- The number and percentage of people who did not answer the question (missing cases): In our example, there are 23 (23%) missing cases; 23 people did not answer the question.
- The frequency (count) and percentage for each response category:

  o   25 people (25%) answered yes, they have engaged in graffiti.
  o   52 people (52%) answered no, they have not engaged in graffiti.

- Comment on valid percent if necessary; that is, if there is a large amount of missing data. In our example, because there is a large amount of missing data (23%), it is useful to do this as missing data can skew your results. Of those who answered this question, 32.5% answered that they have engaged in graffiti, compared to 67.5% who said that they have not engaged in graffiti.
- Comment on cumulative percent if necessary, for example if you need to recode (see section on **crosstabs**). In our example, because there are only two response categories (yes and no), it is not necessary to discuss the cumulative percent.

STATE WHETHER YOU HAVE PROVEN OR DISPROVEN YOUR HYPOTHESIS

In this case, the data have proven the hypothesis. Fewer people have engaged in graffiti than those who have not.

STATE HOW YOUR INFERENCES RELATE TO PREVIOUS RESEARCH
FINDINGS FROM YOUR LITERATURE REVIEW

This involves identifying similarities and differences between your inferences and the existing literature: In this example, the findings from the previous literature have been corroborated, although there may be interesting points to make about the proportion of people who admit to having engaged in graffiti, and how this is similar or different to the previous findings.

STATE HOW YOUR INFERENCES HELP YOU ANSWER YOUR RESEARCH QUESTIONS

Of course, this depends entirely on the nature of the research questions which we have not covered in this example.

Bivariate analysis

Bivariate analysis is 'the examination of the relationship between two variables' (Bryman, 2016: 688). A bivariate analysis can determine whether two variables are related in some way (i.e. if a dependent variable is related to an independent variable). Independent variables usually relate to the respondent's personal characteristics, such as age, gender, ethnicity, and so on. Dependent variables tend to relate to the phenomenon that you are investigating, for example perceptions about some aspect of the criminal justice system. Your bivariate analysis will allow you to ascertain whether variation in the independent variable (for example, someone's age) coincides with a variation in the dependent variables (for example, perceptions of the police).

It is important to stress that bivariate analyses simply allow you to determine if there is a relationship between the variables under study. It does not determine if there is causality. Determining causality (internal validity) is linked to your research design

Table 9.2 Types of bivariate analysis

Type of analysis	Level of measurement		Example
	Independent variable	*Dependent variable*	
Crosstabs	Nominal or ordinal + (< 4 response categories)	Nominal or ordinal + (< 4 response categories)	IV: Gender (nominal) DV: Home security features (nominal)
Cramer's V correlation	At least one variable is nominal	At least one variable is nominal	IV: Gender (nominal) DV: Illegal drugs used (nominal)
Spearman's rho correlation	Ordinal Interval/ratio (scale)	Interval/ratio (scale) Ordinal	IV: Education (ordinal) DV: Victimisation (scale) IV: Age (scale) DV: Worry about being burgled (ordinal)
Pearson's r correlation	Interval/ratio (scale)	Interval/ratio (scale)	IV: Age (scale) DV: Victimisation (scale)

(see Chapter 7 – Research design and sampling): research that utilises a cross-sectional design does not allow for causation to be inferred.

This section will focus on two types of bivariate analysis: crosstabs and correlation. Three types of correlation, Cramer's V, Spearman's rho, and Pearson's r, will be discussed. The type of analysis that you carry out will depend upon the levels of measurement for your two variables. Table 9.2 can help you to ascertain which type of analysis to use, along with the requirements of your central research question.

Crosstabs

Crosstab tables are essentially an extension of the univariate analysis frequency tables that we have already discussed above. The difference is that crosstab tables analyse two variables at the same time, and therefore they allow for the exploration of the association between two variables. Crosstab tables show the relationship between all possible category combinations, and compare the percentages associated with each category in the columns and rows. Crosstab tables also tell you the amount of missing data as a result, for instance, of people not answering the survey question. This is important as a large amount of missing data can skew your results, as we have already seen in relation to frequencies.

In this book, the independent variable is placed in the 'column' and the dependent variable in the 'row'. Note that this is not a universal rule and this needs to be set in SPSS. Comparisons should utilise the percentages rather than the frequencies.

Box 9.3   SPSS instructions for crosstabs

1   To carry out a crosstabs analysis, variables should have a smaller number of response categories. Two response categories per variable is ideal, although a maximum of four is possible. If your variable has more than four response categories (which is almost always the case with ordinal and scale level data), then you must recode it.

2 Recode variables as required. For instructions on recoding see 'Recoding Variables in SPSS': www.youtube.com/watch?v=7qKPB7ntTTI.
3 Click on the 'Analyze' tab located at the top of the screen (you can be in either data view or variable view).
4 Click on 'Descriptive statistics' and then 'Crosstabs'.
5 Put your dependent variable in the 'Row(s):' box.
6 Put your independent variable in the 'Column(s):' box.
7 Click on 'Cells' and check 'Percentages' – 'Column'. Click 'Continue'.
8 Click 'OK'.
9 The output window now opens and you will see the results of your analysis.
10 Copy and paste the 'Crosstabs' tables into a text (Microsoft Word/Pages) document.

Structuring your crosstabs analysis

Imagine that you are studying the relationship between gender and involvement in crime. Your crosstabs analysis would be structured as follows:

State the statistical test being used: Crosstabs

IDENTIFY THE VARIABLES

You need one independent variable and one dependent variable. In this case the independent variable is GENDER and the dependent variable is INVOLVEMENT IN CRIME.

STATE THE HYPOTHESIS

There will be a relationship between the independent and dependent variables; in this case, you might hypothesise that there will be a relationship between gender and involvement in crime, with males being more involved in crime than females, based on your reading of previous research literature and crime statistics.

RESULTS TABLES

Valid	425
Missing	53

Involved in crime	Gender				Total
	Male		Female		
Yes	75	33%	50	25%	125
No	150	67%	150	75%	300
Total	225	100%	200	100%	425

INTERPRET THE TABLE

- Comment on valid and missing numbers and percentages: In our example there are 425 valid cases and 53 missing cases.
- Compare the percentages across the independent variable response categories with each of the dependent variable response categories. Go through each of the dependent variable response categories in turn: In our example 75 of the 225 men (33%) report being involved in crime; 50 of the 200 women (25%) report being involved in crime, which are highlighted in grey; 150 of the 225 men (67%) report not being involved in crime; 150 of the 200 women (75%) report not being involved in crime, which are highlighted in black).
- Calculate the difference (as expressed in percentages) between the categories of the independent variable. Subtract the smaller grey figure from the larger grey figure, and the smaller black figure from the larger black figure. The greater the percentage difference, the bigger the influence of the independent variable: In our example, there is an 8% difference in involvement in crime between men and women, with men the higher, and an 8% difference in non-involvement in crime between men and women, with women the higher).
- How influential is the independent variable? Some argue there is an association between the variables if the difference is greater than 10%: In our example gender appears to have some influence on involvement in crime, but as the difference is 8% this can be considered a relatively small influence).

STATE WHETHER YOU HAVE PROVEN OR DISPROVEN YOUR HYPOTHESIS

In this instance the hypothesis is proven as the empirical data suggests that gender does influence involvement in crime, with men being more involved in crime than women. However, the differences are small as there is only a weak association between the distribution of data in one variable and the distribution in another.

STATE HOW YOUR INFERENCES RELATE TO PREVIOUS RESEARCH
FINDINGS FROM YOUR LITERATURE REVIEW

This involves identifying similarities and differences between your inferences and the existing literature. As the literature and crime statistics suggested that men are likely to be more involved in crime than women, these inferences provide support for this.

STATE HOW YOUR INFERENCES HELP YOU ANSWER YOUR RESEARCH QUESTIONS

This depends entirely on the nature of the research questions which we have not covered in this example.

Correlation

Correlations are analyses that show how two variables vary in relation to one another. Correlations show the

> degree to which the scores (from a set of subjects) on two variables co-relate. That is, the extent to which a variation in the scores on one variable results in a corresponding variation in the scores on the second variable.

(Hinton, 2014: 344)

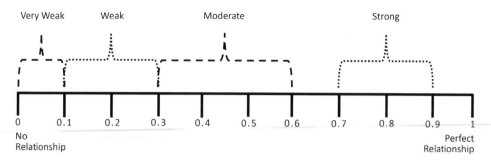

Figure 9.2 Interpreting correlation coefficients.

In this regard, correlations are similar to crosstabs. However, there are some key differences between the two. Firstly, correlations allow you to deal with the different (higher) levels of measurement, namely ordinal and scale level data. Secondly, correlations allow you to work with data that has more than four response categories, which is the realistic limit for crosstabs. Thirdly, correlations allow for a more precise measure of the strength of the relationship than crosstabs.

The type of correlation that is appropriate to use depends upon the variable's level of measurement. The three types of bivariate **correlation coefficient** tests that are covered here are Cramer's V (used when working with nominal variables), Spearman's rho (used when working with ordinal and interval/ratio (scale) variables) and Pearson's r (used when working with interval/ratio (scale) variables).

All three of these tests produce a correlation coefficient which is a measure of the strength of the association between two variables, and in the case of Spearman's rho and Pearson's r also the direction of the relationship. The coefficient provides a numerical representation, which lies between 0 and 1, of how a change in one variable is associated with a change in another. The closer to zero, the weaker the association between the variables, and the closer to 1, the stronger the association. Generally speaking, >0.1 is a very weak relationship, 0.1–0.2 is a weak relationship, 0.3–0.6 is a moderate relationship, and 0.7–0.9 is a strong relationship (see Figure 9.2).

Spearman's rho and Pearson's r also measure the direction of the relationship in addition to its strength. In a positive relationship, the values or the response categories move in the same direction. In the example in Table 9.3, there is a positive relationship between age and how often a person worries about being the victim of a home burglary. As age increases, so does how often a person worries about that eventuality. As you move up the 'age' variable, you also move up the 'worry' variable.

Table 9.3 Positive correlation coefficient in relation to response categories and values

Example of a positive relationship			
Variables	Age		How often do you worry about being the victim of a house burglary?
Response categories	20s		Never
	30s		Yearly
	40s	⬇ ⬇	Monthly
	50s		Weekly
	60s		Daily

Table 9.4 Negative correlation coefficient in relation to response categories and values

Example of a negative relationship			
Variables	Age		How often do you worry about being the victim of a house burglary?
Response categories	20s 30s 40s 50s 60s		Never Yearly Monthly Weekly Daily

Table 9.5 Which correlation coefficient test? (adapted from Bryman, 2016: 340)

Dependent variable / *Independent variable*	*Nominal*	*Ordinal*	*Interval/ratio (scale)*
Nominal	Cramer's V	Cramer's V	Cramer's V
Ordinal	Cramer's V	Spearman's rho	Spearman's rho
Interval/ratio (scale)	Cramer's V	Spearman's rho	Pearson's r

In a negative relationship, the values or response categories move in the opposite direction. In Table 9.4, there is a negative relationship between age and how often a person worries about being the victim of a home burglary. As age increases, the rate at which a person worries about that eventuality decreases. As you move up the 'age' variable, you move down the 'worry' variable.

Table 9.5 (adapted from Bryman, 2016: 340) provides guidance on which correlation coefficient test should be adopted in particular situations. This hinges on the level of measurement of your independent and dependent variables, and as discussed earlier, it is therefore vital to fully understand levels of measurement in order to select the correct correlation coefficient test.

Cramer's V

Cramer's V is the correlation coefficient that should be used whenever a nominal variable is involved in your analysis. This is because it measures the strength of the relationship between a categorical variable and a second variable where it is not possible to evaluate direction. Cramer's V can be used when there are two nominal variables, a nominal variable and an ordinal variable, or a nominal and a scale variable.

Box 9.4   SPSS instructions for Cramer's V

1   Click on 'Analyze', then click 'Descriptive statistics' and then 'Crosstabs'.
2   Put your dependent variable in the 'Row(s):' box.
3   Put your independent variable in the 'Column(s):' box.

4   Click on 'Cells' and check 'Percentages' – 'Column'. Click 'Continue'.
5   Click on 'Statistics' and select 'Phi and Cramer's V'. Click 'Continue'.
6   Click 'OK'.
7   The output window now opens and you will see the results of your analysis.
8   Copy and paste the 'Symmetric Measures' table into a text (Microsoft Word/ Pages) document.

Structuring your Cramer's V analysis

To illustrate how a Cramer's V analysis works, let's return to the example on gender and involvement in crime. Your Cramer's V analysis would look as follows:

State the statistical test being used: Cramer's V

IDENTIFY THE VARIABLES

You need one independent variable and one dependent variable; in this case the independent variable is GENDER and the dependent variable is INVOLVEMENT IN CRIME.

STATE THE HYPOTHESIS

There will be a relationship between the independent and dependent variables; in this case, you might hypothesise that there will be a strong relationship between gender and involvement in crime, based on your reading of previous research literature and crime statistics.

RESULTS TABLE

		Value	*Approximate significance*
	Cramer's V	0.112	0.090
Number of valid cases		425	

INTERPRET THE TABLE

*   Assess the strength of the relationship between the independent and dependent variable. Strength operates on a continuum from 0 to 1, where 0 is no relationship and 1 is a perfect relationship. In our example the strength, highlighted in grey, is 0.112.
*   For analysis, >0.1 = very weak relationship, 0.1–0.2 = weak relationship, 0.3–0.6 = moderate relationship, 0.7–0.9 = strong relationship. Here, the correlation of 0.112 falls between 0.1 and 0.3. In our example there is a weak relationship between gender and involvement in crime.

STATE WHETHER YOU HAVE PROVEN OR DISPROVEN YOUR HYPOTHESIS

In this case the hypothesis is disproven. There is only a weak relationship between gender and involvement in crime.

STATE HOW YOUR INFERENCES RELATE TO PREVIOUS RESEARCH
FINDINGS FROM YOUR LITERATURE REVIEW

This involves identifying similarities and differences between your inferences and the existing literature. Your reading of the literature and crime statistics suggested that there would be a strong relationship between gender and involvement in crime. However, these inferences did not provide support for this.

STATE HOW YOUR INFERENCES HELP YOU ANSWER YOUR RESEARCH QUESTIONS

This depends entirely on the nature of the research questions which we have not covered in this example.

Spearman's rho

The Spearman's rho correlation coefficient measures direction as well as strength. It is used with a pair of ordinal variables, or with an ordinal and a scale variable; at least one of the two variables must always be ordinal.

A positive correlation (+1) denotes that an increase in one variable is associated with an increase in the other variable (for example, the higher someone's age, the more they think the police are effective at catching criminals). A negative correlation (−1) is where an increase in one variable is associated with a decrease in the other variable (e.g. the higher someone's age, the less they think the police are effective at catching criminals).

Box 9.5   SPSS instructions for Spearman's rho

1   Click on the 'Analyze' tab located at the top of the screen (you can be in either data view or variable view).
2   Click on 'Correlate' and then 'Bivariate'.
3   All your variables appear in the list on the left-hand side. Pick your independent variable and dependent variable, one at a time, and move to the 'variable(s):' list on the right using the arrow button (located between the variable list and the variable box).
4   Click 'Correlation Coefficients' and check 'Spearman'.
5   Leave 'Test of significance' as two–tailed and 'flag significant correlations' checked.
6   Click 'OK'.
7   The output window now opens and you will see the results of your analysis.
8   Copy and paste the 'Correlations' table into a text (Microsoft Word/Pages) document.

Structuring your Spearman's rho analysis

To illustrate how a Spearman's rho analysis works, let us return to the earlier example of a study looking at the relationship between age and how often a person worries about being the victim of a home burglary.

State the statistical test being used: Spearman's rho

IDENTIFY THE VARIABLES

You need one independent variable and one dependent variable; in this case, the independent variable is AGE and the dependent variable is HOW OFTEN A PERSON WORRIES ABOUT BEING THE VICTIM OF A HOME BURGLARY.

STATE THE HYPOTHESIS

There will be a positive or negative and a strong, moderate or weak relationship between the independent and dependent variables; in this case, based on previous research, we might hypothesise that there will be a moderate, positive relationship between age and how often a person worries about being the victim of a home burglary.

RESULTS TABLE

		Age	*How often a person worries about being the victim of a home burglary*
Age	Spearman correlation	1	0.345
	Sig. (2-tailed)		0.010
	N	350	350
How often a person worries about being the victim of a home burglary	Spearman correlation	0.345	1
	Sig. (2-tailed)	0.010	
	N	350	350

INTERPRET THE TABLE

- Assess the strength of the relationship between the independent and dependent variable. In our example, the correlation coefficient is 0.345.
- Strength operates on a continuum from 0 to 1, where 0 is no relationship and 1 is a perfect relationship. For analysis, >0.1 = very weak relationship, 0.1–0.2 = weak relationship, 0.3–0.6 = moderate relationship, 0.7–0.9 = strong relationship. In our example, there is a moderate relationship between age and how often a person worries about being the victim of a home burglary.
- Assess the direction of the relationship between the independent and dependent variables. In our example, the Spearman's rho is 0.345, which is a positive correlation coefficient, which means there is a positive relationship between age and how often a person worries about being the victim of a home burglary. The positive relationship means that the older you get, the more often you worry about being the victim of a home burglary. This can be seen in Table 9.6. A table such as this can be included in your own interpretation of your results. A negative Spearman's rho would have indicated a negative relationship between age and how often a person worries about being the victim of a home burglary.
- Optional: If you want to comment on significance (Sig. (2-tailed)), see Hinton (2014).

STATE WHETHER YOU HAVE PROVEN OR DISPROVEN YOUR HYPOTHESIS

In this case the hypothesis is proven. There is a moderate, positive relationship between age and how often a person worries about being the victim of a home burglary. An increase in age sees an increase in how often a person worries about being the victim of a home burglary.

Table 9.6 Assessing the direction of the relationship between age and how often a person worries about being the victim of a home burglary

Direction of relationship between age and how often a person worries about being the victim of a home burglary		
Variables	Age	How often do you worry about being the victim of a home burglary?
Response categories	20s 30s 40s 50s 60s	Never Yearly Monthly Weekly Daily

STATE HOW YOUR INFERENCES RELATE TO PREVIOUS RESEARCH
FINDINGS FROM YOUR LITERATURE REVIEW

Identify similarities and differences between your inferences and the existing literature. In this case our reading of previous research led us to hypothesise that there would be a moderate, positive relationship between age and how often a person worries about being the victim of a home burglary. This proved to be the case.

STATE HOW YOUR INFERENCES HELP YOU ANSWER YOUR RESEARCH QUESTIONS

This depends entirely on the nature of the research questions which we have not covered in this example.

Pearson's r

Like Spearman's rho, the widely used Pearson's r correlation coefficient measures direction as well as strength, but it is used only with two interval/ratio (scale) variables in order to measure their linear relationship. As Field (2009: 791) puts it, Pearson's r is

> a standardized measure of the strength of relationship between two variables. It can take any value from −1 (as one variable changes, the other changes in the opposite direction by the same amount), through 0 (as one variable changes, the other doesn't change at all), to +1 (as one variable changes, the other changes in the same direction by the same amount).

Box 9.6   SPSS instructions for Pearson's r

- Click on the 'Analyze' tab located at the top of the screen (you can be in either data view or variable view).
- Click on 'Correlate' and then 'Bivariate'.
- All your variables appear in the list on the left-hand side. Pick your independent variable and dependent variable, one at a time, and move to the 'variable(s):' list on the right using the arrow button (located between the variable list and the variable box).

- Click 'Correlation Coefficients' and check 'Pearson'.
- Leave 'Test of significance' as two-tailed and 'flag significant correlations' checked.
- Click 'OK'.
- The output window now opens and you will see the results of your analysis.
- Copy and paste the 'Correlations' table into a text (Microsoft Word/Pages) document.

Structuring your Pearson's r analysis

For our step-by-step guide to how a Pearson's r analysis works, we use the example of a study looking at the relationship between age and experiences of victimisation.

State the statistical test being used: Pearson's r

IDENTIFY THE VARIABLES

You need one independent variable and one dependent variable; in this case, the independent variable is AGE and the dependent variable is NUMBER OF TIMES A VICTIM OF CRIME IN THE PAST YEAR.

STATE THE HYPOTHESIS

There will be a positive or negative and a strong, moderate, or weak relationship between the independent and dependent variables; in this case let us assume that our reading of the existing research literature and statistics has led us to hypothesise that there will be a weak, positive relationship between age and number of times a victim of crime in the past year.

RESULTS TABLE

		Age	*Number of times a victim of crime in the past year*
Age	Pearson correlation	1	0.287
	Sig. (2-tailed)		0.004
	N	350	350
Number of times a victim of crime in the past year	Pearson correlation	0.287	1
	Sig. (2-tailed)	0.004	
	N	350	350

INTERPRET THE TABLE

- Assess the strength of the relationship between the independent and dependent variable. In our example, the correlation coefficient is 0.287.
- Strength operates on a continuum from 0 to 1, where 0 is no relationship and 1 is a perfect relationship. For analysis, >0.1 = very weak relationship, 0.1–0.2 = weak relationship, 0.3–0.6 = moderate relationship, 0.7–0.9 = strong relationship. In our example, there is a weak relationship between age and number of times a victim of crime in the past year.

- Assess the direction of the relationship between the independent and dependent variables. In our example, the Pearson's r is 0.287 which is a positive correlation coefficient, which means there is a positive relationship between age and number of times a victim of crime in the past year. The positive relationship means that the older you get, the more likely you are to be a victim of crime in the past year. This can be seen in Table 9.7. A table such as this can be included in your own interpretation of your results. A negative Spearman's rho would have indicated a negative relationship.
- Optional: If you want to comment on significance (Sig. (2-tailed)), see Hinton (2014).

STATE WHETHER YOU HAVE PROVEN OR DISPROVEN YOUR HYPOTHESIS

In this case the hypothesis is proven. There is a weak, positive relationship between age and the number of times someone has been a victim of crime in the past year. An increase in age sees an increase in the chances of being a past-year victim of crime.

STATE HOW YOUR INFERENCES RELATE TO PREVIOUS RESEARCH
FINDINGS FROM YOUR LITERATURE REVIEW

Identify similarities and differences between your inferences and the existing literature. In this case our reading of previous research led us to hypothesise that there would be a weak, positive relationship between age and number of times a victim of crime in the past year. This proved to be the case.

STATE HOW YOUR INFERENCES HELP YOU ANSWER YOUR RESEARCH QUESTIONS

Once again, this depends entirely on the nature of the research questions which we have not covered in this example.

Qualitative data analysis

The purpose of this section is to provide a set of straightforward instructions to conduct a simple, but systematic, qualitative **thematic analysis**. This represents one of many ways of analysing qualitative data, and we introduce it here because it will give you an effective way to analyse the data collected using the qualitative methods outlined in Chapter 8 – Data collection methods, namely: research interviews, focus groups and media analysis.

Table 9.7 Assessing the direction of the relationship between age and number of times a victim of crime in the past year

Direction of relationship between age and number of times a victim of crime in the past year

Variables	Age			Number of times a victim of crime in the past year
Response Values	20			1
	21	↓	↓	2
	22			3
	23			4
	24 . . .			5 . . .

Numerous specialist textbooks provide an in-depth account of a wide variety of qualitative data analysis methods. We recommend seeking out these texts, such as those listed in Box 9.7, to give you a stronger understanding of this technique, as well as an insight into more complex approaches, to supplement the information provided in this chapter.

Box 9.7   Specialist qualitative data analysis textbooks

- Galman, S. (2017). *The Good, the Bad and the Data.* Abingdon: Routledge.
- Silverman, D. (2014). *Interpreting Qualitative Data* (5th ed.). London: SAGE.
- Wincup, E. (2017). *Criminological Research: Understanding Qualitative Methods* (2nd ed.). London: SAGE.

Before exploring the mechanics of 'doing' qualitative data analysis, it is important to consider its theoretical foundations. Denscombe (2008: 287) suggests there are four guiding principles to discovering information from qualitative data analysis:

1   Conclusions should be rooted in the data: the data are the evidence from which all conclusions should be drawn
2   Explanations of the data should emerge from a careful and meticulous reading of the data: the meaning derived from the data is the result of the researcher's interpretation
3   Avoid introducing unwarranted preconceptions: do not make any assumptions or bring any personal bias into the analysis
4   The analysis of data should involve an iterative process: a process that moves back and forth comparing data, sensitising concepts, codes, and themes

Qualitative thematic analysis is where the researcher searches for themes in the data through the systematic process of **coding** and **theme** generation. In this chapter we outline a simple procedure to undertake this type of analysis, which can be followed in a step-by-step fashion. The completion of the analysis will result in the creation of a set of inferences for your qualitative components(s). We break down the analysis process into five stages:

1   Authenticating the data
2   Sensitising concepts
3   Coding
4   Codes to themes
5   Generating themes

Before outlining how to conduct a qualitative thematic analysis, we have a few notes of caution. Due to the nature of qualitative research, be prepared for the analysis to take a substantial amount of time. It cannot be rushed (without compromising the quality of the outcome), so do not leave the analysis until the last minute. Relatedly, at the beginning of the process it can seem like a huge, daunting task, which can lead to avoiding the process. The best remedy is to make a start and work through the process step by step. You may have to take a step back in the process if things are not progressing as planned, which is okay. Research is not a linear or straightforward enterprise. Finally, there is no 'right answer' in qualitative research. Therefore you will have to rely on your academic judgement to create a set of themes that you believe accurately reflect the data, and answers your central research question/qualitative sub-question(s). You can do it!

Authenticating the data

Qualitative thematic analysis begins by getting to know the data and completing the authentication process. This may seem an unnecessary step if you collected the data yourself, but to get the most from your analysis you need to be really familiar with your dataset. Consequently, this is a worthwhile endeavour for the analysis of both primary and secondary qualitative data.

You will authenticate the data on a document-by-document basis. For example, you will complete the following process for each interview transcript or media article in your dataset. Ideally, your document will be saved in a word-processing format (e.g. Microsoft Word or Pages), as you will eventually need to add your own words to the end of each document. You will also code this version of the data in stage three of the analysis process.

The first step of authentication is to read through each document slowly and carefully, avoiding skim reading. At the end write a brief summary (roughly 100 words) of the contents of the document. This stage helps you to bring the overall sentiment of the document into a shortened format, which can be referred to later in the analysis process to remind you about the key details contained in that specific document. This is especially helpful if you have numerous interviews/media analyses to analyse as it provides a quick reference point.

Stage two of the authentication process is to consider how the data were collected. The purpose of this practice is to collate a standardised set of information about each document, which can be used to assess the quality and integrity of the data. Once the themes and inferences have been generated, this information will help you to assess whether your research has high or low levels of **trustworthiness** and **authenticity**. Further information about these evaluative terms can be found in Chapter 10 – Critique. A simple way to record this information is to create a proforma, which you can copy and paste at the end of each document, underneath the summary you have written. The proforma should contain the following information:

- Interview title: This is for administrative purposes, e.g. interview 1.
- Who conducted the interview/created the document?: Was it you? Who created or authored it if it was not you?
- What were the conditions in which it was undertaken?: Was it an interview on a university campus, or by telephone or Skype/FaceTime?
- Are you satisfied this document is not a fake/forgery?: As far as you are aware, is the document legitimate?
- Were the contents witnessed first-hand by you?: Yes or no.
- Has the document been edited in any way?: Yes or no. If yes, provide details. For example, have names and places been removed to maintain participant anonymity? If it is a media article, have any corrections/clarifications been made?

Sensitising concepts

The next stage of the qualitative analysis process is to begin creating the systematic way you are going to search for themes in your data. This involves the creation of a range of **sensitising concepts**. Bryman (2016: 696) defines these as 'a guide in an investigation, so that it points in a general way to what is relevant or important'. Essentially, you have to create a list of terms (sensitising concepts) that will guide you towards information in the text that will help you to answer your central research question. Therefore, your sensitising concepts are the foundation to your thematic analysis and require careful thought and consideration.

Students often have two questions about sensitising concepts: What should they be? And how many do I need? Due to the flexible nature of qualitative research and the way mixed methods research is driven by your central research question or qualitative sub-question(s), there are no definitive answers to these questions. We can point you in the right direction, but ultimately the decision will rest on your own academic judgement. This is simply part of the research process and you should be confident in your decisions; you are on the way to becoming a graduate or postgraduate criminological researcher, so trust your instincts.

There are four different aspects to consider when developing your sensitising concepts: your central research question, previous literature, your quantitative component, and the nature of media articles (for media analysis only), which we will discuss in turn.

The constitution of your sensitising concepts will first and foremost depend on your central research question, or qualitative sub-question(s), and what you are attempting to discover through your qualitative component(s). For example, if your qualitative subsidiary question is 'how do people feel about the police?', then it would be reasonable that one of your sensitising concepts would relate to feelings in some way, for example it could be 'emotions' or 'attitudes'. This would allow you to search the data for instances that relate to this aspect of your question.

Secondly, another source of information to help you create your sensitising concepts is your literature review. Previous research studies will have highlighted a range of factors that are associated with your central research question, so re-visiting the qualitative subsidiary question 'how do people feel about the police?', a range of sensitising concepts could be employed, such as 'confidence' or 'visibility' that have already been highlighted by scholars such as Merry et al. (2012).

Thirdly, in a mixed methods research project you may also find it useful to create sensitising concepts that are linked to your quantitative component. Your sensitising concepts could be developed alongside your quantitative component in a simultaneous study, or your sensitising concepts could emerge from your quantitative inferences if you are employing a sequential design. For example, a quantitative subsidiary question might be: 'what is the relationship between personal characteristics and attitudes towards the police?'. Therefore it would be useful to include sensitising concepts that relate to personal characteristics such as 'age', 'gender', and 'ethnicity'. As you can see, to generate a set of sensitising concepts related to your study, you are pooling a range of information together to identify the most important terms that will help you to locate the most relevant information in your qualitative dataset. Finally, if you are undertaking a media analysis, as well as including sensitising concepts linked to your research questions, the literature, and other data collection components, it is worthwhile considering the nature of media in your analysis. For example, when selecting your dataset of media articles, have you prioritised the collection of articles from tabloid newspapers? If so, then you may want to employ a sensitising concept that examines the language used to talk about your topic of study. For instance, if your central research question is 'what are public attitudes towards the police?', you may have decided to employ a media analysis to determine how tabloid newspapers portray the police. Subsequently, your sensitising concepts should reflect the language used, which could consider aspects such as positive or negative portrayals e.g. 'positive commentary' and 'negative commentary', or maybe the use of colloquial terms e.g. 'slang'. Other media-related aspects to consider include factors such as political affiliation and types of evidence used.

The number of sensitising concepts required for your thematic analysis will depend on the size and scope of your research project, as well as your central research question. For an undergraduate research project it is reasonable to have four or five sensitising concepts. This should be sufficient to generate enough themes to allow you to answer your research questions. As a guide, between one and three is probably too few and anything much above six or seven is likely to be unmanageable. For postgraduate students, the size of your study may allow for more than four or five sensitising concepts to be accommodated, and you may also have a greater amount of time to complete the analysis. However, this does not automatically mean that you should have a greater number of sensitising concepts, as the driving factor is creating a set of sensitising concepts that help you to answer your central research question. Your set of sensitising concepts is likely to build as you work through your analysis. It is okay to add additional sensitising concepts after analysing some of the data and similarly it is okay to discard one if it proves to be irrelevant. Flexibility is one of the advantages of undertaking qualitative data analysis.

Coding

The next stage of the qualitative thematic analysis process is known as coding, which helps you to reduce a large amount of data into a manageable size. This is achieved by using the sensitising concepts to code key information in the dataset. Coding is a methodical procedure. It is the part of thematic analysis that requires the most time, so be sure to set aside a substantial period to complete it. Based on our own and our students' experiences, the stages of coding outlined in Box 9.8 deliver the most satisfactory outcomes. We recommend that you undertake the coding process electronically using a word processor (e.g. Microsoft Word or Pages).

Box 9.8   How to code

Coding is a repetitive, **iterative process**. We suggest that you work through each sensitising concept at a time, analysing all the documents using that same sensitising concept in turn, following the instructions below:

1   Select a sensitising concept, bearing in mind you will work through each sensitising concept in turn.
2   Begin reading through your first document. Wherever you identify something in the text that relates to your sensitising concept, code it.

3 To code in Microsoft Word, highlight the text using the mouse (or with the keyboard using 'shift' and '<' or '>'). Click on the Review tab, then New Comment. In Pages, click on Insert, then Comment. This creates a comment bubble.

4 In the comment bubble you need to record some important information. Firstly, for administrative purposes, you should write the sensitising concept, then insert a colon ':'. For example, for a qualitative component exploring how people feel about the police, with a sensitising concept of 'confidence', it would look like this:

Confidence:

5 Then, in the bubble, you should write a short sentence that briefly explains how the text you have highlighted relates to the sensitising concept in question. For example, the bubble might read:

Confidence: reduced

after police officer did

not call back

There is no right or wrong way to do this. Essentially, these snippets of information are notes you write to yourself to assist the analysis process. You can include more information if you wish.

6 Go through the rest of the document, repeating this process to identify all the detailed meanings that relate to this sensitising concept. Remember, there are no right or wrong answers – it is all down to your individual interpretations.

7 Repeat this process for all the documents to be analysed.

8 Move onto the next sensitising concept and repeat steps 1–7 again. Do this until you have coded all of your transcripts with each sensitising concept.

*** WARNING ***

This is a detailed, reflective process. Avoid rushing in case you miss anything, and always keep your central research question/qualitative subsidiary question(s) in mind, as well as being open to new ideas.

Students often ask how many codes are required for each sensitising concept, as well as how many codes are needed in total. This is another question that does not have a definitive answer, as it all depends on the size of your dataset, the number of sensitising concepts you have created, and your central research question/qualitative subsidiary question(s). You will quickly realise if you do not have enough codes when you begin to undertake the codes to themes stage of the analysis process, which is outlined in the next section. Consider re-examining the documents to see whether greater detail can be added to the existing codes. You may also realise that you need to create a new, more relevant, sensitising concept.

Codes to themes

Once you have coded all the documents in your qualitative dataset, you can begin the process of generating your themes. This can only be undertaken once the coding is complete, so be sure not to cut corners and skip ahead to this stage if you are not ready, as it will only create confusion later.

The first part of the theme generation process is to collate all the codes you have created in the comment bubbles into one manageable document. This will allow you to assess everything that you consider to be relevant to the sensitising concepts across the whole dataset in one place, allowing you to explore the connections between different responses from participants. We recommend that you collate all the codes into a table, which we call the **codes to themes table** as shown in Table 9.8, as this will bring everything together in one place. This will allow you to explore the connections between the different codes and start to think about themes.

The theme generation process begins with some administrative work by creating the codes to themes table. Initially, your first sensitising concept is entered into the first cell on the left-hand side of the row (labelled as cell 'A' in Table 9.8). Starting with your first document, copy and paste all the content from every comment bubble that relates to the first sensitising concept into the 'codes' cell on that row (labelled as cell 'B' in Table 9.8). Include: the comment bubble number, the sensitising concept and your brief explanation. Repeat this process for every sensitising concept. This will be a lengthy process. However, the purpose of a thematic data analysis is to examine the data in-depth to ensure you can draw appropriate and relevant conclusions from your dataset. By undertaking a thorough process you are building trustworthiness into your work; specifically,

Table 9.8 The codes to themes table

Sensitising concept	Codes	Theme
A Sensitising concept 1	B Document 1 [Comment bubble number]: [Sensitising concept 1]: sentence detailing what the data tells you about the sensitising concept Repeat with all comment bubbles Document 2: (and so on . . .) This cell on each row will be full of your codes, making the table look distorted. This is normal.	C What the data and codes tell you about the sensitising concept
Sensitising concept 2		
Sensitising concept 3		
Sensitising concept 4		
Sensitising concept 5* You may not have five sensitising concepts; you may have more. Adapt this table to suit your analysis.		

credibility. Credibility is about making sure the research has been conducted in line with good research practice, which increases the integrity of your research inferences. See Chapter 10 – Critique for more information about the evaluative terminology. Once you have copied and pasted all the comment bubbles from every transcript for each sensitising concept, you are ready to move on to the final part of the thematic analysis process: generating themes.

Generating themes

It can be helpful to think of generating themes like the process of completing a jigsaw puzzle. The analysis that has been undertaken so far, the coding and copying and pasting the codes into the table, has allowed you to start seeing a picture about what the data are telling you. The generation of themes is the final part of the jigsaw, where the overall picture becomes clear and you can see the final product. You can begin to generate themes once you have transferred all the coding information from your comment bubbles into the codes to themes table (Table 9.8). Once you have all this information in one place, you can start to think about the different connections you can make between the data. You do this by working through each sensitising concept at a time. The themes you generate will constitute what the data and codes tell you about each sensitising concept, which should help you to answer your research question. Start with the first sensitising concept. Read through all the codes you've pasted into the table (cell 'B' in Table 9.8) to explore what different connections you can make. Essentially, these themes will emerge from this information, constituting what the data and codes tell you about the sensitising concept.

It is important to examine the codes that relate to each sensitising concept as a whole, rather than concerning yourself with what each individual participant/or document said. At this stage of proceedings it is also vital to ensure you accurately reflect the data in front of you, without making any assumptions about what the participants might think. You can only work with the data that you have. Relatedly, remember that qualitative data analysis is subjective and there is not a set answer that is expected because the inferences you produce will be the product of your own interpretation. Similarly, there is no expectation for you to generate a set number of themes for each sensitising concept, although there should be at least one.

To begin generating themes, you should examine the codes related to your sensitising concept (those in cell 'B' in Table 9.8), and think about the following three aspects suggested by Ryan and Bernard (2003) in turn. They actually propose a further five factors to consider, but we suggest these three are the foundations for a basic thematic analysis:

i) Look for repetitions in the data, so topics that occur frequently. If similar issues are reported by multiple participants or in multiple documents, it is likely that this issue is of central importance to the sensitising concept.
ii) Secondly, look for similarities and differences in the data. For example, consider whether the participants talk about the same issues in similar or different ways. Do people see things differently? If so, how? Can you determine why this is from the data you have?
iii) Finally, think about theory-related material, where you can use theory from the literature to act as a trigger for themes. For example, you may think a particular aspect from the theory is really important to your research project, so you can look for this in the data.

It can be helpful to print out your codes to themes table so you can see all the information in front of you, and you might want to use coloured highlighter pens to show links between the codes. This process can also be done electronically. Again, this is a repetitive process, so expect to read through all the information in the codes cell several times to be able to identify themes. Box 9.9 provides a researcher's account of undertaking this process. Repeat this procedure for all of the sensitising concepts to complete your thematic analysis.

Box 9.9 A researcher's account of generating themes

Here is an example from a project that explored experiences of anti-social behaviour (ASB) victimisation. There is an excerpt from the codes to themes table below that shows the sensitising concept 'ASB Experienced' in the left-hand column, the codes in the middle column, and the themes that have been generated in the right-hand column. One of the purposes of the research was to find out what types of ASB residents had been experiencing.

Table 9.9 Example codes to themes table

INVESTIGATING EXPERIENCES OF ANTI-SOCIAL BEHAVIOUR		
Sensitising Concept	*Codes*	*Themes*
ASB Experienced	TRANSCRIPT 1 1 ASB: ongoing for 6 years 2 ASB: fly-tipping 4 ASB: dog fouling 5 ASB: mistreating dog 6 ASB: dangerous dogs 15 ASB: driving without licence, speeding, no seatbelt 16 ASB: racist remarks 17 ASB: fires in garden in smoke-free zone 20 ASB: verbal abuse (rip f-ing head off) 22 ASB: false accusations of racism 24 ASB: suspected drug dealing 25 ASB: perp using victims address maliciously (court papers) 26 ASB: stalking of neighbour 27 ASB: threats to respondent and neighbours 28 ASB: false accusations of criminal damage 29 ASB: false accusations of killing cat 30 ASB: malicious advertising of van for sale 36 ASB: threatening behaviour 37 ASB: eggs thrown at window 38 ASB: knife thrown over fence	1 Experiencing personal ASB was common 2 Length of victimisation 3 Personal V nuisance ASB 4 New types of ASB

	39 ASB: followed to work
	40 ASB: accosted in supermarket
	41 ASB: name calling
	48 ASB: abusive language
	62 ASB: false accusations of a criminal
	    offence
	91 ASB: throwing stones at house
	
	TRANSCRIPT 2
	 1 ASB: bullying
	 2 ASB: criminal damage
	 3 ASB: threats
	 4 ASB: intimidation (getting in their face)
	 5 ASB: false accusations
	 6 ASB: from neighbours next door and
	    below
	 7 ASB: ongoing for 12 years
	 8 ASB: cut phone and internet lines
	15 ASB: received complaints about them
	    from neighbours	

In reality, the 'ASB Experienced' sensitising concept covered four pages. Therefore, I printed off the materials and laid them out in front of me so I could see all the data together. I read through the information in the codes column several times to ensure I was very familiar with what the participants said.

I read through the data again, looking specifically for instances of repetition. I noticed that many participants talked about experiencing personal ASB, which entails behaviours such as threats and verbal abuse. So I decided this was theme 1 – experiencing personal ASB was common. I also noticed that many participants had experienced ASB for a number of years, so length of victimisation became theme 2.

I then read through the data once more, looking for similarities and differences. This is a little bit trickier to ascertain. It appears that if people were not experiencing personal ASB, they were experiencing nuisance ASB. This is ASB that affects a community. In most cases people were either subject to one type of ASB or another, not necessarily both. So, personal versus nuisance ASB emerged as theme 3.

Finally, I read through the data one last time (you can see how many times I had to do this to achieve the end result), this time looking for theory-related material. In 2004, the Home Office created a typology of ASB that listed many different types of ASB. So, I used this as a starting point to see if the ASB experienced by my participants reflected this typology. I found that it did not. Many more new and different types of ASB were highlighted in the data (e.g. making false accusations), so new types of ASB became my fourth theme. In total, I managed to generate four themes relating to this sensitising concept.

Try to generate at least one theme per sensitising concept. If you have more than one theme per sensitising concept, start to think about which of the themes is most relevant to the findings from previous research that you identified during your literature review.

The themes you generate from completing the codes to themes table represent the inferences from the qualitative component in your mixed methods research project. The next step is to present your data and write up your inferences.

Summary

This chapter has provided a foundational introduction to quantitative and qualitative data analysis techniques. Quantitatively, we focused on running and analysing univariate and bivariate tests in SPSS. Qualitatively, we detailed how to move through the systematic stages to complete a thematic analysis. These different techniques will allow you to analyse data collected by the data collection methods outlined in Chapter 8. Combined, this is sufficient to generate the inferences and meta-inferences for your mixed methods research project. For more experienced researchers, we have signposted you to sources that detail more advanced data analysis techniques, which should allow you to develop a more sophisticated set of meta-inferences. Once you have analysed your data, Chapter 12 – Writing-up provides clear methods of presenting both your statistical data and themes which constitute your inferences.

Learning questions

1 How do the different levels of measurement affect your quantitative analysis?
2 What is the purpose of a sensitising concept?
3 Why is there no set number of codes required to conduct a qualitative thematic analysis?

10 Critique

Introduction

The ability to critically evaluate your own research, as well as others, is an important research skill. This chapter provides a comprehensive overview of how to develop a critique when undertaking a mixed methods research project. The chapter begins by explaining the value of critical analysis to the mixed methods researcher alongside an introduction to the process of critical evaluation in mixed methods research. This is followed by an outline of the established quantitative and qualitative evaluative terminology and how it can be applied, before a full discussion of mixed methods-specific terminology that can be used in a critique.

The importance of critical evaluation

When we talk about critically evaluating research, we are referring to the process of identifying the strengths and weaknesses of a piece of work. Having the skills to be able to critically evaluate criminological research is important for a number of reasons. Firstly, it allows you to appraise the work of others to assess if their findings or inferences/meta-inferences have integrity and are useful to you when developing your own research project. For instance, you may find a research study in an academic journal, which you need to critically evaluate to determine if it is suitable for inclusion in your literature review. A positive appraisal of a piece of work might lead to those findings or inferences/meta-inferences playing an influential role in shaping your own central research question. Similarly, understanding the process of critically evaluating other people's work will also help you to assess the merits of their research process, which will help you to determine the integrity and value of their results. Secondly, being able to identify the strengths and weaknesses associated with different elements of the research process will enable you to select the most appropriate process for your research project. Different research designs and sampling techniques have different advantages and disadvantages (see Chapter 7 – Research design and sampling). Being able to identify these will assist your decision-making when planning your research. Thirdly, the ability to critically evaluate your own research process, inferences and meta-inferences is a vital skill for all researchers. When presenting your work, it is imperative that you can accurately reflect on the quality and integrity of your research so you represent the inferences and meta-inferences truthfully. For example, you should always present your findings as they stand, rather than trying to elaborate them to demonstrate that you have found 'something'. A precise interpretation of the actual inferences and meta-inferences is far more valuable to the process of generating new knowledge and will often attract more marks/credit in an assessment.

Critically evaluating mixed methods research is complicated by utilising multiple research components, as well as the different philosophical considerations of the quantitative and qualitative strategies. Therefore, we suggest that conducting a critique of a mixed methods research project is a step-by-step process, shown in Box 10.1. Initially, you should critically evaluate the inferences from each component using the evaluative terminology that reflects that particular research strategy. To illustrate, for a quantitative component you should critique the inferences using the quantitative terms **reliability** and **validity**; and for a qualitative component you should critique the inferences using the qualitative terms **trustworthiness** and **authenticity**. Applying the strategy-specific evaluative terms to each component will provide a critique that reflects the epistemological and ontological differences between quantitative and qualitative research. This approach will ensure your critique is philosophically accurate and compatible with the key concerns of each strategy. Once the inferences from each component have been combined (see Chapter 6 – Combining the data), a critique of the overall mixed methods meta-inferences should be undertaken using the mixed methods-specific terms **inference quality** and **inference transferability**.

Box 10.1   Research components and their associated evaluative terminology

- Evaluate quantitative component(s) using reliability and validity
- Evaluate qualitative component(s) using trustworthiness and authenticity
- Evaluate mixed methods meta-inferences using inference quality and inference transferability

---

This chapter will now explain the evaluative terminology associated with the quantitative, qualitative and mixed methods strategies to provide the full range of vocabulary that you should use in your mixed methods research project. To develop your understanding, throughout the rest of this chapter we will use an example of a mixed methods project with one quantitative component and one qualitative component that examines students' attitudes towards the police. See Figure 10.1 for all the details.

> **Central Research Question:** What are student attitudes towards the police?

> **Description:** This mixed methods project utilised one QUANT and one QUAL component to investigate undergraduate criminology students' attitudes towards the police. A simultaneous design was employed, with both components given equal priority.

Quantitative Component	**Qualitat ive Component**
The project features of the quantitative component were as follows:	The project features of the qualitative component were as follows:
• Cross-sectional research design	• Cross-sectional research design
• Non-probability convenience sample of first-year undergraduate criminology students	• Non-probability purposive sample of first-year undergraduate criminology students
• Online questionnaire data collection method	• Semi-structured interviews
• 225 responses and a 75% response rate	• 15 participants
• Demographic and attitudinal variables	• Transcripts checked for validatory purposes

Figure 10.1 Example project quantitative component: students' attitudes towards the police.

Quantitative terminology: reliability and validity

For those of you that have studied research methods before, you will probably be familiar with the terms reliability and validity. This is because these terms represent some of the most commonly used criteria to evaluate social research, for both quantitative and qualitative research. However, as we have keenly emphasised the philosophical differences between the quantitative, qualitative, and mixed methods research strategies throughout this book, we will be applying reliability and validity to the quantitative strategy only because of their preoccupation with measurement.

When conducting a mixed methods research project you should evaluate the strengths and weaknesses of each component in turn, applying the strategy-specific terminology. Therefore the quantitative component(s) should be considered using the criteria reliability and validity. This section will outline reliability, before going on to explain four different types of validity: **external validity**, **internal validity**, **ecological validity**, and **construct (measurement) validity**. When explaining each of the terms, we will highlight the part of the research process that determines whether the research project will have a strength or weakness regarding that criterion. For the purposes of applying the criteria that follow, we use the example mixed methods project set out in Figure 10.1.

Reliability

The central focus of reliability is whether the findings from a research project can be repeated. Therefore, if the same study was to take place again, would the same results be found? A researcher utilising quantitative methods would want the answer to this question to be 'yes'. This replicability relies upon the measurement of the concepts to be stable over time. As such, to demonstrate high levels of reliability, a questionnaire question should accurately and consistently measure the same concept every time it is employed. Being able to replicate a study relies on the documentation of a robust research process to ensure that the data are collected in the same way each time. This should allow any researcher to replicate the results if they adopt the same measures and processes.

The extent to which reliability can be inferred is determined by three parts of the research process, namely the research design, sampling and data collection methods employed (see Chapter 7 – Data and sampling and Chapter 8 – Data collection methods). Research designs that afford the researcher more control, such as cross-sectional and experimental designs, can (subject to the skills of the researcher) produce inferences with high levels of reliability. This is because the researcher has the opportunity to employ consistent measures over time. In contrast, research designs where the researcher has less control, or the research is particularly nuanced or unique, such as longitudinal, comparative, and case study designs, will generate inferences with low levels of reliability. The amount of control the researcher can exert is also reflected in the data collection methods that produce high or low levels of reliability in a research project. Data collection methods such as questionnaires, secondary data analysis, and structured observations, where the researcher is in control of the measurement, can produce inferences with high levels of reliability. Subsequently, data collection methods that are heavily influenced by the research participant, such as research interviews and focus groups, will generate inferences with low levels of reliability as they are unlikely to be repeatable. The type of sampling used also affects reliability. For instance, a probability sample will generate inferences with high levels of reliability because the sample is representative of the population being studied. In contrast, if a non-probability sample is used, the researcher does not know if respondents are representative of the population, therefore the results may not be replicable. Box 10.2 explains this in practice.

Box 10.2   Reliability in practice: students' attitudes towards the police

Quantitative component: research details

- Cross-sectional research design
- Non-probability convenience sample of first-year undergraduate criminology students
- Online questionnaire data collection method
- 225 responses and a 75% response rate
- Demographic and attitudinal variables

Applying reliability to the quantitative component of the example study investigating students' attitudes towards the police, both the research design (cross-sectional) and data collection method (online questionnaire) lend themselves to producing a set of inferences with high levels of reliability. This is because a cross-sectional design has characteristics that can be repeated, such as researching more than one case (person) at a single point in time and producing data that can be quantified. Similarly, questionnaire questions are repeatable because the same questions can be used again by the same or different researchers. For both a cross-sectional design and a questionnaire data collection method, the researcher has a high degree of control over the research process, making it easily repeatable. A high level of reliability can be assumed in this research project if the researcher has undertaken a rigorous and clearly documented research process. However, as a non-probability sample was used, the reliability of the inferences will be diminished because there is no knowledge about whether the sample is representative of the population. Consequently, reliability could be judged as moderate overall.

Validity

Bryman (2016) suggests that validity is the most important quality criterion. Validity focuses on the integrity of the inferences from a quantitative component, and can be assessed using the following sub-criteria:

External validity

External validity is the extent to which the inferences can be generalised beyond the context of the research project itself. If the inferences are externally valid, this means that the results can be applied to broader, more general contexts. It is the sampling element of the research process that determines whether the inferences from a research project have high or low levels of external validity. Research projects that use probability sampling, which generates a representative cross-section of the whole population, have the potential to demonstrate a high level of external validity. This is because the representativeness of the sample allows for generalisation. In contrast, research projects that employ non-probability sampling, where there is no indication if the sample is representative of the whole population, will have low levels of external validity. This is due to the lack of representativeness in the sample, which results in a lack of generalisability. Sample size is also important when considering external validity. Students are often concerned about how many respondents they require to achieve high levels of external validity. Unfortunately, there is no set target, as the **response rate** required to determine external validity will depend on the overall size of the population being sampled. For student projects, where the size of the population is usually too large to recruit enough respondents to achieve a high proportion of the population, the emphasis should be on securing a number of respondents that will allow for a robust statistical analysis, which is no fewer than 30 (Denscombe, 2017). See Chapter 7 – Research design and sampling for further information about sampling. Box 10.3 provides an example.

Box 10.3   External validity in practice: students' attitudes towards the police

Quantitative component: research details

- Cross-sectional research design
- Non-probability convenience sample of first-year undergraduate criminology students
- Online questionnaire data collection method
- 225 responses and a 75% response rate
- Demographic and attitudinal variables

Applying external validity to the quantitative component of the example study investigating students' attitudes towards the police, the sampling technique determines whether or not the inferences from this research project will have high levels of external validity or not. As a non-probability convenience sample was employed, the inferences from this research project will have a low level of external validity because the inferences cannot be generalised beyond the immediate context of the research project. This is because researchers using non-probability samples do not know if the sample is representative of the population they are studying. The sample size and response rate were good and could have produced high levels of external validity if probability sampling had been employed.

Internal validity

Internal validity is concerned with causality. Causality is whether one thing causes another. To illustrate, does X (someone's personal characteristics) cause Y (a positive attitude towards the police)? In quantitative research, causation is demonstrated when a change in one variable brings about a change in another variable. Internal validity is the criterion which determines whether a causal relationship really exists. It is the research design part of the research process that governs whether a research project will be able to determine causality, thus internal validity. Research designs which can generate inferences with causation are experimental (because of the manipulation of the independent variable) and longitudinal (because of the time ordering). Both of these types of research design have a before and after situation, which allows for causation to be assessed. It is quite rare to find examples of causality in criminological research studies because of the nature of the research undertaken within the discipline, with fewer experiments and longitudinal studies undertaken compared to a related discipline such as psychology. For example, a classic criminological experiment was conducted by Painter and Farrington (1999) who assessed the effect of improved street lighting on crime using experimental and control areas. See Chapter 7 – Research design and sampling for more details. Box 10.4 illustrates internal validity in practice.

Box 10.4   Internal validity in practice: students' attitudes towards the police

Quantitative component: research details

- Cross-sectional research design
- Non-probability convenience sample of first-year undergraduate criminology students
- Online questionnaire data collection method
- 225 responses and a 75% response rate
- Demographic and attitudinal variables

Applying internal validity to the quantitative component of the example study investigating students' attitudes towards the police, the research design controls whether or not the inferences from this research project will have high levels of internal validity or not. As a cross-sectional design was employed, the inferences from this research project will have a low level of internal validity because the inferences generated will only be able to demonstrate an association or correlation between the variables, as causality cannot be determined. This is because cross-sectional designs collect data at one point in time, so there is not the time ordering of data collection required through multiple data collection points to establish causation. Remember: correlation ≠ causation.

Ecological validity

Ecological validity focuses on whether the inferences from a research project relate to the real-world setting of everyday life. This is an important criterion because social research is often undertaken to obtain a better insight into a particular social phenomenon, therefore being able to accurately reflect that through the inferences ensures there is practical application. The more control the researcher has over the research setting, the less likely it is that the inferences will have high levels of ecological validity. This is because tightly controlled research environments are less likely to reflect a natural setting. Consequently, it is the data collection element of the research process that determines whether a study has the potential for high or low levels of ecological validity. To illustrate, questionnaires and structured observations are unnatural settings which do not accurately reflect everyday life. In contrast, unstructured observations are better able to capture participant behaviour in a natural setting. Because of the nature of quantitative data collection methods and quantitative data, ecological validity is hard to achieve. Therefore, do not be disheartened if your quantitative component has low levels of ecological validity. See Box 10.5 for an example.

Construct validity (measurement validity)

Construct validity, sometimes referred to as **measurement validity**, considers whether the measure employed accurately reflects the concept. The choice and construction of the

Box 10.5   Ecological validity in practice: students' attitudes towards the police

Quantitative component: research details

- Cross-sectional research design
- Non-probability convenience sample of first-year undergraduate criminology students
- Online questionnaire data collection method
- 225 responses and a 75% response rate
- Demographic and attitudinal variables

Applying ecological validity to the quantitative component of the example study investigating students' attitudes towards the police, the data collection method controls whether or not the inferences from this research project will have high levels of ecological validity or not. As a questionnaire data collection method was employed, the inferences from this research project will have a low level of ecological validity because of the unnatural setting created by the participant having to complete a questionnaire. Furthermore, the respondent may provide answers to the questionnaire about their behaviour which they might not undertake in a real-life situation.

variables used in the quantitative component will determine if the research will have high or low levels of construct validity. Some variables are very good at reflecting the concepts they intend to measure, such as demographic questionnaire questions that ask a respondent's age or ethnicity. This is because there are socially accepted standardised responses to these types of question, which will generate high levels of construct validity. Conversely, other types of variables, especially ones that attempt to measure subjective phenomena, can be poor at accurately measuring the concept. This includes any variables attempting to measure attitudes or perceptions. This is because questions that ask respondents to indicate their level of agreement/ disagreement on a Likert scale with a defined statement may not reflect the concept because of individual respondents' interpretation and articulation of their level of agreement/disagreement. For example, respondents' interpretation of the Likert scale may vary because one person's 'agree' might be another person's 'strongly agree'. Therefore, these types of variables will demonstrate low levels of construct validity. Box 10.6 applies this to the example project.

Box 10.6   Construct validity in practice: students' attitudes towards the police

Quantitative component: research details

- Cross-sectional research design
- Non-probability convenience sample of first-year undergraduate criminology students
- Online questionnaire data collection method
- 225 responses and a 75% response rate
- Demographic and attitudinal variables

Applying construct validity to the quantitative component of the example study investigating students' attitudes towards the police, the choice and construction of the variables controls whether or not the inferences from this research project will have high levels of construct validity or not. As a range of demographic and attitudinal variables were used, the inferences from this research project will have both high and low levels of construct validity. This is because the demographic variables, such as age and ethnicity, will produce high construct validity. In comparison, the attitudinal variables, which assessed respondents' levels of confidence in the police, will produce low levels of construct validity. Having variables that span the spectrum of construct validity is acceptable, if the limitations of the variables with low construct validity are acknowledged.

Central Research Question: What are student attitudes towards the police?

Description: This mixed methods project utilised one QUANT and one QUAL component to investigate undergraduate criminology students' attitudes towards the police. A simultaneous design was employed, with both components given equal priority.

Quantitative Component

The project features of the quantitative component were as follows:

- Cross-sectional research design
- Non-probability convenience sample of first-year undergraduate criminology students
- Online questionnaire data collection method
- 225 responses and a 75% response rate
- Demographic and attitudinal variables

Qualitative Component

The project features of the qualitative component were as follows:

- Cross-sectional research design
- Non-probability purposive sample of first-year undergraduate criminology students
- Semi-structured interviews
- 15 participants
- Transcripts checked for validatory purposes

Quantitative Critique

- Moderate reliability
- Low external validity
- Low internal validity
- Low ecological validity
- Elements of high and low construct validity

Figure 10.2 Example project with quantitative critique: students' attitudes towards the police.

As demonstrated above, different parts of the research process determine whether your quantitative component will have high or low levels of reliability and validity. Table 10.1 illustrates the different elements of the research process that affect reliability and validity. In a research project, it is common for some aspects of the research to demonstrate high levels of reliability and validity and others low. It is absolutely fine for this to be the case in your research. Your tutors are not expecting there to be high levels of all the evaluative criteria in your project; the most important thing is that you can correctly apply the terminology, acknowledge why levels might be low and offer potential future alternatives. To summarise this in the context of the example project in Figure 10.2, the quantitative component about students' attitudes towards the police has the following levels of reliability and validity:

Table 10.1 Aspects of the research process that determine reliability and validity

	Reliability	External validity	Internal validity	Ecological validity	Construct validity
Research design	✓		✓		
Sampling	✓	✓			
Data collection method	✓			✓	
Variable					✓

Qualitative terminology: trustworthiness and authenticity

Due to the philosophical differences between the quantitative, qualitative and mixed methods research strategies, it is appropriate to apply the terms trustworthiness and authenticity to evaluate the qualitative component(s) of a mixed methods research project. Some researchers, such as LeCompte and Goetz (1982) and Kirk and Miller (1986), suggest that the quantitative terms reliability and validity can be adapted to encompass qualitative concerns. However, we prefer to use the terms trustworthiness and authenticity, coined by Guba and Lincoln (1986), because they better reflect the interpretivist and constructionist nature of qualitative research (see Chapter 4 – Philosophy for more details about epistemology and ontology). This is contested terrain, so other textbooks and/or researchers may not employ this terminology when evaluating qualitative data.

Trustworthiness and authenticity each have a range of associated criteria. This section will outline the four criteria of trustworthiness, namely: **credibility**, **transferability**, **dependability**, and **confirmability**, before moving on to explain the five criteria associated with authenticity, namely: **fairness**, **ontological authenticity**, **educative authenticity**, **catalytic authenticity**, and **tactical authenticity**. For the purposes of applying the criteria that follow, we will employ an example of a qualitative component from a mixed methods project about students' attitudes towards the police throughout this section; see Figure 10.3. This is the qualitative component of the example project we have used throughout this chapter. Unlike reliability and validity, which are largely determined by the mechanics of the research process (the project's research design, sampling, and data collection method), trustworthiness is influenced by how the researcher undertakes the research and authenticity relates to the wider impact of the research; for instance, how the researcher acts when collecting the data (trustworthiness) and the effect this data collection has upon the participants involved (authenticity). This will be highlighted through

> **Central Research Question:** What are student attitudes towards the police?

> **Description:** This mixed methods project utilised one QUANT and one QUAL component to investigate undergraduate criminology students' attitudes towards the police. A simultaneous design was employed, with both components given equal priority.

Quantitative Component

The project features of the quantitative component were as follows:

- Cross-sectional research design
- Non-probability convenience sample of first-year undergraduate criminology students
- Online questionnaire data collection method
- 225 responses and a 75% response rate
- Demographic and attitudinal variables

Qualitative Component

The project features of the qualitative component were as follows:

- Cross-sectional research design
- Non-probability purposive sample of first-year undergraduate criminology students
- Semi-structured interviews
- 15 part icipants
- Transcripts checked for validatory purposes

Figure 10.3 Example project qualitative component: students' attitudes towards the police.

the criteria that follow, reflecting how the application of trustworthiness and authenticity is much more subjective than when applying reliability and validity. Examples of how to enhance trustworthiness and authenticity in your research will also be provided.

Trustworthiness

Trustworthiness constitutes four criteria to assess the rigour of qualitative research, which align with a range of quantitative evaluative criteria, as seen in Table 10.2. These cross-strategy associations are useful because they will help to broaden your understanding of the notion of critique when considering the strengths and weaknesses of your research across the quantitative and qualitative components. It is also important to remember the prominence of research ethics here, as thorough research demonstrates sound ethical practice. See Chapter 3 – Ethics for further details.

Table 10.2 Trustworthiness criteria and their associated quantitative criteria

Trustworthiness criterion	Associated quantitative evaluative criterion
Credibility	Internal validity
Transferability	External validity
Dependability	Reliability
Confirmability	Objectivity (see Bryman, 2016)

Credibility

For Guba and Lincoln (1986), credibility corresponds to truth value. Credibility reflects the ontological notion that social reality is constructed by actors (people). Consequently, if there is more than one perspective of social reality, it is the way that the researcher arrives at their perspective of social reality (their conclusions) that governs whether the inferences are considered credible (or not). There are two ways that credibility can be ascertained: firstly, by undertaking research that embraces the qualities of good research practice; for example, by collecting the data as intended, and not 'cutting any corners'. This aspect of credibility can be assessed by examining a researcher's methodology. Secondly, the inferences produced can be checked by the research participants to ensure the researcher has correctly interpreted their version of social reality. This is also known as **respondent validation** or member validation (Bryman, 2016). When reflecting on the credibility of your own research, as the researcher it should be simple to determine if credibility is high or low because you will know if the research has been conducted 'properly' and whether respondent validation has taken place. If you are trying to identify if other researchers' work has credibility, you should be able to find information about the research process and any respondent validation in the methodology section of their work. Applying credibility to the qualitative component of the example study investigating students' attitudes towards the police is straightforward if there is knowledge about how the research was conducted. If a proper research process was undertaken, alongside respondent validation, then credibility will be high. If only one of the two aspects have taken place, then credibility can be said to be moderate, and if the research was conducted poorly and without any respondent validation, then credibility will be low.

Guba and Lincoln (1986) suggest a range of ways that you can enhance credibility through the research process; the five most appropriate techniques for student researchers are listed below:

1   Prolonged engagement – with the participants and focus of the research
2   Persistent observation – to obtain an in-depth understanding
3   Triangulation – cross-checking the data (NOT triangulation in the way we talk about it in Chapter 6 – Combining the data)
4   Peer debriefing – talking through your research with a peer or tutor to facilitate an appropriate research process
5   Member checks – like respondent validation, but this can be more informal than supplying copies of the inferences for checking, such as having conversations with participants

Transferability

Transferability is concerned with whether the inferences from a qualitative component can be applied to other similar contexts, which Guba and Lincoln (1986) describe as applicability. This is aligned with the external validity criterion from the quantitative strategy. However, application of the inferences to different contexts is difficult to attain in qualitative research because the emphasis is on generating an in-depth account of a specific phenomenon, rather than the measurement and generalisation associated with the quantitative strategy. Nevertheless, producing an in-depth qualitative account in one context can act as a benchmark for determining whether the inferences could be transferred to a similar context. The identification of transferability rests firmly with the 'eye of the beholder'; based on how the researcher has designed their research project and interpreted the inferences. To illustrate, the qualitative component that investigated students' attitudes towards the police consisted of 15 interviews with first-year undergraduate criminology students at one university. If the inferences were very in-depth, detailed, and repetitive between participants, with congruent similarities and differences, it would be appropriate to suggest that the inferences would have a high level of transferability to a similar context. This could be a different group of 15 first-year undergraduate criminology students from the same institution. Nevertheless, transferability could be considered low if the other context being studied was markedly different; for example, the participants being final-year undergraduate students and/or students from a different institution. The application of transferability really highlights the subjective nature of the trustworthiness criteria.

According to Guba and Lincoln (1986), trustworthiness can be enhanced by producing 'thick, descriptive data'. This should provide a clear narrative and understanding about the context being studied, so you or other researchers can determine whether the inferences can be appropriately applied to different contexts. However, they provide a caveat that suggests the exact 'thickness' of the data required is unclear, which is one of the challenges of undertaking qualitative research.

Dependability

Dependability focuses on the research process and how the strength of the inferences can be judged by assessing how the research was carried out; for example, how the researcher conducted various elements of the research process such as data collection and data analysis. Guba and Lincoln (1986) associate this with consistency. This holds similarities to the reliability criterion from the quantitative strategy and in terms of research practice is linked to credibility. To achieve high levels of dependability, Guba and Lincoln (1986) suggest undertaking an 'auditing approach' whereby all details of the research process are diligently noted through thorough and accurate record-keeping. This audit trail can then be assessed by other researchers to ascertain the quality of the inferences. According to Bryman (2016), this criterion has not been widely adopted. It is easy to see why, because it is rare for others to assess your work in such detail and vice versa, even for students undertaking assessed coursework. However, undertaking an auditing approach can be personally beneficial for individual researchers. They can reflect upon their research practice and then decide if their research exhibits dependability. Consequently, it would most likely be for the researchers who conducted the qualitative component research into students' attitudes towards the police to judge for themselves whether their research demonstrated high levels of dependability, or not, based upon their auditing records. As such, they would appraise their audit/research notes to ascertain if the research had been completed in a thorough manner, such as completing respondent validation with all participants.

Confirmability

Confirmability is the aspect of trustworthiness that focuses on whether the research has been conducted in the most value-free and neutral way possible. Guba and Lincoln (1986) consider this criterion to be concerned with neutrality. Qualitative research cannot be free from researchers' values, but inferences can be achieved with minimal personal influence or bias. Again, this criterion is usually best assessed by the researcher themselves when reflecting on the integrity of their inferences. This is another instance where Guba and Lincoln (1986) suggest that an auditing approach can enhance this criterion. However, unless an audit is undertaken by other researchers or a tutor, it would be difficult for someone other than the researcher to accurately determine confirmability. Therefore, the researchers who conducted the qualitative component that researched students' attitudes towards the police would be best placed to comment on the confirmability of the inferences. For instance, they will know from conducting the research whether there was a bias in selecting participants, or the way the interviews were conducted. Biased participant recruitment would involve deliberately selecting people because they held provocative views about the police, which would impact on the inferences generated.

Authenticity

Authenticity contains five criteria, which are all related to the impact that qualitative research can have on both the research participants and wider society. Guba and Lincoln (1986) concede that these criteria require further development, but as they currently stand, the criteria are a useful tool for researchers to reflect upon the wider impact of their research, even at undergraduate level.

Fairness

Fairness is rooted in the ontological notion of constructionism (for more information on ontology see Chapter 4 – Philosophy). Guba and Lincoln (1986) suggest that it is important for researchers to reveal the different values and constructions that participants attribute to the social world. Therefore, fairness is concerned with whether the research presents these different perspectives and their associated values. Guba and Lincoln (1986) suggest that fairness is achieved by providing all participants with the same opportunities to articulate their version(s) of reality. A researcher can facilitate this by ensuring that all participants are treated equally, regardless of their and/or the researcher's views. For instance, using the example about researching students' attitudes towards the police, in an interview setting the researcher must retain a neutral stance when asking questions and probing responses, even if their views about the police completely contradict those of the participant. An unfair approach would involve the researcher asking leading questions, which is something that should be avoided.

Ontological authenticity

Ontological authenticity considers whether the research participants, be that individuals or groups, gain a better understanding of the social world through taking part in the research project. Guba and Lincoln (1986) suggest that participating in research may provide individuals with an improved 'conscious experiencing' of the world they live in. This knowledge may then be applied to the participants' everyday life. We apply ontological authenticity, and the remaining three types of authenticity to the example project, at the end of this section because of the nature of these criteria.

Educative authenticity

Educative authenticity is concerned with whether engaging in a research project helps the participants to develop a better understanding and appreciation of other people's views. This could be achieved through hearing different people's perspectives when involved in a focus group. However, educative authenticity is less likely when the data collection is undertaken with a single participant who does not have any interaction with other people taking part in the research, such as a single interview setting.

Catalytic authenticity

Catalytic authenticity is focused on action, and whether a research project stimulates participants and the wider community to do something following their engagement with the research. A participant may be inspired to begin campaigning about the topic that is at the centre of the research, with the research having given them the impetus to take action. Similarly, someone reading about the research project may also be prompted to take action based on what they have learned about the topic. In both instances, some kind of follow-up investigation would be required to know whether people had 'done something' following the research.

Tactical authenticity

Tactical authenticity is also concerned with action, specifically whether participating in a research project empowers individuals and gives them the requisite knowledge and/ or skills to be able to take such action. This is because, according to Guba and Lincoln (1986), change will only be effective if individuals have the power to make a change. For instance, taking part in a research project may give a participant the necessary information to be able to take action, such as learning about different organisations that they can contact/become involved with.

By nature, the authenticity criteria are more difficult to determine and less tangible than the other evaluative criteria we have examined. It is difficult to know if a participant has individually benefited in all the different ways. A simple solution is to ask them, and this might form part of an informal conversation during the participant validation element of the research process. You could enquire about their levels of understanding about the research topic and whether they have taken any action following their participation in the research project. This checking process should be built in to the tasks you need to complete when collecting your data and be part of your auditing process (see 'Dependability' for more details).

For the example study used in this chapter, a qualitative component researching students' attitudes towards the police, the impact the research has had on the participants is not known based on the details that have been provided. You may find this is the case in your research if you have used a secondary dataset for the qualitative component of your mixed methods research project. Similarly, you might not know about the impact that your own primary data collection has had on the participants; either because you did not enquire, or the participants were not forthcoming with a response. This is not an ideal situation as it would be better to know if the research being undertaken has had some kind of impact. However, the most important thing is to be transparent about your research process, so when writing-up your section on authenticity, you can state the specific criteria that cannot be determined if you are not in possession of the details.

Overall, as demonstrated above, the manner in which the qualitative component is carried out determines the levels of trustworthiness and authenticity. Figure 10.4 illustrates the extent of trustworthiness and authenticity in the example project about students' attitudes towards the police. Similar to reliability and validity, it is common that not all the criteria will be 'high'. It is fine for your research to have a mixture of high, low and unknown levels of trustworthiness and authenticity. Remember to use the correct terminology and suggest why you have made those judgements about your inferences.

Central Research Question: What are student attitudes towards the police?

Description: This mixed methods project utilised one QUANT and one QUAL component to investigate undergraduate criminology students' attitudes towards the police. A simultaneous design was employed, with both components given equal priority.

Quantitative Component

The project features of the quantitative component were as follows:

- Cross-sectional research design
- Non-probability convenience sample of first-year undergraduate criminology students
- Online questionnaire data collection method
- 225 responses and a 75% response rate
- Demographic and attitudinal variables

Qualitative Component

The project features of the qualitative component were as follows:

- Cross-sectional research design
- Non-probability purposive sample of first-year undergraduate criminology students
- Semi-structured interviews
- 15 part icipants
- Transcripts checked for validatory purposes

Quantitative Critique

- Moderate reliability
- Low external validity
- Low internal validity
- Low ecological validity
- Elements of high and low construct validity

Qualitative Critique

- High credibility
- High transferability
- High dependability
- High confirmability
- High fairness
- Unknown ontological authenticity
- Unknown educative authenticity
- Unknown catalytic authenticity
- Unknown tactical authenticity

Figure 10.4 Example project with qualitative critique: students' attitudes towards the police.

Mixed methods terminology: inference quality and inference transferability

Having examined how to evaluate inferences using reliability, validity, trustworthiness and authenticity, our attention now turns to appraising meta-inferences. These are the conclusions and interpretations drawn across the quantitative and qualitative components; they are essentially your overall mixed methods findings once the data has been combined. This section will explain how to evaluate meta-inferences and provide a range of terminology to help you to do so.

As mixed methods research is a comparatively new area of research methods, there has been a lot of debate about the evaluative criteria that should be used to assess the quality of meta-inferences. As more mixed methods research has been undertaken, and a greater number of people have been thinking about how to conduct the mixed methods research process, a range of new terminology has been created. However, in comparison to the more established terms of reliability, validity, trustworthiness, and authenticity, there has been relatively little written about how to evaluate meta-inferences, which is why this section contains fewer terms than the sections above.

Like many other aspects of mixed methods research, the disputes between scholars have predominantly focused on the contrasting epistemological and ontological concerns of the quantitative and qualitative strategies. Subsequently, different researchers have promoted the use of different terminology. Creswell and Plano Clark (2011: 239) suggest that researchers using mixed methods should aim for validity in their meta-inferences. They characterise validity as the result of a process which involves 'employing strategies that address potential issues in data collection, data analysis, and the interpretations that might compromise the merging or connecting of the quantitative and qualitative strands of the study and the conclusions drawn from the combination'. However, the term validity is not acceptable to all mixed methods researchers because of its alignment with quantitative epistemology and ontology. Even Creswell and Plano Clark (2011) admit that the term is often over-used and meaningless to mixed methods research. Therefore, to counteract the issues with using paradigm-specific evaluative terminology, Teddlie and Tashakkori (2003, 2010) use the term inference quality to judge the value of the conclusions and interpretations that are the product of combining the data in a mixed methods research project. They also use the term inference transferability to deal with concerns around generalisation. These are the two terms that we use to evaluate meta-inferences.

Inference quality

To assess inference quality, Greene (2007: 167) suggests a multiplistic stance should be adopted that:

- focuses on the available data support for the inferences, using data of multiple and diverse kinds
- could include criteria or stances from different methodological traditions
- attends to the nature and extent of the better understanding that is reached with this mixed methods design, as this is the overall aim of mixed methods inquiry.

Consequently, if these criteria are satisfied, the meta-inferences would be deemed to have high levels of inference quality. This multiplistic stance also highlights how criteria from different methodological traditions (e.g. quantitative and qualitative) can be used in the critiquing process, which is what we have advocated throughout this chapter. To simplify Greene's (2007) approach for researchers new to using mixed methods, we suggest that inference quality can be determined through an appraisal of the factors shown in Box 10.7.

Box 10.7   Factors that determine inference quality

- A systematic, rigorous, and ethical data collection process with a clear rationale provided for the way the inferences from the quantitative and qualitative components have been combined
- An evaluation of the quantitative component(s) using reliability and validity, and an assessment of the qualitative component(s) using trustworthiness and authenticity
- Whether the meta-inferences provide a better understanding of the social world by answering the central research question and/or subsidiary questions.

Inference transferability

Teddlie and Tashakkori (2003) also use the term inference transferability to reflect the quantitative notions of external validity and qualitative concerns with transferability. Therefore, if the inferences from the quantitative and qualitative components had high levels of external validity and transferability respectively, then inference transferability would also be high. If the circumstance arose where the quantitative and qualitative components differed in their levels of external validity and transferability (for example, one was high and one was low), you would need to reflect upon the priority afforded to each component to determine the overall levels of inference transferability. This will require you to use your academic judgement, so be sure to be clear and transparent in your decision-making process and support your decisions with evidence where possible, such as the inferences from each component. You should be prepared to make these sorts of decisions throughout a mixed methods research project, which is where a thorough knowledge and understanding of the mixed methods research methodology will help. If you are unsure about the decisions you have made, check back through this book and seek help from your research supervisor or peer. Sometimes talking through the scenario out loud can help clarify your thoughts. Box 10.8 discusses inference quality and inference transferability in relation to the example project, with Figure 10.5 completing the critique for the example project.

Box 10.8   Inference quality and inference transferability in practice: students' attitudes towards the police

Using the example project that investigated students' attitudes towards the police, we can consider inference quality and inference transferability using the determining factors in Box 10.7 as a guide. Because reliability and the four different types of validity range from high to low, with a similar picture for trustworthiness and authenticity, it is appropriate to suggest that the inference quality of the meta-inferences is moderate. The same judgement could be made about inference transferability, given that external validity is low and transferability is high. As you can see, there is no clear-cut answer here and that is what you should expect

in your research. As usual, the main thing is to justify your deci
aspect to consider when evaluating the meta-inferences generate
methods project is the overarching strengths and weaknesses of
ods strategy. A range of advantages and disadvantages relating to the ˙
methods can be found in Chapter 1 – Introduction to mixed methods.

Central Research Question: What are student attitudes towards the police?

Description: This mixed methods project utilised one QUANT and one QUAL component to investigate undergraduate criminology students' attitudes towards the police. A simultaneous design was employed, with both components given equal priority.

Quantitative Component

The project features of the quantitative component were as follows:

- Cross-sectional research design
- Non-probability convenience sample of first-year undergraduate criminology students
- Online questionnaire data collection method
- 225 responses and a 75% response rate
- Demographic and attitudinal variables

Qualitative Component

The project features of the qualitative component were as follows:

- Cross-sectional research design
- Non-probability purposive sample of first-year undergraduate criminology students
- Semi-structured interviews
- 15 participants
- Transcripts checked for validatory purposes

Quantitative Critique

- Moderate reliability
- Low external validity
- Low internal validity
- Low ecological validity
- Elements of high and low construct validity

Qualitative Critique

- High credibility
- High transferability
- High dependability
- High confirmability
- High fairness
- Unknown ontological authenticity
- Unknown educative authenticity
- Unknown catalytic authenticity
- Unknown tactical authenticity

Mixed Methods Critique

- Moderate inference quality
- Moderate inference transferability

Figure 10.5 Example project with mixed methods critique: students' attitudes towards the police.

Summary

This chapter details how to undertake a critique of a mixed methods research project. Similar to many other chapters in this book, the emphasis has been on demonstrating how to employ a systematic process to logically assess the strengths and weaknesses of your mixed methods work. Consequently, when undertaking your critique it is important to evaluate the inferences from each component using the appropriate evaluative criteria for each research strategy in a clear and consistent manner. The quantitative component(s) should be evaluated using the terms reliability and validity, and the qualitative components using trustworthiness and authenticity. Once all the components have been assessed, a full appraisal of the meta-inferences should be undertaken using the terms inference quality and inference transferability. The crucial element is to ensure you present your critique in a way that truthfully and accurately reflects the quality of the inferences and meta-inferences. Even if there are prevailing integrity issues, always articulate your research project in a way that supports the decisions you have made when planning your project, as you will have justified these decisions elsewhere.

Learning questions

1   Why is it important to critique your research?
2   How many evaluative terms are there? Which ones relate to which strategy?
3   What are the factors that determine inference quality?

11 Troubleshooting

Introduction

This chapter discusses how it is possible to deal with those situations where your research does not go according to plan. It is divided into three sections. Firstly, we will examine some of the potential solutions to common problems that may be encountered in mixed methods research. Secondly, we will look at a worked example to show how trouble-shooting might work in a real-life situation. Finally, a number of experienced mixed methods researchers will provide their top tips for success.

The very nature of mixed methods research, in particular the fact that two or more components of data collection are taking place, means that there is greater potential for things to go wrong (Waters, 2009). Yet mixed methods research also provides added opportunities for flexibility precisely because there is more than one component involved in the project. With this in mind, the chapter will offer practical advice on what to do when things go wrong and suggest how mixed methods can be used to one's advantage in these situations.

Solutions to common problems in mixed methods research

Because of the added complexity of any mixed methods research project, potential issues can occur at a multitude of points along the way. The best way to deal with problems is to avoid them in the first place, and the best way to do this is to ensure you are comfort-able in conducting both your quantitative and qualitative components. Often research-ers (including those that teach you) are trained more heavily in either quantitative or qualitative research methods, and students also often have a stronger inclination towards one approach over the other, perhaps because of the analysis involved. For example, some are more comfortable carrying out statistical analysis of quantitative data than thematic analysis of qualitative data. Thus, it can sometimes be challenging to become fluent in both quantitative and qualitative approaches, but doing so will help your project to proceed smoothly. It is also worth stressing how important it is to have a well-designed research plan which is rigorous and thought through. Your resources, especially as a student, are limited. The sampling and data collection phases of your research are the most labour intensive (and potentially costly) of the entire research process. The quality of your research in these phases will have direct implications for your attempts to analyse your data, and ultimately develop inferences and meta-inferences. The data collected for each component need to be of good quality in order to ensure that the subsequent phases of the research progress smoothly.

Of course, even with the best planning, difficulties can still arise. As a result, it is useful to understand what can go wrong in mixed methods projects before you begin planning your research so that you can attempt to avoid difficult situations as far as possible, or at least be fully aware of the means that exist to resolve them if they do occur. Watkins and Gioia (2015: 123) suggest adopting a 'preparing for the worst' strategy. This means that you have a 'back-up plan' if things do not go as anticipated. They suggest that writing a list of '*if* . . . *then* . . .' statements can be useful in trying to think about what might go wrong and how it can be addressed. They give the following example: '*If* we cannot recruit a sufficient number of study participants during the 2-week recruitment period, *then* we will expand our recruitment locations to include churches and local athletic facilities'. However, it may be the case that you are reading this section whilst in the midst of an unforeseen research crisis; no matter, much of the advice that follows can be implemented partway through a project. Indeed, one of the beauties of mixed methods research projects is that they offer the researcher a greater amount of flexibility. There is more space within the project to be adaptable, and there is the possibility that one component of the research can compensate for another that has proven problematic. If one component does not go entirely to plan, then mixed methods usually offers the opportunity for alterations and adjustments to other components in order to keep the overall research project viable.

The remainder of this section highlights six solutions to common problems that can arise in mixed methods research, all of which can be put into practice during the process of carrying out the project. This is by no means an exhaustive list of potential solutions, but it does cover those issues that you are most likely to encounter in your own projects, and it should provide insights into how best to tackle any other pitfalls you might face.

1. Changing priority

If one of your components does not go to plan, then it is sometimes possible to change the priority of your components. For example, it might be the case that you fail to recruit enough participants or collect sufficient data for what was intended to be the dominant component. Depending on the nature of your study, the component which lacks sufficient data could potentially become the subordinate component, and a component that was intended to be subordinate can instead become dominant. An example of this is Waters' research on older illegal drug users.

Waters says:

> When it came to operationalising the research, I encountered serious difficulties in recruiting participants. The main difficulty was that potential interviewees were unwilling to speak on the record about their engagement in an illegal activity

(Waters, 2015). As a result of this, I shifted priority towards the quantitative component. This meant undertaking a more detailed analysis and discussion of the British Crime Survey, so whilst the project remained simultaneous in nature, the quantitative component assumed a greater role in terms of priority. The research thus changed from a 'QUANT / QUAL } →' design to a 'QUANT / qual } →' design. Thus, I inadvertently came to realise one of the strengths of the mixed methods approach; if something does not go to plan with one component of mixed methods research, all is not necessarily lost as in certain circumstances mixed methods allows some degree of flexibility. Although certain aspects of the project, including some of the objectives, did need revising, I was still able to answer my central research question and address the broad aims of the study with this small adjustment. In my case, a simple change in priority enabled me to finish and make the most of my project.

2. Changing sequence

There are a number of reasons why you might need to change the sequence of your design. These include time constraints, practical considerations, recruitment issues, access issues, or a need to maintain the momentum of your project. For example, it might be necessary to capitalise on participants' involvement in the research project at a certain point in time; in a situation where individuals have completed an online questionnaire and have agreed to a follow-up interview, it might make little sense to wait until all the questionnaires have been completed before embarking on the interviews. In this situation it is likely to be beneficial to conduct the interview as quickly as possible before the contact has gone 'cold', even if this involves a change from a sequential to a simultaneous design. Conversely, you may have planned for a simultaneous design, but ethical or access issues might bring about a delay on one of your components, necessitating a switch to a sequential design. An example of a change in sequence is Banks et al.'s study on the family members of problem gamblers.

Banks et al. say:

> Although the research team devised a sequential (QUANT → QUAL) approach to data collection, with qualitative semi-structured interviews following the administration of the (largely) quantitative questionnaire, as data collection progressed, individual components of the research design were conducted simultaneously (QUANT / QUAL } →). Questionnaires were used to recruit participants for interviews and thus the qualitative component of the research was designed to follow the quantitative component. However, the research team quickly recognised the need to immediately follow-up questionnaire respondents who stated that they were willing to speak with a researcher, in order to successfully timetable an interview. In addition, some prospective research participants, who had not (yet) completed the questionnaire, contacted the research team directly to be interviewed. Thus, it quickly became evident that questionnaire data collection and semi-structured interviews needed to be conducted simultaneously.

3. Changing the method of data collection

Because a mixed methods design involves multiple data collection methods, there is greater flexibility and scope to alter those methods if required. Although changing your data collection methods during the course of a project is not ideal, sometimes there is no alternative. It might be appropriate if it has proved impossible to recruit enough participants to a particular component, if you have been denied access or ethical approval, or if it has proved impossible to source sufficient data. Changing the data collection method might be as straightforward as swapping a hard-copy questionnaire for an online one, or swapping an interview for a focus group. Note that substitutions such as these might also affect priority and sequence, and may also require further ethical approval. An example of changing the method of data collection can be seen in Robinson's 'Working It Out for Yourself' project.

Robinson says:

> I set out to gain participants for my study through volunteering in youth projects with the intention of recruiting young people to engage in creative activities outside of the project space. I did not explicitly set out to do ethnographic studies of my three settings but have found myself relying rather more on observation and interactions within the groups where I have been working than anticipated. That means I have less by way of systematic recording than I would otherwise have done but I do have a lot of material, including from activities and interviews.

4. Supporting or replacing one component with another

If a primary data collection component does not go to plan, this can potentially be supported by, or even replaced with, a secondary data collection component. It is also possible to change the priority of components, as we have seen above. Similarly, if a secondary dataset turns out not to be as useful as initially intended, this can be backed up by a primary data collection component. Once again, this comes with the potential for a complete change in priority if deemed necessary. An example of a study where the secondary data proved to be flawed was Cubellis' research on sexual victimisation, disclosure and accountability.

Cubellis says:

> One of the greatest difficulties encountered when conducting the qualitative portion of the study was the reliance on data that was not collected for the purpose of qualitative content analysis. While the use of secondary data analysis poses benefits in terms of the length of time it takes to complete research projects, it also limits the amount of information the researcher has and the possible avenues they can take to examine the data. It was not uncommon for there to be a lack of information in the Boy Scouts of America (BSA) files, making it difficult to ascertain what abuse was alleged to have occurred or how exactly the BSA responded. While this was ultimately out of my control, it was a factor I had to take into consideration when trying to qualitatively analyse the data available to me. Based on this, I had to be selective about the cases that I would use for content and case study analysis, recognizing that I would not be able to use all of the cases because of the lack of information in some.

5. Adopting different strategies for the recruitment of participants

Participant recruitment can be challenging in any research, and this is often magnified in mixed methods projects as there can be a need to recruit for more than one component. Persuading people to take part in your research when there is no immediately obvious benefit to them can make sample building a thankless task. However, in mixed methods research, these difficulties can be somewhat alleviated. For instance, if your mixed methods project involves sample building across more than one component, it may be appropriate to construct slightly smaller samples than would otherwise be the case, as your sampling and data in one component can buttress your sampling and data in another. This might make the task of creating a sample a slightly less onerous one. In addition, if one sample-building strategy has proven to be ineffective for an initial component, then a different strategy can be adopted for subsequent components. This trial-and-error approach is much easier to implement in mixed methods projects, especially in a sequential study where the lessons learned from earlier phases can be applied to later phases. One good example of this might be the use of online recruitment strategies designed to support traditional offline strategies, as in the work of Banks et al.

Banks et al. say:

> To date, research exploring the gambling–family nexus had been based on small sample sizes and populations accessing treatment or help services, limiting generalisability. In order to maximise our response rate, access hard to reach participants, and those in distant locations across the UK, the research team developed an online questionnaire and distributed it through the microblogging service Twitter, as well as an assortment of other on- and offline networks and groups. Each Twitter user is, on average, connected to 208 other individuals, presenting an effective system through which the questionnaire could be circulated amongst service users, co-workers, family members, friends and other relevant individuals. This enabled us to disseminate our link to a wide range of gambling related groups and communities across the UK. The research team worked hard to develop the network prior to distribution, and to ensure that a wide range of stakeholders supported this process. Sheffield Hallam University's media department was also actively involved in the ongoing promotion of this research and hard copies of the questionnaire were also prepared and distributed to relevant agencies. Disseminating the questionnaire through multiple starting points maximised both the scale and the representativeness of the sample. Moreover, as Griffiths' (2010) review of internet-based research techniques notes, online questionnaires allow relatively large scale samples to be surveyed quickly and efficiently whilst lowering the social desirability and increasing the levels of honesty of respondents.

6. Becoming a single method study

This is the nuclear option for extreme cases! It involves abandoning the mixed methods element of the project and reverting to single method research. As we have seen, there are a range of reasons why a component in your research may not work. There may be access issues, ethical constraints, an inability to recruit, or other external factors that prevent you from collecting data in one of your components. In cases where components are not salvageable through the adoption of different data collection methods, the use of secondary data findings, and so on, it is possible to simply drop the problematic components and retain the one viable component, therefore turning the project into a single method study. Of course, this is not an option available to those who are conducting single method studies, and is perhaps the best example of the flexibility afforded by mixed methods.

Whilst this is a drastic course of action that requires a great deal of thought before being committed to, it is worth noting that there is nothing inherent in mixed methods research that makes it superior to single method research. As Bryman (2016: 649) puts it, 'there is no point collecting more data simply on the basis that "more is better"'. Therefore, if you can generate a satisfactory answer to your central research question through the use of just a single method, and you have run into insurmountable difficulties with your mixed methods, then reversion to a single method study is a viable option of last resort.

Troubleshooting: a worked example

The following is a worked example of how troubleshooting in a mixed methods project might work. It is intended to give you a flavour of the decision-making processes involved in troubleshooting, and how this might play out in a real-life situation.

Imagine that a student researcher is conducting a sequential mixed methods study where the components are of equal priority (QUANT → QUAL). The timeline for carrying out data collection is four months and the plan is to collect data through quantitative questionnaires followed by qualitative participant observations. The topic of the study is the effects of CCTV surveillance on people's behaviour. A convenience sample of 200 people who take the online questionnaire is constructed. Participants are asked to leave contact information on the questionnaire if they are willing to participate in the second phase of the study. After three months the online questionnaire is closed. Forty people have provided contact information. Some have given e-mail addresses and others have given telephone numbers. The researcher starts contacting people and has underestimated how long it will take to construct a sample for the qualitative component. The researcher manages to re-instigate contact with 20 people but only five of these are comfortable and willing to consent to participant observation. The target sample was at least 10.

This is not an unlikely scenario in mixed methods research. In this situation, there are two key issues. First, the potential qualitative sample is too small because people do not want to participate in the observation of their behaviours. Second, the deadlines for the data collection cannot be met because the researcher underestimated the amount of time the qualitative component would take. Now is the time for troubleshooting!

One feasible solution to the first problem is to attempt to recruit participants using different strategies (solution 5 above). In this case, this might mean broadening the search for willing qualitative participants to include individuals who did not take part in the initial quantitative questionnaire. A convenience sample consisting of friends and family or fellow students can often be useful here, as these are people who know and trust you, although of course this can greatly reduce the pool of potential participants and is only appropriate in certain circumstances where the sample is not required to have particular characteristics. It might also have a negative impact on the quality of your inferences.

It might also be possible to complement the qualitative data collection method with another one, such as interviews (solution 3 above). The researcher would need to get in touch with their tutor, research supervisor, or a representative of their university ethics committee in order to get approval for an additional data collection method. Then they would seek to get back in contact with those participants who provided their details and ask if they would be willing to partake in telephone interviews instead.

A further possibility would be to support the qualitative component with an additional secondary data component (solution 4 above). This would require the researcher to seek out any studies that have looked at the same or a similar issue, in order to ascertain whether data collected for that study could potentially support the inferences of the researcher's own truncated qualitative component. Increasingly, researchers are making their full datasets available alongside the published results of their studies, so this is becoming an ever more feasible course of action. Of course, a good researcher should already know what research has been conducted in their area of study, so this can often be a useful and relatively straightforward way around a difficult problem, although great care must be taken to ensure that the secondary data are relevant and appropriate to the task at hand (see also Table 8.1 for a list of secondary data sources).

If these alternatives do not bear fruit, then it might be necessary to change the priority of the study (solution 1 above). In this example, dominance would be given to the quantitative component and the qualitative component would become subordinate (QUANT → qual). The nature of the finished work would be very different if this course was pursued, but it would still have the potential to provide an answer to the central research question, which of course is the main consideration when troubleshooting.

The second issue is falling behind the research timeline. One way that this could be addressed would be to change the sequence of the study (solution 2 above). Rather than conducting the research sequentially (QUANT → QUAL), with the qualitative component following on from the quantitative component, once it became apparent that time was an issue the study could have been carried out simultaneously (QUANT / QUAL} →). This would require questionnaire participants who left their details being contacted immediately and asked if they would be willing to participate in observations or interviews straight away. The disadvantage of this would be that the quantitative phase of the project could not inform the qualitative phase to the same degree as in a sequentially designed study, and so the nature of the project would be quite different, but the advantage would be that the entire process of data collection would be completed much more quickly and it would therefore be easier to meet any self- or externally imposed deadline. If this option is not taken, then realistically if there is a deadline which is not adjustable (for instance, an assessed deadline), the time needs to be gained in later parts of the research process (for instance, during the analysis or writing-up phases). Of course, this may affect the quality of the final product. It is extremely common for data collection to take longer than planned, especially for mixed methods research where multiple data collection efforts are required, so switching the sequence of the study can be a useful solution if time is becoming a problem.

As this example shows, sometimes you have to make difficult decisions as a researcher; you need to be flexible and consider alternatives whilst also bearing in mind the consequences of your decisions; ultimately, being a mixed methods researcher means being pragmatic (see Chapter 4 – Philosophy). In the end, the possibility always remains that you could simply abandon the idea of doing a mixed methods study completely, scrap the component or components that are causing difficulties, and conduct a single method study instead (solution 6 above). In this example, a sample of 200 participants having completed a quantitative questionnaire should still yield a large amount of data, and whilst abandoning the qualitative component might result in a study that lacks the more in-depth and nuanced data that a qualitative component can provide, it should still be possible to offer some kind of answer to the central research question.

Top tips

This section provides a number of 'top tips' for mixed methods projects based upon the experiences of a number of seasoned mixed methods researchers. We would like to thank everyone who contributed to this section: James Banks, Jacky Burrows, Beth Collinson, Michelle Cubellis, Joanna Large, Deborah Platts-Fowler, and Anne Robinson.

- Make sure you allocate enough time for planning and development. A truly mixed method project requires time at inception and development to determine what methods you want to use and how you are going to use these methods to address your inquiry. It is important for the researcher to know what specific aspects of their research question the different types of methods will address, and how the data will be combined. This is undoubtedly a task that takes more time than I expected. [MC]
- Do not assume that established 'methods' are somehow fixed. Read the core texts, but also look at the most current debates relating to your chosen approach and topic. [JBu]
- Ensure you have a clear purpose for each method so you are not simply collecting data for the sake of it. If you have a series of research questions, it can be helpful to try and map your methods to your research questions. [JL]
- In designing large research projects, there is a risk that mixed methods are not really 'mixed'. Quantitative and qualitative components may be designed separately by researchers who have little interest in the other. This is not necessarily a problem, except where the lack of communication, especially in the earlier stages, compromises combining the data. A top tip for achieving data assimilation is to ensure an integrated research team. [DPF]
- Keep good field notes – you never know when you might need to draw on them more heavily than anticipated. [AR]
- It is important that researchers are flexible when devising and undertaking their research. [JBa]
- Be flexible about what you do and exploit any opportunities that are presented to you. [AR]
- I've found that when managing such a large amount of data, organisation is key. Creating databases from the onset of your project assists this process and makes data collection much more manageable. I kept a database with participants' contact details and logged each time I had contacted them. Colour codes indicated when they were due their six-month follow-up. [BC]
- When I began analysing my secondary data, it became apparent that the dataset was incomplete in many areas. While using secondary data can save time and be beneficial in many ways, you have to remain mindful that if you haven't collected the data yourself, you can't get too caught up when it doesn't pan out how you would have hoped. [BC]
- Remember that you should make a note of all issues that arise and that you should be transparent about these in your final work. Issues can be discussed in the methodology section of your work, or in the limitations section of your discussion.
- Be prepared for hiccups along the way. With any research project – qualitative, quantitative or both – you are bound to face challenges during the process; it's inevitable. [BC]
- Celebrate small victories. Set yourself interim goals and reward yourself when you achieve them.

Summary

This chapter has looked at how to deal with the problems that you might encounter when things do not go to plan with mixed methods research. Mixed methods tends to increase the chances of things going wrong because by its very nature it involves data collection for more than one component and both quantitative and qualitative methods. However, the greater scope that mixed methods work brings also affords the researcher greater flexibility so that there are usually good options available to address difficulties.

The chapter began by introducing some of the potential solutions available to common problems with mixed methods. Discussion centred on changing the priority of the components, changing the sequence, changing the method of data collection, supporting or replacing one component with another, adopting different strategies for the recruitment of participants, and turning the study into a single method piece of research. We then went on to look at a worked example, which gave a flavour of the kinds of decisions researchers must make when things do go wrong in order to salvage their project. Finally, a number of experienced mixed methods researchers provided their top tips.

Perhaps the most important message is that it is almost inevitable that mixed methods research will never quite go as planned; however, by being properly prepared and aware of the options available to you, even if your own project does not proceed smoothly, there is always a way to address the problems that you face.

Learning questions

1   What could potentially go wrong in your research?
2   What could you do to address these problems, or at least minimise the negative effects?
3   Is it possible to create a contingency plan at the outset of your research project? What would this look like?

12 Writing-up

Introduction

You could undertake the most amazing mixed methods research project, but if you cannot communicate your study effectively in writing, the importance of your work will not be fully understood. This chapter is dedicated to helping you successfully articulate your research project in written form. The chapter begins by providing an outline structure to write-up mixed methods research, before discussing each of the constituent parts in detail. We cover the: abstract and introduction, literature review, methodology, inferences, discussion (including meta-inferences and critique), conclusion, and appendices. In each section, we consider the structure and content required, alongside a range of tips and tricks to help you maximise the quality of your account. The chapter concludes with a section on proof-reading and terminology checking, to ensure you produce a polished piece of work, before providing a checklist to work through when undertaking your writing. Throughout the chapter, we provide example sections of writing about mixed methods research which model good practice to illustrate what your write-up should look like.

How to write-up mixed methods research

It is vitally important to present your mixed methods research in a way that makes logical sense and reflects the systematic research process you undertook. Mixed methods research projects are similar to single method projects because there is a core requirement to discuss elements of the research process such as the literature review. However, many mixed methods research projects comprise a complex research design and methodology. Therefore, you need to think carefully about the most suitable way of presenting your work to reflect the data collection processes from your multiple components, as well as the inferences generated. Heap and Waters (2018) have created a basic structure for a mixed methods research report/dissertation, which can be seen in Box 12.1.

Box 12.1   Basic structure for a mixed methods research project (adapted from Heap and Waters, 2018)

- Abstract
- Introduction
- Literature review
- Methodology (including mixed methods philosophy, mixed methods design, research design, sampling and ethics)
- Component 1 inferences/higher priority inferences if simultaneous
- Component 2 inferences/lower priority inferences if simultaneous
- Component 3 inferences (including as many components as necessary)
- Discussion of meta-inferences and critique
- Conclusion
- References
- Appendices

You will notice this structure looks like a single method project in many respects. However, the content and structure of sections such as the methodology and discussion are quite different to a single method project, with the distinctions explained in-depth later in the chapter.

When planning to write-up your research, the other thing to bear in mind is the word count you have been given. This is usually specified at the start of a research project or assignment, and is generally in the region of 8,000–10,000 words for an undergraduate dissertation. At the outset, this can seem a daunting figure, with many students wondering how they will ever write that many words. This is completely normal; however, you will quickly see the words mount up, especially when you are reporting on multiple components from a mixed methods project. As every mixed methods project is driven by the research question, every write-up will look slightly different; see Chapter 13 – Case studies for real-world examples. Therefore, we cannot provide any definitive guidance about suggested word counts for each section. A useful first step is to try to map out your write-up using bullet points, like the layout used in Box 12.1. Then, allocate estimated word counts to each section and check this with your research supervisor. See Box 12.2 for an example. Doing this exercise serves two purposes: firstly, it makes the overall word count appear less intimidating and much more manageable. Secondly, it gives you something to aim for when writing, so you can structure and plan each section appropriately to ensure you are not wildly under or over the word count. You are also aiming to write quality words, as well as the required quantity of words, so careful planning will ensure you have your words in the right place. This approach potentially saves time (and stress) later in the writing-up process. Finally, remember that you are setting approximate word counts, which can be revised according to the needs of your research project.

Box 12.2   Example of planning approximate word counts for each section of the write-up

This example is based on an undergraduate dissertation with a 10,000-word maximum limit. The mixed methods research project has a sequential design, with two components of equal priority. If the components did not have equal priority, you should consider allocating more words to the component with greater priority.

- Abstract – not usually in the word count
- Introduction – 750 words
- Literature review – 2,000 words
- Methodology (including ethics) – 2,000 words
- Component 1 – 1,350 words
- Component 2 – 1,350 words
- Discussion of inferences, meta-inferences and critique – 1,550 words
- Conclusion – 1,000 words
- References – not usually in the word count
- Appendices – not usually in the word count
- TOTAL = 10,000 words

Abstract and introduction

Students are often anxious about the abstract and introduction to their research reports, typically because they have not had to write anything like this before. Both sections are usually the last parts of your report to write, which seems counter-intuitive. But there is no need to worry about them until you are well into the writing-up phase. This is also why it is important to think about your word count from the outset, as you do not want to come to write these sections only to find you do not have any words left!

An abstract provides a summary of the whole research project, including the key meta-inferences, which is why it needs to be written last. Its purpose is to provide the reader with a holistic account of the project, so they have an overall indication of the research undertaken and what was found. When conducting your research, you will have read many abstracts because they are a core feature of journal articles; and this is what you are trying to emulate. It is well worth re-visiting three or four abstracts from the research studies that relate most to your central research question, to give you a flavour of how similar research has been summarised. The style abstracts adopt will vary, but a range of core features will be apparent. You will also notice that abstracts are written in the third-person, and your abstract should be the same. Writing an abstract can be difficult because you need to be concise. Abstracts are often in the region of between 150 and 300 words. You only need to include a sentence or two about five key things:

1   The problem being investigated
2   Reference to a key theory/research study if replicating previous research
3   The research strategy and mixed methods design
4   Data collection details for each component (research design, data collection methods, sample size, and participant information)
5   The key inferences and meta-inferences.

Figure 12.1 provides an example abstract from a mixed methods research project by Heap (2010), which contains all the required information as demonstrated in the annotation.

The introduction is generally written second-to-last. This section is used to set the scene for your research project and should provide the reader with insight into the purpose, contents and structure of the report/dissertation. There are generally five main parts to an introduction:

1   Brief outline of the topic area – this should familiarise the reader with the research topic, including any appropriate definitions. Be careful here not to encroach on the literature review; simply set the scene.

2   Central research question and context – links the topic area to the focus of your research, with a clear indication of your central research question.

3   Rationale – explain why the research is relevant to the topic area and why the central research question needs to be answered (without encroaching on the literature review).

4   Subsidiary question(s), aims, and objectives – this part highlights the mixed methods nature of your research project and provides details about each component. Essentially, it should demonstrate how you have gone about answering your central research question.

5   Chapter breakdown – outlines the chapters that follow, including an overview of the core content in each one.

The introduction is another section that needs to be precise, because of the limited word count. You must also be careful to ensure you do not repeat information from other

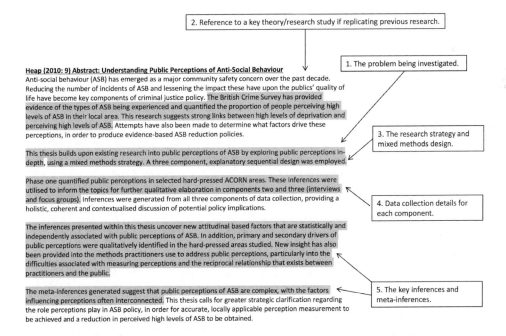

Figure 12.1 Annotated abstract from Heap (2010) *Understanding public perceptions of anti-social behaviour.*

chapters. For example, your brief overview of the topic should not be the same as the introductory paragraph to your literature review and you must avoid the temptation to talk about your inferences and meta-inferences. Think of your introduction as a more basic, simple introduction to what is likely to be a complex research process. This chapter is a good piece of work to put to 'the Grandma test', where you discuss your work with a non-criminologist to check that it makes sense; see Chapter 2 – Creating a mixed methods question and project planning for further information.

Literature review

The literature review is a significant part of your write-up because it is the opening chance to showcase your knowledge about the topic you are researching. It is also the first chapter that you will begin to write. Chapter 2 – Creating a mixed methods question and project planning details a range of different techniques to find the most appropriate literature. Once you have gathered a suitable amount of relevant literature, you need to craft your literature review section into a critical, holistic overview of the topic. Denscombe (2017: 375) states that a literature review should be 'an analysis of the overall picture which highlights the main features and provides strengths and weaknesses of the available knowledge on the topic'. To achieve this, you will need to **synthesise** the literature into a coherent piece, rather than reporting the findings of previous research studies in turn. Writing about each piece of literature in a list-type format will do little to inform the reader about the cross-cutting debates in your area of study and, most importantly, you will not adequately demonstrate an understanding of the context of your research.

Many students struggle with the concept of synthesising literature because it is difficult to know what information to put where, and working this out takes time and practice. Table 12.1 provides a basic framework for the creation of a synthesised literature review. It is based on the premise of you pooling information together from a variety of different sources, and analysing similar aspects from each source alongside one another. You should populate the rows of the table with the information from each source, then to synthesise the information you should write-up the details column by column. For instance, once the table is complete, the 'Results' column will provide a comprehensive overview of the

Table 12.1 Synthesising a literature review

Article *Information (note full citation for reference list)*	*Main idea* • *Aim* • *Purpose* • *Intended outcome*	*Methodology* • *Strategy* • *Design* • *Sampling* • *Data collection method(s)*	*Results* • *Main findings*	*Critique* • *Strengths* • *Weaknesses* • *Gaps?*	*Link to your central research question* • *Topic?* • *Methodology?* • *Implications for your research?*
Use this row to summarise each column in turn . . . →	*Column summary:*	*Column summary:*	*Column summary:*	*Column summary:*	*Column summary:*

main findings from all the studies you have identified that relate to your topic area. There is a final row at the bottom of the table that provides space for you to pool together the information you have collected.

Once you have completed the table using all the sources you have collated, do a quick check to see if you have any gaps. As such, if you have only found quantitative studies, are there any qualitative or mixed methods studies that are relevant to your work? If substantial gaps are identified, it may mean that you need to alter your central research question, subsidiary question(s), aims and objectives slightly, which is acceptable at this stage. When you are sure the table is complete, you can begin synthesising the contents. Ideally this process should take place before you finalise the research design, sampling and data collection methods for each component so it can help inform your decision-making, although in reality this might take place side by side.

You create the synthesis by writing-up the table column by column, moving from left to right; use the 'Column summary' cell in the final row to bring all the information together. Remember, you are trying to assess your research topic as a whole, so be sure to keep in mind the bigger picture as you complete this process. Furthermore, you need to critically analyse the literature; see Chapter 2 – Creating a mixed methods question and project planning for details.

Start by assessing all the contents of the 'Main idea' column to determine the general approach research studies have taken in relation to your topic. This will be different for every research project, but there will likely be clusters of research into specific areas relating to your central research question. For instance, if you are examining public attitudes towards the police, there may be a group of studies relating to gender and attitudes, some about age and attitudes, and others on ethnicity and attitudes. Some studies may also include more than one focus. Group common themes together and discuss them as a whole.

Next, move on to the 'Methodology' column (see Chapter 7 – Research design and sampling, Chapter 8 – Data collection methods and Chapter 9 – Data analysis for information); looking across all the studies, are they mainly quantitative, qualitative, or mixed methods? Does a specific research design feature more frequently than others, how were participants sampled and what data collection methods were regularly used? Again, there are likely to be some commonalities here across all of the sources you have collated. Establish which methods have been used most frequently and explain this. Also, identify flaws in the methods used and suggest how your project will improve on this approach.

Then examine the 'Results' column (see Chapter 6 – Combining the data and Chapter 9 – Data analysis). This is an important one because it will tell you the current state of knowledge about the topic you intend to research. Consider what the main findings are. Are some findings replicated? Are there any findings that contradict each other? In this section, attempt to provide a succinct overview of the key things you know. Try to avoid simply writing-up the findings from each author as a list. Moving on to the 'Critique' column (see Chapter 10 – Critique), determine the methodological strengths and weaknesses of existing research into your topic. Remember to think about all your sources together here; for example, are all the studies quantitative? Consequently, what inherent methodological weaknesses are apparent?

Finally, contemplate the 'Link to your central research question' column. Do the literature and previous studies you have found relate to your proposed research? Does your planned research share a methodology with existing studies? It might be that examining the literature prompts you to revise your central research question, subsidiary question(s), aims, and objectives. This is completely normal and all part of the research planning process. These implications should be in a final paragraph, which sets the scene for the methodological information, which will be the next chapter of your work. See Chapter 2 – Creating a mixed methods question and project planning for more information. Box 12.3 provides a range of sentence stems to help you construct a synthesised literature review and articulate your ideas.

Box 12.3   Sentence stems for creating a synthesised literature review

Writing a synthesised literature review can be a challenging task. Below are a range of sentence stems that can be used to help introduce your findings in relation to each of the column headings from the synthesis table (Table 12.1).

Main idea

- Most of the studies focused on examining . . .
- In contrast, [X number of] studies investigated . . .
- Of the studies presented in the literature, the general aim was to find . . .

Methodology

- The studies within the literature review chiefly utilised a [quantitative/qualitative/mixed methods] strategy . . .
- Within the studies a range of sampling techniques were employed, with [X] being the most popular . . .
- Common data collection methods include . . .

Results

- The main findings relating to [X topic] are . . .
- Other repeated findings include . . .
- Less frequent, but interesting findings were that . . .

Critique

- The main strengths of the research conducted into [X] are . . .
- A frequently occurring limitation of the studies presented in the literature review is . . .
- Having considered previous studies, it is apparent there is a gap in knowledge relating to . . .

Link to your central research question

- The central research question in this study will aim to replicate . . .
- As a result of reviewing the literature, the central research question for this study was revised to include [X] . . .
- From reviewing the literature, it is important that this research employs [X] methodology

As well as synthesising the literature you have found, it is also worth thinking about what not to do. Punch (2016) has created a list of four things to avoid doing in a literature review; see Box 12.4.

Box 12.4   Things to avoid in a literature review (Punch, 2016: 74–75)

Try your best to avoid the following four factors in your literature review. Do not:

- *Use too many direct quotations* – you need to paraphrase the literature to demonstrate your understanding. Also, avoid stringing quotes together. You should be creating the narrative of your literature review, not using the quotations to do this on your behalf.
- *Rely too heavily on secondary sources* [generic textbooks] – ideally you should read the primary, first-hand account of the literature whenever possible.
- *Neglect practitioner-oriented literature* – avoid overlooking practice-based information. From a criminology and criminal justice perspective this includes government reports and policies, as well as publications from agencies and charities (e.g. The Howard League for Penal Reform).
- *Include everything you have ever read* – only use literature relevant to the central research question/methodology. It is quality, not quantity, that counts.

Methodology

When writing-up any research project it is crucial to provide an honest account of the research process undertaken, including all methodological decisions and any mistakes or things that did not go according to plan. This forms your methodology chapter, which is usually written-up after you have drafted your literature review. A methodology chapter should accurately reflect on how and, perhaps most importantly, why you designed and conducted your research project as you did, in order to justify your decision-making. To create and execute a mixed methods research project you will have undertaken a systematic planning process, as outlined in Chapter 2 – Creating a mixed methods question and project planning. The purpose of this chapter is to explain this process in detail. It is imperative that it reflects what you did, rather than simply describing the different parts of the data collection process. Do not simply describe what a particular methodological technique is; explain how you employed it in your work.

Denscombe (2017: 362) suggests a methodology section should achieve three things:

1   Describe how the research was conducted
      This includes providing specific details about the project, as well as information about the 'what, when, where, how, and who' of the research undertaken.
2   Justify these procedures
      Explain why you made the decisions you did and provide evidence to support your claims. Denscombe (2017) suggests you should consider factors such as the: reasonableness, suitability, appropriateness and reliability of the methods, which impacted on your decision-making.

3   Acknowledge any limitations to the methods employed

    It is essential to recognise that your research has inherent strengths and weaknesses associated with the methodology employed. In this section you should focus on these, rather than other strengths and weaknesses associated with the way you could have conducted the research. Other strengths and weaknesses can be examined in the discussion chapter, which we explain later in the chapter.

When writing-up your methodology, you will need to provide a description of the research, justify your decisions and acknowledge the strengths and weaknesses, with reference to each of the different parts of the research process (philosophical rationale, research strategy, mixed methods design, combining the data, research design, sampling, data collection methods, data analysis, and ethical considerations). It is probably easiest to write-up the methodology with sub-headings. For example, a sub-section on research strategy will contain the description, justification, and strengths and weaknesses related to the mixed methods strategy. This approach is much more reader-friendly.

    The parts of the research process you will need to discuss in your methodology section include:

- Philosophical rationale
- Research strategy (mixed methods)
- Mixed methods design (priority and sequence decisions)
- Proposed method of combining the data
- Research design
- Sampling
- Data collection methods
- Methods of data analysis
- Ethical considerations

Articulating your philosophical stance

When you write-up research philosophy, you need to think holistically about your research project. Your epistemology, ontology, research strategy, approach to theory, and general methodology all need to come together into a coherent whole. Before you begin writing, you need to make sure that you have selected the approaches that fit together (see Table 4.2 in Chapter 4 – Philosophy). For a mixed methods piece of work, you need to ensure that you are properly applying pragmatism and multiple realities to your research project, making sure that they align with your central research question, subsidiary question(s), research aims, and research objectives.

    When talking about philosophy you need to make sure you that you are *applying* the terms to your project. Avoid being overly descriptive and writing things like 'according to Heap and Waters (2018) pragmatism is . . .' and simply listing the key features of pragmatism. You can assume the person reading your work has an understanding of the key terminology, particularly if it is a university assignment. Instead, you should aim to write sentences such as 'pragmatism is the most appropriate epistemology for this project because . . .'. This demonstrates an understanding of the term and justifies why it has been selected for your research project.

Explaining project planning decisions

Remember, the information included in the methodology section should be accurate and detailed. The actual numbers and dates of things should be detailed, such as the number of participants and when the research was conducted. This provides a clear picture to the reader and will allow other researchers to replicate your research project. Box 12.5 provides good and bad written examples of a data collection methods section, discussing a quantitative component. You will notice how both examples contain Denscombe's (2017) three must-haves, which are articulated in a synthesised format. However, you will see that each example is communicated very differently, with the good example demonstrating a much more comprehensive approach and positive tone than the bad one.

Box 12.5   Written example of a data collection methods section of a methodology

Here are two examples of written work relating to the data collection methods part of a methodology chapter:

Good practice: detailed, well justified, and emphasises the strengths

An online questionnaire was developed as the data collection method for the quantitative component. It contained 25 closed questions, with all responses measured using a five-point Likert scale to assess the extent of agreement towards the questions posed (strongly agree, agree, neither agree nor disagree, disagree, strongly disagree). The questionnaire was created on the Qualtrics platform and circulated to potential participants via email. Utilising a questionnaire allowed for a large amount of quantitative data to be collected and analysed, with a consistent set of questions posed each time. This facilitates replication and avoids interview effects. An online questionnaire required no financial expenditure and could be created quickly, which suited the short time constraints of the project. Using a questionnaire to collect data does not afford the depth of insight provided by an interview; however, it will provide enough detail to adequately answer the quantitative sub-question. Issues concerning low levels of ecological validity are offset by the qualitative component.

Bad practice: superficial, poorly justified, and emphasises the weaknesses

A questionnaire was used for the quantitative component. It was circulated online and created quickly using an online platform. A questionnaire had to be used because there was no other option with such little time to do the research. Focus groups would have been a much better way of collecting the data required because in questionnaires you cannot prompt or probe the respondent for better answers. It is also impersonal and you have to ask simple questions because you cannot rely on the literacy of the person doing the questionnaire to understand the question.

A useful tip to bear in mind when writing about your chosen methodology is to imagine that you are trying to 'sell' the reader your ideas. You want to convince them that you have planned the best project possible, given the constraints you had to work within (e.g. time, financial, ethical). Adopting a salesperson mind-set should help you to write about your project positively, and avoid any slippage towards a negative portrayal. Just be careful not to go too far into salesperson-mode; remember that the details need to be truthful, accurate and written in the third-person.

Communicating ethical practice

It is worthwhile including three elements in all ethics sections of a written report, namely: details of your ethical approval, the actions you have taken to ensure your research upholds ethical principles, and acknowledgement of a code/statement of ethics from a professional body, such as the British Society of Criminology Statement of Ethics (2015).

You should state that your research has received ethical approval from the relevant gatekeeper and detail what this entailed. Approval was likely to be granted by your university's research ethics committee or possibly your research supervisor. It can be useful to briefly outline the process undertaken, the completion of specific paperwork and the provision of research instruments for scrutiny. If you have been given a reference number associated with your ethical approval, it is good practice to include this in your written work too.

It is also necessary to detail how you have upheld the notions of ethical practice with reference to the ethical principles, which are discussed in Chapter 3 – Ethics. When writing, be careful to ensure you write from the perspective of an ethically conscientious researcher, rather than a researcher that resents the constraints that adhering to research ethics can sometimes impose. Box 12.6 provides an indication of good and bad practice in this respect.

Box 12.6   Research ethics: the conscientious researcher vs the resentful researcher

Throughout your write-up you should aim to portray a professional picture of your research practice. The way you describe your approach to research ethics sends a clear signal about your stance. The two contrasting write-ups below provide examples of how you should and should not articulate the ethical decisions relating to your research. The examples demonstrate that how you write about something can make a substantial difference to the way it is received by the reader.

Good practice: the conscientious researcher

In this project, every effort was made to safeguard the welfare of participants and the researcher. To avoid causing psychological harm to a potentially vulnerable sample population, only questions about perceptions of sexual assault were asked.

Bad practice: the resentful researcher

This project was limited by the fact that only questions about perceptions of sexual assault could be asked, which meant that real-world experiences could not be obtained. This was because the research ethics committee declined the proposed research, which restricted the scope of this study and constrained the findings.

Finally, referring to a code/statement of ethics from a professional body situates your ethical considerations within the discipline of criminology. It serves as an indication that you are aware of contemporary ethical debates relating to your topic and reflects an understanding of wider ethical issues. This part does not have to be lengthy, but it should relate to your own ethical decision-making process. To illustrate, you may have followed the advice provided in the British Society of Criminology Statement of Ethics (2015) about the recruitment of vulnerable participants for your research. Try to make these sorts of detailed links to the code/statement, rather than making general statements about an overall adherence to the guidelines.

There is no specific order in which the three ethical elements need to be discussed. The structure and presentation of this section will be determined by provisions you have made to undertake ethically sound research. The main thing is to be clear about the process you have undertaken and be explicit about the ethical decisions and considerations you have made.

Inferences

The inferences generated by your data collection components are the star attraction of your mixed methods research project. Therefore, care should be taken to present them well. It goes without saying that all data should be presented clearly and accurately. However, in a mixed methods project you also need to think about the order in which you present your data. The structure of your data presentation should be logical and ideally reflect the systematic research process you undertook. You will also need to consider your mixed methods design decisions, particularly issues of sequence and priority, to ensure your presentation matches your process. As outlined earlier in this chapter, you should present the data from each component separately; consequently you will need to demonstrate your quantitative and qualitative analytical prowess. The following sub-sections discuss the presentation of quantitative and qualitative data respectively.

Presenting quantitative data

A wealth of different analyses can be undertaken using quantitative data, so the purpose of this section is to provide a framework for writing-up any type of quantitative analysis. The advice provided here relates to the analysis techniques outlined in Chapter 9 – Data analysis. You will probably not have space to include the details of every statistical test you conduct. Therefore, you should prioritise the inclusion of tests that best answer your central research question. Generally, each statistical test you do present should be displayed in a consistent format, with a table or other visual representation of the data presented alongside the write-up to evidence what has been found. All write-ups should include the details in the bullet points below. Box 12.7 provides an example of these points written-up in practice.

- State the statistical test being used.
- Identify the variable(s).
- State the hypothesis.
- Results table (can be copied and pasted from SPSS).
- Interpret the table (include numerical values and percentages as appropriate): clearly state what the table is saying and what it means in relation to the variables used. What is included in this section will depend on the type of statistical test being used.

- State whether you have proven or disproven your hypothesis.
- State how your results relate to previous research findings from your literature review.
- State how your results help you answer your research questions.

Box 12.7   A basic example of effectively presenting quantitative data

The example shows a basic write-up from a quantitative component of a mixed methods project about public attitudes towards the police, where a Spearman's rho correlation test has been conducted.

It is hypothesised that there will be a moderate positive relationship between police visibility and confidence in the ability of the police to keep people safe, with greater visibility equating to greater confidence (Merry et al., 2012). A Spearman's rho correlation test was undertaken using the two ordinal variables 'SEEPOLICE' and 'SAFEO'.

Table 1 Correlation of police visibility and confidence in the ability of the police to keep people safe

		How often do you see a police officer in the area that you live? The area that you live is defined as being within a 15-minute walk of your home.	How confident are you that the police are effective at keeping people safe?
How often do you see a police officer in the area that you live? The area that you live is defined as being within a 15-minute walk of your home.	Spearman correlation	1	0.004
	Sig. (2-tailed)		0.957
	N	244	241
How confident are you that the police are effective at keeping people safe?	Spearman correlation	0.004	1
	Sig. (2-tailed)	0.957	
	N	241	241

Table 1 details the correlation coefficient value of 0.004. This is a very weak positive correlation, which demonstrates there is little relationship between police visibility and confidence in the ability of the police to keep people safe. However, it does show that the response categories in the variables are moving in the same direction, thus greater visibility reflects more confidence. This result disproves the hypothesis and is in contrast to research conducted by Merry et al. (2012), who noted that police visibility was found to aid confidence levels. It provides some indication about how police visibility can affect attitudes towards the police, but it is less conclusive than the independent variables that relate to personal characteristics when considering the central research question.

Presenting qualitative data

There are a variety of ways of analysing qualitative data, with the following advice tailored to writing-up the basic thematic analysis described in Chapter 9 – Data analysis. When writing-up a thematic analysis, there are a range of things to include for each theme, as indicated in the bullet points below. An example can be found in Figure 12.2, which has been annotated to demonstrate each of the core components as well as how to reference your own data:

- Introductory statement about the theme
- References to the data (correctly cited)

  o Paraphrasing
  o Direct quotation

- Synthesis to previous research and/or an established theory
- Links to the central research question/subsidiary question

Discussion

The discussion chapter in a mixed methods project should contain two core topics: a discussion of the meta-inferences and a critique of your research process. This section outlines how you should present your meta-inferences, before moving on to spend a substantial amount of time considering critique.

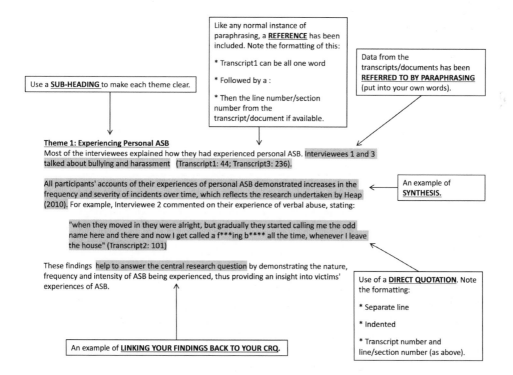

Figure 12.2 Annotated example of writing-up a theme from a qualitative thematic analysis.

Presenting meta-inferences

The meta-inferences you generate are the reason why you undertook your mixed methods research project in the first place and they should answer your central research question. For information about how to develop a set of meta-inferences based on the way you combine your quantitative and qualitative components, see Chapter 6 – Combining the data.

The contents of your meta-inferences will vary depending on the data collection methods used in your quantitative and qualitative components, the way the data were combined, and ultimately by your central research question. As such, it is difficult to be too prescriptive about how your meta-inferences should be presented. However, meta-inferences should always be:

- Clear, succinct, and to the point
- Accessible to a non-specialist audience (think of 'The grandma test' from Chapter 2 – Creating a mixed methods question and project planning)
- Provide an answer to the central research question

Sometimes mixed methods research projects can generate multiple meta-inferences, which students can find overwhelming to report as a coherent set. In such circumstances, it may be helpful to bullet point the meta-inferences or put them in a table. Furthermore, you may wish to select roughly three of your meta-inferences that best answer your central research question to be your key meta-inferences, which you explain in detail. Focusing on a smaller number of key areas will also be beneficial when writing your conclusion as you will be able to concisely refer to the central points.

When you detail your key meta-inferences be sure to relate them to the literature you discuss in your literature review and when you wrote up your inferences. As outlined in Chapter 2 – Creating a mixed methods question and project planning, this is often a timely juncture to conduct a final literature research for any issues arising from your inferences.

Critique in the discussion

The critique section, which forms part of the discussion or evaluation chapter, is one of the most important elements of writing-up your research. It provides you with the opportunity to showcase and apply your knowledge about a range of methodological factors that include: the research process, the full spectrum of evaluative terminology, the interpretation of your inferences and meta-inferences, and whether your research has answered your central research question. Therefore investing time in sharpening this section is energy well spent. You should also be prepared to use these skills elsewhere in your writing, for instance in the literature review, where you will be required to critique the work of others.

Some students believe that the main purpose of a critique section is to show how wonderfully well the research has gone, by putting an inaccurate positive spin on the work that has been carried out. Instead, it is far more valuable for your development as a researcher (and more likely to mean you will gain higher marks on an assessed task) if you truthfully report both the strengths and weaknesses of your research and explain why they have occurred. For example, you may not have been able to recruit as many participants as expected. Be transparent about any mistakes made and the actions you took to remedy the issue(s). An exact representation is much better than over-claiming what you did, or have really found. It is also important to note that it does not particularly matter if you cannot fully answer your central research question, as it is often the process that you have embarked upon to reach your conclusion that is prioritised. This section will outline seven factors to consider, including how to: articulate your research in a critical but positive way, use key terminology, and frame your critique consistently. It will then move on to discuss how to structure and plan a critique section, enabling you to produce a logical appraisal of your research.

1. Articulating your critique positively

Providing an honest account of your research does not mean that your critique should only focus on the things that could have been better; quite the opposite. The language that you use to articulate your project defines how your research is interpreted by the reader and you should endeavour to convey your critique as positively as possible, whilst being transparent about the reality of the strengths and weaknesses. The two examples provided in Box 12.8 each report the same information about the levels of external validity present in an example study about students' attitudes towards the police (which is also outlined in Chapter 10 – Critique). The examples demonstrate that it is how you write about something that influences the reader's perception of the content.

Box 12.8 Examples of good and bad practice when writing a critique

Both of these examples discuss a quantitative component that used an online questionnaire to assess students' attitudes towards the police. A non-probability convenience sampling technique was used, resulting in low levels of external validity. Instead of focusing on the disadvantages of the said practice, you should always try to highlight and justify the advantages of using that method and why you selected that approach, even when reporting a weakness in your research.

Good practice: a positive critique

A non-probability convenience sampling technique was employed to quickly gather the opinions of students that were close to hand. This facilitated a large number of respondents, but means the inferences have low external validity because they cannot be generalised.

Bad practice: a negative critique

There was not the time to produce a random probability sampling frame so a non-probability convenience technique had to be used instead, which meant the findings have low levels of external validity because the inferences cannot be generalised.

These examples provide a snapshot of written work about one evaluative criterion. Try to imagine reading a whole section that constantly focuses on the disadvantages of the research practice that was undertaken. It paints an unnecessarily negative picture of the research process and undermines the initial justifications and decision-making that took place when the research project was planned and reported in your methodology. The reader may begin to question why you made those decisions in the first place. Therefore, aim to model the good practice example that foregrounds the advantages, which will create a more positive impression of your research even when acknowledging any weaknesses.

2. Using key terminology

A further way to ensure you write a convincing critique is to use the correct research methods terminology. There are a lot of specific terms to include in an evaluative section when using mixed methods; up to 16. Using the correct methodological terms will demonstrate to the reader (in many cases the person marking your work) that you have a sound grasp of the technical aspects of the topic. Furthermore, it will allow you to clearly articulate your points through the production of a concise summary of the strengths and weaknesses, which is useful for reports that have a restricted or limited word count. When assessing the merits of the inferences generated by different components, it is important to use the correct terminology for the associated research strategy. Use Table 12.2 to double-check that you have used the correct terminology for each strategy and your meta-inferences. Students can often get the quantitative and qualitative terms mixed up, and with the added dimension of mixed methods, there are even more terms to contend with.

Table 12.2 Research strategies and their associated evaluative terms

Strategy	Associated evaluative terms
Quantitative	Reliability Validity (4 criteria) — External validity — Internal validity — Ecological validity — Construct validity
Qualitative	Trustworthiness (4 criteria) — Credibility — Transferability — Dependability — Confirmability Authenticity (5 criteria) — Fairness — Ontological authenticity — Educative authenticity — Catalytic authenticity — Tactical authenticity
Mixed methods	Inference quality Inference transferability

3. Framing your critique

As well as writing with a positive tone and using the correct methodological terminology, it is useful to use a consistent means of framing your critique across all the three strategies that you are commenting on (quantitative, qualitative, and mixed methods). You may have noticed that here and throughout Chapter 10 – Critique we use the terms *high* and *low* when referring to the evaluative criteria. To illustrate, 'the research demonstrated high levels of reliability' or 'the internal validity was low in this research'. Also see the examples provided in Chapter 10, Boxes 10.2 to 10.8, which further demonstrate the use of these terms in practice. Using 'high' and 'low' provides a consistent benchmark for your critique that is non-strategy-specific. It also affords you the opportunity to suggest that a criterion with features of high and low aspects can be 'fairly high', 'fairly low', or 'moderate'. With a criterion such as construct validity, where some variables demonstrate high levels and some variables low levels, there is the option to make a judgement about the overall level of construct validity being somewhere in between high and low, such as moderate.

4. Planning your write-up

From your experience of completing a range of academic work to date, you may have found that some pieces of written work can be produced quickly. In contrast, a critique section is something that requires meticulous planning to make sure all the relevant content is included. So be sure to leave enough time to complete this process. Your planning process should include some thinking about structure, content, and synthesis that are outlined below.

5. Structure

Throughout this book we have detailed how conducting mixed methods research is a systematic process and this should also be reflected in all aspects of your write-up. The critique section should look broadly like the process diagram in Figure 12.3, but should reflect the structure of the mixed methods project you have undertaken. For instance, you should critique the components in the sequence in which they were conducted and presented, as this reflects your research project. If the components were conducted simultaneously, the first component to be reported should be the one with greater priority. If everything is equal, then simply select one component to report first, but ensure you consistently report this component first throughout your entire write-up.

6. Content

Once you have decided on the structure for your critique section, it is time to think about the content. The section(s) on the quantitative component(s) should focus on the research process that you undertook and how your decision-making resulted in high or low levels of reliability, internal validity, external validity, ecological validity, and construct validity. The section(s) on the qualitative component(s) should reflect on the impact your research has had upon the participants and wider society by using all nine of the evaluative criteria to assess whether there are high or low levels of trustworthiness (credibility, transferability, dependability and confirmability) and authenticity (fairness, ontological authenticity, educative authenticity, catalytic authenticity and tactical authenticity). Remember that it

The structure of a critique section for a QUANT/QUAL mixed methods project:

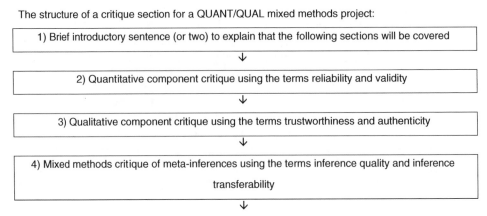

Figure 12.3 Suggested structure for a critique section.

is okay to state that trustworthiness and authenticity cannot be determined if you do not have the information from which to form a judgement. Finally, your section on mixed methods will need to conclude whether the meta-inferences exhibit high or low levels of inference quality and inference transferability. That equates to 16 different criteria that you need to assess and discuss.

7. Synthesis

As well as the order and contents of the section, also consider how you are going to structure each part (e.g. the quantitative component(s), the qualitative component(s), and the mixed methods meta-inferences). There are two basic approaches to the actual structure of the write-up for the component: the list approach and the synthesis approach. The list approach is simply that you would list the different evaluative criteria and indicate if they are high or low, using examples from your research to support your claims. For example:

> *In the quantitative component, reliability was high because a cross-sectional research design was used alongside a questionnaire data collection method. The internal validity was low because a cross-sectional research design was used, meaning that causation could not be determined. Ecological validity was also low because a questionnaire data collection was used which did not reflect the real world . . .*

Listing your critique is one way to ensure you cover all the evaluative terminology by going through each one in turn, but it does make the section a little disjointed and repetitive. In contrast, the synthesis approach is a much more sophisticated way of writing-up your critique section and we would encourage you to attempt this method. To synthesise your writing you would group your ideas together by topic, rather than discussing each criterion in turn (listing them). Bringing together similar elements of the evaluative criteria will provide a critical account of your research that has a greater sense of flow.

As such, you would discuss each component in term, noting the criteria that are high and then outlining the criteria that are low. This style should utilise fewer words than the list approach, which is helpful if your word limit is tight, and a synthesis should also avoid too much repetition. Synthesising your critique section can be achieved in two straightforward ways. Firstly, you could group your write-up based on whether the criteria evidenced are high or low. To illustrate:

> *The qualitative component demonstrated high levels of trustworthiness, specifically credibility, dependability, and confirmability, as well as the authenticity criterion fairness. This is because the research process was thorough, a meticulous research audit was conducted, and the researcher acted as neutrally as possible, which facilitated a range of perspectives. In contrast, transferability was low because of a lack of in-depth data. Furthermore, ontological authenticity, educative authenticity, catalytic authenticity, and tactical authenticity could not be determined because feedback from the participants about the impact of the research was not obtained . . .*

Alternatively, in the case of the quantitative component, the grouping could be based on the research process. For instance:

> *For the quantitative component, the cross-sectional research design produced a high level of reliability because the research could be repeated, but a low level of internal validity due to the inability to determine causation. The online questionnaire data collection method afforded a high level of reliability because the same concepts can be consistently measured over time, but because of a lack of real-world applicability, ecological validity was low . . .*

The type of synthesis you employ will depend on the type of research project you have designed and the range of strengths and weaknesses from your inferences and meta-inferences. You may wish to include a mixture of the list and synthesis approaches, and/or use different types of synthesis to report on the different components.

Conclusion

The conclusion section draws everything together from your mixed methods research project, and is ultimately where you provide your definitive answer to your central research question. In order to do this, you should explain your research and what you found. This is where some students struggle because they repeat the information already provided in the chapters about the different components. There is no need to go through your whole project again in the conclusion. You should succinctly state what you have found, possibly listing your main meta-inferences. Then you can begin to analyse your meta-inferences by considering the implications of your research; what do they mean and who are they meaningful to? For instance, do your meta-inferences suggest that an element of criminal justice practice should be reconsidered? Or does your research call for better support services to be made available to victims? Try to think about the wider discipline of criminology here, and situate your findings in a meaningful and relatable context. Furthermore, you should also consider what your research adds to the field of study. Do your meta-inferences confirm or contradict previous research? Is there a reason why your meta-inferences have occurred and what does this mean? Be positive about what you have found, locate your work within the discipline and be distinct about your contribution to the field.

The next part of your conclusion should reflect on the things about your research project that you would do differently if you had the chance to do it again. It is important to be honest here about any shortcomings or problems you faced that had an impact on the research project. For example, did you leave participant recruitment for your qualitative component too late? Would you have selected a different sampling technique in hindsight? If everything went as planned, think about how you could improve your project. Could you have phrased some of the questions on your quantitative questionnaire differently to get a more nuanced dataset? Could you have recruited a more representative cross-section of participants for your qualitative component if you used a probability sample? It is not necessary to hide mistakes or issues that arose during the project. They happen to all researchers regardless of experience and are simply part of the research process.

A final section of your conclusion should consider any emerging policy-related issues from your research project and meta-inferences. Has there been a big criminal justice event since you designed your project that has produced a defining moment in your field of study, for example the Manchester Arena bombing or the Westminster Bridge terrorist attacks that took place in 2017? Has there been a new policy announcement since you started your project, such as the introduction of police body-worn cameras? Think carefully about your topic and any related events. Adding a policy element to your conclusion takes the analysis to a more sophisticated level, demonstrating you have reflected upon your meta-inferences in relation to the real world. You can even make suggestions for new policies. Finally, based on your meta-inferences, you should offer some suggestions for future research projects. This should highlight any ongoing gaps in knowledge and indicate how they could be filled. For instance, briefly suggest what a future research project might investigate.

Appendices

The appendix of a research report/dissertation contains a range of supplementary information that may be useful to the reader, in a way that supports the claims you have made in the report itself. The contents of the appendices are not usually included in the word count. The appendices are always situated at the end of the document after the reference list and should be presented in the order that they are referred to within the main body of work. You may find that your institution stipulates what documents your appendix should contain, but if not, the following information is commonly included:

- Literature review tables
- Ethical approval paperwork
- Participant invitation letter(s)
- Information sheet(s)
- Blank consent form(s)
- Debriefing material(s)
- Research instruments (e.g. questionnaire/interview schedule)
- Supplementary tables and figures of quantitative analysis
- Evidence of qualitative analysis (e.g. a thematic coding table and coded interview transcripts)

Make sure each item in the appendix is clearly labelled, for example Appendix 1, Appendix 2, and so on. Furthermore, ensure this matches the description provided in the text. For instance, if you say that Appendix 1 is your ethical approval form, ensure your ethical approval form is presented as Appendix 1 in the appendix. This sounds quite obvious, but it is something that is easy to overlook.

Proof-reading and terminology checking

The final stage of presenting your work is to thoroughly check each section to ensure that you are using the correct quantitative, qualitative, and mixed methods terminology. Using research terminology accurately demonstrates your understanding of your research topic and mixed methods methodology, as well as often being a more concise way of writing about something. Use the Glossary of key terms at the back of this book as a guide.

In addition, remember to check for typographical and grammatical errors. It is often helpful for someone else to help you proof-read, especially if they are not a criminologist. A lay perspective is useful because they will also highlight any sections that are unclear or need re-writing. Sometimes institutions offer proof-reading services; check your virtual learning environment for details, or ask at the library. If you cannot find anyone to proof-read for you, do not worry. A good way to check if your work makes sense is to read it aloud. You may feel a little silly at first, but it is a great way to spot errors in your written work.

Writing-up checklist

To help with your writing-up we have created a checklist to ensure you include all the key points discussed in this chapter, and throughout the book. We have tried to make this as generic as possible so it is relevant to all mixed methods research projects. However, your project is unique so do not see this as an exhaustive list, but more as a starting point. The quantitative and qualitative components in the checklist do not represent the order in which you need to report these sections in (your presentation should reflect your process); it is simply to provide information about what should be included in the write-up for each component.

- Abstract
  - The problem being investigated
  - Reference to a key theory/research study if replicating previous research
  - The research strategy and mixed methods design
  - Data collection details for each component
  - The key inferences and meta-inferences
- Introduction
  - Brief introduction to the topic area
  - Central research question and context
  - Rationale
  - Subsidiary question(s), aims, and objectives
  - Chapter breakdown
- Literature review
  - Synthesised
  - Main ideas

- o   Methodology
- o   Findings
- o   Critique
- o   Implications for your central research question

- Methodology

  - o   Philosophical rationale
  - o   Research strategy
  - o   Mixed methods design (priority and sequence decisions)
  - o   Proposed way of combining the data
  - o   Research design
  - o   Sampling
  - o   Data collection methods
  - o   Methods of data analysis
  - o   Ethical considerations

- Quantitative component

  - o   Hypothesis
  - o   Form of analysis
  - o   Interpret the table – including numbers/values in the write-up
  - o   Explain the meaning of the results
  - o   Link back to hypothesis – proved or disproved
  - o   Related to previous studies from literature review
  - o   Related to research questions

- Qualitative component

  - o   Outline the theme
  - o   Refer to the data (correctly referenced)
  - o   Paraphrasing
  - o   Direct quotation
  - o   Synthesis to previous research and/or an established theory
  - o   Links to the central research question/subsidiary question

- Discussion of meta-inferences and critique

  - o   Key meta-inferences discussed in relation to the literature
  - o   Critique
  - o   Quantitative component(s)
  - o   Qualitative component(s)
  - o   Mixed methods

- Conclusion

  - o   Main meta-inferences and answer central research question
  - o   Emerging policy issues and things you would do differently
  - o   Implications and suggestions for future research

- References

  - o   All listed in alphabetical order and formatted correctly (e.g. APA 6th)

- Appendices (which may include)
  - o Literature review tables
  - o Ethical approval paperwork
  - o Participant invitation letter(s)
  - o Information sheet(s)
  - o Blank consent form(s)
  - o Debriefing material(s)
  - o Research instruments (e.g. questionnaire/interview schedule)
  - o Supplementary tables and figures of quantitative analysis
  - o Evidence of qualitative analysis (e.g. a thematic coding table and coded interview transcripts)

Summary

This chapter has provided a detailed overview about how to write-up a mixed methods research project. The focus has been on providing a generic template for any mixed methods project that can be adapted to suit the needs of your research. We have said throughout this book that undertaking mixed methods research is more complex than doing single method research, and this comes to the fore when writing-up.

When using mixed methods it is likely that you will have a lot of information to write-up, often within the same word limit constraints as those using a single method. Use the resources and tips in this chapter, as well as the Glossary of key terms at the back of the book, to create a concise write-up that details your research in a positive light. If you have completed your mixed methods project, you will have worked extremely hard to get to this point, so ensure your write-up does your research justice. Good luck! ☺

Learning questions

1 What does synthesising your literature review chapter entail?
2 How are you going to structure the presentation of your quantitative and qualitative components in your written work? (Hint: this should be based on sequence and priority.)
3 Why should you communicate your research in a positive light?

13 Case studies

Catrin Andersson

CHAPTER OVERVIEW

- Introduction
- Case study 1: Criminality, consumption and the counterfeiting of fashion goods: a consumer perspective
- Case study 2: Evaluation of the Gateway Protection Programme
- Case study 3: Families living with problem gambling
- Case study 4: Sexual victimization, disclosure, and accountability: organizational responses of the Boy Scouts of America to child sexual abuse
- Case study 5: Investigating recovery capital whilst identifying gender similarities and differences in pathways to recovery from problematic alcohol use: a mixed methods study
- Summary
- Learning questions

Introduction

This chapter presents five case studies of mixed methods projects from the UK and the USA. Different criminological topics are coved in the case studies, including: deviant leisure, refugees, gambling, addiction, child sexual abuse, and recovery from substance use. The case studies are written by the original authors of the research and provide a concrete illustration of the concepts and themes introduced throughout this book. To help you draw parallels with the rest of the book, each case study is divided into six parts: A summary of the study, philosophy (see Chapter 4), mixed methods design (see Chapter 5), methodology (see Chapters 7 and 8), inferences and meta-inference (see Chapters 6 and 9), and conclusion. In the conclusion to each case study, the authors highlight the impact of their research (Bornmann, 2012; Kingsley, 2015), demonstrating the usefulness of mixed methods research in criminology. From this chapter you will see that mixed methods research can be conducted by a range of means, which are articulated in a variety of ways. The central lesson to take from this is the importance of clarity and justification in your research planning and process.

Case study 1: Criminality, consumption and the counterfeiting of fashion goods: a consumer perspective

Joanna Large

University of Bristol

Summary of study

The past decade has seen heightened attention towards the potentially harmful consequences of intellectual property crime. In particular, there are concerns about the damage to industry and the global economy, alongside increasing recognition of links with
'organised' crime and terrorism. As a result, a plethora of policy initiatives have sought
to reduce the problem of counterfeiting and piracy, of which the underlying principle
is consumer responsibility. However, this research argues that the principle of consumer
responsibility is based on a number of assumptions. This is prominent when the specific
example of fashion counterfeiting is examined. Therefore, the aim of this mixed methods
research was to explore consumers' perceptions about fashion counterfeiting and how
they relate to their fashion purchasing and assumptions underpinning anti-counterfeiting
policy in the UK. The main central research question is 'What perceptions do consumers
have about fashion counterfeiting and how do they relate to their fashion purchasing and
assumptions underpinning anti-counterfeiting policy?' In addition, the following subsidiary questions were posed:

- What perceptions and understandings do consumers have about fashion counterfeiting?
- How do consumers' perceptions about fashion counterfeiting relate to their con-
  sumption patterns?
- Who buys counterfeit fashion items and who does not?
- Why do people buy fashion counterfeit items or not?
- What are the different consumption patterns buying fashion and/or fashion counter-
  feit items?
- What factors shape consumers' behaviour and attitudes towards buying fashion coun-
  terfeit items?
- What are the key assumptions about fashion counterfeiting that currently inform
  policy?
- How do these assumptions relate to consumer perceptions and behaviours?

Philosophy

This mixed methods research set out to explore a topic that had been largely unexplored
within criminology and required an approach that was interdisciplinary and iterative.
Stemming from an interpretivist paradigm, the research process was guided by the idea of
'adaptive theory' (Layder, 1998). Adaptive theory takes on board a number of important
principles that were felt to be important for research of such an exploratory nature. In particular, adaptive theory allows an acknowledgement that no research is 'theory neutral'. It
allows for movement between collecting data and developing inferences and going back to
more data collection without inferences being fixed in stone, thus keeping in line with an
inductive approach. Adaptive theory also allows for a 'wide search for relevant data', which
was important for an interdisciplinary thesis, and essentially 'a genuine willingness to utilize
appropriately both quantitative and qualitative data sources' (Bottoms, 2008: 98–99).

Mixed methods design

It was initially perceived that this would be a qualitative research project, and follow
strictly in the qualitative tradition. However, as the research proposal progressed into a
feasible project, it became apparent that because of the lack of existing data in this area, a
quantitative method such as a questionnaire making use of a larger sample would enable

a much broader picture to be gained and generate some initial exploratory data (Bryman, 2008). On the other hand, it was felt that using only a quantitative data collection method would be insufficient in exploring the overall research aim, and the methodology naturally progressed into one that took a mixed methods approach comprising three components.

This research adopted a multi-phase sequential mixed methods design, with equal priority of the three components. As such, this project sought to use a quantitative component to provide a sense of context, followed by two qualitative components to provide a more in-depth understanding that formed the primary emphasis of the research. Therefore, the three components working in tandem with each other were implemented. Initially, a quantitative self-completion questionnaire (online and paper version) was conducted. This provided a way of exploring consumer perceptions and behaviours and identifying themes to explore in the qualitative work, which is characteristic of multi-phase sequential design. Next, building upon preliminary data observations, the project made use of a series of qualitative semi-structured interviews and qualitative focus groups that explored these early observations and allowed for the generation of new and more detailed insights. It was hoped that by implementing this mix of methods, the research would provide data that were 'mutually illuminating' (Bryman, 2008: 603).

Methodology

The research adopted a cross-sectional design, capturing data at a single point in time. Data collected were completed for the three different components (i.e. questionnaire, semi-structured interviews and focus groups) through three interwoven sampling processes. First, because of the lack of an existing sampling frame and the exploratory nature of the questionnaire, a non-probability sampling method was employed for the three components, utilising a mixture of purposive and snowball sampling methods. The questionnaire received 807 responses. Demographic information was collected on each participant's age, gender, ethnicity, location, employment status and average monthly spend on fashion goods. Second, a purposive sampling strategy was primarily used for the semi-structured interviews to target consumers who had previously knowingly bought counterfeit fashion, those who had never knowingly purchased counterfeit fashion and those who identified as 'non-fashion' consumers. Some participants were recruited via the questionnaire (respondents had an option to provide contact details for a follow-up interview); other respondents were approached via interview invitation flyers, posters (e.g. in places like charity shops and hair salons), online discussion forums, email distribution lists, and through contacts and word of mouth. Twenty-seven interviews were conducted in total. Profiles describing demographic characteristics and consumption habits were created for each interview participant and included in the project proposal as an appendix. Third, making use of an opportunistic approach to target a particular age group, identified as retrospectively important in the earlier research phases, two focus groups – with a total of 19 participants – were carried out with young people (aged 16–18 years).

Quantitative and qualitative analyses were carried out on data from the three components. Reflecting the non-probability sampling strategy and aim for the questionnaire data to generate exploratory themes, statistical analysis examining patterns and potential relationships in the data was the focus of the quantitative analysis of the questionnaires data. All qualitative data generated through the interviews and focus groups were analysed using a thematic approach.

Inferences and meta-inferences

The inferences from the quantitative analyses found support for the idea suggested by Ledbury Research (2007) who argued that 'there is little to distinguish demographically between those who buy counterfeits and those who do not'. This meant that there was little evidence to support common assumptions that those who buy counterfeits are from a lower socio-economic background. Further, this supported Rutter and Bryce's (2008) work that criticised the idea that counterfeit consumers can be positioned as 'Other'. Another finding was that the situation, including the cost of the product and the location of where the counterfeit product was being sold, was important in understanding counterfeit fashion purchasing. This reflected other research on consumer behaviour with regards to counterfeits that suggests people buy counterfeits because of the 'price advantages' they offer (BASCAP, 2009; Ledbury Research, 2007). UK consumers were also much more likely to buy counterfeits when they were abroad than in the UK (when not purchasing products from the internet). The quantitative analyses also found that counterfeit fashion purchasing tended to be infrequent and occasional.

A considerable proportion of the questionnaire was devoted to examining attitudes towards fashion counterfeiting and respondents were asked to rate their agreement with a number of statements. The inferences here demonstrated that the consumption of fashion counterfeits was largely seen as unproblematic, socially acceptable, and, for some, a legitimate way of consuming versions of products they would not otherwise be able to access. This acceptability towards counterfeits was closely associated with the popular perception that fashion counterfeiting is a 'victimless crime' that is not, on the whole, considered harmful. Respondents tended to disagree with the idea that public policing resources should be spent on tackling counterfeiting.

Inferences from the qualitative components of the research allowed for a much greater interrogation of the themes covered on the questionnaire, but also allowed for new insights to be gathered that were not covered by the questionnaire. The most striking finding here was how, although respondents might describe fashion counterfeiting as something that is relatively harmless, their explanations of counterfeiting suggested that they actually very much recognised the harms, victims, and impacts of counterfeiting. It was interesting to find that many participants did not recognise counterfeiting as a crime problem, but instead talked about counterfeiting in relation to social harm. Many described concerns in terms of ethics – issues such as child labour, labour exploitation and risks to workers. However, many people also described how they had these same concerns about the legitimate fashion industry – from value retailers to luxury brands. This meant that for many people, the argument that they should not buy counterfeits because they are harmful – a key message in anti-counterfeiting consumer responsibility policy advocated by law and regulatory agencies – was just not something they took seriously.

Meta-inferences suggest that the consumption of counterfeit fashion goods happens within the broader reasons why people buy fashion more generally: it is a situated everyday part of consumption and leisure practices. Whilst situational and contextual factors (such as cost, location, and availability) are important on the surface level, there is also something important about the product, or the way it is marketed, that drives consumer desire.

In terms of exploring consumer views in relation to fashion counterfeiting and harm, the research inferences challenge focusing on a narrow understanding of crime and harm. Consumers were generally unconcerned about potential financial harm to the legitimate industry, or indeed wider loss of tax revenue. However, many were acutely aware of the potential ethical issues associated with the counterfeit fashion industry.

Many consumers recognised the ethical issues of manufacturing and producing counterfeits, but also the association of ethical issues with the manufacture and production of fashion goods more generally. Although fashion companies would likely deny poor practices, consumers did often hold these perceptions. This reinforces the need to consider the consumption of counterfeit fashion within the context of consuming fashion generally. But, if we are to do this, there must be recognition that many consumers view the illegitimate counterfeit industry in a similar light to the legitimate fashion industry. This has important implications for criminology's tendency to focus on legally defined conceptions of crime. The research also found some strong views against fashion counterfeiting, although interestingly, this tended to relate to personal views on identity and style, as opposed to concerns about the harms of counterfeiting.

The research was able to conclude that there are real challenges for the consumer responsibility-focused policy approach to tackling the problem of counterfeiting. These challenges arose for a number of reasons, stemming partly from the issue that this kind of policy starts by making assumptions about consumer behaviour, coupled with a generic understanding of counterfeiting and too simplistic understandings of issues around supply and demand. The mixed methods research found that to understand fashion counterfeiting, a broader awareness of how this relates to legitimate fashion consumption is needed.

Conclusion

This mixed methods project provided the first criminological exploration into understanding the consumption of counterfeit fashion. Employing a multi-phase sequential mixed methods design highlighted the importance of interrogating surface-level assumptions and the ability of mixed methods research to generate meta-inferences which are 'mutually illuminating' (Bryman, 2008). It also demonstrated the complexities of the relationships between perceptions and behaviour and, importantly for criminology, how public perceptions and understandings of crime, harm and victimisation may be much more complex than they first appear. Importantly, respondents tended to be supportive of the idea of counterfeiting as a 'victimless crime' and not very harmful, yet would go on to talk about issues that, especially within a critical criminological perspective, are absolutely relevant to criminologists.

Case study 2: Evaluation of the Gateway Protection Programme

Deborah Platts-Fowler and David Robinson

Victoria University of Wellington and University of Sheffield

Summary of study

The Gateway Protection Programme (GPP) is the UK quota refugee scheme co-funded by the UK Border Agency and the European Refugee Fund (ERFIII). The scheme provides 12 months of material and social assistance to help refugees resettle. This mixed methods research evaluated the scheme for refugees who arrived in the UK between February and May 2009 using an explanatory sequential mixed methods design.

The research had two aims: to investigate how the GPP was being delivered by different organisations across a number of resettlement sites; and to explore the resettlement experiences of refugees during their first 18 months of life in the UK. In addressing the second aim, the research used a mixed methods design – a questionnaire and focus groups – and was longitudinal to explore changes over time. The research questions included:

- Which aspects of the GPP provision are valued by refugees and how have these supported integration?
- What are the social and anti-social experiences of refugees, particularly racial discrimination and hate crime?
- Do refugee experiences vary by nationality, gender, GPP provider, or resettlement site and why?

Philosophy

There was a strong appetite for quantitative data for this study, as is often the case when evaluating government programmes. This is understandable given the need for public accountability; the requirement to show that citizens' money has been well spent. The interest in quantitative data is also about the 'killer graph' – the chart that demonstrates success instantly. However, the rationale for qualitative data was also strong for this study. If we are to understand why government programmes are successful, and not merely if they are, talking to people and even ethnographic observation are important methods of research. If the line of inquiry is not too rigid, these qualitative methods may also reveal answers to questions that one might not have thought to ask; highlighting the value of inductive inquiry, where theories can be developed from the data and not merely tested by the data. Of course, the value of quantitative methods is not merely in testing a theory, but also in assessing its generalisability across a range of social groups and situations. This type of detail undermines the 'killer graph' or the 'killer statistic', so it may not get the airtime it deserves. Arguably, this is why some researchers are sceptical of quantitative methods (e.g. Young, 2011). Instead, these critics might focus on qualifying how quantitative data are collected and represented.

This study was underpinned by a pragmatic and holistic approach to research, supporting the use of whatever methodological tools are required to answer the research questions (Teddlie and Tashakkori, 2009). For this study, it was necessary to describe experiences and outcomes across the entire cohort of refugees over the specified period, supporting the use of a questionnaire. The decision to use a qualitative component in conjunction with a quantitative component was rooted in the ontological perspective of multiple realities. Social phenomena can rarely be extracted from the social context. Studying the experiences of Iraqi refugees in two different resettlement sites, although they were supported by the same agency, was underpinned by the understanding that the physical and social place will likely affect resettlement experiences and integration; which is exactly what the study concluded (Platts-Fowler and Robinson, 2015).

For this study, it was important to understand the why, for whom and in what circumstances, in addition to how many. A complementarity understanding of quantitative and qualitative data was the main reason for using mixed methods. Another reason was the potential to use the qualitative inferences to inform the quantitative design and the questionnaire inferences to inform the qualitative design. This mutually beneficial understanding of mixed methods will be discussed in more detail below.

Mixed methods design

Mixed methods were used to grasp the nature and the extent of the refugee programme's impact on perceptions and outcomes. The first questionnaire was designed and administered ahead of the focus groups. This was a pragmatic decision to maximise the response rate, leaving enough time within the scope of the project to send out reminder letters, known to increase postal responses. Another reason was to use the questionnaire responses to inform the sampling and development of the topic guides for the focus groups. The mixed methods design was multi-phase sequential with equal priority of the different components. This is an iterative process as a development technique, with the quantitative element informing the qualitative element and vice versa. The focus group data informed the questionnaires administered at 12 and 18 months. Most questions remained unchanged to facilitate longitudinal analysis, but others were removed or added to assess how widely some of the qualitative inferences applied across the cohort.

Mixed methods were primarily also used in this study to achieve 'expansion', with the questionnaire providing the breadth and the focus group discussions the depth. In other words, the quantitative data contributed to understanding of 'how much' and the qualitative data contributed more to the 'how and why' research questions. In addition, complementarity was used. Both the questionnaire and focus groups explored refugee resettlement and integration, even using the same themes, but they were able to target distinct issues. The women–only focus groups were used to explore issues affecting women. It was especially important to take this approach, because often men assisted their female relatives to complete their questionnaires, particularly if their literacy levels were higher.

Methodology

The main strand of the study was focused on the resettlement experiences of refugees entering the UK as part of the GPP, and therefore a longitudinal design was implemented. Data on refugee experiences were collected at three stages – at six, 12, and 18 months after arrival into the UK. The GPP provision lasted only 12 months. The data collection at 18 months was to assess how refugees were faring independently, focusing on their ability and willingness to access mainstream services and informal social support. Data collection comprised a questionnaire sent to all GPP refugees arriving in the UK between February and May 2009; and a series of focus groups with a selected sample. The focus groups provided an opportunity to investigate refugee experiences, perceptions and outcomes in more depth; to explore causal processes; and to capture the day-to-day reality of their new lives in the UK.

The questionnaire consisted largely of closed questions. Many had been used in previous evaluations of Gateway and others were drawn from national surveys, providing benchmarks with the general population. The questions covered topics integral to the aims of the GPP, as well as important indicators of integration highlighted within the academic literature. Ager and Strang's theoretical framework (2004) was used to inform the research, as it is widely acknowledged as a useful starting point for thinking about integration (Refugee Action, 2008). This focused the research on issues such as housing, employment, English-language proficiency, health and well-being, notions of belonging, and social relationships.

The research cohort included all adult refugees arriving in the UK as part of the GPP between February and May 2009. This provided 146 potential participants, including

105 from Iraq, 18 from the Democratic Republic of Congo (DRC) and 23 Rohingya, a minority ethnic group from Burma. All were invited to take part in the questionnaire at all three stages unless they specifically opted out, which few did. Six focus groups, involving 35 participants, were conducted across the study period. Participants were purposively sampled according to their resettlement site, demographic characteristics (age, gender, marital status), and their responses to questionnaire questions. For example, one focus group was convened for refugees who had reported some employment or volunteering experience in the UK.

The questionnaire response rates were high by usual standards. For the first questionnaire, 89% of the cohort responded. By the third questionnaire just under half (49%) of the original sample submitted a response. This compares to 45% for a typical mail questionnaire (Shih and Xitao Fan, 2008). The dropout rate was mainly due to the loss of Iraqi participants. This was likely due to the different approach taken with Iraqi refugees in administering the questionnaire. It may also be explained by respondent mobility, again mainly Iraqis, moving home and leaving no way to contact them.

Selected focus group participants were initially contacted by telephone, by a community researcher or interpreter. The call was used to discuss the purpose and practicalities of the focus group and to determine willingness and ability to participate. To facilitate the participation of women, childcare was offered. All refugees receiving a questionnaire or participating in a focus group were given a £10 voucher as a 'thank you'. It was anticipated this gift might also be an incentive to participate. There was an ethical concern that refugees might feel pressured to participate to maintain their refugee status in the UK. Hence, the voluntary nature of the research was emphasised whenever possible. In one of the focus groups, participants sought clarification about the limitations on foreign travel as refugees. This provided an opportunity to emphasise the researchers' independence from the Home Office; and also an opportunity to offer something back to participants by liaising with the Home Office to ensure the relevant information was disseminated to the refugees.

Due to the small target population and decreasing response rates leading to smaller sample sizes, quantitative analyses were not statistically significant. Instead the quantitative data were analysed descriptively, to highlight patterns and any variability between nationality groups and resettlement sites. The focus groups were audio recorded, translated, and transcribed, to facilitate detailed content analysis (using NVivo software). The data were thematically coded using the same themes developed for the questionnaire, informed by the aims of the GPP and Ager and Strang's (2004) work on indicators of integration.

Inferences and meta-inferences

Funders of the GPP were especially interested in employment outcomes for refugees. They clearly wanted the research to demonstrate if the provision was having a positive economic impact. Thus, questions about employment were asked at all three stages. This turned out to have been a wasted opportunity to ask about other issues because only three Iraqi men had experienced paid work by the end of the study. DRC and Rohingya refugees had been living in refugee camps before arriving in the UK; and, before this, their persecution had limited opportunities for education and employment. Consequently, the DRC and Rohingya refugees were still getting accustomed to living in homes with central heating and washing machines; their English-language ability was too low for even voluntary work; and mental and physical health needs remained a priority.

The mixed methods study highlighted different resettlement experiences in different sites within the UK. The quantitative data highlighted that Iraqis resettled in Sheffield were reporting better experiences of local amenities and social relations than Iraqis in Hull. The contributing factors were explored in focus groups, revealing that a longer history of migration to Sheffield was largely responsible. The ethnic diversity in Sheffield had promoted the development of culturally appropriate services and fostered greater tolerance. In Hull, some of the refugees reported repeat experience of racial harassment and lower perceptions of community cohesion. They felt visibly different and easy targets for racial abuse, being resettled in parts of the city that were predominated by whites.

The inferences demonstrate how integration is sensitive to interactions between people and place, despite proceeding under the same general operative processes. The inferences also point to the importance of tailored provision. Refugees are not a homogeneous group and provision that acknowledges the prior experience of specific cohorts can ensure appropriate and time-relevant provision to fulfil economic goals and social responsibilities.

Conclusion

This mixed methods study demonstrates the possibilities and benefits of using quantitative and qualitative methods to improve research design and inferences. In this instance, mixed methods was employed to explore the resettlement experiences of refugees during their first 18 months of life in the UK. The meta-inferences demonstrate how integration is sensitive to interactions between people and place, despite proceeding under the same general operative processes. The meta-inferences also point to the importance of tailored provision. Refugees are not a homogeneous group and provision that acknowledges the prior experience of specific cohorts can ensure appropriate and time-relevant support to fulfil economic goals and social responsibilities.

Case study 3: Families living with problem gambling

James Banks, Catrin Andersson, David Best, Michael Edwards, and Jaime Waters

Sheffield Hallam University

Summary of study

Commercial gambling in Britain has grown to become one of the most accessible and heterogeneous gambling marketplaces in the world (Wardle et al., 2014). Off- and online gambling opportunities continue to multiply, with casinos, sports and horse race betting, bingo and a host of charitable lotteries now offered by in the region of 3,000 different operators (Miers, 2016). The widespread availability of gambling is associated with a multitude of 'serious harms for individuals, families and society' including underage gambling, increased rates of problem gambling, unemployment, debt, deterioration in personal health and self-esteem, familial dysfunction, family breakdown, and crime and victimisation (Orford, 2011: 24). While there is a developing research agenda exploring the social cost of the widespread availability of gambling on UK society, which has provided early evidence of a range of gambling-related harms, there is, to date, relatively little research that has explored the relationship between gambling problems and families. This research extends beyond the focus of the problem gambler, to incorporate the experiences of family members.

This mixed methods research study explored the relationship between problem gambling and its influence on families in the UK using a convergent parallel design. Whilst the current literature indicates that problem gambling can have a significant impact on families, their relationship remains under-explored, and family members' voices have not been heard sufficiently in the gambling research literature. In response, this programme of research provided the first UK examination of problem gambling from the perspective of the family member(s). It explored the impact of problem gambling on different family members, the coping strategies they employ and their help seeking behaviours using mixed methods. The aim was to explore the relationship between problem gambling and families in the UK in order to enhance the quality of life of problem gamblers and family members. The objectives were:

- To explore the impact of problem gambling on families;
- To examine how family members cope with gambling problems, and what adverse events they experience;
- To identify how families find out about and access information regarding help and/or treatment services, and how effective these services are perceived to be;
- To use the meta-inferences to help shape best practice relating to the education, prevention and treatment of gambling related harm, and to inform further research in this area. This may include the development of an information hub and self-help materials for families of problem gamblers.

Philosophy

Given that the experiences of gamblers' family members are an uncharted area of research, this study benefited from a flexible philosophical approach. This study adopted a pragmatist epistemological position in order to have a responsive and multifaceted approach to gambling related experiences in family members. Recognition of the multiple realities relating to problem gambling and families underpinned the research team's decision to utilise a mixed methods approach to data collection and indeed as a framework for the entire scope of the project. In turn, this ontological position shaped the questionnaire design and interview schedule that focused on securing a holistic view of the impact of problem gambling through the perspectives of different family members.

Mixed methods design

This research set out to use an explanatory sequential design with equal priority given to the quantitative and qualitative components, but changed to a convergent parallel design partway through the study. Quantitative data were collected through the questionnaire and qualitative data primarily through interviews, but also through a questionnaire. Although the research team devised a sequential approach to data collection, with qualitative semi-structured interviews following the administration of the (largely) quantitative questionnaire, as data collection progressed, individual components of the research design were conducted simultaneously. Questionnaires were used to recruit participants for interviews and thus the qualitative component of the research was designed to follow the quantitative component. However, the research team quickly recognised the need to immediately follow up questionnaire respondents who stated that they were willing to speak with a researcher, in order to successfully timetable an interview. In addition, some prospective research participants, who had not (yet) completed the questionnaire, contacted the research team directly to be interviewed. Thus, it quickly became evident that questionnaire data collection and semi-structured interviews needed to be conducted simultaneously. Data were collected using online questionnaires (n=233) and semi-structured interviews (n=35), and analysed using quantitative analysis (SPSS) and thematic analysis, respectively.

Methodology

The study employed a cross-sectional research design. Primary data were collected at one point in time for each participant, ranging between November 2017 and March 2018. This design also allowed the examination of patterns of association in the quantitative component and the examination of more than one case in both the quantitative and qualitative components.

A non-probability convenience sampling strategy was employed in this study to secure research samples for both the questionnaire and interviews. The population for this study was UK residents, the sample consisting of those residents responding to calls for participation in either the questionnaire and/or the interviews, and the unit of analysis being the individual family member. The principal method of distributing the Families Living with Problem Gambling questionnaire was through a web-link to a SurveyMonkey version of the questionnaire. Questionnaire respondents were self-selecting, responding to the research team's calls for participation through Twitter. Interviewees were also self-selecting, leaving their contact details at the end of the questionnaire or contacting a member of the research team directly. Interviewees consisted of family members both where there has been a successful outcome in terms of their loved one's problem gambling and where there is ongoing problem gambling. Interviews lasted for between 30 and 90 minutes and were conducted either face-to-face or over the telephone. Interviews were tape recorded and transcribed in preparation for analysis. Interviews resulted in rich qualitative data that complemented and augmented the quantitative data derived through the survey method, in turn enhancing the research team's understanding of problem gambling and families.

The Families Living with Problem Gambling questionnaire responses were downloaded into an SPSS file. Quantitative data were cleaned and recoded for the purposes of data analysis. Descriptive statistics and bivariate analyses were conducted using SPSS 22. In addition, qualitative responses to questions exploring the impacts of problem gambling on family members and their help seeking behaviour were aggregated and subject to thematic analysis. Qualitative data derived from the semi-structured interviews were also analysed thematically.

Inferences and meta-inferences

The analyses are currently being conducted but some preliminary analysis suggests several key inferences:

- Questionnaire and interview data indicate that problem gambling can impair relationships and lead to emotional, financial and health difficulties.
- Problem gambling can affect spouses, children, adult children, and parents, as well as the overall family, and although the harms experienced by individual family members may be different, they are inextricably interwoven.

- Family members adopt a range of coping strategies to mitigate the effects of problem gambling on themselves and others.
- Family members also seek help from a variety of individuals, groups, and organisations, including family and friends, online, telephone and face-to-face gambling support and information services, primary care, and counselling services.
- Family members also identified a number of internal and external barriers to help-seeking.

Conclusion

This convergent parallel mixed methods study provided a unique investigation into the experiences of family members of problem gamblers. These family members have a range of negative experiences and the support offered to this group needs to increase. This study has shown some of the advantages of mixed methods research as it offers a flexible and iterative approach to research, which sometimes includes changing the methodology.

Case study 4: Sexual victimization, disclosure, and accountability: organizational responses of the Boy Scouts of America to child sexual abuse

Michelle Cubellis

Central Connecticut State University

Summary of study

Child sexual abuse has been a highly publicized and controversial topic worldwide because of the vulnerability of children. However, there have been several recent child sexual abuse (CSA) scandals in the US, garnering even more attention and concern. With the exposure of the American Catholic Church abuse scandal in 2002, public attention became focused on the Archdiocese's poor and prolonged response to these events. This crisis was not the sole case of widespread sexual violence and institutional failure. In October 2012, Boy Scouts of America (BSA) files from 1959 to 1991 containing reports of CSA were publicly released. Research on organizations caring for children, including juvenile facilities, schools, and childcare organizations, has found alarming rates of CSA, ranging from 3.7% to 50.3% of children in these institutions (Beck et al., 2010; Shakeshaft, 2004; Wolfe et al., 2003).

While there appears to be some research on organizational CSA, these studies focus primarily on incidence and prevention of abuse, and not on organizational responses to abuse. Using a convergent parallel design, this mixed methods research addressed the factors of the abuse and the organization that influenced the BSA's response. The study asked the following research questions:

- What are the characteristics of abusers and abuse incidents in the BSA?
- How did the BSA learn of abuse and what was their response to these allegations?

Philosophy

While prior research focuses heavily on the types of sexual offending and nature of sexual offending within youth organizations, such as the BSA, very little attention is paid to the response of these organizations to allegations of sexual offending by their members. To this end, this research investigated more specifically what the BSA did when they learned about allegations of sexual abuse, and what specific characteristics of the alleged abused could have influenced their decision. This research took a pragmatic philosophical approach, recognizing that while quantitative analysis could provide an overall picture of what was happening in the BSA, it would not provide the intricate details of what happened in each case and the steps the organization took to address abuse allegations.

Mixed methods design

While the project initially focused solely on quantitative data analysis, initial coding of the first few files during the proposal development phase suggested that more information could be obtained through qualitative analysis as well. The files featured rich information, including rationalizations, justifications, and excuses, that would be lost if only quantitative analysis was conducted. The mixed methods design of this study was convergent parallel with equal priority, where both quantitative and qualitative methods were carried out on separate pieces of the data and then combined. It was hoped that the information obtained in the qualitative analysis could help explain in greater detail the reaction of the BSA to sexual abuse allegations, as well as the overall characteristics common of abuse by organization members. Rather than use the inferences from the quantitative and qualitative analysis for triangulation, the inferences were instead used in a concurrent transformative design. The combination of these components was important to understand overall how the BSA responded to allegations of sexual abuse by their members, and to delve more in-depth into why they may have reacted in these ways based on the unique features of each case.

The data obtained from the mixed method design were used according to a complementarity approach, whereby the results from both the quantitative and qualitative components of the study were used to understand the response of the BSA from different perspectives. The quantitative analysis approach focused on how the BSA was most likely to respond, and how factors about the offender or their role in the organization influenced this response. The content analysis and case study component of the study sought to expand on this, by understanding the actual steps taken by the organization when responding and the justifications or rationalizations used to support the actions taken.

Methodology

The current study relied on both longitudinal and cross-sectional analysis to understand the nature of sexual offending within the BSA and the organization's response to offending by adult members. The primary data used were publicly available records of sexual offending within the BSA. The records were mandated to be released by the BSA after a successful lawsuit was filed against the organization in 2012 by an individual who was sexually victimized while a youth member. A total of 2,379 records with both qualitative and quantitative data, ranging from 1959–1991, were released. These files were publicly available on the website of the attorney who represented the former scout, and were downloaded for inclusion in the study. These reports feature detailed information about the abuse incident, the offender, and the BSA's response to the allegations of abuse.

For the study, the roughly 2,300 files were coded by the researcher and three research assistants for general information about the offender, victim, event, and important dates or details, as well as the presence of justifications/rationalizations offered by the BSA. Intercoder reliability was frequently conducted on the coded files to ensure that all coding occurred according to the codebook created for the study and that there was agreement across coders. In many instances, text within the files was not legible. On these occasions, anything that was not legible in the files was removed.

The quantitative analyses included multivariate analysis, survival analysis, and intervention analysis. These were conducted on the 2,379 cases in addition to qualitative content analysis. Quantitative analysis was conducted to provide an overall picture of the incidence and prevalence of sexual abuse by members of the BSA during the time period of released filed. Qualitative content analysis was used to provide more in-depth understanding of select instances of organizational responses to allegations of CSA, as well as to address the applicability of rationalization tactics to these institutional responses. The content analysis relied on both inductive category development and deductive category application. For the study, the deductive categories were the eight rationalization tactics outlined by Sykes and Matza (1957). Inductive category development was used to determine if additional responses to abuse allegations that did not fit into one of the prescribed categories were present in the files. In addition, in-depth case studies were conducted of a few select cases to gain a deeper understanding of how the BSA responded to abuse.

Inferences and meta-inferences

Inferences from the quantitative analysis revealed that the majority of offenders in the organization were younger Scoutmasters and had been a part of the organization prior to their offending. Most cases featured isolated incidents rather than numerous abuse incidents, and victims often disclosed their abuse to a parent or immediate family member. These inferences represented the first information known about offenders within the BSA. The BSA's reliance on informal responses, such as removing the offender or referring to treatment, when dealing with abuse allegations against members suggests that the organization was aware of the harm that could occur to its reputation and mission had allegations been made public.

These inferences also suggested a calculated effort on the part of the BSA to deal with allegations as quietly as possible in order to maintain their legitimacy and standing within society. Qualitative content analysis and case study analysis revealed that the organization did in fact use rationalization tactics, relying heavily on the denial of responsibility and metaphor of the ledger justifications.

All of these inferences suggest that when addressing CSA, the response of the organization is an important factor in determining how abuse is handled and whether appropriate steps are taken to ensure it doesn't happen again. These inferences have important ramifications for the field of criminology, suggesting that focus on the incidence and prevalence of CSA in the BSA, or other youth-serving organizations, does not provide enough information to truly understand how deviance occurs within organizations or at the organizational level and why it occurs, and to implement policies and procedures to reduce it.

Conclusion

While the majority of research on CSA in youth organizations focuses on questions of incidence and prevalence, very little focuses on the actual response of the organization, the possible response options available to the organization and what factors may prompt them to act in a certain way. A large reason this information is lacking is due to the reliance on quantitative datasets that do not lend themselves to qualitative analysis. This largely occurs because qualitative data on CSA allegations are either lacking or very difficult to obtain. The files from the BSA represent a unique case in which qualitative analysis could be completed. In the case of my study, the detail provided in the BSA files permitted me to conduct content and case study analysis. This research is especially useful as a guide for how quantitative and qualitative data can be used to provide a more complete picture of how organizations respond to CSA by members. While the use of quantitative data is useful for understanding the overall picture of abuse and responses, they lack the depth of understanding and richness of detail that can be obtained through qualitative analysis, thus warranting a pragmatic approach of mixed methods.

Case study 5: Investigating recovery capital whilst identifying gender similarities and differences in pathways to recovery from problematic alcohol use: a mixed methods study

Beth Collinson

Sheffield Hallam University

Summary of study

Estimates show 9% of men and 3% of UK women exhibit signs of alcohol dependence (NHS, 2015). As a result of this prevalence, recovery from alcohol dependence has emerged in public policy and national strategy in both England and Scotland. While 'recovery' in the context of substance use remains a contested concept (see Neale et al., 2013), Best and Laudet (2010: 2) suggest that recovery is 'a lived experience of improved quality of life and a sense of empowerment'. Recovery-focused policy goes beyond abstinence, encouraging participation in fulfilling activities as a recovery goal and exhorting the virtues of citizenship (Sobell et al., 1996). Best and Laudet (2010) further recognise that for an individual to rebuild their life and overcome addiction, access to a wide range of support services outside of treatment is essential.

This study, currently being undertaken for a doctoral thesis, engages in both primary and secondary data collection across three components and foregrounds working alongside individuals in recovery from alcohol dependency. The central research question for this project is: How does recovery capital differ by gender in pathways to recovery from problematic alcohol use? Additionally, there are four subsidiary questions:

1   How well do existing measures capture the three elements of recovery capital?
2   How would we go about developing adequate measures that assess recovery resources at the social and community level, and establish norms for those measures? How does personal, social, and community capital differ by gender?
3   How does each aspect of recovery capital differ by gender at different stages of their recovery journeys? Are there different predictors of recovery outcomes by gender?
4   What are the key parameters of community capital and how are they related to stigma and exclusion, and how can we demonstrate the impact of community capital on personal recovery pathways whilst identifying gender differences?

Philosophy

This research draws on the epistemological stance of pragmatism, supporting the multi-faceted view that knowledge 'is both constructed and based on the reality of the world we experience and live in' (Onwuegbuzie et al., 2009: 122). Pragmatism is particularly advantageous in this study because it aims to measure concrete aspects of recovery (e.g. the three elements of recovery capital) but at the same time capture the lived experiences of individuals in recovery from substance use, proving a fuller picture and deeper understanding. Similarly, the ontological approach is multiple realities, a position in which the emphasis is not on having an objective or subjective view. Instead, the social world is understood by exploring it from different perspectives, which for this research involves looking at recovery from different viewpoints.

Mixed methods design

In answer to the sequence question, this project is both sequential and simultaneous. As for the priority question, one of the components is dominant, with the other two components being subordinate. Secondary data analysis (quant) was undertaken first, influencing the sampling and planning of the following two components (QUANT/qual), illustrating an element of development. Ultimately, complementarity will be used to create the meta-inferences for the project. The notation for this design is: quant → QUANT / qual } →.

Methodology

The research, undertaken with local charity Sheffield Alcohol Support Service (SASS), includes the three following components:

1   Secondary data analysis of SASS data (quant)
2   REC-CAP questionnaire (QUANT)
3   Asset mapping and audio recording (qual)

Each component will now be discussed in terms of research design, sampling, and data collection.

Component 1

Component 1 consisted of the secondary analysis of data collected by SASS (quant), which employed a cross-sectional research design. All new service users were administered a user-friendly version of the Assessment of Recovery Capital (ARC) (Groshkova, Best, and White, 2012) designed specifically for SASS, at their entry to the service and at a four-week follow-up. These data created a baseline of information of new service users. From an initial observation, the dataset seemed fairly substantial (300 records), but further analysis indicated there were only 62 records completed over the two time frames. The data were subject to statistical analysis using SPSS, identifying basic gender similarities and differences in pathways to recovery.

Whilst the sample for this component was not randomly selected and the inferences cannot be generalised, the results will contribute to knowledge regarding factors that play a role in the process of change through one's recovery journey and identity transition. Due to the relatively small sample size, any recommendations made within this stage of data collection had to be regarded as tentative. As the sample size was much smaller than expected, this component decreased in priority, resulting in it becoming subordinate. Also, as the secondary data analysis did not successfully identify levels of community engagement amongst the recovery community, development was used to re-fashion component 2 to predominantly focus on this. Priority was adjusted to match this shift in design, with component 2 now becoming dominant.

Component 2

The aim of this component was to attempt to capture the key elements of recovery capital and to translate this into a summary of recovery strengths and barriers that can be used to support the ongoing recovery pathway and journey (Best et al., 2016). The REC-CAP (Best et al., 2016), a standardised quantitative questionnaire (QUANT) which encapsulates the key elements of personal, social, and community capital, was deemed the most appropriate way to achieve this. The REC-CAP can be quantified and used in a systematic way to measure the progress of individuals on their recovery journey. To do this successfully, the questionnaires needs to be administrated over two time points, making this component longitudinal in its research design.

At entry to the service, SASS staff informed all new service users about the research project. Those who consented to their contact details being passed on to the research team were contacted about taking part in the study. In the end, 100 new service users at SASS completed the REC-CAP upon entry to the service. From this baseline measure, follow-up REC-CAP questionnaires were administered to the same cohort after six months, including both those who retained contact with the service and those who did not. Although every service user had the same chance to participant in the research, not all consented, resulting in the creation of a self-selecting, convenience sample. While this type of sampling may be one of the quicker techniques to carry out, questions can be raised regarding the representativeness of the data.

While administrating the REC-CAP alone would have helped to answer some of the subsidiary questions, the aim was to combine this with a qualitative method to enhance the richness of the data. To achieve this, a third component was used to explore when and with whom different genders are connecting and how community engagement and social networks help construct and maintain recovery. In terms of mixed methods design, component 2 (QUANT) and component 3 (qual) were simultaneous, with both components having been developed out of component 1 (quant). Both employed a cross-sectional research design.

Component 3

The last component entailed qualitative asset mapping with service users at SASS (qual). The main aim of this component was to see what organisations, activities, and groups are being utilised by the recovery community, and which assets within the community may be going unrecognised. This stage of data collection involved a self-selecting convenience sample. Service users at SASS on the same days as the researcher were briefed on the research project and given the opportunity to participate. In accordance with the primary elements of the Social Identity Model of Recovery (SIMOR) (Best et al., 2016), service users were asked to record whether individuals associated with the asset they identify are in recovery, non-users, social users, or active users. By utilising SIMOR (Best et al., 2016), the research can identify which assets within the community may facilitate and/or hinder an individual's recovery process due to unsupportive sobriety/supportive sobriety network ties. The conversation between researcher and participant whilst they created the map was also audio recorded and transcribed. The transcriptions were analysed using NVivo 11 to provide a richer understanding as to why an individual may feel connected to a group, why an asset is accessible, what the expense associated with a particular asset is, and why individuals may choose to avoid accessing certain assets. Implementing a qualitative component of this type should shed light on what exactly provides therapeutic value and beneficial impact for service users. This research is the first time the REC-CAP (component 2) has been combined with the asset mapping technique (component 3), offering a novel aspect for this research and greater potential for the meta-inferences.

Conclusion

The mixed methods doctoral project discussed in this case study employed three components: secondary analysis of SASS data (quant), the REC-CAP questionnaire (QUANT), and asset mapping and audio recording (qual). The components chosen and developed for the purpose of the study aim to provide a richer understanding of the central research question and, in this context, seemed most appropriate to use. Data collection is still underway; therefore inferences and meta-inferences are still to be developed. Due to the nature of the research, the data should be as accessible as possible. It is expected that meta-inferences will advance current knowledge within the field: identifying whether gender similarities are prevalent within the recovery populations and how recovery capital for these individuals differs over time. By combining the data from the three components using complementarity, the meaningfulness of these meta-inferences will be enhanced. The meta-inferences will be able to guide policy and practice in the field, informing appropriate treatment and community supports for those in recovery from problematic alcohol use.

Summary

This chapter illustrates what mixed methods research projects look like in practice and provides examples of how the concepts and terminology that have been used throughout this book are applied in the field. The authors of the case studies have employed different research philosophies, mixed methods designs, methodologies and ways of combining the data to create the inferences and meta-inferences needed to answer their central research question. They have also shown the importance of a clear decision-making process and a logical approach to research planning, which foregrounds the central research question, for the production of sophisticated and robust inferences and meta-inferences. Hopefully the case studies presented here have shown you the breadth and diversity of criminological mixed methods research and have inspired you to try it in your next project.

Learning questions

1   What lessons can you take from the case studies?
2   How might you apply these lessons to your own research?
3   Can you identify any common themes across the project planning decisions made in the case studies?

Glossary of key terms

abductive   Refers to the relationship between theory and research, where there is a back-and-forth relationship between theory generation and theory testing, with theories being successively tested and developed as the research progresses (see 'deductive' and 'inductive' for related approaches).

absolute confidentiality   Where all information is kept confidential no matter how serious a disclosure may be (within the laws of the land).

abstract   In academic terms, this refers to a brief summary of the purpose of a research project that is presented at the start of a written account. It is often the last piece of a project to be written-up.

anonymity   When individuals are not identifiable as having taken part in a study. It is preserved by withholding a participant's name and any other details that might identify or associate them with the research.

appendix/appendices   A range of supplementary information that may be useful to the reader in a way that supports the claims you have made in the report itself, but is too detailed/lengthy to be in the main body of the written work.

authenticity   Qualitative evaluative term that contains five criteria (see fairness, ontological authenticity, educative authenticity, catalytic authenticity, and tactical authenticity), which are all related to the impact that qualitative research can have on both the research participants and wider society.

bivariate   'Two variables'. The analysis and investigation of the relationship between two variables.

case study research   Research design that allows a researcher to focus in-depth on one phenomenon, such as a person, setting, or institution. In mixed methods this is employed as an overarching design across all components.

catalytic authenticity   Criterion of authenticity (qualitative). It is action focused, and evaluates whether a research project stimulates people to do something following their engagement in the study.

central research question   'The overarching question that defines the scope, scale, and conduct of a research project' (Gilbert, 2008: 512), and the factor which drives your mixed methods research project.

cluster sampling   Involves using naturally occurring, pre-existing groups as the sample population that reflect the population being studied.

code/statement of ethics   Often published by professional bodies, a code or statement of ethics is a set of ethical principles which the body expects members to adhere to.

codes to theme table   Table used to systematically record qualitative data as part of a thematic analysis.

coding   Systematic process of highlighting text in qualitative data that helps you to reduce a large amount of data to a manageable size.

coercion   Where someone is persuaded or forced to do something they do not wish to do. In relation to research, this term is generally associated with forcing someone to consent to take part.

comparative research   Research design that examines similar phenomena in two or more contrasting cases, and as a result it is applied as an overarching design for a whole mixed methods project. It is usually employed in cross-cultural studies to explore the similarities and differences between countries.

complementarity   Used in mixed methods research where two or more methods are used to investigate distinct, albeit often overlapping, aspects of a phenomenon in order to produce rich, deep understanding.

component   Constituent parts of your mixed methods design that, when combined, make up your mixed methods research. They are either quantitative or qualitative. Mixed methods requires a minimum of one quantitative component and one qualitative component.

concepts   Building blocks of central research questions; a term that helpfully allows us to group ideas together in a manageable way, such as behaviours, attitudes, and characteristics.

confidentiality   The promise to keep something private, limiting the access to that information. Also see absolute confidentiality and limited confidentiality.

confirmability   Criterion of trustworthiness (qualitative). It focuses on whether the research has been conducted in the most value-free and neutral way possible.

consent form   Written document that participants sign as proof of their agreement to take part in a research project. The researcher signs this too and both parties should keep a copy for their records.

construct validity   Type of validity (quantitative). It considers whether the measure employed accurately reflects the concept being assessed.

constructionism   Ontological position which argues that social reality is created though social interaction, and is continually being revised. This position aligns with the interpretivist epistemology.

convenience sampling   Where the sample selected is the most convenient and readily available to the researcher.

convergent parallel design   Mixed methods design which involves the simultaneous collection of quantitative and qualitative data, typically of equal priority.

correlation coefficient   The number (statistic) that shows the nature of the relationship between two variables and how they vary in relation to one another.

covert research   Research where the participants do not know they are taking part in a study at the time the data is collected, and/or the researcher does not reveal their real identity. See also overt research.

Cramer's V   Correlation coefficient for nominal level variables, measuring relationship strength.

credibility   Criterion of trustworthiness (qualitative). It reflects the ontological notion that social reality is constructed by actors (people). Consequently, if there is more than one perspective of social reality, it is the way that the researcher arrives at their perspective of social reality (their conclusions) that governs whether the inferences are considered credible (or not).

cross-sectional research   Research design where data is collected at a single point in time, and there is more than one case (participant). For quantitative data specifically, this also provides the opportunity to collect quantifiable data, and consider patterns of association.

crosstabs   Analysis of two variables at the same time, allowing for exploration of the association between the two. Crosstab tables show the relationship between all possible category combinations, and compare the percentages associated with each category in the columns and rows.

debriefing   Takes place between the researcher and participant after the data has been collected. It gives the participant the opportunity to ask any questions, and allows the researcher to provide the participant with additional support.

deception   Where researchers deliberately misrepresent the details of their study to withhold information from participants (who have provided their informed consent). The purpose is to elicit information or observe behaviour from the participants that might not be revealed if the full details of the study were known.

deductive   Refers to the relationship between theory and research, where research is conducted based on a hypothesis that utilises existing theory (see 'inductive' for a contrasting approach).

dependability   Criterion of trustworthiness (qualitative). It focuses on the research process and how the strength of the inferences can be judged by assessing how the research was carried out.

dependent variable   Variable that changes in relation to the independent variable, also known as 'outcome variable'. It is the variable/concept that you want to find out about.

descriptive research questions   Find out what is going on. They allow researchers to create a benchmark, which in turn creates the opportunity for explanatory research. Term coined by De Vaus (2001).

development   Technique of mixed methods research involving the employment of a sequential design, with the inferences drawn from the first component used to help inform the development of the second component. This approach is employed to increase the robustness of the inferences and any concepts generated as a result.

dominant   For a non-equivalent answer to the priority question, the component(s) that has priority.

ecological validity   Type of validity (quantitative). It focuses on whether the inferences from a research project relate to the real-world setting of everyday life.

educative authenticity   Criterion of authenticity (qualitative). It is concerned with whether engaging in a research project helps the participants to develop a better understanding and appreciation of other people's views.

epistemology   The branch of philosophy concerned with the theory of knowledge. It focuses on the questions of what knowledge is (which can vary between disciplines) and how it is acquired.

ethical approval   Given once your research project proposal is deemed to uphold ethical research practice by the body that grants permission to undertake research. This is usually a Research Ethics Committee (UK) or Institutional Review Board (USA) in a university setting.

expansion   Refers to mixed methods research that provides breadth and depth to the exploration of a particular phenomenon. This approach reflects the philosophically pragmatic notion of selecting the most appropriate tool for the job at hand.

experimental research   Research design chiefly associated with the quantitative strategy, involving the empirical testing of a hypothesis under controlled conditions to examine the relationship between specific variables.

explanatory research questions   Find out why something is going on. Term coined by De Vaus (2001).

explanatory sequential design   Mixed methods design in which the quantitative data collection occurs before the qualitative data collection. Priority can rest with any of the components.

explicit coercion   Where an obvious threat of harm is made to secure consent in a research context. See also coercion and implicit coercion.

exploratory sequential design   Mixed methods design in which the qualitative data collection occurs before the quantitative data collection. Priority can rest with any of the components.

external validity   Type of validity (quantitative). It is the extent to which quantitative inferences can be generalised beyond the context of the research project. If the inferences are externally valid, this means that the results can be applied to broader, more general contexts.

fairness   Criterion of authenticity (qualitative). It is concerned with whether the research presents these different perspectives and their associated values.

focus group   Data collection method consisting of a handful of people participating in a guided group discussion about a particular topic or issue.

focus group script   Set of instructions and questions used for carrying out a focus group.

frequency   Number of times a value or category occurs as an answer in one variable. A frequency table clearly illustrates this in both count and percentage and is the starting point for most analyses.

gatekeeper   Refers to an organisation, group, or person that controls access to something. In research this usually relates to the ethical approval process, or access to a certain population or group of people.

General Data Protection Regulation (GDPR)   The General Data Protection Regulation (GDPR) came into force in May 2018, replacing the Data Protection Act (1998). Under the GDPR data processing must be lawful, fair, and transparent, with researchers classed as either a data controller (someone who decides the purpose and processing of personal data) or a data processor (someone who processes personal data on behalf of a data controller).

hypothesis   Informed prediction about the outcome of your analysis. It is informed because it is based upon the existing research literature in the particular field that the research is taking place in.

implicit coercion   Where individuals are under the impression that they have no choice but to take part in a research project. See also coercion and explicit coercion.

indefinite triangulation   Offering a more flexible approach; the same basic principle of using one or more methods to answer the same question is applied, but its purpose is not to check the validity of the inferences from each component.

independent variable   Variable that is not changed by other variables, hence it is independent. Sometimes referred to as the 'influencing' variable (as it influences the dependent variable).

inductive   Refers to the relationship between theory and research, where theory or theories are generated by the research itself (see 'deductive' for a contrasting approach).

inference quality   Evaluative term used in mixed methods research to judge the value of the conclusions and interpretations that stem from the integration of findings from each component of the research. It is the mixed methods equivalent of the evaluative term 'validity'.

inference transferability   Mixed methods-specific evaluative term, which deals with concerns around the generalisation of inferences and meta-inferences.

inferences   The conclusions and interpretations from each single component (quantitative or qualitative) of a mixed methods research project.

information sheet   Document provided to potential research participants providing information about the study to enable informed consent.

informed consent   Refers to the practice of giving potential research participants enough information to make an informed decision about whether to participate in the research.

initiation   Mixed methods research where new perspectives or paradoxes emerge. This may not have been the purpose of the mixed methods research, but the inferences generated from each component of the research allow for further analysis to be undertaken to create new knowledge and ideas.

internal validity   Type of validity (quantitative). It is the criterion which determines whether a causal relationship really exists.

interpretivism   Epistemological position that asserts that knowledge is socially created and subjective.

interval/ratio   Level of measurement with the greatest amount of precision. Variables are continuous, and the response categories are of numerical value, with equal distance between the values. Also known as 'scale'.

interview   Method of data collection involving purposeful conversations with participants, where their responses are the data.

interview schedule   Set of instructions and questions used for carrying out an interview.

iterative process   Where you arrive at an answer following the repeated analysis of data.

level of measurement   Expresses the nature and level of detail of the responses for a variable. There are three levels of measurement: nominal, ordinal, and interval/ratio (scale).

limited confidentiality   Where a researcher makes it clear to participants in advance that certain disclosures cannot be treated confidentially, such as criminal offences that have taken place.

literature review   Critical overview and analysis of the literature (books, journal articles, research reports and other relevant sources) which relates to the research topic being studied in relation to the central research question.

longitudinal research   Research design concerned with the collection and analysis of data over time. Data collection takes place with the same sample of participants on two or more distinct occasions and is assessed to determine any changes.

measurement validity   See construct validity.

measures of central tendency   Trio of statistics that provide ways of describing the typical or central value in the distribution of values. They help you to identify the middle point of the data in various ways.

media analysis   Examination, interpretation, and critique of media content and outputs.

meta–inferences   Inferences (conclusions and interpretations) brought together from across all of the quantitative and qualitative components.

mixed methods   Systematic and rigorous bringing together of quantitative and qualitative research methods and data into a coherent whole, where this whole is greater than the sum of its individual component parts, in order to answer a central research question.

mixed methods design   Element of a mixed methods study where decisions on the priority question and the sequence question are made. The answers to these questions, and the way the answers are combined, result in an overall mixed methods design.

multi methods   See multiple methods.

multiple methods   Use of two or more qualitative OR quantitative research methods or data collection tools in a single study. This distinguishes it from mixed methods, which requires the use of quantitative and qualitative methods.

multiple realities   Ontological position often associated with mixed methods research. It suggests that there is no single 'correct' ontological understanding of the social world, and instead there are multiple understandings of reality that each have some validity.

multi-stage sampling   Where more than one stage of sampling is required, with each new sample being drawn from the existing sample.

nominal   Lowest level of measurement. Variables are categorical, consisting of two or more categories with no ordering of values or relationship between the categories. The values/categories cannot be numerical.

non-probability sampling   Used when there is an unknown population. As a result, each person within the population does not have an equal chance (probability) of being included in the sample.

objective   Based on 'facts' alone and not influenced by one's personal beliefs or feelings.

objectivism   Ontological position that asserts that social reality exists independently of our existence as social actors and it is therefore possible to uncover 'truths' about that reality. This position is associated with positivistic epistemology.

observation   Data collection method where the researcher directly witnesses events. Observations can be quantitative, qualitative, in the field, or online.

observation schedule   Document that facilitates the recording of what a researcher witnesses when in the field.

ontological authenticity   Criterion of authenticity (qualitative). It considers whether the research participants, be that individuals or groups, gain a better understanding of the social world through taking part in the research project.

ontology   The study of the nature of social reality. Ontology asks what constitutes social reality and how we can come to understand that reality.

operationalise   To put something into practice.

ordinal   Middle level of measurement, between nominal and interval/ratio. Variables are categorical with a logical order or a relationship between the categories; however, the spacing between the categories can be uneven and is not meaningful.

overt research   Where participants have the study clearly explained to them in advance and voluntarily take part. See also covert research.

Pearson's r   Correlation coefficient for scale level variables, measuring relationship strength and direction.

population   The entire number of units (people or datasets) from which a sample is selected.

positivism   Epistemological position which takes an approach akin to that of natural science to social research. It values empiricism, neutrality, and the 'scientific' method.

pragmatism   Epistemological position often adopted in mixed methods research. Pragmatism seeks to bypass the debates around positivism and interpretivism by taking a practical stance that focuses on the research questions at hand, utilising the most appropriate research tools available to provide the 'best' possible outcome.

primary data   Data collected by you that is tailored to your research project and the specifics of your central research question.

primary source   The original version of a document, as opposed to secondary. See also secondary source.

priority question   Question that researchers must answer when designing a mixed methods project: Are the qualitative and the quantitative components of equivalent priority or is one component of greater priority than the other?

privacy   The right of an individual or group to withhold information about themselves. Researchers should respect a participant's right not to answer certain questions that they might consider to be too personal.

probability sampling   Aims to obtain a representative sample where the inferences can be generalised from the sample to the population.

professional body   Organisation that aims to further the interests and knowledge related to a profession, such as the British Society of Criminology.

pseudonym   Made-up name given to research participants in order to preserve their anonymity.

purposive sampling   Where the researcher purposely selects participants or a dataset based on the known characteristics of the people/data involved.

qualitative   Use and prioritisation of words (and pictures and sounds) as data in social research.

quantitative   Use and prioritisation of numbers as data in social research.

questionnaire   Method of data collection involving a series of written questions designed to gather data from respondents for the purpose of analysis. It is also the name for the actual set of questions that are being asked. Sometimes used synonymously with 'survey'.

quota sampling   Occurs when specific quotas (strata) are selected for inclusion in the sample based on their proportion of the population. However, quota sampling is not random as the researcher decides who is selected for inclusion; hence it is different to stratified sampling.

random sampling   Where every person in the population has the same and equal chance of being selected to take part.

reliability   Refers to whether the findings from a research project can be repeated, and considers whether the measures used are stable.

representative   Refers to the composition of a sample. If deemed to be representative, the sample will accurately reflect the composition of the population being studied.

research aim   Details what your project broadly hopes to achieve. You may have one for your whole mixed methods project, and/or one for each of the components.

research objective   Facilitates the operationalisation of your central research question, any subsidiary question(s) and your research aims by specifically detailing what it is you intend to do in your research project.

research strategy   Overarching approach taken in a research endeavour to methodology, data collection and the nature of data. See quantitative, qualitative, and mixed methods for examples of specific research strategies.

respondent validation   Where the inferences produced by a researcher are checked by research participants to ensure the researcher has correctly interpreted the participants' version of social reality.

response rate   Defined as the number of people from the sample who actually participate in the research, usually expressed as a percentage.

sample   The proportion of the population studied when it is not feasible to engage with every member of the population under investigation.

sampling frame   Lists all the people (units) in the population, which is used to select the sample.

scale   See interval/ratio.

secondary data   Data collected by another researcher for a different piece of research, which are then made available to others for additional analysis.

secondary source   Uses primary sources to create a second-hand account of the original document. For example, a textbook provides a secondary account of a range of original, primary sources. See also primary source.

sensitising concept   Term that will guide you towards the information qualitative data that consists of words, which will help you to answer your central research question.

sequence question   Question that researchers must answer when designing a mixed methods project: In what order do the quantitative and qualitative components occur, simultaneously or sequentially?

snowball sampling   Where initial small numbers of participants inform the researcher about other participants that may be willing to engage in the research.

Spearman's rho   Correlation coefficient for ordinal (or ordinal and scale) level variables, measuring relationship strength and direction.

stratified sampling   Where different sub-groups of the population, which are essential to the central research question, are prioritised by the researcher to ensure they are adequately represented in the sample.

subjective   Based on or influenced by personal beliefs or feelings rather than facts alone.

subordinate   For a non-equivalent answer to the priority question, the component(s) that does not have priority.

subsidiary question   Question employed in a component that helps you to answer your central research question. Specific quantitative and qualitative concerns can be acknowledged by employing subsidiary questions, or sub-questions, in each component.

synthesise   To bring together pieces of information into a coherent whole by grouping common themes and making connections between ideas.

systematic (research) process   Refers to the notion of ensuring your research follows an orderly, logical, and well-justified method.

systematic sampling   Where a sample is selected through a systematic method, usually by picking the 'nth' case.

tactical authenticity   Criterion of authenticity (qualitative). It is concerned with action, specifically whether participating in a research project empowers individuals and gives them the requisite knowledge and/or skills to be able to take such action.

thematic analysis   Where the researcher searches for themes in qualitative data through the systematic process of coding and theme generation, which produces the inferences for your qualitative component(s).

theme   Generated by the process of qualitative thematic analysis, it constitutes what the data and codes tell you about each sensitising concept, which should help you to answer your research question.

theoretical sampling   Where participants or secondary data are selected because they help to build a theoretical understanding by answering the central research question.

theoretical saturation   Point at which no new material is generated by including additional participants in the research. It is usually associated with qualitative data collection components.

transferability   Criterion of trustworthiness (qualitative). It is concerned with whether the inferences from a qualitative component can be applied to other similar contexts. A qualitative version of the quantitative term 'external validity'.

triangulation   Used in mixed methods research where two or more methods are used to investigate the same phenomenon. The aim is to seek a convergence and corroboration of the inferences generated from each research component to create meta-inferences.

triangulation as epistemological dialogue or juxtaposition   Where the use of mixed methods is not as simple as providing different kinds of information about the same phenomenon, but is about constituting the world in different ways. This approach relates to the theoretical influences of constructionism and postmodernism.

trustworthiness   Constitutes four criteria to assess the rigour of qualitative research, namely: credibility, transferability, dependability, and confirmability.

univariate   'One variable'. The analysis and investigation of one variable.

validity   Focuses on the integrity of the inferences from a quantitative component and contains four types: construct (measurement), ecological, external, and internal.

within-method triangulation   Quantitative and qualitative data are collected through the same data collection method, for example through a questionnaire.

References

Adorjan, M. and Ricciardelli, R. (Eds.). (2016). *Engaging with ethics in international criminological research*. Abingdon: Routledge.

Ager, A. and Strang, A. (2004). *Indicators of integration final report*. London. Retrieved 16/07/2018 from http://webarchive.nationalarchives.gov.uk/20110218141321/http:/rds.homeoffice.gov.uk/rds/pdfs04/dpr28.pdf.

Armitage, R. and Monchuk, L. (2011). Sustaining the crime reduction impact of Secured by Design: 1999 to 2009. *Security Journal*, 24(4), 320–343.

Atkinson, R. and Flint, J. (2001). *Accessing hidden and hard-to-reach populations: Snowball research strategies* (Social Research Update No. 33). Guildford: Department of Sociology, University of Surrey.

Bacchus, L., Buller, A.M., Ferrari, G., Brzank, P. and Feder, G. (2018). 'It's always good to ask': A mixed methods study on the perceived role of sexual health practitioners asking gay and bisexual men about experiences of domestic violence and abuse. *Journal of Mixed Methods Research*, 12(2), 221–243.

Bachman, R. and Schutt, R. (2011). *Fundamentals of research in criminology and criminal justice* (2nd ed.). Los Angeles, CA: SAGE.

Banks, J., Andersson, C., Best, D., Edwards, M. and Waters, J. (2018). *Families living with problem gambling*. London: GambleAware.

BASCAP. (2009). *Research report on consumer attitudes and perceptions of counterfeiting and piracy*. Business Action to Stop Counterfeiting and Piracy. Retrieved 21/08/2011 from www.iccwbo.org/uploadedFiles/BASCAP/Pages/BASCAP-Consumer%20Research%20Report_Final.pdf.

Beck, A.J., Harrison, P.M. and Guerino, P. (2010). *Sexual victimization in juvenile facilities reported by youth, 2008–09* (NCJ Report No. 228416). Retrieved 02/12/2014 from http://bjs.ojp.usdoj.gov/content/pub/pdf/svjfry09.pdf.

Berg, B.L. (2001). *Qualitative research methods for the social sciences* (4th ed.). Ann Arbor, MI: Allyn and Bacon.

Best, D. and Laudet, A. (2010). *The potential of recovery capital*. London: RSA.

Best, D., Albertson, K., Irving, J., Lightowlers, C., Mama-Rudd, A. and Chaggar, A. (2015). *The UK life in recovery survey 2015: The first national UK survey of addiction recovery experiences*. Sheffield: Helena Kennedy Centre for International Justice.

Best, D., Beckwith, M., Haslam, C., Alexander Haslam, S., Jetten, J., Mawson, E. and Lubman, D.I. (2016). Overcoming alcohol and other drug addiction as a process of social identity transition: The social identity model of recovery (SIMOR). *Addiction Research and Theory*, 24(2), 111–123.

Best, D., Bliuc, A.-M., Iqbal, M., Upton, K. and Hodgkins, S. (2018). Mapping social identity change in online networks of recovery. *Addiction Research and Theory*, 26(3), 163–173.

Best, D., Irving, J. and Albertson, K. (2017). Recovery and desistance: what the emerging recovery movement in the alcohol and drug area can learn from models of desistance from offending. *Addiction Research and Theory*, 25(1), 1–10. doi: 10.1080/16066359.2016.1185661.

Best, D., Irving, J., Cano, I., Andersson, C. and Edwards, M. (2016). *An evaluation of intuitive recovery: Interim report*. Sheffield: Helena Kennedy Centre for International Justice.

Best, D., Irving, J., Collinson, B., Andersson, C. and Edwards, M. (2017). Recovery networks and community connections: Identifying connection needs and community linkage opportunities in early recovery populations. *Alcoholism Treatment Quarterly*, 35(1), 2–15.

Best, D., Lubman, D., Savic, M., Wilson, A., Dingle, G., Haslam, S.A., Haslam, C. and Jetten, J. (2014). Social and transitional identity: Exploring social networks and their significance in a therapeutic community setting. *Therapeutic Communities: The International Journal of Therapeutic Communities*, 35(1), 10–20.

Biernacki, P. and Waldorf, D. (1981). Snowball sampling: Problems and techniques of chain referral sampling. *Sociological Methods and Research*, 10, 141–163.

Bliuc, A.-M., Best, D., Iqbal, M. and Upton, K. (2017). Building addiction recovery capital through online participation in a recovery community. *Social Science and Medicine*, 193, 110–117. https://doi.org/10.1016/j.socscimed.2017.09.050.

Bloch, S. (2018). Place-based elicitation: Interviewing graffiti writers at the scene of the crime. *Journal of Contemporary Ethnography*, 47(2), 171–198. doi.org/10.1177/0891241616639640.

Bornmann, L. (2012). *Measuring the societal impact of research*. EMBO reports 13, 673-676. Retrieved 16/07/2018 from www.ncbi.nlm.nih.gov/pmc/articles/PMC3410397/pdf/embor201299a.pdf.

Bottoms, A. (2008). The relationship between theory and empirical observations in criminology. In R.D. King and E. Wincup (Eds.), *Doing research on crime and justice* (2nd ed.). Oxford: Oxford University Press.

Brace, I. (2013). *Questionnaire design* (3rd ed.). London: Kogan Page.

British Library. (2018). *EThOS: e-theses online service*. Retrieved 16/07/2018 from http://ethos.bl.uk/Home.do;jsessionid=CCF311DD23328CEB1E14F462D1D8BAF4.

British Society of Criminology. (2015). *Statement of ethics*. Retrieved 16/07/2018 from www.britsoccrim.org/documents/BSCEthics2015.pdf.

Bryant, A. and Charmaz, K. (2007). *The SAGE handbook of grounded theory*. London: SAGE.

Bryman, A. (1988). *Quantity and quality in social research*. London: Routledge.

Bryman, A. (2006). Integrating quantitative and qualitative research: How is it done? *Qualitative Research*, 6, 97–113.

Bryman, A. (2008). *Social research methods* (3rd ed.). Oxford: Oxford University Press.

Bryman, A. (2011). *Social research methods* (4th ed.). Oxford: Oxford University Press.

Bryman, A. (2016). *Social research methods* (5th ed.). Oxford: Oxford University Press.

Burns, T. and Sinfield, S. (2012). *Essential study skills: The complete guide to success at university* (3rd ed.). London: SAGE.

Burrows, J. (2018). When 'sexting' becomes 'revenge porn': An investigation of victim-blaming in cases involving the malicious use of intimate media (unpublished master's dissertation). University of Manchester, UK.

Cabrera, N. (2011). Using a sequential exploratory mixed-method design to examine racial hyperprivilege in higher education. *New Directions for Institutional Research*, 2011(151), 77–91. doi: 10.1002/ir.400.

Campbell, D. and Fiske, D. (1959). Convergent and discriminant validation by the multitrait-multimethod matrix. *Psychological Bulletin*, 56(2), 81–105.

Cashmore, E. (2006). *Celebrity culture*. Abingdon: Routledge.

Caulfield, L. and Hill, J. (2014). *Criminological research for beginners: A student's guide*. London: Routledge.

Charmaz, K. (2009). Shifting the grounds: Constructivist grounded theory methods. In J.M. Morse, P.N. Stern, J. Corbin, B. Bowers, K. Charmaz and A. Clarke (Eds.), *Developing grounded theory: The second generation*. Walnut Creek, CA: Left Coast Press.

Cherry, M. and Dickson, R. (2017). Defining my review question and identifying inclusion and exclusion criteria. In A. Boland, G.M. Cherry and R. Dickson (Eds.), *Doing a systematic review*. London: SAGE.

Chonody, J., Ferman, B., Amitrani-Welsh, J. and Martin, T. (2013). Violence through the eyes of youth: A photovoice exploration. *Journal of Community Psychology*, 41(1), 84–101. doi:10.1002/jcop.21515.

Cicourel, A. (1974). *Cognitive sociology*. Harmondsworth: Penguin.

Cohen, J. (1988). *Statistical power analysis for the behavioural sciences* (2nd ed.). New York: Routledge.

Cohen, S. (1972). *Folk devils and moral panics: The creation of the Mods and Rockers*. London: MacGibbon and Kee.

Collinson, B. (in progress). Investigating recovery capital whilst identifying gender similarities and differences in pathways to recovery: A mixed methods study (unpublished doctoral thesis). Sheffield Hallam University, Sheffield.

Cottrell, S. (2011). *Critical thinking skills: Developing effective analysis and argument* (2nd ed.). London: SAGE.

Creswell, J. (2015). *A concise introduction to mixed methods research*. London: SAGE.

Creswell, J. and Plano Clark, V. (2011). *Designing and conducting mixed methods research* (2nd ed.). Thousand Oaks, CA: SAGE.

Crowther-Dowey, C. and Fussey, P. (2013). *Researching crime: Approaches, methods and application*. Basingstoke: Palgrave Macmillan.

Cruwys, T., Steffens, N.K., Haslam, S., Haslam, C., Jetten, J. and Dingle, G. (2016). Social identity mapping (SIM): A procedure for visual representation and assessment of subjective group memberships. *British Journal of Social Psychology*, 55(4), 613–642. doi: 10.1111/bjso.12155.

Cubellis, M. (2015). Sexual victimization, disclosure and accountability: Organizational responses of the Boy Scouts of America to child sexual abuse (unpublished doctoral thesis). The City University of New York, New York.

Cullen, F.T. (2013). The corruption of benevolence revisited: Why editorial snooping is a bad idea. *The Criminologist*, 38, 22–26.

Davies, P. (2011). Formulating criminological research questions. In P. Davies, P. Francis and V. Jupp (Eds.), *Doing criminological research* (2nd ed.). London: SAGE.

Davies, P., Francis, P. and Jupp, V. (Eds.). (2011). *Doing criminological research* (2nd ed.). London: SAGE.

Denscombe, M. (1983). Interviews, accounts and ethnographic research on teachers. In M. Hammersley (Ed.), *The ethnography of schooling*. Driffield: Nafferton Books.

Denscombe, M. (2002). *Ground rules for good research: A 10 point guide for social researchers*. Maidenhead: Open University Press.

Denscombe, M. (2007). *The good research guide for small-scale social research projects* (3rd ed.). Maidenhead: McGraw-Hill.

Denscombe, M. (2008). Communities of practice: A research paradigm for the mixed methods approach. *Journal of Mixed Methods Research*, 2(3), 270–283. https://doi.org/10.1177/1558689808316807.

Denscombe, M. (2010). *Ground rules for social research: Guidelines for good practice* (4th ed.). Maidenhead: McGraw-Hill.

Denscombe, M. (2014). *The good research guide: For small-scale social research projects* (5th ed.). Maidenhead: Open University Press.

Denscombe, M. (2017). *The good research guide: For small-scale social research projects* (6th ed.). London: McGraw-Hill.

Denzin, N. (1970). *The research act in sociology*. Chicago, IL: Aldine.

Denzin, N. (2012). Triangulation 2.0. *Journal of Mixed Methods Research*, 6(2), 80–88.

De Vaus, D. (2001). *Research design in social research*. London: SAGE.

De Vaus, D. (2014). *Surveys in social research* (6th ed.). London: Routledge.

Duffy, L. (2015). Achieving a sustainable livelihood after leaving intimate partner violence: Challenges and opportunities. *Journal of Family Violence*, 30(4), 403–417. doi.org/10.1007/s10896-015-9686-x.

Durnescu, I. (2017). The five stages of prisoner reentry: Toward a process theory. *International Journal of Offender Therapy and Comparative Criminology*, 62(8), 2195–2215. doi.org/10.1177/0306624X17706889.

Erzberger, C. and Kelle, U. (2003). Making inferences in mixed methods: The rules of integration. In A. Tashakkori and C. Teddlie (Eds.), *Handbook of mixed methods in social and behavioral research*. London: SAGE.

Erzberger, C. and Prein, G. (1997). Triangulation: Validity and empirically based hypothesis construction. *Quality and Quantity*, 2, 141–154.

European Network of Research Ethics Committees. (2018). *Welcome to EUREC*. Retrieved 01/04/2018 from www.eurecnet.org/index.html.

Farrington, D. (2006). Key longitudinal-experimental studies in criminology. *Journal of Experimental Criminology*, 2, 121–141.

Field, A. (2018). *Discovering statistics using IBM SPSS statistics* (5th ed.). London: SAGE.

Finch, E. and Fafinski, S. (2016). *Criminology skills* (2nd ed.). Oxford: Oxford University Press.

Fitzgibbon, W. and Stengel, C. (2017). Women's voices made visible: Photovoice in visual criminology. *Punishment & Society*, 20(4), 411–431. doi.org/10.1177/1462474517700137.

Flick, U. (2004). Triangulation in qualitative research. In U. Flick, E. von Kardoff and I. Steinke (Eds.), *A companion to qualitative research*. London: SAGE.

Gilbert, N. (Ed.). (2008). *Researching social life* (3rd ed.). London: SAGE.

Glaser, A. and Strauss, A. (1967). *The discovery of grounded theory*. Chicago, IL: Aldine.

Goffman, A. (2014). *On the run: Fugitive life in an American city*. New York: Picador.

Google Dictionary. (2017). *Triangulation*. Retrieved 01/09/2017 from www.google.co.uk/search?client=safariandrls=enandq=triangulationandie=UTF-8andoe=UTF-8andgfe_rd=cranddcr=0andei=gCXaWY3lIJLDaNKukHA.

Greene, J. (2007). *Mixed methods in social inquiry*. San Francisco, CA: Jossey-Bass.

Greene, J., Caracelli, V. and Graham, W. (1989). Toward a conceptual framework for mixed-method evaluation designs. *Educational Evaluation and Policy Analysis*, 11(3), 255–274.

Griffiths, M.D. (2010). The use of online methodologies in data collection for gambling and gaming addictions. *International Journal of Mental Health and Addiction*, 8, 8–20.

Groshkova, T., Best, D. and White, W. (2012). The assessment of recovery capital: Properties and psychometrics of a measure of addiction recovery strengths. *Drug Alcohol Review*, 32(2), 187–194. doi: 10.1111/j.1465-3362.2012.00489.x.

Guba, E. and Lincoln, Y. (1986). But is it rigorous? Trustworthiness and authenticity in naturalistic evaluation. In D. Williams (Ed.), *Naturalistic evaluation*. San Francisco, CA: Jossey-Bass.

Hagan, F. (2005). *Essentials of research methods in criminal justice and criminology*. London: Pearson.

Halfpenny, P. and Procter, R. (2015). *Innovations in digital research methods*. London: SAGE.

Hall, S., Critcher, C., Jefferson, T., Clarke, J. and Roberts, B. (1978). *Policing the crisis: Mugging, the state, and law and order*. London: Macmillan.

Hammersley, M. (1992). The paradigm wars: Reports from the front. *British Journal of Sociology of Education*, 13, 131–143.

Hammersley, M. (2008). Troubles with triangulation. In M. Bergman (Ed.), *Advances in mixed methods research*. London: SAGE.

Harrits, G. (2011). More than method? A discussion of paradigm differences within mixed methods research. *Journal of Mixed Methods Research*, 5(2), 150–166.

Haslam, C., Dingle, G., Best, D., Mackenzie, J. and Beckwith, M. (2017). Social identity mapping: Measuring social identity change in recovery from addiction. In S. Buckingham and D. Best (Eds.), *Addiction, behavioral change and social identity: The path to resilience and recovery*. Abingdon: Routledge.

Haslam, S. A., Jetten, J., Postmes, T. and Haslam, C. (2009). Social identity, health and well-being: An emerging agenda for applied psychology. *Applied Psychology: An International Review*, 58(1), 1–23.

Heap, V. (2010). Understanding public perceptions of anti-social behaviour: Problems and policy responses (unpublished doctoral thesis). University of Huddersfield, Huddersfield.

Heap, V. and Waters, J. (2018). Using mixed methods in criminological research. In P. Davies and P. Francis (Eds.), *Doing criminological research* (3rd ed.). London: SAGE.

Hesse-Biber, S.N. (2010). *Mixed methods research: Merging theory with practice*. New York: Guilford Press.

Hewson, C., Vogel, C. and Laurent, D. (2016). *Internet research methods* (2nd ed.). London: SAGE.

Holdaway S. (1984). *Inside the British police: A force at work*. Oxford: Blackwell.

Hollis-Peel, M.E. and Welsh, B.C. (2014). What makes a guardian capable? A test of guardianship in action. *Security Journal*, 27(3), 320–337.

Humphreys, L. (1970). *Tearoom trade: Impersonal sex in public places*. London: Duckworth Overlook.

Janis, I. (1972). *Victims of groupthink*. New York: Houghton Mifflin.

Jetten, J., Haslam, C., Haslam, S.A. and Branscombe, N. (2009). The social cure. *Scientific American Mind*, 20(5), 26–33.

Jick, T.D. (1979). Mixing quantitative and qualitative methods: Triangulation in action. *Administrative Science Quarterly*, 24, 602–611.

Johnson, R. and Onwuegbuzie, A. (2004). Mixed methods research: A research paradigm whose time has come. *Educational Researcher*, 33(7), 14–26.

Johnson, R., Onwuegbuzie, A. and Turner, L. (2007). Toward a definition of mixed methods research. *Journal of Mixed Method Research*, 1(2), 1–22.

Jonathan-Zamir, T. and Weisburd, D. (2013). The effects of security threats on antecedents of police legitimacy: Findings from a quasi-experiment in Israel. *Journal of Research in Crime and Delinquency*, 50(1), 3–32.

King, A. (2008). Keeping a safe distance: Individualism and the less punitive public. *British Journal of Criminology*, 48, 190–208. doi: 10.1093/bjc/azm069.

King A. and Maruna, S. (2005). The function of fiction for a punitive public. In P. Mason (Ed.), *Captured by the media*. London: Willan.

King, A. and Maruna, S. (2009). Is a conservative just a liberal who has been mugged?: Exploring the origins of punitive views. *Punishment and Society*, 11(2), 147–169. doi. org/10.1177/1462474508101490.

King, A. and Maruna, S. (2011). Shame, materialism, and moral indignation in the east of England: An empirical look at Ranulf's thesis. In S. Karstedt, I. Loader and H. Strang (Eds.), *Emotions, crime and justice*. Oxford: Hart.

Kingsley, D. (2015). *What is 'research impact' in an interconnected world?* University of Cambridge Office of Scholarly Communication. Retrieved 17/07/2018 from https://unlockingresearch. blog.lib.cam.ac.uk/?p=252.

Kirk, J. and Miller, M. (1986). *Reliability and validity in qualitative research*. Newbury Park, CA: SAGE.

Large, J. (2011). Criminality, consumption and the counterfeiting of fashion goods (unpublished doctoral thesis). Leeds University, Leeds.

Large, J. (2015). 'Get real, don't buy fakes': Fashion fakes and flawed policy – the problem with taking a consumer-responsibility approach to reducing the 'problem' of counterfeiting. *Criminology and Criminal Justice*, 15(2), 169–185.

Latané, B. and Darley, J. (1968). Group inhibition of bystander intervention in emergencies. *Journal of Personality and Social Psychology*, 10(3), 215–221.

Layder, D. (1993). *New strategies in social research*. Cambridge: Polity Press.

Layder, D. (1998). *Sociological practice: Linking theory and social research*. London: SAGE.

Leahy-Harland, S. and Bull, R. (2017). Police strategies and suspect responses in real-life serious crime interviews. *Journal of Police and Criminal Psychology*, 32(2), 138. doi.org/10.1007/s11896-016-9207-8.

LeCompte, M. and Goetz, J. (1982). Problems of reliability and validity in ethnographic research. *Review of Educational Research*, 52, 31–60.

Ledbury Research. (2007). *Counterfeiting luxury: Exposing the myths* (2nd ed.). Davenport Lyons. Retrieved 22/09/2010 from www.a-cg.com.

Lipscomb, M. (2008). Mixed method nursing studies: A critical realist critique. *Nursing Philosophy*, 9(1), 32–45.

Lubet, S. (2015). *Ethics on the run*. Retrieved 01/04/2018 from http://newramblerreview.com/ images/files/Steven-Lubet_review-of_Alice-Goffman.pdf.

Maruna, S. (2010). Mixed methods research: Why not go both ways? In A. Piquero and D. Weisburd (Eds.), *Handbook of quantitative criminology*. New York: Springer.

Maruna, S. and King, A. (2004). Public opinion and community penalties. In A. Bottoms, S. Rex and G. Robinson (Eds.), *Alternatives to prison: Options for an insecure society*. Cullompton: Willan Publishing.

Maruna, S. and King, A. (2009). 'Once a criminal, always a criminal?': Redeemability and the psychology of punitive public attitudes. *European Journal of Criminal Policy and Research*, 15, 7–24.

Masterman, M. (1970). The nature of a paradigm. In I. Lakatos and A. Musgrave (Eds.), *Criticism and the growth of knowledge*. Cambridge: Cambridge University Press.

Mathison, S. (1988). Why triangulate? *Educational Researcher*, 17(2), 13–17.

Mayoh, J. and Onwuegbuzie, A. (2015). Toward a conceptualization of mixed methods phenomenological research. *Journal of Mixed Methods Research*, 9(1), 91–107.

Merry, S., Power, N., McManus, M. and Alison, L. (2012). Drivers of public trust and confidence in police in the UK. *International Journal of Police Science and Management*, 14(2), 118–135.

Mertens, D.M. (2009). *Transformative research and education*. New York: Guilford Press.

Metcalfe, M. (2006). *Reading critically at university*. London: SAGE.

Miers, D. (2016). Social responsibility and harm minimization in commercial gambling in Great Britain. *Gaming Law Review and Economics*, 20(2), 164–176.

Milgram, S. (1963). Behavioral study of obedience. *Journal of Abnormal and Social Psychology*, 67, 371–378.

Minke, L. (2011). The effects of mixing offenders with non-offenders: Findings from a danish quasi-experiment. *Journal of Scandinavian Studies in Criminology and Crime Prevention*, 12(1), 80–99.

Morgan, G. (2006). *Images of organization*. London: SAGE.

Morse, J. and Niehaus, L. (2009). *Mixed method design: Principles and procedures*. Abingdon: Routledge.

Moxon, D. and Waters, J. (2017). *Illegal drug use through the lifecourse: A study of 'hidden' older users*. Abingdon: Routledge.

Neale, J., Nettleton, S. and Pickering, L. (2013). Does recovery-oriented treatment prompt heroin users prematurely into detoxification and abstinence programmes?: Qualitative study. *Drug and Alcohol Dependence*, 127(1), 163–169.

Neale, J., Finch, E., Marsden, J., Mitcheson, L., Rose, D., Strang, J., Tompkins, C., Wheeler, C. and Wykes, T. (2014). How should we measure addiction recovery? Analysis of service provider perspectives using online Delphi groups. *Drugs: Education, Prevention and Policy*, 21(4), 310–323.

Nelson, M., Wooditch, A. and Gabbidon, S. (2014). Is criminology out-of-date? A research note on the use of common types of data. *Journal of Criminal Justice Education*, 25(1), 16–33. doi:10.1080/10511253.2013.798005.

Neuman, W.L. (2000). *Social research methods: Qualitative and quantitative approaches* (4th ed.). Boston, MA: Allyn and Bacon.

Newburn, T. (2017). *Criminology* (4th ed.). London: Routledge.

NHS. (2015). *Statistics on alcohol: England, 2015*. Retrieved 01/07/2018 from https://files.digital.nhs.uk/publicationimport/pub17xxx/pub17712/alc-eng-2015-rep.pdf.

Noaks, L. and Wincup, E. (2004). *Criminological research: Understanding qualitative methods*. London: SAGE.

Oakley, A. (1999). Paradigm wars: Some thoughts on a personal and public trajectory. *International Journal of Social Research Methodology*, 2, 247–254.

O'Leary, Z. (2017). *The essential guide to doing your research project* (3rd ed.). Los Angeles, CA: SAGE.

Oliver, P. (2010). *The student's guide to research ethics* (2nd ed.). Maidenhead: McGraw-Hill.

Onwuegbuzie, A. and Leech, N. (2006). Linking research questions to mixed methods data analysis procedures. *The Qualitative Report*, 11(3), 474–498.

Onwuegbuzie, A. and Frels, R. (2013). Toward a new research philosophy for addressing social justice issues: Critical dialectical pluralism. *International Journal of Multiple Research Approaches*, 7(1), 9–26.

Onwuegbuzie, A., Johnson, B. and Mt Collins, K. (2009). Call for mixed analysis: A philosophical framework for combining qualitative and quantitative approaches. *International Journal of Multiple Research Approaches*, 3(2), 114–139.

Orford, J. (2011). *An unsafe bet? The dangerous rise of gambling and the debate we should be having*. Hoboken, NJ: Wiley-Blackwell.

Oxford Dictionary. (2018). *Definition of 'systematic'*. Retrieved 15/03/2018 from https://en.oxforddictionaries.com/definition/systematic.

Painter, K. and Farrington, D. (1999). Improved street lighting: Crime reducing effects and cost-benefit analyses. *Security Journal*, 12, 17–32.

Patten, M. and Newhart, M. (2017). *Understanding research methods: An overview of the essentials* (10th ed.). Abingdon: Routledge.

Pawson, R. and Tilley, N. (1997). *Realistic evaluation*. London: SAGE.

Pennebaker, J., Boyd, R., Jordan, K. and Blackburn, K. (2015). *The development and psychometric properties of LIWC2015*. UT Faculty/Researcher Works.

Phillips, J. (2013). Probation workers' practice and practice ideals in a culture of control (unpublished doctoral thesis). University of Cambridge, Cambridge. https://doi.org/10.17863/CAM.16552.

Phillips, L. and Lindsay, M. (2011). Prison to society: A mixed methods analysis of coping with reentry. *International Journal of Offender Therapy and Comparative Criminology*, 55(1), 136–154.

Pitak-Arnnop, P., Dhanuthai, K., Hemprich, A. and Pausch, N. (2012). Morality, ethics, norms and research misconduct. *Journal of Conservative Dentistry*, 15(1), 92–93.

Plano Clark, V. and Creswell, J. (2008). Methodological selections. In V. Plano Clark and J. Creswell (Eds.), *The mixed methods reader*. Thousand Oaks, CA: SAGE.

Plano Clark, V. and Badiee, M. (2010). Research questions in mixed methods research. In A. Tashakkori and C. Teddlie (Eds.), *SAGE handbook of mixed methods in social and behavioral research*. Thousand Oaks, CA: SAGE. doi: 10.4135/9781506335193.

Platts-Fowler, D. and Robinson, D. (2011). *An evaluation of the gateway protection programme*. Centre for Regional Economic and Social Research, Sheffield Hallam University. Retrieved 12/10/2018 from www.shu.ac.uk/research/cresr/sites/shu.ac.uk/files/eval-gateway-protection-programme.pdf.

Platts-Fowler, D. and Robinson, D. (2015). A place for integration: Refugee experiences in two English cities. *Population, Space and Place*, 21(5), 476–491. https://doi.org/10.1002/psp.1928.

Punch, K. (2016). *Developing effective research proposals* (3rd ed.). London: SAGE.

Raddon, A. (n.d.). *Early stage research training: Epistemology and ontology in social science research*. University of Leicester.

Raynor, P. (2004). The probation service 'pathfinders': Finding the path and losing the way? *Criminal Justice*, 4, 309–325.

Raynor, P. (2008). Community penalties and Home Office research: On the way back to 'nothing works'? *Criminology and Criminal Justice*, 8, 73–87.

Refugee Action. (2008). *Gateway protection programme good practice guide*. London. Retrieved 17/07/2018 from www.refugeecouncil.org.uk.

Rock, P. and Holdaway, S. (1998). Thinking about criminology: 'Facts are bits of biography'. In S. Holdaway and P. Rock (Eds.), *Thinking about criminology*. London: UCL Press.

Rumsey, S. (2008). *How to find information: A guide for researchers* (2nd ed.). London: Open University Press.

Rutter, J. and Bryce, J. (2008). The consumption of counterfeit goods: 'Here be pirates'. *Sociology*, 42(6), 1146–1164.

Ryan, G. and Bernard, H. (2003). Techniques to identify themes. *Field Methods*, 15, 85–109.

Sarantakos, S. (2005). *Social research* (3rd ed.). Basingstoke: Palgrave Macmillan.

Shakeshaft, C. (2004). *Educator sexual misconduct: A synthesis of existing literature*. US Department of Education, Office of the Under Secretary. Retrieved 17/07/2018 from www2.ed.gov/rschstat/research/pubs/misconductreview/report.pdf.

Shih, T.-H. and Xitao Fan, X. (2008). Comparing response rates from web and mail surveys: A meta-analysis. *Field Methods*, 20(3), 249–271. doi: 10.1177/1525822X08317085.

Shon, P. (2015). *How to read journal articles in the social sciences* (2nd ed.). London: SAGE.

Silverman, D. (2007). *A very short, fairly interesting and reasonably cheap book about qualitative research*. London: SAGE.

Sobell, L., Cunningham, J. and Sobell, M. (1996). Recovery from alcohol problems with and without treatment: prevalence in two population surveys. *American Journal of Public Health*, 86(7), 966–972.

Sutherland, A., Brunton-Smith, I. and Jackson, J. (2013). Collective efficacy, deprivation and violence in London. *The British Journal of Criminology*, 53(6), 1050–1074. doi.org/10.1093/bjc/azt050.

Sykes, G. and Matza, D. (1957). Techniques of neutralization: A theory of delinquency. *American Sociological Review*, 22(6), 664–670. doi: 10.2307/2089195.

Tashakkori, A. and Teddlie, C. (1998). *Mixed methodology: Combining qualitative and quantitative approaches*. Thousand Oaks, CA: SAGE.

Tashakkori, A. and Teddlie, C. (2003). *Handbook of mixed methods in social and behavioral research*. Thousand Oaks, CA: SAGE.

Tashakkori, A. and Teddlie, C. (2010). *SAGE handbook of mixed methods in social and behavioral research*. Thousand Oaks, CA: SAGE.

Teddlie, C. and Tashakkori, A. (2003). Major issues and controversies in the use of mixed methods in the social and behavioral sciences. In A. Tashakkori and C. Teddlie (Eds.), *Handbook of mixed methods in social and behavioral research*. Thousand Oaks, CA: SAGE.

Teddlie, C. and Tashakkori, A. (2006). A general typology of research designs featuring mixed methods. *Research in the Schools*, 13(1), 12–28.

Teddlie, C. and Tashakkori, A. (2009). *Foundations of mixed methods research: Integrating quantitative and qualitative approaches in the social and behavioural sciences*. Thousand Oaks, CA: SAGE.

Teddlie, C. and Tashakkori, A. (2010). Overview of contemporary issues in mixed methods research. In A. Tashakkori and C. Teddlie (Eds.), *SAGE handbook of mixed methods in social and behavioral research*. Thousand Oaks, CA: SAGE.

Teddlie, C. and Yu, F. (2007). Mixed methods sampling: A typology with examples. *Journal of Mixed Methods Research*, 1(1), 77–100.

Treadwell, J. and Wakeman, S. (forthcoming). *Criminological ethnography: An introduction*. London: SAGE.

University of Southampton. (2017). *Qualitative v quantitative*. Retrieved 17/07/2018 from www.erm.ecs.soton.ac.uk/theme7/qualitative_vs_quantitative.html.

Van Koppen, M. and De Poot, C. (2013). The truck driver who bought a café: Offenders on their involvement mechanisms for organized crime. *European Journal of Criminology*, 10(1), 74–88. doi.org/10.1177/1477370812456346.

Walliman, N. (2016). *Social research methods* (2nd ed.). London: SAGE.

Wardle, H., Keily, R., Astbury, G. and Reith, G. (2014). 'Risky places?': Mapping gambling machine density and socio-economic deprivation. *Journal of Gambling Studies*, 30(1), 201–212.

Wardle, H., Moody, A., Spence, S., Orford, J., Volberg, R., Jotangia, D., Griffiths, M., Hussey, D. and Dobbie, F. (2011). *British gambling prevalence survey 2010*. London: National Centre for Social Research.

Waters, J. (2009). Illegal drug use among older adults (unpublished doctoral thesis). University of Sheffield, Sheffield.

Waters, J. (2015). Snowball sampling: A cautionary tale involving a study of older drug users. *International Journal of Social Research Methodology*, 18(4), 367–380.

Waters, J., Westaby, C., Fowler, A. and Phillips, J. (forthcoming). Doing criminological research: An emotional labour perspective. In J. Phillips, J. Waters, C. Westaby and A. Fowler (Eds.), *Emotional labour in criminal justice and criminology*. Abingdon: Routledge.

Watkins, D. and Gioia, D. (2015). *Mixed methods research: Pocket guide to social work research methods*. Oxford: Oxford University Press.

Webb, E., Campbell, D., Schwartz, R. and Sechrest, L. (1966). *Unobtrusive measures*. Chicago, IL: Rand McNally.

Wincup, E. (2017). More carrots, less sticks: The role of incentives in drug treatment. *Addiction*, 112(5), 761–762. doi.org/10.1111/add.13667.

Winlow, S. and Hall, S. (2012). What is an 'ethics committee'?: Academic governance in an epoch of belief and incredulity. *The British Journal of Criminology*, 52(2), 400–416.

Winlow, S., Hobbs, D., Lister, S. and Hadfield, P. (2001). Get ready to duck: Bouncers and the ethnographic realities of research on violent groups. *British Journal of Criminology*, 41, 536–548.

Wolfe, D., Jaffe, P., Jette, J. and Poisson, S. (2003). The impact of child abuse in community institutions and organizations: Advancing professional and scientific understanding. *Clinical Psychology: Science and Practice*, 10(2), 179–191.

World Health Organization. (2018). *Global health ethics*. Retrieved 10/04/2018 from www.who.int/ethics/en.

Young, J. (2011). *The criminological imagination*. Cambridge: Polity Press.

Young, M. (1991). *An inside job: Policing and police culture in Britain*. Oxford: Oxford University Press.

Zimbardo, P. (1973). On the ethics of intervention in human psychological research: With special reference to the Stanford prison experiment. *Cognition*, 2(2), 243–256.

Index